Sriranga Veeraraghavan

Shell Programming in 24 Hours

SECOND EDITION

SAMS

201 West 103rd St., Indianapolis, Indiana, 46290 USA

Sams Teach Yourself Shell Programming in 24 Hours, Second Edition

International Standard Book Number: 0-672-32358-3

Library of Congress Catalog Card Number: 2001096631

Printed in the United States of America

First Printing: April 2002

05 04 03 02 4 3 2 1

Trademarks

All terms mentioned in this book that are known to be trademarks or service marks have been appropriately capitalized. Sams cannot attest to the accuracy of this information. Use of a term in this book should not be regarded as affecting the validity of any trademark or service mark.

Warning and Disclaimer

Every effort has been made to make this book as complete and as accurate as possible, but no warranty or fitness is implied. The information provided is on an "as is" basis. The authors and the publisher shall have neither liability nor responsibility to any person or entity with respect to any loss or damages arising from the information contained in this book.

Acquisitions Editor
Katie Purdum

Development Editor
Steve Rowe

Technical Editor
Michael Watson

Managing Editor
Charlotte Clapp

Project Editor
Natalie Harris

Copy Editors
Kezia Endsley
Rhonda Tinch-Mize

Indexer
Kelly Castell

Proofreaders
Linda Seifert
Karen Whitehouse

Interior Design
Gary Adair

Cover Design
Aren Howell

Page Layout
Stacey Richwine-DeRome

Contents at a Glance

Contents

About the Author

Sriranga Veeraraghavan is a material scientist by training and a software engineer by trade. He has several years of software development experience in C, Java, Perl, and Bourne Shell and has contributed to several books, including *Solaris 8: Complete Reference*, *UNIX Unleashed* and *Special Edition Using UNIX*. Sriranga graduated from the University of California at Berkeley in 1997 and is presently pursuing further studies. He is currently employed in the Server Appliance group at Sun Microsystems, Inc. Before joining Sun, Sriranga was employed at Cisco Systems, Inc. Among other interests, Sriranga enjoys mountain biking, classical music, and playing Marathon with his brother Srivathsa. Sriranga can be reached via e-mail at `ranga@soda.berkeley.edu`.

Dedication

For my grandmother, who taught me to love the English language.

For my mother, who taught me to love programming languages.

Acknowledgments

Writing a book on shell programming is a daunting task, due to the myriad UNIX versions and shell versions that are available. Thanks to the hard work of my development editor Steve Rowe, my technical editor Michael Watson, and my copy editor Kezia Endsley, I was able to make sure the book covered the material completely and correctly. Their suggestions and comments have helped enormously.

In addition to the technical side of the book, the task of coordinating and managing the publishing process is a difficult one. The assistance of my acquisitions editor, Kathryn Purdum, in handling all of the editorial issues and patiently working with me to keep this book on schedule was invaluable.

Working on a book takes a lot of time and makes it difficult to concentrate on work and family activities. Thanks to the support of my manager, Larry Coryell, my parents, my brother Srivathsa, and my uncle and aunt Srinvasa and Suma, I was able to balance work, family, and authoring.

Thanks to everyone else on the excellent team at Sams who worked on this book. Without their support, this book would not exist.

Tell Us What You Think!

As the reader of this book, *you* are our most important critic and commentator. We value your opinion and want to know what we're doing right, what we could do better, what areas you'd like to see us publish in, and any other words of wisdom you're willing to pass our way.

You can email or write me directly to let me know what you did or didn't like about this book—as well as what we can do to make our books stronger.

Please note that I cannot help you with technical problems related to the topic of this book, and that due to the high volume of mail I receive, I might not be able to reply to every message.

When you write, please be sure to include this book's title and author as well as your name and phone or fax number. I will carefully review your comments and share them with the author and editors who worked on the book.

Email: `opensource@samspublishing.com`

Mail: Mark Taber
Sams Publishing
201 West 103rd Street
Indianapolis, IN 46290 USA

Introduction

In recent years, the UNIX operating system has seen a huge boost in its popularity, especially with the emergence of Linux. For programmers and users of UNIX, this comes as no surprise: UNIX was designed to provide an environment that's powerful yet easy to use.

One of the main strengths of UNIX is that it comes with a large collection of standard programs. These programs perform a wide variety of tasks from listing your files to reading e-mail. Unlike other operating systems, one of the key features of UNIX is that these programs can be combined to perform complicated tasks and solve your problems.

One of the most powerful standard programs available in UNIX is the shell. The *shell* is a program that provides a consistent and easy-to-use environment for executing programs in UNIX. If you have ever used a UNIX system, you have interacted with the shell.

The main responsibility of the shell is to read the commands you type and then ask the UNIX kernel to perform these commands. In addition to this, the shell provides several sophisticated programming constructs that enable you to make decisions, repeatedly execute commands, create functions, and store values in variables.

This book concentrates on the standard UNIX shell called the Bourne shell. When Dennis Ritche and Ken Thompson were developing much of UNIX in the early 1970s, they used a very simple shell. The first real shell, written by Stephen Bourne, appeared in the mid 1970s. The original Bourne shell has changed slightly over the years; some features were added and others were removed, but its syntax and its resulting power have remained the same.

The most attractive feature of the shell is that it enables you to create scripts. *Scripts* are files that contain a list of commands you want to run. Because every script is contained in a file and every file has a name, scripts enable you to combine existing programs to create completely new programs that solve your problems. This book teaches you how to create, execute, modify, and debug shell scripts quickly and easily. After you get used to writing scripts, you will find yourself solving more and more problems with them.

How This Book Is Organized

This book assumes that you have some familiarity with UNIX and know how to log in, create, and edit files, as well as how to work with files and directories to a limited extent. If you haven't used UNIX in a while or you aren't familiar with one of these topics, don't worry; the first part of this book reviews this material thoroughly.

This book is divided into three parts:

- Part I is an introduction to UNIX, the shell, and some common tools.
- Part II covers programming using the shell.
- Part III covers advanced topics in shell programming.

Part I consists of Chapters 1 through 7. The following material is covered in the individual chapters:

- Chapter 1, "Shell Basics," discusses several important concepts related to the shell and describes the different versions of the shell.
- Chapter 2, "Script Basics," describes the process of creating and running a shell script. It also covers the login process and the different modes in which the shell executes.
- Chapters 3, "Working with Files," and 4, "Working with Directories," provide an overview of the commands used when working with files and directories. These chapters show you how to list the contents of a directory, view the contents of a file, and manipulate files and directories.
- Chapter 5, "Input and Output" covers the `echo`, `printf`, and `read` commands along with the < and > input redirection operators. This chapter also covers using file descriptors.
- Chapter 6, "Manipulating File Attributes," introduces the concept of file attributes. It covers the different types of files along with how to modify a file's permissions.
- Chapter 7, "Processes," shows you how to start and stop a process. It also explains the term *process ID* and how you can view them.

By this point, you should have a good foundation in the UNIX basics. This will enable you to start writing shell scripts that solve real problems using the concepts covered in Part II. Part II is the heart of this book, consisting of Chapters 8 through 18. It teaches you about all the tools available when programming in the shell. The following material is covered in these chapters:

- Chapter 8, "Variables," explains the use of variables in shell programming, shows you how to create and delete variables, and explains the concept of environment variables.
- Chapters 9, "Substitution," and 10, "Quoting," cover the topics of substitution and quoting. Chapter 9 shows you the four main types of substitution: filename, variable, command, and arithmetic substitution. Chapter 10 shows you the behavior of the different types of quoting and its affect on substitution.

- Chapters 11, "Flow Control," and 12, "Loops," provide complete coverage of flow control and looping. The flow control constructs `if` and `case` are covered along with the loop constructs `for` and `while`.
- Chapter 13, "Parameters," shows you how to write scripts that use command-line arguments. The special variables and the `getopts` command are covered in detail.
- Chapter 14, "Functions," discusses shell functions. Functions provide a mapping between a name and a set of commands. Learning to use functions in a shell script is a powerful technique that helps you solve complicated problems.
- Chapters 15, "Text Filters," 16, "Filtering Text with Regular Expressions," and 17, "Filtering Text with `awk`," cover text filtering. These chapters show you how to use a variety of UNIX commands including `grep`, `tr`, `sed`, and `awk`.
- Chapter 18, "Other Tools," provides an introduction to some tools that are used in shell programming. Some of the commands that are discussed include `type`, `find`, `bc`, and `expr`.

At this point, you will know enough about the shell and the external tools available in UNIX that you can solve most problems. The last part of the book, Part III, is designed to help you solve the most difficult problems encountered in shell programming. Part III spans Chapters 19 through 24 and covers the following material:

- Chapter 19, "Signals," explains the concept of signals and shows you how to deliver a signal and how to deal with a signal using the `trap` command.
- Chapter 20, "Debugging," discusses the shell's built-in debugging tools. It shows you how to use syntax checking and shell tracing to track down bugs and fix them.
- Chapters 21, "Problem Solving with Functions," and 22, "Problem Solving with Shell Scripts," cover problem solving. Chapter 21 covers problems that can be solved using functions. Chapter 22 introduces some real-world problems and shows you how to solve them using a shell script.
- Chapter 23, "Scripting for Portability," covers the topic of portability. In this chapter, you will rewrite several scripts from previous chapters to be portable to different versions of UNIX.
- Chapter 24, "Shell Programming FAQs," is a question-and-answer chapter. Several common programming questions are presented along with detailed answers and examples.

Each chapter in this book includes complete syntax descriptions for the various commands along with several examples to illustrate the use of commands. The examples are designed to show you how to apply the commands to solve real problems. At the end of each chapter are a few questions that you can use to check your progress. Some of the questions are short answers, whereas others require you to write scripts.

After Chapter 24, four appendixes are available for your reference:

- Appendix A, "Command Quick Reference," provides a complete command reference.
- Appendix B, "Glossary," contains the terms used in this book.
- Appendix C, "Answers to Questions," contains the answers to all the questions in the book.
- Appendix D, "Shell Function Library," contains a listing of the shell function library discussed in Chapter 21, "Problem Solving with Functions."

About the Examples

As you work through the chapters, try typing in the examples to get a better feeling for how the computer responds and how each command works. After you get an example working, try experimenting with the example by changing commands. Don't be afraid to experiment. Experiments (both successes and failures) teach you important things about UNIX and the shell.

Many of the examples and the answers to the questions are available for downloading from the following URL:

`http://www.csua.berkeley.edu/~ranga/downloads/tysp2.tar.Z`

After you have downloaded this file, change to the directory where the file was saved and execute the following commands:

```
$ uncompress tysp2.tar.Z
$ tar -xvf tysp2.tar
```

This creates a directory named `tysp2` that contains the examples from this book.

There is no warranty of any kind on the examples in this book. Much effort has been placed into making the examples as portable as possible. To this end the examples have been tested on the following versions of UNIX:

- Sun Solaris versions 2.5.1 to 8
- Hewlett-Packard HP-UX versions 10.10 to 11.0
- OpenBSD versions 2.6 to 2.9
- Apple MacOS X 10.0 to 10.1.2
- Red Hat Linux versions 4.2, 5.1, 5.2, 6.0, and 6.2
- FreeBSD versions 2.2.6 and 4.0 to 4.3

It is possible that some of the examples might not work on other versions of UNIX. If you encounter a problem or have a suggestion about improvements to the examples or the content of the book, please feel free to contact me at the following e-mail address:

`ranga@soda.berkeley.edu`

I appreciate any suggestions and feedback you have regarding this book.

Conventions Used in This Book

Features in this book include the following:

Notes give you comments and asides about the topic at hand, as well as full explanations of certain concepts.

Tips provide great shortcuts and hints on how to program in shell more effectively.

Cautions warn you against making your life miserable and avoiding the pitfalls in programming.

New terms appear in *italic*. Each of the new terms covered in a chapter is listed at the end of that chapter in the "Terms" section.

At the end of each chapter, you'll find the handy Summary and Quiz sections (with answers found in Appendix C).

In addition, you'll find various typographic conventions throughout this book:

- Commands, variables, directories, and files appear in text in a special `monospaced font`.
- Commands and such that you type appear in **boldface type**.
- Placeholders in syntax descriptions appear in a *`monospaced italic`* typeface. This indicates that you will replace the placeholder with the actual filename, parameter, or other element that it represents.

Part I

Introduction to UNIX and Shell Tools

Hour

HOUR 1

Shell Basics

My father is an avid woodworker. He has a tool chest that holds all his woodworking tools, from screwdrivers and chisels to power sanders and power drills. Over the years, he has used his tools to build everything from a toy bridge to a shed. By applying the same tools, he has been able to build all the elements required in his projects.

In many ways, shell programming is similar to woodworking. A woodworking project requires a design for the project and its elements along with the right tools. In shell programming, the project design is provided by the programmer and the tools are *utilities* or *commands* provided by UNIX. There are simple commands such as `ls` and `cd`, and there are also commands such as `awk` and `sed`, which are the power tools in UNIX.

The simple commands are easy to learn. You probably already know how to use many of them. The power tools take longer to learn, but after mastering them almost any problem can be tackled. This book covers both the simple tools and the power tools, with the main focus on the most powerful tool in UNIX, the shell. In this chapter you will learn about

- Simple, complex, and compound commands
- Command separators
- Different types of shells

What Is a Command?

A *command* is a file containing a set of instructions that UNIX can run or *execute*. In operating systems such as Mac OS or Windows, commands are executed by clicking their icons. In UNIX, a command is executed by typing in its name and pressing Enter or Return. For example, in order to execute the `date` command, use the following:

```
$ date [ENTER]
Wed Dec  9 08:49:13 PST 1998
$
```

The purpose of the `date` command is to display the current day, date, time, and year. Notice that after the command finishes executing, the character `$` is displayed. This character is the *prompt*. When a prompt is present, the name of a command can be given for execution. The shell reads the command name and tries to execute it. While the command executes, the prompt is not displayed. When the command finishes executing, the prompt is displayed again.

The `$` character is a prompt for you to enter a command. It is not part of the command itself.

For example, to execute the `date` command, only the word `date` is typed at the prompt. Don't type `$ date`. Some systems might display an error message if you type `$ date` instead of `date`.

Here is another example of executing the `who` command:

```
$ who
vathsa     tty1     Dec  6 19:36
ranga      ttyp0    Dec  9 09:23
$
```

The `who` command displays a list of all the people, or users, who are currently using the UNIX machine. The first column of the output lists the usernames of the people who are logged in. On this system, there are two users, `vathsa` and `ranga`. The second column lists the terminals they are logged in to, and the final column lists the time they logged in. The output varies from system to system. On some versions of UNIX or Linux, there might be additional columns in the output. Try it on your system to see who is logged in.

For those readers who are not familiar with the process of logging in to a UNIX system, the details are discussed in Chapter 2, "Script Basics."

Simple Commands

The commands `who` and `date` are examples of simple commands. A *simple command* is one that can be executed by just specifying the command name at the prompt. The syntax for executing a simple command is

```
$ cmd
```

Here *cmd* is the name of the command to be executed.

Simple commands in UNIX can be small commands such as `who` and `date`, or they can be large commands such as a Web browser or spreadsheet program. Most commands in UNIX can be executed as simple commands.

Complex Commands

A *complex command* consists of a command name followed by a list of arguments. *Arguments* are modifiers specified after the command name and are used to alter the behavior of the command. The syntax for a complex command is

```
$ cmd arg1 arg2 arg3 ... argN
```

Here *cmd* is the name of the command you want to execute, and *arg1* through *argN* are the arguments you want to give *cmd*. As an example, you can use the `who` command to determine information about yourself by executing it as follows:

```
$ who am i
ranga       pts/0        Dec  9 08:49
$
```

In this mode, `who` omits information about the other users and just prints information about you. This is an example of a complex command. Here, the *cmd* is `who` and the arguments, *arg1* and *arg2*, are `am` and `i`. These arguments change the behavior of the `who` command. Most commands accept arguments that modify their behavior.

> Although you can specify any arguments you want to a command, most commands only understand a handful of arguments. Some commands ignore arguments they do not understand, whereas others display error messages. The `man` command, discussed in Chapter 2, can help determine the arguments a command understands.

When `who` was executed as a simple command, it displayed information about all the users who were logged in. This is referred to as the *default behavior* for the `who` command. The default behavior of a command is the output produced by the command when it is executed as a simple command.

Compound Commands

It is possible to combine simple and complex commands into *compound commands*. A compound command consists of a list of simple and complex commands, with each command separated by a semicolon, ;. The syntax for a complex command is

```
$ cmd1 ; cmd2 ; cmd3 ; ... ; cmdN ;
```

Here, *cmd1* through *cmdN* are either simple or complex commands. The order of execution is *cmd1*, followed by *cmd2*, followed by *cmd3*, and so on. When *cmdN* finishes executing, the prompt is returned.

An example of a complex command is

```
$ date ; who am i ;
Wed Dec  9 10:10:10 PST 1998
ranga      pts/0        Dec  9 08:49
$
```

Here the compound command consists of the simple command `date` and the complex command `who am i`. The `date` command is executed first, followed by the `who am i` command. The behavior of the previous complex command is the same as if each of the commands were executed as follows:

```
$ date
Wed Dec  9 10:25:34 PST 1998
$ who am i
ranga      pts/0        Dec  9 08:49
$
```

The difference between executing commands in this fashion and using a compound command is that in a compound command, the prompt is returned only after all the commands that compose the complex command have been executed.

Command Separators

The semicolon character (;) is treated as a *command separator*. Command separators indicate where one command ends and another begins. If a command separator is not used to separate each of the individual commands in a complex command, the system will not be able to distinguish between the ending of one command and the beginning of the next command.

For example, if the previous example is executed without the first semicolon, such as shown here,

```
$ date who am i
```

the system will produce an error message similar to the following:

```
date: bad conversion
```

In this case, `date` thinks that it is being executed as a complex command with the arguments `who`, `am`, and `i`. The `date` command is confused by these arguments and displays an error message. When using complex commands, remember to use the semicolon character.

You can also terminate individual simple and complex commands using the semicolon character. Both of the following commands produce the same output:

```
$ date
$ date ;
```

In the first case, the simple command `date` executes, and the prompt returns. In the second case, the shell thinks that a complex command is executing. It begins by executing the first command in the complex command (in this case, `date`). When this command finishes, the shell tries to execute the next command. In this case, no other commands are left to execute, so the prompt returns.

You will frequently see the semicolon used to terminate simple and complex commands in scripts. Because the semicolon is required to terminate commands in other languages, such as C, Perl, and Java, many script programmers use it the same way in scripts. There is no overhead in using the semicolon for this purpose.

What Is the Shell?

The *shell* provides you with an interface to the UNIX system. It reads input from you and executes the programs you specified. While the programs are executing, it displays their output. For this reason, the shell is often referred to as the UNIX system's *command interpreter*. For users familiar with Windows, the UNIX shell is similar to the DOS shell, `COMMAND.COM`.

The real power of the shell lies in the fact that it is much more than a command interpreter. It is also a powerful programming language, complete with conditional statements, loops, and functions.

If you are familiar with these types of statements from other programming languages, you can learn shell programming quickly. If you haven't seen these before, don't fret. By working through the examples and exercises in this book, you will learn how to effectively use all these statements.

The Shell Prompt

The *prompt*, `$`, discussed earlier in this chapter, is printed by the shell. When the prompt is displayed, you can type in a command. The shell waits for you to press Enter or Return before reading your input. The command to execute is determined by examining the first *word* of your input. A word is a set of characters separated by a space or tab. The shell treats input as follows:

```
$ word1 word2 word3 ... wordN
```

The first word, *`word1`*, is always assumed to be the name of the command to execute. If there is only one word, as in the following example, the shell simply executes the command:

```
$ date
```

If there are multiple words as follows,

```
$ who am i
```

the extra words are passed as arguments to the command specified by *`word1`*.

Different Types of Shells

The prompt on your system might be different from the simple `$` used in this book. The actual prompt that is displayed depends on the type of shell you are using. In UNIX, there are two major types of shells:

- Bourne (includes `sh`, `ksh`, `bash`, and `zsh`)
- C (includes `csh` and `tcsh`)

If you are using most Bourne-type shells, the last character of the default prompt is the dollar sign character, `$`. If you are using a C-type shell or `zsh`, the last character of the default prompt is the percent character, `%`.

This book covers Bourne-type shells. Unless explicitly noted, the examples and exercise answers in this book will work with any Bourne-type shell. The C-type shells have several problems that make them unsuitable for shell programming, thus they are not covered in this book. For more information on this topic, refer to the following article:

`http://www.faqs.org/faqs/unix-faq/shell/csh-whynot/`

In UNIX, there are two types of accounts, regular accounts and the root account. Normal users are given *regular* accounts. The *root* account is an account with special privileges that the administrator of a UNIX system

> (called the *sysadmin*) uses to perform maintenance and upgrades.
>
> When the root account is used, both Bourne-type and C-type shells display the # character as the last character of the prompt.
>
> Use extreme caution when executing commands as the root user because the commands affect the whole system. None of the examples in this book require that you have access to the root account to execute them.

Bourne Shell

The original UNIX shell was written at AT&T Bell Labs in New Jersey during the mid-1970s by Steve Bourne. Because the Bourne shell was the first shell to appear on UNIX systems, it is often referred to as "the shell." Historically, it was installed as `/bin/sh`.

In addition to being a command interpreter, the Bourne shell is a powerful language with a programming syntax similar to that of the ALGOL language. Steve Bourne had written a ALGOL-68 compiler when he was at Cambridge University in England and liked the syntax of that language so much that he modeled the syntax of the shell after it.

Some of the features of the Bourne shell are

- Process control (see Chapter 7, "Processes")
- Variables (see Chapter 8, "Variables")
- Regular expressions (see Chapter 9, "Substitution")
- Flow control (see Chapter 11, "Flow Control," and Chapter 12, "Loops")
- Powerful input and output controls (see Chapter 5, "Input and Output")
- Functions (see Chapter 14, "Functions")

One of the main complaints against the Bourne shell is that, although it is excellent for programming, it is hard to use interactively. Some of the major drawbacks are

- Lack of filename completion
- Lack of command history or command editing
- Difficulty in executing multiple background processes

C Shell

The C shell was written at the University of California at Berkeley in the early 1980s by Bill Joy. C shell was designed to make the shell easier to use interactively. It first appeared in BSD UNIX and was later incorporated into AT&T's version of UNIX. C shell is usually installed as `/bin/csh`.

The C shell updated the shell's syntax from the older ALGOL-like syntax to a more modern C-like syntax. At the time, most people felt that this change would simplify shell programming for Berkeley's UNIX programmers, who were well versed in C and its syntax. As it turned out, C shell could not be used for much more than the most trivial scripts because of the following flaws:

- Weak input and output controls
- Lack of functions
- Confusing syntax

Although the C shell did not catch on for scripts, it has become extremely popular for interactive use. Some of the key improvements responsible for this popularity are:

- *Command History.* Previously executed commands can be recalled for re-execution. The command can also be edited before it is re-executed.
- *Aliases.* C shell allows for the creation of short mnemonic names that can be entered in lieu of the full command names. Aliases are a simplified form of the Bourne shell functions.
- *File Name Completion.* The C shell can automatically complete a filename after a few characters of the file's name have been entered.
- *Job Controls.* The C shell allows for the execution of multiple background processes and allows for their control via the `jobs` command.

The TENEX/TOPS C shell, `tcsh`, is a newer version of the C shell that features several usability enhancements. For example, it can scroll through the command history using the up and down arrow keys and it allows for the editing of commands using right and left arrow keys. For more information on `tcsh`, refer to the following URL:

`http://www.dubois.ws/software/csh-tcsh-book/`

The Korn Shell

For many years, the only shells to choose from were the Bourne shell and the C shell. This meant that most users had to learn two shells, the Bourne shell for programming and the C shell for interactive use. To rectify this situation, David Korn of AT&T Bell Labs wrote the Korn Shell, `ksh`. It incorporates all the C shell's interactive features while preserving the Bourne shell's ALGOL-like syntax. The Korn Shell is usually installed as `/bin/ksh` or `/usr/bin/ksh`.

Some of the additional features that the Korn Shell adds to the Bourne shell are

- Command history and history substitution
- Command aliases and functions

- Filename completion
- Arrays (see Chapter 8)
- Built-in integer arithmetic (see Chapter 9)

In general ksh is fully compatible with sh. Some minor differences exist that can affect the execution of a script. Where appropriate, such differences are noted in this book.

There are several variants of ksh. The official version is pre-installed on most commercial versions of UNIX, such as Solaris and HP-UX. For other systems, it is available in binary form from

http://www.kornshell.com

Most non-commercial versions of UNIX, such as Linux and BSD, use the public domain version of the Korn Shell, pdksh. Eric Gisin created pdksh using Charles Forsyth's public domain V7 shell along with parts of the BRL shell. Currently, pdksh is maintained by Michael Rendell. It is available in both source and binary forms from

http://web.cs.mun.ca/~michael/pdksh/

For the shell programmer, there is no difference between the official and the public domain versions of ksh—scripts that run in one version will run in the other. For users, the official version provides a few nice features such as command line completion with the Tab key rather than the Esc key.

Another variant of ksh is the POSIX shell. The Institute of Electrical and Electronics Engineers (IEEE) created the POSIX standards in order to help programmers write portable programs that are compatible with a wide range of systems. One particular standard, the 1003.2/ISO 9945.2 Shell and Tools specification, specifies the syntax and behavior of a portable shell, which is essentially the syntax and behavior of ksh. Most commercial UNIX vendors are slowly adapting the POSIX standards. HP is currently shipping the POSIX shell as the default shell, /bin/sh, on all of its new HP-UX systems.

Bourne Again Shell

The Bourne Again Shell, bash, was written by Brian Fox of the Free Software Foundation as a replacement for the Bourne shell. At present bash is maintained by Chet Ramey. It incorporates most of the features of csh, tcsh, and ksh while retaining compatibility with the original Bourne shell and compliance with the POSIX standard.

Most Linux distributions, such as Red Hat, Debian, and Slackware, ship with bash installed as /bin/bash and /bin/sh. Because of licensing restrictions, the original Bourne shell cannot be easily distributed with Linux. Since bash is compatible with the Bourne shell, most Linux distributions have chosen to use a copy of bash in place of a genuine Bourne shell.

For non-Linux systems, `bash` is available in both source and binary forms from

`http://cnswww.cns.cwru.edu/~chet/bash/bashtop.html`

Some features that `bash` includes, in addition to those of the Korn Shell, are

- Name completion for variable names, usernames, hostnames, commands, and filenames
- Spelling correction for pathnames in the `cd` command
- Arrays of unlimited size
- Integer arithmetic in any base between 2 and 64

The Z Shell

The Z shell, `zsh`, was written by Paul Falstad while he was a student at Princeton University. It is extremely customizable and is mostly compatible with `ksh`.

On Mac OS X systems, `zsh` is installed as `/bin/zsh` and /bin/sh. Because of licensing issues, Apple has chosen not to distribute the original Bourne shell with Mac OS X. Apple distributes `zsh` as its Bourne shell replacement.

For non-Mac OS X systems, `zsh` is available from

`http://zsh.sunsite.dk/`

In addition to the features of `ksh` and `bash`, some additional features of `zsh` are

- Highly configurable command-line editing
- Fully programmable filename, username, hostname, and history completion
- Highly customizable keyboard mappings

Summary

This chapter covered shell basics, including the execution of simple commands, complex commands, and compound commands. The concept of a shell and several different shells, including `ksh`, `bash`, and `zsh`, were described. The next chapter, "Script Basics," explores the function of the shell in greater detail, starting with interactive and non-interactive uses of the shell.

1

Questions

1. Classify each of the following as simple, complex, or compound commands:

   ```
   $ ls
   $ date ; uptime
   $ ls -l
   $ echo "hello world"
   ```

   If you haven't seen some of these commands before, try them out on your system. As you progress through the book, each will be formally introduced.

2. What is the effect of putting a semicolon at the end of a single simple or complex command?

   For example, will the output of the following commands be different?

   ```
   $ who am i
   $ who am i ;
   ```

3. What are the two major types of shells? Give an example of a shell that falls into each type.

Terms

Arguments Arguments are command modifiers that change the behavior of a command.

Command Separators A command separator indicates where one command ends and another begins. The most common command separator is the semicolon character (`;`).

Commands A command is a program that can be executed. To execute a command, type its name and press Enter or Return.

Complex Commands A complex command is a command that consists of a command name and a list of arguments.

Compound Commands A compound command consists of a list of simple and complex commands separated by the semicolon character (`;`).

Default Behavior The default behavior of a command is the output generated by a command when it is run as a simple command.

Prompt The prompt is displayed by the shell. When the prompt is present, the shell can be given a command to execute. In this book, the `$` character is used to indicate the prompt.

Shell The shell is an interface to the UNIX system. It reads input and executes programs based on that input. When a program has finished executing, it displays that program's output. The shell is sometimes called a command interpreter.

Simple Commands A simple command is a command that can be executed by giving just its name at the prompt.

Words Words are sets of characters separated by spaces and tabs.

HOUR 2

Script Basics

Chapter 1, "Shell Basics," introduced the concept of a shell and commands, and described how the shell reads input and executes the specified commands. This chapter expands on those basic concepts to explain in greater detail what the shell is and how it works, including the login and logout process as it relates to the shell.

This chapter also explains how to group commands that are normally executed interactively into a file, thus creating a program or script. Scripts are the power behind the shell because they allow commands to be grouped together to create new commands.

Specifically, the topics covered in this chapter are

- The UNIX System
- Shell Initialization
- Getting Help

The UNIX System

The UNIX system consists of two main components:

- Utilities
- Kernel

Utilities are programs that can be executed. The programs `who` and `date` from the previous chapter are examples of utilities.

Commands are slightly different from utilities. The term *utility* refers to the name of a program, whereas the term *command* refers to the program and any arguments are specified to that program in order to change its behavior. For simple commands, the term *command* is sometimes used in place of the term *utility*.

The kernel is the heart of the UNIX system. It provides utilities with a means of accessing the computer's hardware. It also handles scheduling and executing commands.

When a computer is powered off, both the kernel and the utilities are stored on the hard drives. When the computer boots, the kernel is loaded from disk into memory and remains in memory until the computer is turned off. Utilities, on the other hand, are stored in files on disk and loaded into memory only when they are requested for execution. For example, when the following command is executed,

```
$ who
```

the kernel loads the `who` command from a file on disk, places it in memory, and starts executing it. When the program finishes executing, it remains in the machine's memory for a short period of time before it is removed. This enables frequently used commands to execute faster. Consider what happens when the `date` command is executed three times in quick succession:

```
$ date
Sun Dec 27 09:42:37 PST 1998
$ date
Sun Dec 27 09:42:38 PST 1998
$ date
Sun Dec 27 09:42:39 PST 1998
```

The first time the `date` command might need to be loaded from the computer's hard disk, but the second and third time the `date` command usually remains in the computer's memory, allowing it to execute faster. Try it on your system and see if you notice a slight delay the first time and no delay the second and third times.

Commands and Files

In UNIX most commands are stored in separate files on disk. For example, the `who` and `date` commands are stored in two separate files named `who` and `date` on the disk; they are not part of the shell. This allows for new commands to be added and bugs in existing commands to be fixed without modifying the shell.

If you are unfamiliar with the concept of a file, don't panic! Files are covered in the next chapter.

Logging In

Just like `date`, the shell is a program that is stored on disk. The main difference is that the shell is loaded into memory when you log in and stays in memory until you log out.

When you first connect to a UNIX system, a login prompt will be presented. Usually it looks similar to

```
login:
```

Here you need to enter a *username*, which is your identity on a UNIX system. After entering a username, another prompt will be presented:

```
login: ranga
Password:
```

Here you need to enter the password corresponding to the username you entered. Your username, password, and associated files are called your *user account*. The system administrator is responsible for creating your user account and providing you with the username and password associated with it.

After reading both the username and password, the system looks through the user database, normally located in the file `/etc/passwd`, for an entry matching the information that was provided. If a match is found, the shell associated with that entry is executed; otherwise, an error is displayed.

For those of you who are not familiar with UNIX file and directory names, such as `/etc/passwd`, these topics are covered in Chapter 3, "Working with Files," and Chapter 4, "Working with Directories."

Files and directories are discussed very briefly in this chapter. A general idea about files and directories from other operating systems is sufficient to understand the examples.

The following is a sample entry from `/etc/passwd` on my system:

```
ranga:x:500:100:Sriranga Veeraraghavan:/home/ranga:/bin/bash
```

The entry is composed of several fields, each separated from the other fields by a colon, :. Later chapters will explain the information stored in each field. For now, only the last two fields are important. The last field stores the shell associated with the account. The second from the last field stores the *home directory* for the account. The home directory is where you first start out after logging in. In some documentation, you will see home directories denoted by a tilde, ~, or a tilde followed by a slash, `~/`. In the previous example, the shell is `/bin/bash` and the home directory is `/home/ranga`. Your shell and home directory will most likely be different.

In most cases, the system administrator will assign you the default shell for a particular version of UNIX. In some cases, there are two defaults and the system administrator can choose between them based on his personal preferences.

The default shells for some common versions of UNIX are as follows:

- Solaris uses Bourne shell or C Shell.
- HP-UX uses POSIX shell.
- BSD uses Korn Shell or C Shell.
- Mac OS X uses Z Shell or C Shell.
- Linux uses the Bourne Again Shell.

For the sake of brevity, we assume that you have been assigned Bourne shell, Korn Shell (`ksh`), Bourne Again Shell (`bash`), or Z Shell (`zsh`) as your shell.

Shell Modes and Initialization

In this section, we will first discuss the startup procedure for the various Bourne-type shells, and then we will examine the different modes of execution for a shell.

Initialization Procedures

After you log in, a shell is executed on your behalf. When this shell starts executing, it is *uninitialized*. In this state, several parameters required for its proper operation are not defined. The shell undergoes a process called *initialization* that defines these parameters. The steps and files involved in initialization are different in each shell, so we will examine the process used by each of the Bourne-type shells individually. In general each of the shells uses default or system-wide configuration files located in the `/etc` directory along with a set of personal configuration files located in your home directory.

Bourne Shell

Bourne shell initialization has four steps and involves the initialization files (also called init files) `/etc/profile` and `.profile`. The process is as follows:

1. The shell checks to see whether the file `/etc/profile` exists.
2. If it exists, the shell reads it; otherwise, the shell skips it.
3. The shell checks to see whether the file `.profile` exists in your home directory.
4. If it exists, the shell reads it; otherwise, the shell skips it.

After these steps have been performed, the prompt is displayed. The default prompt for Bourne shell is `$` (a dollar sign followed by a space).

Korn Shell

Korn Shell (`ksh`) closely resembles Bourne shell initialization. It has six steps and involves the init files `/etc/profile`, `.profile`, and `.kshrc`:

1. `ksh` checks to see whether the file `/etc/profile` exists.
2. If it exists, `ksh` reads it; otherwise, `ksh` skips it.
3. `ksh` checks to see whether the file `.profile` exists in your home directory.
4. If it exists, `ksh` reads it; otherwise, `ksh` skips it.
5. `ksh` checks to see whether the file `.kshrc` exists in your home directory.
6. If it exists, `ksh` reads it; otherwise, `ksh` skips it.

After these steps have been performed, the prompt is displayed. The default prompt for `ksh` is `$` (a dollar sign followed by a space).

Bourne Again Shell

Bourne Again shell (`bash`) initialization is a bit longer than Korn shell and Bourne shell initialization. It has eight steps and involves the init files `/etc/profile`, `.bash_profile`, `.bash_login`, and `.profile`:

1. `bash` checks to see whether the file `/etc/profile` exists.
2. If it exists, `bash` reads it; otherwise, `bash` skips it.
3. `bash` checks to see whether the file `.bash_profile` exists in your home directory.
4. If it exists, `bash` reads it; otherwise, `bash` skips it.
5. `bash` checks to see whether the file `.bash_login` exists in your home directory.
6. If it exists, `bash` reads it; otherwise, `bash` skips it.
7. `bash` checks to see whether the file `.profile` exists in your home directory.
8. If it exists, `bash` reads it; otherwise, `bash` skips it.

After these steps have been performed, a prompt is displayed. The default prompt for bash is bash$ (the string bash$ followed by a space).

Z Shell

Z shell (zsh) initialization is quite long and does not resemble the initialization process of the other shells. It has 16 steps and involves the init files /etc/zshenv, .zshenv, /etc/zprofile, .zprofile, /etc/zlogin, and .zlogin:

1. zsh checks to see whether the file /etc/zshenv exists.
2. If it exists, zsh reads it; otherwise, zsh skips it.
3. zsh checks to see whether the file .zshenv exists in your home directory.
4. If it exists, zsh reads it; otherwise, zsh skips it.
5. zsh checks to see whether the file /etc/zprofile exists.
6. If it exists, zsh reads it; otherwise, zsh skips it.
7. zsh checks to see whether the file .zprofile exists in your home directory.
8. If it exists, zsh reads it; otherwise, zsh skips it.
9. zsh checks to see whether the file /etc/zshrc exists.
10. If it exists, zsh reads it; otherwise, zsh skips it.
11. zsh checks to see whether the file .zshrc exists in your home directory.
12. If it exists, zsh reads it; otherwise, zsh skips it.
13. zsh checks to see whether the file /etc/zlogin exists.
14. If it exists, zsh reads it; otherwise, zsh skips it.
15. zsh checks to see whether the file .zlogin exists in your home directory.
16. If it exists, zsh reads it; otherwise, zsh skips it.

After these steps have been performed, a prompt is displayed. The default prompt for zsh is *host*%. Here *host* is the hostname of your system. For example, on a system named mars, the default zsh prompt would be mars%.

Initialization File Contents

Usually a shell's init files are quite short. The purpose of these files is to provide a complete working environment with as little overhead as possible. In this section, we will look at the basic settings required for Bourne shell. If you are using a different shell, you can put these settings into an init file used by that shell.

The init file `.profile` contains all of your shell initialization settings. You can add as much customization information as you want to this file. The minimum set of information that you need to configure includes

- A list of directories in which to locate commands
- A list of directories in which to locate manual pages for commands

Setting PATH

When you type the command,

```
$ date
```

the shell has to locate the command `date` before it can be executed. The `PATH` variable-specifies the directories in which the shell should look for commands. The most basic setting is as follows:

```
PATH=/bin:/usr/bin
```

Each of the individual entries separated by the colon character, `:`, should be directories. Directories are discussed in Chapter 4.

If you request the shell to execute a command and it cannot find it in any of the directories given in the `PATH` variable, a message similar to the following appears:

```
$ hello
hello: not found
```

Setting MANPATH

In UNIX, online help has been available since the beginning. The next section, "Getting Help," discusses how to access the online help using the `man` command. In order for this command to work properly, you have to tell the shell where the help pages are located. This information is specified using the `MANPATH`. A common setting is

```
MANPATH=/usr/man:/usr/share/man
```

Similar to the path, each of the individual entries separated by the colon character, `:`, are directories.

When you use the `man` command to request online help, it searches every directory given in the `MANPATH` for an online help page corresponding to the topic you requested. For example, the command

```
$ man who
```

looks for the online help page corresponding to the `who` command. If this page is found, it is displayed.

Interactive and Non-Interactive Shells

Shell can run in two different modes: interactive and non-interactive. In *interactive mode*, the shell expects to read input from you and execute the commands that you specify. This mode is called interactive because it interacts with the user . In *non-interactive* mode, the shell does not interact with the user; instead it reads commands stored in a file and executes them. When it reaches the end of the file, it exits.

Most people are familiar with interactive mode: log in, execute some commands in the shell, and log out.

Starting an Interactive Shell

To start a shell in interactive mode, you can type in its name at the prompt. For example, the following command starts `bash` in interactive mode:

```
$ /bin/bash
bash$
```

The first prompt, `$`, that is displayed by the shell started on your behalf when you logged in; the second prompt, `bash$`, is displayed by the `bash` you started.

At this point, we have two interactive shells: The first one is waiting for the other to finish. At first glance, this does not sound extremely useful, but there are cases in which it can be quite helpful. For example, if you need to make changes to the shell's settings, the easiest way to test your changes is to start another shell, perform and verify the changes, and then exit back to the original, unaltered shell.

To exit from the second shell, you can use the `exit` command:

```
bash$ exit
$
```

This returns you to the original shell. If you type `exit` here, the system will log you out. The `exit` command works in all Bourne-type shells.

Starting a Non-Interactive Shell

You can start a shell in non-interactive mode as follows:

```
$ /bin/sh filename
```

Here *`filename`* is the name of a file that contains commands to execute. As an example, consider the compound command:

```
$ date ; who
```

Let's put these commands into a file called `logins`. First open a file called `logins` in an editor and type in this command and save the file. Now you can execute the commands in this file using the command:

```
$ /bin/sh logins
```

This executes the compound command and displays its output. This is the first example of a shell script or shell program. Basically, a *shell script* is a file that contains a list of commands. When the shell executes the commands contained in the file, it does so without interacting with the user. For this reason, when the shell is used to execute a shell script, it is said to execute in non-interactive mode.

Making a Shell Script Executable

One of the most important tasks in writing shell scripts is making the shell script executable and making sure that the correct shell is invoked on the script.

In a previous example, you created the `logins` script that executes the following compound command:

```
date ; who ;
```

If you wanted to run the script by just typing its name, you need to do two things:

- Mark the file as executable.
- Make sure that the right shell is used to execute the script.

To make this script executable, you need to execute a command of the form:

```
chmod a+x filename
```

The `chmod` command, when used in this form, marks the file specified by *`filename`* as executable. For a complete discussion of `chmod` and its function, see Chapter 6, "Manipulating File Attributes." As an example, the following command marks the file `logins` executable:

```
$ chmod a+x $logins
```

To ensure that the correct shell is used to execute a script, you must add a *magic* line, of the following form, as the first line of the script:

```
#!shell
```

Here *`shell`* is the name of the shell that should be used to execute the script. In most cases, you will want to use `/bin/sh` as `shell`, but if you want to use `ksh` for your scripts, you can specify `/bin/ksh` instead. Without a magic line, the current shell is always used to evaluate a script, regardless of which shell the script was written for. If you omit the magic line from your scripts, `csh` and `tcsh` users might not be able to run them correctly.

> **The Magic of `#!/bin/sh`**
>
> The `#!/bin/sh` must be the first line of a shell script in order for `sh` to be used to run the script. If this appears on any other line, it is treated as a comment and ignored by all shells.

After this addition, the `logins` script contains two lines:

```
#/bin/sh
date ; who ;
```

Now it is possible to execute the script by just typing in its name:

```
$ logins
Tue Sep 18 18:44:12 PDT 2001
ranga    console  Sep 12 10:22
```

Comments

The magic first line for the shell script, `#!/bin/sh`, introduces the concept of comments. A *comment* is a statement embedded in a shell script that is not intended for execution by the shell. In shell scripts, comments start with the `#` character. Everything between the `#` and end of the line are considered part of the comment and are ignored by the shell.

Adding comments to a script is quite simple: Open the script using an editor and add lines that start with the `#` character. For example, to add the following line to the `logins` shell script,

```
# print out the date and who's logged on
```

you can open the file `logins` with an editor and insert this line as the second line in the file. Now the script has three lines:

```
#!/bin/sh
# print out the date and who's logged on
date ; who ;
```

There is no change in the output of the script because comments are ignored. Comments do not slow down a script because the shell just skips them.

You can also add comments to lines that contain commands by adding the `#` character after the commands. For example, you can add a comment to the line `date ; who ;` as follows:

```
date ; who ; # execute the date and who commands
```

When you are writing a shell script, make sure to use comments to explain what the script is doing. If someone else has to look at your shell script, it will help him to understand how your script functions. Comments can also help you figure out what your script is doing, months or years after you wrote it.

Getting Help

As you read through this book, you will want to get more information about the commands and features that are discussed. Much of this information is available by using the online help features of UNIX. Some other resources include Web sites that cover shell programming and Usenet newsgroups.

man

Every version of UNIX comes with an extensive collection of online help pages called *man pages* (short for *manual pages*). The man pages are the authoritative source about your UNIX system. They contain complete information about both the kernel and all the utilities.

You can access man pages by using the `man` command:

```
man cmd
```

Here, *cmd* is the name of a command that you want more information about. As an example,

```
$ man uptime
```

displays the following man page on a Solaris machine:

```
User Commands                                        uptime(1)

NAME
     uptime - show how long the system has been up

SYNOPSIS
     uptime

DESCRIPTION
     The uptime command prints the current time,  the  length  of
     time  the system has been up, and the average number of jobs
     in the run queue over the last 1, 5 and 15 minutes.  It  is,
     essentially,  the first line of a w(1) command.

EXAMPLE
     Below is an example of the output uptime provides:
          example% uptime
```

```
        10:47am  up 27 day(s), 50 mins,  1 user,
        ➥load average: 0.18, 0.26, 0.20

SEE ALSO
     w(1), who(1), whodo(1M), attributes(5)

NOTES
     who -b gives the time the system was last booted.
```

Man Page Sections

As you can see from the output in the previous example, a man page is divided into several sections that are described in Table 2.1. Almost every man page will include these sections. The content and style of the material in the sections differs from system to system.

TABLE 2.1 Sections in a Man Page

Section	*Description*
NAME	This section gives the name of the command along with a short description of it.
SYNOPSIS	This section describes all the different modes in which the command can be run. If a command accepts arguments, they are shown in this section.
DESCRIPTION	This section includes a verbose description of the command. If a command accepts arguments, each argument will be fully explained in this section.
EXAMPLE	This section contains an example demonstrating how to execute the command. It might also contain some sample output. Not all man pages contain this section.
SEE ALSO	This section lists other commands that are related to the command.
NOTES	This section usually lists some additional information about the command. Sometimes it lists the known bugs.

Most man pages include all the sections given in Table 2.1 and might include one or two optional sections described in Table 2.2.

TABLE 2.2 Optional Sections Found in Man Pages

Section	*Description*
AVAILABILITY	This section describes the versions of UNIX that include support for a given command. Sometimes it lists the optional software packages you need to purchase from the vendor to gain extra functionality from a command.
KNOWN BUGS	This section usually lists one or more known problems with the command. If you encounter a problem that is not included in this section, it should be reported to the vendor or author.

TABLE 2.2 continued

Section	*Description*
`FILES`	This section lists the files that are required for the command to function correctly. It might also list the files that can be used to configure a command.
`AUTHORS` or `CONTACTS`	These sections list the commands' author or authors and provide contact information such as e-mail or postal addresses.
`STANDARDS COMPLIANCE`	If the behavior of a command is specified by a standards organization such as ISO (International Standards Organization), IEEE (Institute of Electrical and Electronic Engineers), or ANSI (American National Standards Institute), this section lists the relevant standard or standards.

Try using the `man` command to get more information on some of the commands discussed in this chapter.

If the `man` command cannot find a man page corresponding to the command you requested, it issues an error message. For example, the command

```
$ man apple
```

produces an error message similar to the following on my system:

```
No manual entry for apple
```

The exact error message depends on your version of UNIX.

UNIX System Manuals

The term manual page comes from the original versions of UNIX, when the online pages were available as large bound manuals. In all, there were eight different manuals covering the main topics of the UNIX system. These manuals are described in Table 2.3.

TABLE 2.3 The UNIX System Manuals

Manual Section	*Description*
1	Covers commands.
2	Covers UNIX *system calls*. System calls are used inside a program, such as `date`, to ask the kernel for a service.
3	Covers libraries. Libraries are used to store non–kernel-related functions used by C programmers.
4	Covers file formats. For example, the format file `/etc/passwd` is documented in this section.

TABLE 2.3 continued

Manual Section	*Description*
5	A secondary section that covers file formats.
6	Includes instructions for playing games on UNIX. (UNIX wasn't always a serious academic and business operating system; it started out as a gaming platform!)
7	Covers device drivers.
8	Covers system maintenance.

In the printed version, you had to know the section where you needed to look for a particular manual page. The big advantage of `man` over the printed manual is that `man` looks in all the sections of the manual for the information you requested, making it much easier to get help.

Online Resources

In addition to `man`, there are several Usenet newsgroups, Web sites, and e-mail lists that are good sources of information about the different shells and shell programming.

The main Usenet newsgroup for shell programming questions and information is `comp.unix.shell`. Before posting a question, you should read the *frequently asked questions (FAQ)* for the newsgroup. The FAQ is located at

`http://www.faqs.org/faqs/unix-faq/shell/intro/`

Often you will find that your question, or something very similar to it, has an answer in this or one of the other FAQ's mentioned later.

For questions regarding the Bourne Again shell (`bash`), you can subscribe to the `bash` e-mail list: `bug-bash@gnu.org`. A subscription form is located at

`http://mail.gnu.org/mailman/listinfo/bug-bash`

If you prefer reading news to e-mail, the e-mail list is available as the newsgroup `gnu.bash.bug`. Before posting to the newsgroup, you should read the `bash` FAQ located at

`http://www.faqs.org/faqs/unix-faq/shell/bash/`

For questions regarding the Z Shell (`zsh`), you can subscribe to the zsh-users mailing list: `zsh-users@sunsite.dk`. Subscription instructions can be found at

`http://zsh.sunsite.dk/Arc/mlist.html`

Before posting to the mailing list, you should read the zsh FAQ located at

```
http://www.faqs.org/faqs/unix-faq/shell/zsh/
```

The following Web sites are also excellent references for shell programming:

```
http://www-h.eng.cam.ac.uk/help/tpl/unix/scripts/scripts.html
http://www.shelldorado.com/
```

The first site contains a tutorial on shell programming written by Tim Love at Cambridge University. The second site is an archive of shell scripts and shell programming information maintained by Heiner Steven of Sun Microsystems.

Summary

This chapter covered what the shell is and how it operates in greater detail. The init process for the various shells was described along with a brief description of the basic information required in the init file .profile. The different modes of operation for the shell, interactive and non-interactive, were also covered. Shell programming relies on the non-interactive mode because it enables commands specified in a file to be executed.

We also covered man and man pages, the online help system in UNIX. Finally, online sources for shell programming information, such as Usenet newsgroups, Web sites, and e-mail lists, were covered.

The next chapter formally introduces the concept of files by showing you how to list files, view the contents of files, and manipulate files.

Questions

1. What are the two files used by the shell to initialize itself?
2. Why do you need to set PATH and MANPATH?
3. What is the purpose of the following line in a shell script?

   ```
   #!/bin/sh
   ```

4. What command should you use to access the online help?

Terms

Commands A command is comprised of the name of a program along with zero or more arguments. You might see the term command used instead of the term utility for simple commands, where only the program name is given.

Comments A comment is a statement that is embedded in a shell script but is not executed by the shell.

Home Directory The home directory is where you first start out after logging in.

Interactive Mode In interactive mode, the shell reads input from the user and executes the specified commands. This mode is called interactive because the shell is interacting with a user.

Kernel The kernel is the heart of the UNIX system. It provides utilities with a means of accessing a machine's hardware. It also handles scheduling and executing commands.

Man Pages Every version of UNIX comes with an extensive collection of online help pages called man pages (short for manual pages). The man pages are the authoritative source about your UNIX system. They contain complete information about both the kernel and all the utilities.

Non-interactive Mode In non-interactive mode, the shell does not interact with the user; instead it reads commands stored in a file and executes them. When the shell reaches the end of the file, it exits.

Shell Initialization After a shell is started, it undergoes a phase called initialization in which important parameters are set up.

Shell Script A shell script is a list of commands stored in a file.

Uninitialized Shell An uninitialized shell is one that has not yet read its init files in order to set up the parameters required for its proper operation.

Utilities Utilities are programs, such as `who` and `date`, that can be executed.

HOUR 3

Working with Files

In UNIX there are two basic types of files: ordinary and special. An *ordinary* file contains data, text, or program instructions. Almost all of the files on a UNIX system are ordinary files. This chapter covers operations on ordinary files.

Special files are mainly used to provide access to hardware such as hard drives, CD-ROM drives, modems, and Ethernet adapters. Some special files are similar to aliases or shortcuts and enable you to access a single file using different names. Special files are covered in Chapter 6, “Manipulating File Attributes.”

Both ordinary and special files are stored in directories. *Directories* are similar to folders in the Mac OS or Windows, and they are covered in detail in Chapter 4, “Working with Directories.”

In this chapter, we will examine ordinary files, concentrating on the following topics:

- Listing files
- File contents
- Manipulating files

Listing Files

We'll start by using the `ls` (short for **list**) command to list the contents of the current directory:

```
$ ls
```

The output will be similar to the following:

```
Desktop         Icon            Music           Sites
Documents       Library         Pictures        Temporary Items
Downloads       Movies          Public
```

We can tell that several items are in the current directory, but this output does not tell us whether these items are files or directories. To find out which of the items are files and which are directories, we can specify the `-F` *option* to `ls`. An option is an argument that starts with the hyphen or dash character, '`-`'.

The following example illustrates the use of the `-F` option of `ls`:

```
$ ls -F
```

Now the output for the directory is slightly different:

```
Desktop/        Icon            Music/          Sites/
Documents/      Library/        Pictures/       Temporary Items/
Downloads/      Movies/         Public/
```

As you can see, some of the items now have a `/` at the end, incicating each of these items is a directory. The other items, such as `icon`, have no character appended to them. This indicates that they are ordinary files.

When the `-F` option is specified to `ls`, it appends a character indicating the file type of each of the items it lists. The exact character depends on your version of `ls`. For ordinary files, no character is appended. For special files, a character such as `!`, `@`, or `#` is appended to the filename. For more information on the `-F` options, check the UNIX manual page for the `ls` command. You can do this as follows:

```
$ man ls
```

Options Are Case Sensitive

The options that can be specified to a command, such as `ls`, are case sensitive. When specifying an option, you need to make sure that you have specified the correct case for the option. For example, the output from the `-F` option to `ls` is different from the output produced when the `-f` option is specified.

So far, you have seen `ls` list more than one file on a line. Although this is fine for humans reading the output, it is hard to manipulate in a shell script. Shell scripts are geared toward dealing with lines of text, not the individual words on a line. Although external tools, such as the `awk` language covered in Chapter 17, "Filtering Text with `awk`," can be used to deal with multiple words on a line, it is much easier to manipulate the output when each file is listed on a separate line. You can modify the output of `ls` to this format by using the `-1` option. For example,

```
$ ls -1
```

produces the following listing:

```
Desktop
Documents
Downloads
Icon
Library
Movies
Music
Pictures
Public
Sites
Temporary Items
```

3

Hidden Files

In the examples you have seen thus far, the output has listed only the visible files and directories. You can also use `ls` to list invisible or hidden files and directories. An *invisible* or *hidden* file is one whose first character is a dot or period (`.`). Many programs, including the shell, use such files to store configuration information. Some common examples of invisible files include

- `.profile`, the Bourne shell (`sh`) initialization script
- `.kshrc`, the Korn Shell (`ksh`) initialization script
- `.cshrc`, the C Shell (`csh`) initialization script
- `.rhosts`, the remote shell configuration file

All files that do not start with the `.` character are considered *visible*.

To list invisible files, specify the `-a` option to `ls`:

```
$ ls -a
```

The directory listing now resembles this:

```
.                   .FBCLockFolder      Icon                Public
..                  .ssh                Library             Sites
.CFUserTextEncoding Desktop             Movies              Temporary Items
```

```
.DS_Store           Documents           Music
.FBCIndex           Downloads           Pictures
```

As you can see, this directory contains several invisible files.

Notice that in this output, the file type information is missing. To get the file type information, specify the `-F` and the `-a` options as follows:

```
$ ls -a -F
```

The output changes to the following:

```
./                       .ssh/               Movies/
../                      Desktop/            Music/
.CFUserTextEncoding      Documents/          Pictures/
.DS_Store                Downloads/          Public/
.FBCIndex                Icon?               Sites/
.FBCLockFolder/          Library/            Temporary Items/
```

With the file type information, you see that there are two invisible directories (`.` and `..`). These directories are special entries present in all directories. The first one, `.`, represents the current directory, whereas the second one, `..`, represents the parent directory. These concepts are discussed in greater detail in Chapter 4.

Option Grouping

In the previous example, you specified the options to `ls` separately. You could have grouped the options together, as follows:

```
$ ls -aF
$ ls -Fa
```

Both of these commands are equivalent to the following command:

```
$ ls -a -F
```

The order of the options does not matter to `ls`. As an example of option grouping, consider the following equivalent commands:

```
ls -1 -a -F
ls -1aF
ls -a1F
ls -Fa1
```

All permutations of the options `-1`, `-a`, and `-F` produce the same output:

```
./
../
.CFUserTextEncoding
.DS_Store
```

```
.FBCIndex
.FBCLockFolder/
.ssh/
Desktop/
Documents/
Downloads/
Icon?
Library/
Movies/
Music/
Pictures/
Public/
Sites/
Temporary Items/
```


File Contents

In the last section we looked at listing files and directories with the `ls` command. In this section we will look at the `cat` and `wc` commands. The `cat` command lets you view the contents of a file. The `wc` command gives you information about the number of words and lines in a file.

cat

To view the contents of a file, we can use the `cat` (short for con**cat**enate) command as follows:

```
cat [opts] file1 ... fileN
```

Here `opts` are one or more of the options understood by `cat`, and `file1...fileN` are the names of the files whose contents should be printed. The options, `opts`, are optional and can be omitted. Two commonly used options are discussed later in this section.

The following example illustrates the use of `cat`:

```
$ cat fruits
```

This command prints the contents of a file called `fruits`:

```
Fruit           Price/lbs       Quantity
Banana          $0.89           100
Peach           $0.79           65
Kiwi            $1.50           22
Pineapple       $1.29           35
Apple           $0.99           78
```

If more than one file is specified, the output includes the contents of both files concatenated together. For example, the following command outputs the contents of the files `fruits` and `users`:

```
$ cat fruits users
Fruit           Price/lbs       Quantity
Banana          $0.89           100
Peach           $0.79           65
Kiwi            $1.50           22
Pineapple       $1.29           35
Apple           $0.99           78

ranga
vathsa
amma
```

Numbering Lines

The `-n` option of `cat` will number each line of output. It can be used as follows:

```
$ cat -n fruits
```

This produces the output

```
     1  Fruit           Price/lbs       Quantity
     2  Banana          $0.89           100
     3  Peach           $0.79           65
     4  Kiwi            $1.50           22
     5  Pineapple       $1.29           35
     6  Apple           $0.99           78
     7
```

From this output, you can see that the last line in this file is blank. We can ask `cat` to skip numbering blank lines using the `-b` option as follows:

```
$ cat -b fruits
```

Now the output resembles the following:

```
     1  Fruit           Price/lbs       Quantity
     2  Banana          $0.89           100
     3  Peach           $0.79           65
     4  Kiwi            $1.50           22
     5  Pineapple       $1.29           35
     6  Apple           $0.99           78
```

The blank line is still presented in the output, but it is not numbered. If the blank line occurs in the middle of a file, it is printed but not numbered:

```
$ cat -b hosts
     1  127.0.0.1       localhost           loopback

     2  128.32.43.52    soda.berkeley.edu   soda
```

If multiple files are specified, the contents of the files are concatenated in the output, but line numbering is restarted at 1 for each file. As an illustration, the following command,

```
$ cat -b fruits users
```

produces the output

```
     1  Fruit          Price/lbs      Quantity
     2  Banana         $0.89          100
     3  Peach          $0.79          65
     4  Kiwi           $1.50          22
     5  Pineapple      $1.29          35
     6  Apple          $0.99          78

     1  ranga
     2  vathsa
     3  amma
```


wc

Now let's look at getting some information about the contents of a file. Using the `wc` command (short for **w**ord **c**ount), we can get a count of the total number of lines, words, and characters contained in a file. The basic syntax of this command is:

```
wc [opts] files
```

Here `opts` are one or more of the options given in Table 3.1, and `files` are the files you want examined. The options, *`opts`*, are optional and can be omitted.

TABLE 3.1 `wc` Options

Option	*Description*
`-l`	Count of the number of lines.
`-w`	Count of the number of words.
`-m`	Count of the number of characters. This option is available on Mac OS X, OpenBSD, Solaris, and HP-UX. This option is not available on FreeBSD and Linux systems.
`-c`	Count of the number of characters. This option is the Linux and FreeBSD equivalents of the `-m` option.

When no options are specified, the default behavior of `wc` is to print out a summary of the number of lines, words, and characters contained in a file. For example, the command

```
$ wc fruits
```

produces the following output:

```
       8      18     219 fruits
```

The first number, in this case `8`, is the number of lines in the file. The second number, in this case `18`, is the number of words in the file. The third number, in this case `219`, is the number of characters in the file. At the end of the line, the filename is listed. When multiple files are specified, the filename helps to identify the information associated with a particular file.

If more than one file is specified, `wc` gives the counts for each file along with a total. For example, the command

```
$ wc fruits users
```

produces output similar to the following:

```
       8      18     219 fruits
       3       3      18 users
      11      21     237 total
```

The output on your system might be slightly different.

Counting Lines

To count the number of lines, the `-l` (as in lines) option can be used. For example, the command

```
$ wc -l fruits
```

produces the output

```
       8 fruits
```

The first number, in this case `8`, is the number of lines in the file. The name of the file is listed at the end of the line.

When multiple files are specified, the number of lines in each file is listed along with the total number of lines in all of the specified files. As an example, the command

```
$ wc -l fruits users
```

produces the output

```
       8 fruits
       3 users
      11 total
```

Counting Words

To count the number of words in a file, the `-w` (as in words) option can be used. For example, the command

```
$ wc -w fruits
```

produces the output

```
    18 hosts
```

The first number, in this case `18`, is the number of words in the file. The name of the file is listed at the end of the line.

When multiple files are specified, the number of words in each file is listed along with the total number of words in all of the specified files. As an example, the command

```
$ wc -w fruits users
```

produces the output

```
    18 fruits
     3 users
    21 total
```


Counting Characters

To count the number of characters, we need to use either the `-m` or the `-c` option. The `-m` option is available on Mac OS X, OpenBSD, Solaris, and HP-UX. On FreeBSD and Linux systems, the `-c` option should be used instead.

For example, on Solaris the command

```
$ wc -m fruits
```

produces the output

```
     219 fruits
```

The same output is produced on Linux and FreeBSD systems using the command

```
$ wc -c fruits
```

The first number, in this case `219`, is the number of characters in the file. The name of the file is listed at the end of the line.

When multiple files are specified, the number of characters in each file is listed along with the total number of characters in all the specified files. As an example, the command

```
$ wc -m fruits users
```

produces the output

```
219 hosts
 18 users
237 total
```

Combining Options

The options to `wc` can be grouped together and specified in any order. For example, to obtain a count of the number of lines and words in the file `fruits`, we can use any of the following commands:

```
$ wc -w -l fruits
$ wc -l -w fruits
$ wc -wl fruits
$ wc -lw fruits
```

The output from each of these commands is identical:

```
8      18 fruits
```

The output lists the number of words in the files, followed by the number of lines in the file. The filename is specified at the end of the line. When multiple files are specified, the information for each file is listed along with the appropriate total values.

Manipulating Files

In the preceding sections, you looked at listing files and viewing their content. In this section, you will look at copying, renaming, and removing files using the `cp`, `mv`, and `rm` commands.

Copying Files (`cp`)

The `cp` command (short for copy) is used to make a copy of a file. The basic syntax of the command is

```
cp src dest
```

Here `src` is the name of the file to be copied (the source) and `dest` is the name of the copy (the destination). For example, the following command creates a copy of the file `fruits` in a file named `fruits.sav`:

```
$ cp fruits fruits.sav
```

If *`dest`* is the name of a directory, a copy with the same name as *`src`* is created in *`dest`*. For example, the command

```
$ cp fruits Documents/
```

creates a copy of the file `fruits` in the directory `Documents`.

It is also possible to specify multiple source files to `cp`, provided that the destination, `dest`, is a directory. The syntax for copying multiple files is

```
$ cp src1 ... srcN dest
```

Here `src1 ... srcN` are the source files and `dest` is the destination directory. As an example, the following command

```
$ cp fruits users Documents/
```

creates a copy the files `fruits` and `users` in the directory `Documents`.

Interactive Mode

The default behavior of `cp` is to automatically overwrite the destination file if it exists. This behavior can lead to problems. The `-i` option (short for interactive) can be used to prevent such problems. In interactive mode, `cp` prompts for confirmation before overwriting any files.

3

Assuming that the file `fruits.sav` exists, the following command

```
$ cp -i fruits fruits.sav
```

results in a prompt similar to the following:

```
overwrite fruits.sav? (y/n)
```

If `y` (yes) is chosen, the file `fruits.sav` is overwritten; otherwise the file is untouched. The actual prompt varies among the different versions of UNIX.

Common Errors

When an error is encountered, `cp` generates a message. Some common error conditions follow:

- The source, *`src`*, is a directory.
- The source, *`src`*, does not exist.
- The destination, *`dest`*, is not a directory when multiple sources, *`src1 ... srcN`*, are specified.
- A non-existent destination, *`dest`*, is specified along with multiple sources, *`src1 ... srcN`*.
- One of the sources in *`src1 ... srcN`* is not a file.

The first error type is illustrated by the following command:

```
$ cp Downloads/ fruits
```

Because *`src`* (`Downloads` in this case) is a directory, an error message similar to the following is generated:

```
cp: Downloads: is a directory
```

In this example, `dest` was the file `fruits`; the same error would have been generated if `dest` was a directory.

The second error type is illustrated by the following command:

```
$ cp fritus fruits.sav
cp: cannot access fritus: No such file or directory
```

Here the filename `fruits` has been misspelled `fritus`, resulting in an error. In this example `dest` was the file `fruits.sav`; the same error would have been generated if *`dest`* was a directory.

The third error type is illustrated by the following command:

```
$ cp fruits users fruits.sav
usage: cp [-R [-H | -L | -P]] [-f | -i] [-p] src target
       cp [-R [-H | -L | -P]] [-f | -i] [-p] src1 ... srcN directory
```

Because *`dest`*, in this case `fruits.sav`, is not a directory, a usage statement that highlights the proper syntax for a `cp` command is presented. The output might be different on your system because some versions of `cp` do not display the usage information.

If the file `fruits.sav` does not exist, the error message is

```
cp: fruits.sav: No such file or directory
```

This illustrates the fourth error type.

The fifth error type is illustrated by the following command:

```
$ cp fruits Downloads/ users Documents/
cp: Downloads is a directory (not copied).
```

Although `cp` reports an error for the directory `Downloads`, the other files are correctly copied to the directory `Documents`.

Renaming Files (`mv`)

The `mv` command (short for move) can be used to change the name of a file. The basic syntax is

```
mv src dest
```

Here `src` is the original name of the file and `dest` is the new name of the file. For example, the command

```
$ mv fruits fruits.sav
```

changes the name of the file `fruits` to `fruits.sav`. There is no output from `mv` if the name change is successful.

If `src` does not exist, an error will be generated. For example,

```
$ mv cp fritus fruits.sav
mv: fritus: cannot access: No such file or directory
```

Similar to `cp`, `mv` does not report an error if `dest` already exists. The old file is automatically overwritten. This problem can be avoided by specifying the `-i` option (short for interactive). In interactive mode, `mv` prompts for confirmation before overwriting any files.

Assuming that the file `fruits.sav` already exists, the command

```
$ mv -i fruits fruits.sav
```

results in a confirmation prompt similar to the following:

```
overwrite fruits.sav?
```

If `y` (yes) is chosen, the file `fruits.sav` is overwritten; otherwise the file is untouched. The actual prompt varies among the different versions of UNIX.

Removing Files (`rm`)

The `rm` command (short for remove) can be used to remove or delete files. Its syntax is

```
rm file1 ... fileN
```

Here `file1 ... fileN` is a list of one or more files to remove. For example, the command

```
$ rm fruits users
```

removes the files `fruits` and `users`.

Because there is no way to recover files that have been removed using `rm`, you should make sure that you specify only those files you really want removed. One way to ensure this is by specifying the `-i` option (short for interactive). In interactive mode, `rm` prompts before removing every file. For example, the command

```
$ rm -i fruits users
```

produces confirmation prompts similar to the following:

```
fruits: ? (n/y) y
users: ? (n/y) n
```

In this case, you answered `y` (yes) to removing `fruits` and `n` (no) to removing `users`. Thus, the file `fruits` was removed, but the file `users` was untouched.

3

Common Errors

The two most common errors when using `rm` are

- One of the specified files does not exist.
- One of the specified files is a directory.

The first error type is illustrated by the following command:

```
$ rm users fritus hosts
rm: fritus non-existent
```

Because the file `fruits` is misspelled as `fritus`, it cannot be removed. The other two files are removed correctly.

The second error type is illustrated by the following command:

```
$ rm fruits users Documents/
rm: Documents directory
```

The `rm` command is unable to remove directories and presents an error message stating this fact. It removes the two other files correctly.

Summary

In this chapter, the following topics were discussed:

- Listing files using `ls`
- Viewing the content of a file using `cat`
- Counting the words, lines, and characters in a file using `wc`
- Copying files using `cp`
- Renaming files using `mv`
- Removing files using `rm`

Knowing how to perform each of these basic tasks is essential to becoming a good shell programmer. In the chapters ahead, you will use these basics to create scripts for solving real-world problems.

Questions

1. What are invisible files? How can they be listed with `ls`?
2. Is there any difference in the output of the following commands?
   a. `$ ls -a1`
   b. `$ ls -1 -a`
   c. `$ ls -1a`
3. Which options should be specified to `wc` to count just the number of lines and characters in a file?
4. Given that `hw1`, `hw2`, `ch1`, and `ch2` are files and `book` and `homework` are directories, which of the following commands generates an error message?
   a. `$ cp hw1 ch2 homework`
   b. `$ cp hw1 homework hw2 book`
   c. `$ rm hw1 homework ch1`
   d. `$ rm hw2 ch2`

3

Terms

Directories Directories are used to hold ordinary and special files. Directories are similar to folders in Mac OS or Windows.

Invisible Files An invisible file is one whose first character is a dot or period (`.`). Many programs (including the shell) use such files to store configuration information. Invisible files are also referred to as hidden files.

Option An option is an argument that starts with the hyphen or dash character, '`-`'.

Ordinary File An ordinary file is a file that contains data, text, or program instructions. Almost all the files on a UNIX system are ordinary files.

Special Files Special files are mainly used to provide access to hardware such as hard drives, CD-ROM drives, modems, and Ethernet adapters. Some special files are similar to aliases or shortcuts and enable you to access a single file using different names.

HOUR 4

Working with Directories

UNIX uses a hierarchical structure for organizing files and directories, which is referred to as a *directory tree*. The tree has a single root node, slash (/); all other directories are contained below it.

Every directory, including /, can store both files and other directories. Every file is stored in a directory, and every directory, except /, is stored within a directory.

This is slightly different from the multi-root hierarchical structure used by Windows and Mac OS. In those operating systems, all devices (floppy disk drives, CD-ROMs, hard drives, and so on) are located at the same top-most level. The UNIX model is slightly different, but after you've adjusted to it, it is extremely convenient.

This chapter introduces the directory tree and shows you how to manipulate its building blocks: directories. Specifically, the topics we will cover are

- The Directory tree
- Switching directories
- Listing files and directories
- Manipulating directories

The Directory Tree

To understand the origin and advantages of the directory tree, let's consider a project that requires organization: writing a book. When you start out, it is easiest to put all the documents related to the book in one location. As you work on the book, you might find it hard to locate the material related to a particular chapter.

If you are writing the book with pen and paper, the easiest solution to this problem is to take all the pages related to the first chapter and put them into a folder labeled Chapter 1. As you write more chapters, you can put the material related to these chapters into separate folders. If you stick to this method, you will have many separate folders by the time you finish the book. You might put all the folders into a box and label that box with the name of the book. (Then you can stack the boxes in your closet.)

By grouping the material for the different chapters into folders and grouping the folders into boxes, the multitude of pages required to write a book becomes organized and easily accessible. When you want to see Chapter 5 from a particular book, you can grab that box from your closet and look at the folder pertaining to Chapter 5.

You can use this same method for projects on a computer. When you start out, all the files for the book might be in your home directory, but as you write more chapters, you can create directories to store the material relating to a particular chapter. Finally, you can group all of those directories into a directory named after the book.

As you can probably see, this arrangement creates an upside-down *tree* with a root at the top and directories *branching* off from the root. The files stored in the directories can be thought of as *leaves*.

This brings up the notion of *parent* directories and *child* or *subdirectories*. For example, consider two directories A and B, where directory A contains directory B. In this case, A is called the parent of B, and B is called a child of A.

The only limitation on the depth of the directory tree is that the *absolute path* to a file cannot have more than 1,024 characters. Absolute paths are covered later in the chapter.

Filenames

Every file and directory has a name associated with it. This name is referred to as that file or directory's *filename*. Every file and directory is also associated with the name of its parent. When a filename is combined with the parent directory's name, the result is called a *pathname*. Two examples of pathnames are

```
/home/ranga/docs/book/ch5.doc
/usr/local/bin/
```

As you can see, a pathname consists of several words separated by slashes, `/`. The individual words in a pathname are the names of files or directories. Taken together, the words and the slashes make up the pathname. The last word in a pathname is the actual name of the file or directory being referenced. The rest of the words are the names of its parent directories. In the first pathname of the previous example, the filename is `ch5.doc`.

Strictly speaking, a filename can be up to 255 characters long and can contain any ASCII character except `/`. In general, the characters used in pathnames are the alphanumeric characters (`a` to `z`, `A` to `Z`, and `0` to `9`) along with periods (`.`), hyphens (`-`), and underscores (`_`). Other characters, such as space, tab, and the shell's special characters (`!`, `#`, `$`, `%`, `&`, `*`, `(`, `)`, `|`, `\`, `"`, `'`, `?`, `{`, `}`, `[`, `]`, `` ` ``, `<`, `>`, `;` and `:`), are usually avoided because many programs cannot deal with them properly. For example, consider a file with the following name:

```
A Farewell To Arms
```

Most programs will treat this as four separate files named `A`, `Farewell`, `To`, and `Arms`. A workaround for this problem is covered in Chapter 10, "Quoting."

One thing to keep in mind about filenames is that two files in the same directory cannot have the same name. Both of the following pathnames refer to the same file:

```
/home/ranga/docs/ch5.doc
/home/ranga/docs/ch5.doc
```

whereas the following pathnames refer to the different files:

```
/home/ranga/docs/ch5.doc
/home/ranga/docs/books/ch5.doc
```

Filenames are also case sensitive: You can have two files in the same directory whose names differ only by case. For example, the following pathnames refer to different files:

```
/home/ranga/docs/ch5.doc
/home/ranga/docs/CH5.doc
```

Pathnames

In order to access a file or directory, its pathname must be specified. As you have seen, a pathname consists of two parts: the name of the directory and the names of its parents. UNIX offers two ways to specify the names of the parent directory, leading to two types of pathnames:

- Absolute
- Relative

> **An Analogy for Pathnames**
>
> The following statements illustrate the difference between absolute and relative pathnames:
>
> "I live in San Jose."
>
> "I live in San Jose, California, USA."
>
> The first statement gives only the city in which I live. It does not give any more information, thus it is a relative location. It could be located in any state or country containing a city called San Jose. The second statement fully qualifies the location, thus it is an absolute location.

Absolute Pathnames

An *absolute* pathname represents the location of a file or directory starting from the root directory and listing all the directories between the root and the file or directory of interest. Because absolute pathnames list the path from the root directory, they always start with the slash (`/`) character. Regardless of what the current directory is, an absolute path points to an exact location of a file or directory. The following is an example of an absolute pathname:

```
/home/ranga/work/bugs.txt
```

This absolute path tells you that the file `bugs.txt` is located in the directory `work`, which is located in the directory `ranga`, which in turn is located in the directory `home`. The slash at the beginning of the path tells you that the directory `home` is located in the root directory.

Relative Pathnames

A *relative* pathname enables you to access files and directories by specifying a path to that file or directory within your current directory. When your current directory changes, the relative pathname to a file can also change.

To find out what the current directory is, use the `pwd` command (short for **p**rint **w**orking **d**irectory), which prints the name of the directory in which you are currently located. For example,

```
$ pwd
/home/ranga/pub
```

tells us that the current directory is `/home/ranga/pub`.

When you're specifying a relative pathname, the slash character is not present at the beginning of the pathname. The relative pathname is a list of the directories located between your current directory and the file or directory you are representing.

If you are pointing to a directory in your pathname that is below your current one, you can access it by specifying its name. For example, the directory name `docs/` refers to the directory `docs` located in the current directory.

In order to access the current directory's parent directory or other directories at a higher level in the tree than the current level, use the special name of two dots (`..`). The UNIX filesystem uses two dots (`..`) to represent the directory above you in the tree, and a single dot (`.`) to represent your current directory.

Let's look at an example that illustrates how relative pathnames are used. Assuming that the current directory is

```
/home/ranga/work
```

the relative pathname

```
../docs/ch5.doc
```

represents the file

```
/home/ranga/docs/ch5.doc
```

whereas

```
./docs/ch5.doc
```

represents the file

```
/home/ranga/work/docs/ch5.doc
```

You can also refer to this file using the following relative path:

```
docs/ch5.doc
```

You do not have to append `/` to the beginning of pathnames referring to files or directories located within the current directory or its subdirectories.

Switching Directories

Now that we have covered the basics of the directory tree, let's look at moving around the tree using the `cd` (short for *change directory*) command.

Home Directories

First print the working directory:

```
$ pwd
/home/ranga
```

The preceding example should indicate to you that I am in my home directory. Your home directory is the initial directory where you start when you log in to a UNIX machine. The easiest way to determine the location of your home directory is to do the following:

```
$ cd
$ pwd
/home/ranga
```

When you issue the `cd` command without arguments, it changes the current directory to your home directory. After the `cd` command completes, the `pwd` command prints the working directory, which happens to be your home directory.

Changing Directories

You can use the `cd` command to do more than change to a home directory; it can be used to change to any directory by specifying a valid absolute or relative path. The syntax is as follows:

```
cd dir
```

Here *`dir`* is the name of the directory that you want to change to. For example, the command

```
$ cd /usr/local/bin
```

changes to the directory `/usr/local/bin`. Regardless of the directory we were in before, this command always places us in the directory `/usr/local/bin`. That is the advantage of using an absolute path. Let's look at another example. Say that the current directory is

```
$ pwd
/home/ranga
```

From this directory, we can `cd` to the directory `/usr/local/bin` using the following relative path:

```
$ cd ../../usr/local/bin
```

Changing the current directory means that all your relative path specifications must be relative to the new directory rather than the old one. For example, consider the following sequence of commands:

```
$ pwd
/home/ranga/docs
$ cat names
ranga
vathsa
amma
$ cd /usr/local
```

```
$ cat names
cat: cannot open names
```

When the first cat command was issued, the working directory was /home/ranga/docs. The file, names, was located in this directory, thus the cat command found it and displayed its contents.

After the cd command, the working directory became /usr/local. Because there was no file called names in that directory, cat produced an error message stating that it could not open the file. To access the file names from the new directory, you need to specify either the absolute path to the file or a relative path from the current directory.

Common Errors

The most common errors with cd are

- Specifying more than one argument
- Trying to cd to a file
- Trying to cd to a directory that does not exist

An example of specifying more than one argument is seen here:

```
$ cd /home /tmp /var
$ pwd
/home
```


As you can see, cd uses only its first argument. The other arguments are ignored. Sometimes, in shell programming, this becomes an issue. When you issue a cd command in a shell script, you need make sure that you end up in the correct directory.

Let's now take a look at trying to cd to a file. An example of this is as follows:

```
$ pwd
/home/ranga
$ cd docs/ch5.doc
cd: docs/ch5.doc: Not a directory
$ pwd
/home/ranga
```

Here, we tried to change to a location that was not a directory, and cd reported an error. If this error occurs, the working directory does not change. The output from pwd illustrates this.

Finally, let's try to cd to a directory that does not exist:

```
$ pwd
/home/ranga
$ cd final_exam_answers
cd: final_exam_answers: No such file or directory
```

```
$ pwd
/home/ranga
```

Here, we tried to change into the directory `final_exam_answers`, a directory that did not exist, thus `cd` reported an error. The final `pwd` command shows that the working directory did not change.

Listing Files and Directories

In Chapter 3, "Working with Files," you looked at using the `ls` command to list the files in the current directory. Now let's look at using the `ls` command to list the files in any directory.

Listing Directories

To list the files in a directory, you can use the following syntax:

```
ls dir
```

Here, *`dir`* is the absolute or relative pathname of the directory whose contents you want listed.

For example, both of the following commands will list the contents of the directory `/usr/local` (assuming that the working directory is `/home/ranga`):

```
$ ls /usr/local
$ ls ../../usr/local
```

On my system, the listing resembles

```
X11          bin          gimp         jikes        sbin
ace          doc          include      lib          share
atalk        etc          info         man          turboj-1.1.0
```

The listing on your system might look quite different.

You can use any of the options you covered in Chapter 3 to change the output. For example, the command

```
$ ls -aF /usr/local
```

produces the output

```
./           atalk/       gimp/        lib/         turboj-1.1.0/
../          bin/         include/     man/
X11/         doc/         info/        sbin/
ace/         etc/         jikes/       share/
```

You can also specify more than one directory as an argument. For example,

```
$ ls /home /usr/local
```

produces the following output on my system:

```
/home:
amma    ftp     httpd   ranga   vathsa

/usr/local:
X11          bin          gimp         jikes        sbin
ace          doc          include      lib          share
atalk        etc          info         man          turboj-1.1.0
```

A blank line separates the contents of each directory.

Listing Files

You can mix files and directories as arguments to `ls`:

```
$ ls .profile docs/ /usr/local /bin/sh
```

This produces a listing of the specified files and the contents of the directories. If you don't want the contents of a directory listed, you need to specify the `-d` option to `ls`. This forces `ls` to display only the name of the directory, not its contents:

```
$ ls -d /home/ranga
/home/ranga
```

The `-d` option can be combined with any of the other `ls` options. An example of this is

```
$ ls -aFd /usr/local /home/ranga /bin/sh
/bin/sh*      /home/ranga/  /usr/local/
```


Common Errors

If the file or directory you specify does not exist, `ls` reports an error. For example,

```
$ ls tomorrows_stock_prices.txt
tomorrows_stock_prices.txt: No such file or directory
```

If you specify several arguments instead of one, `ls` will report errors only for those files or directories that do not exist. It correctly lists the others. For example,

```
$ ls tomorrows_stock_prices.txt /usr/local .profile
```

produces an error message

```
tomorrows_stock_prices.txt: No such file or directory
/usr/local:
X11          bin          gimp         jikes        sbin
ace          doc          include      lib          share
atalk        etc          info         man          turboj-1.1.0

.profile
```

Manipulating Directories

The most common ways of manipulating a directory are

- Creating a directory
- Copying a directory
- Moving a directory
- Removing a directory

Creating Directories

You can create directories with the `mkdir` command (short for make directory). Its syntax is

```
mkdir dir
```

Here, *`dir`* is the absolute or relative pathname of the directory you want to create. For example, the command

```
$ mkdir hw1
```

creates the directory `hw1` in the current directory. Here is another example:

```
$ mkdir /tmp/test-dir
```

This command creates the directory `test-dir` in the `/tmp` directory. The `mkdir` command produces no output if it successfully creates the requested directory.

If more than one directory is specified, `mkdir` will try to create each of the directories. For example,

```
$ mkdir docs pub
```

creates the directories `docs` and `pub` under the current directory.

Creating Parent Directories

Sometimes when you want to create a directory, one or more of its parent directories might not exist. If this is the case, `mkdir` issues an error message. For example,

```
$ mkdir /tmp/ch4/tst
mkdir: Failed to make directory "/tmp/ch4/tst"; No such file or directory
```

In order to create the parent directories, you can specify the `-p` (p as in parent) option to `mkdir`. For example,

```
$ mkdir -p /tmp/ch4/tst
```

will create all the required parent directories. In order to create this directory, `mkdir` will use the following procedure:

1. `mkdir` checks whether the directory `/tmp` exists. If it does not exist, `mkdir` creates it.
2. `mkdir` checks whether the directory `/tmp/ch04` exists. If it does not exist, `mkdir` creates it.
3. `mkdir` checks whether the directory `/tmp/ch04/test1` exists. If it does not, `mkdir` creates it.

Common Errors

The most common error in using `mkdir` is trying to create a directory that already exists. If the directory `/tmp/ch04` already exists, the command

```
$ mkdir /tmp/ch04
```

generates an error message similar to the following:

```
mkdir: cannot make directory '/tmp/ch04': File exists
```

An error also occurs if you try to create a directory with the same name as a file. For example, the following commands

```
$ ls -F docs/names.txt
names
$ mkdir docs/names
```

result in the error message

```
mkdir: cannot make directory 'docs/names': File exists
```

If you specify more than one argument to `mkdir`, it creates as many of these directories as it can. An error message is generated for each directory that could not be created.

4

Copying Files and Directories

In Chapter 3, you looked at using the `cp` command to copy files. Now let's look at using it to copy directories.

To copy a directory, you need to specify the `-r` option to `cp`. The syntax is as follows:

```
cp -r src dest
```

Here, *`src`* is the pathname of the directory you want to copy, and *`dest`* is the pathname where you want the copy to be placed. When the `-r` option is specified, all files and directories located under *`src`* are copied to *`dest`*. For example,

```
$ cp -r docs/book /mnt/zip
```

copies the directory `book` located in the `docs` directory to the directory `/mnt/zip`. If the directory `book` does not exist under `/mnt/book`, it will be created.

Copying Multiple Directories

You can copy multiple directories in much the same way as copying multiple files. If `cp` encounters more than one source, all the source directories are copied to the destination directory. The destination directory is assumed to be the last argument. For example, the command

```
$ cp -r docs/book docs/school work/src /mnt/zip
```

copies the directories `school` and `book`, located in the directory `docs`, to `/mnt/zip`. It also copies the directory `src`, located in the directory `work`, to `/mnt/zip`. After the copies finish, `/mnt/zip` resembles the following:

```
$ ls -aF /mnt/zip
./    ../    book/    school/    src/
```

You can also mix files and directories in the argument list. For example,

```
$ cp -r .profile docs/book .kshrc doc/names work/src /mnt/jaz
```

copies all the requested files and directories to the directory `/mnt/jaz`.

If the argument list consists of only files, the `-r` option has no effect.

Common Errors

The most common problem related to copying directories is using a destination that is not a directory. An example of this is

```
$ cp -r docs /mnt/zip/backup
cp: cannot create directory '/mnt/zip/backup': File exists
$ ls -F /mnt/zip/backup
/mnt/zip/backup
```

As you can see, the `cp` operation fails because a file called `/mnt/zip/backup` already exists.

Moving Files and Directories

In the previous chapter we looked at using `mv` to rename files, but its real purpose is to move files and directories between different locations in the directory tree. The basic syntax is:

```
mv src dest
```

Here, *src* is the name of the file or directory you want to move, and *dest* is the directory where you want the file or directory to end up. For example,

```
$ mv /home/ranga/names /tmp
```

moves the file `names` located in the directory `/home/ranga` to the directory `/tmp`.

Moving a directory is exactly the same:

```
$ mv docs/ work/
```

moves the directory `docs` into the directory `work`. To move the directory `docs` back to the current directory, you can use the command:

```
$ mv work/docs .
```

One nice feature of `mv` is that you can move and rename a file or directory all in one command. For example,

```
$ mv docs/names /tmp/names.txt
```

moves the file `names` in the directory `docs` to the directory `/tmp` and renames it `names.txt`.

Moving Multiple Items

Just as you can with `cp`, you can specify more than one file or directory as the source. For example,

```
$ mv work/ docs/ .profile pub/
```

moves the directories `work` and `docs` along with the file `.profile` into the directory `pub`.

When you are moving multiple items, you cannot rename them. If you want to rename an item and move it, you must use a separate `mv` command for each item.

Common Errors

Two common errors that can occur when using `mv` are

- Moving multiple files and directories to a directory that does not exist
- Moving files and directories to a file

These cases produce the same error message, so look at one example that illustrates what happens:

```
$ mv .profile docs pub /mnt/jaz/backup
mv: when moving multiple files, last argument must be a directory
$ ls -aF /mnt/jaz
./          ../          archive/     lost+found/  old/
```

As you can see, no directory named `backup` exists in the `/mnt/jaz` directory, so `mv` reports an error. The same error is reported if `backup` happens to be a file.

Removing Directories

Two commands can be used to remove directories:

- `rmdir`
- `rm -r`

The first command, `rmdir` (short for remove directory), can only be used to remove empty directories. It is considered "safe" because in the worst case, you just lose an empty directory that can be easily recreated with `mkdir`.

The second command, `rm -r`, removes a directory and all of its contents. It is considered "unsafe" because it is possible to accidentally delete an entire system.

> When using `rm` to remove either files or directories, make sure that you remove only those files that you don't want.
>
> There is no way to restore files deleted with `rm`, so mistakes can be very hard to recover from.

`rmdir`

The syntax for `rmdir` is

```
rmdir dir1 ... dirN
```

Here, `dir1 ... dirN` are the directories you want removed. At least one directory must be specified. For example, the command

```
$ rmdir ch01 ch02 ch03
```

removes the directories `ch01`, `ch02`, and `ch03` if they are empty. The `rmdir` command produces no output if it is successful.

Common Errors

Common errors that might occur when using `rmdir` include

- Trying to remove a directory that is not empty
- Trying to remove files with `rmdir`

For the first case, you need to know how to determine whether a directory is empty. You can do this by using the `-A` option of the `ls` command. An empty directory produces no output. If there is some output, the directory you specified is not empty.

For example, if the directory `bar` is empty, the following command

```
$ ls -A bar
```

returns nothing. This directory can be removed with `rmdir`.

Now say that the directory `docs` is not empty. The following command

```
$ rmdir docs
```

produces an error message

```
rmdir: docs: Directory not empty
```

To illustrate the second type of error, assume that `names` is a file. The following command

```
$ rmdir names
```

produces an error message

```
rmdir: names: Not a directory
```

rm -r

You can specify the `-r` option to `rm` to remove a directory and its contents. The syntax is as follows:

```
rm -r dir1 ... dirN
```

Here `dir1 ... dirN` are the names of the directories you want removed. For example, the command

```
$ rm -r ch01/
```

removes the directory `ch01` and its contents. This command produces no output.

You can specify a combination of files and directories as follows:

```
$ rm -r ch01/ test1.txt ch01-old.txt ch02/
```

In order to make `rm` safer, you can combine the `-r` and `-i` options.

4

Common Errors

The most common error that can occur when using `rm` is trying to remove a file or directory that does not exist. In this case, `rm` reports an error. For example, if the directory `midterm_answers` does not exist, trying to remove it will fail as follows:

```
$ rm -r midterm_answers
rm: midterm_answers: No such file or directory
```

Summary

In this chapter, we have looked at working with directories. Specifically, the following topics were covered:

- Working with filenames and pathnames
- Switching directories
- Listing files and directories
- Creating directories
- Copying and moving directories
- Removing directories

We reviewed each of these topics because it is important to know how to perform these functions when writing shell scripts. As you go further into this book, you will begin to see that directory manipulations occur quite frequently in shell scripts.

Questions

1. Which of the following are absolute pathnames? Which are relative?
   a. `/usr/local/bin`
   b. `../../home/ranga`
   c. `docs/book/ch01`
   d. `/`
2. What is the output of the `pwd` command after the following sequence of `cd` commands have been issued?
```
$ cd /usr/local
$ cd bin
$ cd ../../tmp
$ cd
```
3. What command should be used to copy the directory `/usr/local` to `/opt/pgms`?
4. What command(s) should be used to move the directory `/usr/local` to `/opt/pgms`?
5. Given the following listing for the directory `backup`, can the `rmdir` command be used to remove this directory? If not, please give a command that can be used.
```
$ ls -a backup
./    ../   sysbak-980322 sysbak-980112
```

Terms

Absolute Pathname The absolute pathname represents the location of a file or directory starting from / and listing all the directories between / and the file or directory of interest. The pathname /etc/hosts is an absolute pathname.

Directory Tree The hierarchical structure used in UNIX for organizing files and directories.

Filename The name of a file. The name of the file /etc/hosts is hosts.

Parent Directory The directory that contains a given directory. If directory B is contained within directory A, directory A is considered the parent directory of B.

Pathname The filename of a file combined with the filenames of its parent directories. The pathname of the file hosts located in the directory /etc is /etc/hosts.

Relative Pathname The relative pathname represents the location of a file or directory relative to the current directory. The pathname ../etc/hosts is a relative pathname.

Root The root directory, /, is the top-most directory in the UNIX directory tree.

Subdirectory A directory that is contained within another directory. If directory A contains directory B, directory B is considered a subdirectory of A.

HOUR 5

Input and Output

Until now, you have been looking at commands that output messages. In this chapter, you will look at the different types of output available to shell scripts. You will also discover the mechanisms used to obtain *input* from users. Specifically, the areas that you will cover are

- Output to the screen
- Output to a file
- Input from a file
- Input from users

Output

As you have seen in previous chapters, most commands produce output. For example, the command

```
$ date
```

produces the current date in the terminal window:

```
Thu Nov 12 16:32:35 PST 2001
```

When a command produces output that is written to the terminal, you say that the program has printed its output to the *Standard Output*, or STDOUT. When you run the `date` command, it prints the date to STDOUT. You have also seen commands produce error messages, such as:

```
$ ln -s ch01.doc ch01-01.doc
ln: cannot create ch01-1.doc: File Exists
```

Error messages are not written to STDOUT, but instead they are written to a special type of output called *Standard Error* or STDERR, which is reserved for error messages. Most commands use STDERR for error messages and STDOUT for informational messages. You will look at STDERR later in this chapter. In this section, you will look at how shell scripts can use STDOUT to output messages to each of the following:

- The terminal (STDOUT)
- A file
- The terminal and a file

Output to the Terminal

Two common commands that can be used to output messages to STDOUT are `echo` and `printf`. The `echo` command is mostly used for printing strings that require simple formatting. The `printf` command is the shell version of the C language function `printf`. It provides a high degree of flexibility in formatting output.

echo

The syntax for `echo` is as follows

```
echo str
```

Here *`str`* is the message you want printed. For example, the command

```
$ echo Hi
```

produces the following output:

```
Hi
```

You can also embed spaces in the output as follows:

```
$ echo Safeway has fresh fruit
Safeway has fresh fruit
```

In addition to spaces, you can embed punctuation marks and formatting escape sequences in the *`str`*.

Embedding Punctuation Marks

Punctuation marks are used when you need to ask the user a question, complete a sentence, or issue a warning. For example, the following command might be used as the prompt in an install script:

```
echo Do you want to install?
```

Usually, significant error messages are terminated with the exclamation point. For example, the following command

```
echo ERROR: Could not find required libraries! Exiting.
```

might be found in a script that configures a program for execution. You can also use any combination of the punctuation marks. For example, the following command uses the comma (`,`), question mark (`?`), and exclamation point(`!`) punctuation marks:

```
$ echo Eliza, where the devil are my slippers?!?
Eliza, where the devil are my slippers?!?
```

Formatting with Escape Sequences

The output in the previous examples consisted of single lines with words separated by spaces. Frequently, output needs to be formatted into columns or multiple lines. By using *escape sequences,* you can format the output of `echo`. An escape sequence is a special sequence of characters that represents another character. When the shell encounters an escape sequence, it substitutes the escape sequence with a different character. The `echo` command understands several formatting escape sequences, the most common of which are given in Table 5.1.

TABLE 5.1 Escape Sequences for the `echo` Command

Escape Sequence	*Description*
`\n`	Prints a newline character
`\t`	Prints a tab character
`\c`	Prints a string without a default trailing newline

The escape sequences for the `echo` command, given in Table 5.1, do not work with all shells. These escape sequences work in the Bourne Shell (`/bin/sh` or `/sbin/sh` on Solaris) and Korn Shell (`ksh`). They do not work with `bash` or `zsh`. The `printf` command, covered later in this chapter, can be used as a work-around for this limitation in `bash` and `zsh`.

The `\n` escape sequence is normally used when you need to generate more than one line of output. For example, the command

```
$ FRUIT_BASKET="apple orange pear"
$ echo "Your fruit basket contains:\n$FRUIT_BASKET"
Your fruit basket contains:
apple orange pear
```

generates a list of fruit preceded by a description of the list. This example illustrates two important aspects of using `escape` sequences:

- The entire input string, *`str`*, is quoted.
- The escape sequence appears in the middle of the string, *`str`*, and is not separated by spaces.

Whenever an escape sequence is used in the input string to `echo`, the string must be quoted to prevent the shell from expanding the escape sequence on the command line. Quoting is explained in detail in Chapter 10, "Quoting". Furthermore, the input string is a specification of how the output should look; spaces should not be used to separate the escape sequences unless that is how the output needs to be formatted.

It is possible to rewrite any `echo` command that uses the `\n` escape sequence as several `echo` commands. For example, you can generate the same output as in the previous example using two echo commands:

```
$ echo "Your fruit basket contains:"
$ echo $FRUIT_BASKET
```

Another commonly used escape sequence is the `\t` sequence, which generates a tab in the output. Usually it is used when you need to make a small table or generate tabular output that is only a few lines long. As an example, the following command generates a small table of two users along with their usernames:

```
$ echo "Name \tUser Name\nSriranga\tranga\nSrivathsa\tvathsa"
Name    User Name
Sriranga        ranga
Srivathsa       vathsa
```

As you can see from the output, the heading `User Name` is not centered over its column. You can fix this by adding another tab:

```
$ echo "Name\t\tUser Name\nSriranga\tranga\nSrivathsa\tvathsa"
Name            User Name
Sriranga        ranga
Srivathsa       vathsa
```

For generating large tables, the `printf` command, covered in the next section, is preferred because it provides a greater degree of control over the size of each column in the table.

The \c sequence is frequently used in shell scripts that need to generate user prompts or diagnostic output. As you have seen in the previous example, the default behavior of echo is to add a newline at the end of its output. When you are generating a prompt, this is not the most user-friendly behavior. When the \c escape sequence is used, echo does not output a newline when it finishes printing its input string. The following example illustrates the use of this option:

```
$ echo "Do you want to play a game? (y/n) \c"
```

It produces the following message:

```
Do you want to play a game (y/n)?
```

Some versions of echo do not understand the \c escape sequence. These versions of echo treat \c literally and the resulting output will look like the following:

```
$ echo "Please enter your name \c"
echo Please enter your name \c
$
```

In these versions of echo, you need to use the -n option instead of \c. In Chapter 23, "Scripting for Portability," you will develop a mechanism that handles this difference automatically.

printf

The printf command is similar to the echo command, in that it enables you to print messages to STDOUT. In its most basic form, its usage is identical to echo. For example, the following echo command:

```
$ echo "Is that a mango?"
```

is identical to the printf command:

```
$ printf "Is that a mango?\n"
```

The only major difference is that the string specified to printf explicitly requires the \n escape sequence at the end of a string, in order for a newline to print. The echo command prints the newline automatically.

> The printf command is located in the directory /usr/bin on Linux, Solaris, MacOS X, and HP-UX machines. The printf command is a built-in command in bash.

5

The power of `printf` comes from its capability to perform complicated formatting by using format specifications. The basic syntax for this is as follows:

```
printf format arguments
```

Here, *`format`* is a string that contains one or more of the formatting sequences, and *`arguments`* are strings that correspond to the formatting sequences specified in *`format`*. For those who are familiar with the C language `printf` function, the formatting sequences supported by the `printf` command are identical. The formatting sequences have the form:

```
%[-]m.nx
```

Here `%` starts the formatting sequence and *`x`* identifies the formatting sequences type. Table 5.2 gives possible values of *`x`*.

TABLE 5.2 Formatting Sequence Types

Letter	*Description*
`s`	String
`c`	Character
`d`	Decimal (integer) number
`x`	Hexadecimal number
`o`	Octal number
`e`	Exponential floating-point number
`f`	Fixed floating-point number
`g`	Compact floating-point number

Depending on the value of *`x`*, the integers *`m`* and *`n`* are interpreted differently. Usually *`m`* is the minimum length of a field, and *`n`* is the maximum length of a field. If you specify a real number format, *`n`* is treated as the precision that should be used. The hyphen (`-`) left justifies a field. By default, all fields are right justified.

The following commands illustrate the use of `printf`:

```
printf "%16s\t%16s\n" "Name" "User Name"
printf "%16s\t%16s\n" "Sriranga" "ranga"
printf "%16s\t%16s\n" "Srivathsa" "vathsa"
```

The format `%16s\t%16s\n` specifies that the output string should be separated in two columns, each 16 characters long and separated by a space. The output of these commands will be similar to the following:

```
            Name           User Name
        Sriranga               ranga
       Srivathsa              vathsa
```

As you can see, the headings and the columns are not aligned properly. You can fix this by adding a - to the format specification:

```
printf "%-16s\t%-16s\n" "Name" "User Name"
printf "%-16s\t%-16s\n" "Sriranga" "ranga"
printf "%-16s\t%-16s\n" "Srivathsa" "vathsa"
```

The ouput of these commands will be similar to the following:

```
Name                    User Name
Sriranga                ranga
Srivathsa               vathsa
```

To format numbers, specify a number formatting sequence, such as `%f`, `%e`, or `%g`, instead of the string formatting sequence, `%s`. One of the questions at the end of this chapter familiarizes you with using number formats.

Output Redirection

In the process of developing a shell script, you often need to capture the output of a command and store it in a file. When the output is in a file, it can be easily edited and modified. The process of capturing the output of a command and storing it in a file is called *output redirection* because it redirects the output of a command into a file instead of the screen. To redirect the output of a command or a script to a file, instead of `STDOUT`, use the output redirection operator, >, as follows:

```
cmd > file
list > file
```

The first form redirects the output of the command *`cmd`* to the file specified by *`file`*, whereas the second redirects the output of list *`list`* to the file specified *`file`*. If *`file`* exists, its contents are overwritten; if *`file`* does not exist, it is created. For example, the command

5

```
date > now
```

redirects the output of the `date` command into the file `now`. The output does not appear on the terminal, but it is placed into the file instead. If you view the file `now`, you find the output of the `date` command:

```
$ cat now
Sat Nov 14 11:14:01 PST 1998
```

You can also redirect the output of lists as follows:

```
{ date; uptime; who ; } > mylog
```

Here the output of the commands `date`, `uptime`, and `who` is redirected into the file `mylog`.

When you redirect output to a file using the output redirection operator, the shell overwrites the data in that file with the output of the command you specified. For example, the command

```
$ date > now
```

overwrites all the data in the file `now` with the output of the `date` command. For this reason, you should take extra care and make sure the file you specified does not contain important information.

Appending to a File

Overwriting a file simply by redirecting output to it is often undesirable. Fortunately, the shell provides a second form of output redirection with the >> operator, which appends output to a file. The basic syntax is as follows:

```
cmd >> file
list >> file
```

In these forms, output is appended to the end of *`file`*. If the file does not exist it is created. For example, you can prevent the loss of data from the file `mylog` each time a date is added by using the following command:

```
{ date; uptime; who ; } >> mylog
```

If you view the contents of `mylog`, you find that it contains the output of both lists:

```
11:15am  up 79 days, 14:48,  5 users,  load average: 0.00, 0.00, 0.00
ranga    tty1     Aug 26 14:12
ranga    ttyp2    Aug 26 14:13 (:0.0)
ranga    ttyp0    Oct 27 19:42 (:0.0)
amma     ttyp3    Oct 30 08:20 (localhost)
ranga    ttyp4    Nov 14 11:13 (rishi.bosland.u)
Sat Nov 14 11:15:54 PST 1998
 11:16am  up 79 days, 14:48,  5 users,  load average: 0.00, 0.00, 0.00
ranga    tty1     Aug 26 14:12
ranga    ttyp2    Aug 26 14:13 (:0.0)
ranga    ttyp0    Oct 27 19:42 (:0.0)
amma     ttyp3    Oct 30 08:20 (localhost)
ranga    ttyp4    Nov 14 11:13 (rishi.bosland.u)
```

Redirecting Output to a File and the Screen

In certain instances, you need to direct the output of a script to a file and onto the terminal. An example of this is shell scripts that are required to produce a log file of their activities. For interactive scripts, the log file cannot just contain the script's output redirected to a file.

To redirect output to a file and the screen, you can use the `tee` command. The basic syntax is as follows:

```
cmd | tee file
```

Here *cmd* is the name of a command, such as `ls`, and *file* is the name of the file where you want the output written. For example, the command

```
$ date | tee now
```

produces the following output on the terminal:

```
Sat Nov 14 19:50:16 PST 2001
```

The same output is written to the file `now`.

Input

Many UNIX programs are interactive and read input from the user. To use such programs in shell scripts, you need to provide them with input in a non-interactive manner. Also, scripts often need to ask the user for input in order to execute commands correctly.

To provide input to interactive programs or to read input from the user, you need to use input redirection. In this section, you will look at the following methods in detail:

- Input redirection from files
- Reading input from a user
- Redirecting the output of one command to the input of another

Input Redirection

When you need to use an interactive command, such as `mail` in a script, you need to provide the command with input. One method for doing this is to store the input of the command in a file and then tell the command to read input from that file. You can accomplish this using input redirection. The input can be redirected in a manner similar to output redirection. In general, input redirection is

```
cmd < file
```

Here the contents of *file* become the input for *cmd*. As an example, the following command is an excellent use of redirection:

```
Mail ranga@soda.berkeley.edu < Final_Exam_Answers
```

Here the input to the `Mail` command, which becomes the body of the mail message, is the file `Final_Exam_Answers`. In this particular example, a professor might perform this function, and the file might contain the answers to a current final exam.

Here Documents

An additional use of input redirection is in the creation of *here* documents. Say you need to send a list of phone numbers or URLs to the printer. You can enter the information that you want to send to the printer into the here document and then send that here document to the printer. This is much simpler than using a temporary file, which needs to be created and then should be deleted.

The general form for a here document is as follows:

```
cmd << delimiter
document
delimiter
```

Here the shell interprets the << operator as an instruction to read input until it finds a line containing the specified *`delimiter`*. All the input lines up to the line containing the *`delimiter`* are then fed into the standard input of the *`cmd`*. The *`delimiter`* tells the shell that the here document has completed. Without it, the shell continues to read input forever. The *`delimiter`* must be a single word that does not contain spaces or tabs. For example, to print a quick list of URLs, you can use the following here document:

```
lpr << MYURLS
     http://www.csua.berkeley.edu/~ranga/
     http://www.cisco.com/
     http://www.marathon.org/story/
     http://www.gnu.org/
MYURLS
```

To strip the tabs in this example, you can give the << operator a - option.

You can also combine here documents with output redirection as follows:

```
cmd > file << delimiter
document
delimiter
```

If used in this form, the output of *`cmd`* is redirected to the specified *`file`*, and the input of *`cmd`* becomes the here document. For example, you can use the following command to create a file with the short list of URLs given previously:

```
cat > urls << MYURLS
     http://www.csua.berkeley.edu/~ranga/
     http://www.cisco.com/
     http://www.marathon.org/story/
     http://www.gnu.org/
MYURLS
```

Reading User Input

A common task in shell scripts is to prompt users for input and then read their responses. You can use the `read` command to read a user's response and store it in a variable. Variables are explained in detail in Chapter 8, "Variables." The syntax of the `read` command is as follows:

```
read name
```

It reads the entire line of user input until the user presses Enter and assigns the input string to the variable specified by *name*. The following example illustrates the use of `read`:

```
echo "What is your name? \c"
read NAME
```

The user's response is stored in the variable `NAME`.

On some versions of `echo`, the `\c` in the previous example will appear literally in the output as follows:

```
What is your name? \c
```

If you experience this behavior, you should use the following `echo` command instead of the one given in the previous example:

```
echo -n "What is your name?"
```


Pipelines

Most commands in UNIX that are designed to work with files can also read input from STDIN. This enables you to use one program to filter the output of another. Using one program to manipulate the output of another program is one of the most common tasks in shell programming. This section provides a short description of this technique; Chapters 15, 16, and 17 contain much more detailed examples.

You can redirect the output of one command to the input of another command using a *pipeline*, which connects several commands together with *pipes* as follows:

```
cmd1 | cmd2 | ... | cmdN
```

The pipe character, `|`, connects the standard output of *cmd1* to the standard input of *cmd2*, and so on. The commands can be as simple or complex as are required. The following commands illustrates the use of pipelines:

```
tail -f /var/adm/messages | more
ps -ael | grep "$UID" | more
```

In the first example, the standard output of the `tail` command is piped into the standard input of the `more` command, which enables the output to be viewed one screen at a time. In the second example, the standard output of `ps` is connected to the standard input of `grep`, and the standard output of `grep` is connected to the standard input of `more`, so that the output of `grep` can be viewed one screen at a time. The `tail` and `grep` commands are explained in detail in Chapter 15, "Text Filters."

One important thing about pipelines is that each command is executed as a separate process, and the exit status of a pipeline is the exit status of the last command.

It is vital to remember this fact when writing scripts that must do error handling.

File Descriptors

When you issue any command, three files are opened and associated with that command. In the shell, each of these files is represented by a small integer called a file descriptor. A *file descriptor* is a mechanism by which you can associate a number with a filename and then use that number to read and write from the file. File descriptors are often referred to as *file handles*.

The three files opened for each command along with their corresponding file descriptors are

- Standard Input (STDIN), 0
- Standard Output (STDOUT), 1
- Standard Error (STDERR), 2

The integer following each of these files is its file descriptor. Usually, these files are associated with the user's terminal, but they can be redirected into other files. In the previous examples in this chapter, you have used input and output redirection using the default file descriptors. This section introduces the general form of input and output redirection.

Associating Files with a File Descriptor

You can associate any file with file descriptors using the `exec` command. Associating a file with a file description is useful when you need to redirect output or input to a file many times but you don't want to repeat the filename several times. To open a file for writing, use one of the following forms:

```
exec n>file
exec n>>file
```

Here *n* is an integer, and *file* is the name of the file to be opened for writing. The first form overwrites the specified *file* if it exists. The second form appends to the specified *file*. For example, the following command

```
$ exec 4>fd4.out
```

associates the file `fd4.out` with the file descriptor 4.

Use output redirection of STDOUT with care. If you accidentally redirect STDOUT, your commands may appear to stop working. For example, the following command:

```
$ exec 1>fd1.out
```

redirects STDOUT to the file `fd1.out`. If you execute this command, the output from all your commands will be placed in the file `fd1.out`. You will not see any output on your terminal.

To open a file for reading, you can use the following form:

```
exec n<file
```

Here *n* is an integer, and *file* is the name of the file to be opened for reading.

General Input/Output Redirection

You can perform general output redirection by combining a file descriptor and an output redirection operator. The general forms are

```
cmd n> file
cmd n>> file
```

Here *cmd* is the name of a command, such as `ls`; *n* is a file descriptor (integer) and *file* is the name of the file. The first form redirects the output of *cmd* to the specified *file*, whereas the second form appends the output of *cmd* to the specified *file*. For example, you can write the standard output redirection in the general form as follows:

```
cmd 1> file
cmd 1>> file
```

Here the 1 explicitly states that STDOUT is being redirected into the given file.

General input redirection is similar to general output redirection. It is performed as follows:

```
cmd n<file
```

Here *cmd* is the name of a command, such as `ls`; *n* is a file descriptor (integer) and *file* is the name of the file. For example, the standard input redirection can be written in the general form as follows:

```
cmd 0<file
```

Redirecting STDOUT and STDERR to Separate Files

One of the most common uses of file descriptors is to redirect STDOUT and STDERR to separate files. The basic syntax is

```
cmd 1> file1 2> file2
```

Here STDOUT of the command *cmd* is redirected to *file1*, and the STDERR (error messages) is redirected to *file2*. Often the STDOUT file descriptor, 1, is omitted, so a shorter form is

```
cmd > file1 2> file2
```

You can also use the append operator in place of either standard redirect operator:

```
cmd >> file1 2> file2
cmd > file1 2>> file2
cmd >> file1 2>> file2
```

The first form appends STDOUT to *file1* and redirects STDERR to *file2*. The second form redirects STDOUT to *file1* and appends STDERR to *file2*. The third form appends STDOUT to *file1* and appends STDERR to *file2*.

The following example illustrates the first form:

```
ln -s ch05.doc ./docs >> /tmp/ln.log 2> /dev/null
```

Here the STDOUT of `ln` is appended to the file `/tmp/ln.log`, and the STDERR is redirected to the file `/dev/null`, in order to discard it.

The file `/dev/null` is a special file available on all UNIX systems used to discard output. It is sometimes referred to as the *bit bucket*. If you redirect the output of a command into `/dev/null`, it is discarded. For example, the command

```
rm file > /dev/null
```

discards the output of the `rm` command.

If you use `cat` to display the contents of `/dev/null` to a *file*, the file's contents are erased:

```
$ cat /dev/null > file
```

After this command, the *file* still exists, but its size is zero.

Redirecting STDOUT and STDERR to the Same File

You looked at how to use file descriptors to redirect STDOUT and STDERR to different files, but sometimes you need to redirect both to the same file. In general, you can do this as follows

```
cmd > file 2>&1
list > file 2>&1
```

Here STDOUT (file description 1) and STDERR (file descriptor 2) of *cmd* are redirected into the specified *file*. Here is a situation where it is necessary to redirect both the standard output and the standard error:

```
rm -rf /tmp/my_tmp_dir > /dev/null 2>&1 ; mkdir /tmp/my_tmp_dir
```

In this case you are not interested in the error message or the informational message printed by the `rm` command. You only want to remove the directory, thus its output, or any error message it prints, is redirected to `/dev/null`.

If you have a command or list that should append its standard error and standard output to a file, you can use one of the following forms of output redirection:

```
cmd >> file 2>&1
list >> file 2>&1
```

An example of a command that might require this is

```
rdate -s ntp.nasa.gov >> /var/log/rdate.log 2>&1
```

Here you are using the `rdate` command to synchronize the time of the local machine to an Internet time server and you want to keep a log of all the messages.

5

Printing a Message to STDOUT

You can also use this form of output redirection to output error messages on STDERR. The basic syntax is

```
echo str 1>&2
printf format args 1>&2
```

You might also see these commands with the STDOUT file descriptor, `1`, omitted:

```
echo string >&2
printf format args >&2
```

Redirecting Two File Descriptors

You can redirect the output from one file descriptor to another file descriptor using the general form of output redirection:

```
n>&m
```

Here *n* and *m* are file descriptors (integers). When you let *n*=1 and *m*=2, STDERR is redirected to STDOUT. The general form of output redirection is often combined with `exec` to duplicate an already open output file description:

```
exec n>&m
```

Here *n* is a new file descriptor and *m* is an open output file descriptor. For example if the file descriptor `4` is opened as follows:

```
exec 4>out.txt
```

then the command:

```
exec 5>&4
```

causes file descriptor `5` to become a duplicate of file descriptor `4`. Given these two `exec` commands, the output of the following command:

```
date 1>&5
```

will end up in the file `out.txt`.

The general form of input redirection is similar to the general form of output redirection:

```
n<&m
```

Here, *n* and *m* are file descriptors (integers). The general form of output redirection is often combined with `exec` to duplicate an already open input file description:

```
exec n<&m
```

Here *n* is a new file descriptor and *m* is an open input file descriptor. In the following example, file descriptor `6` becomes a duplicate of STDIN:

```
exec 6<&0
```

Closing File Descriptors

The following syntax can be used to close an open file descriptor:

```
exec n>-
```

Here *n* is an open file descriptor. When a file descriptor is closed, trying to read or write from it results in an error. The following example closes the previously opened file descriptor `4`:

```
exec 4>-
```

Summary

In this chapter, you learned about the concept of input and output and examined the `echo` and `printf` commands that are used to produce messages from within shell scripts. You also learned about output redirection, and covered the methods of redirecting and appending the output of a command to a file. You also learned about the concept of a file descriptor and saw several aspects of its use, including opening files for reading and writing, closing files, and redirecting the output of two file descriptors to one source.

In subsequent chapters, you will expand on the material covered here, and you will see many more applications of both input and output redirection along with the use of file descriptors.

Questions

1. Which file descriptors are associated with STDOUT, STDERR and STDIN?
2. Use `printf` to convert the numbers 16, 255, and 65535 into hexadecimal and octal.
3. Given the following script:

   ```
   exec 4>out.txt
   exec 5>&4
   exec 1>&5
   date
   ```

   Where does the output from `date` end up?

Terms

Escape sequence A special sequence of characters that represents another character.

File descriptor An integer that is associated with a file. Enables you to read and write from a file using the integer instead of the file's name.

Input redirection In UNIX, the process of sending input to a command from a file.

Output redirection In UNIX, the process of capturing the output of a command and storing it in a file. It redirects the output of a command into a file instead of the screen.

STDERR Standard Error. A special type of output used for error messages. The file descriptor for STDERR is 2.

STDIN Standard Input. User input is read from STDIN. The file descriptor for STDIN is 0.

STDOUT Standard Output. The output of scripts is usually to STDOUT. The file descriptor for STDOUT is 1.

HOUR 6

Manipulating File Attributes

In addition to files and directories, UNIX supports several special file types along with a set of attributes for each file and directory. Shell scripts are often called upon to create special files and manipulate file attributes. This chapter discusses the following topics related to special files and file attributes:

- Creating links
- Modifying file permissions
- Modifying file ownership and group membership

File Types

UNIX files can contain important data and executable programs or they can represent devices, directories, or pointers to other files. This section looks at the different types of files available under UNIX.

Determining a File's Type

You can determine a file's type by using the `-l` option of the `ls` command. When this option is specified the output of `ls` contains a file's type and its attributes in addition to its name. For example, the command

```
$ ls -l /home/ranga/.profile
```

produces the following output:

```
-rwxr-xr-x    1 ranga     users        2368 Jul 11 15:57 .profile*
```

As you can see, the very first character in the output is a hyphen (`-`). This indicates that this is a regular file. For special files, the first character is one of the letters given in Table 6.1. The subsequent sections describe each of these special files in detail.

TABLE 6.1 Special Characters for Different File Types

Character	*File Type*
`-`	Regular file
`l`	Symbolic link
`c`	Character special
`b`	Block special
`p`	Named pipe
`d`	Directory file

To obtain file type information for a directory, you need to specify the `-d` option along with the `-l` option. For example, in order to obtain file type information for the directory `/home/ranga`, you use the following command:

```
$ ls -ld /home/ranga
```

This produces the following output:

```
drwxr-xr-x   27 ranga     users        2048 Jul 23 23:49 /home/ranga/
```

Regular Files

Regular files are the most common type of files on UNIX systems. They can be used to store any kind of data, including binary data that the system can execute. Often determining that a file is a regular one tells you very little about the file. Usually you need to know whether a particular file is a binary program, a shell script, or a C language library. In these instances, the `file` command is very useful. Its syntax is as follows:

```
file filename
```

Here, *filename* is the name of the file you want more information about. For example, the command:

```
$ file /bin/sh
```

will produce output similar to the following:

```
/bin/sh: ELF 32-bit MSB executable SPARC Version 1,
➥statically linked, stripped
```

Based on this output, you can tell that the file, `/bin/sh`, is an executable program for SPARC-based system. The output on your system will most likely be different.

Links

A *link* is a file that points to another file on the system. Links are useful for maintaining multiple copies of a file in several locations on the system without using up storage for the copies. Because a link just points to another file, changing the content of the link alters the content of the original file. Similarly, altering the content of the original file appears to alter the content of the link.

UNIX supports two types of links, *hard links* and *symbolic links*.

Hard Links

A hard link is a special directory entry that points to another file. Hard links have some limitations:

- A hard link cannot point to a directory; it can only point to a file.
- Hard links are indistinguishable from the file that it points to; there is no way to tell if a particular file is a hard link or the original file.

Hard links can be created using the `ln` (short for link) command. Its syntax is as follows:

```
ln src target
```

Here *src* is the pathname that the pathname *target* should point to. For example, if you want the hard link `banana` to point to the file `apple`, you can create the link as follows:

```
$ ln apple banana
```

If there is a problem creating the hard link, `ln` displays an error message; otherwise, it displays no output.

When a hard link is moved from one directory to another, it can continue to point to the original file without any problems. For example, consider the following commands:

```
$ echo I drink lemonade in the summer > lemonade
$ cat lemonade
I drink lemonade in the summer
```

```
$ ln lemonade summer_drink
$ cat summer_drink
I drink lemonade in the summer
$ mv summer_drink ..
$ cat ../summer_drink
I drink lemonade in the summer
```

As you can see from the output, the file `summer_drink` continues to point to the original file even after it is moved out of the directory where it was created.

When a hard link is removed, the original file that it points to is not affected; only the link is deleted. If the original file is deleted, the entry for the original file is removed, but its content remains on disk until the link is deleted. For example:

```
$ echo  Pomegranates are very juicy > juicy
$ ln juicy pomegranate
$ cat pomegranate
Pomegranates are very juicy
$ rm juicy
$ cat pomegranate juicy
Pomegranates are very juicy
cat: juicy: No such file or directory
```

As you can see the file `pomegranate` continues to point to the content of the file `juicy` even after the file juicy has been removed.

If a file has multiple hard links to it, simply removing the file will not be sufficient to free up the disk space; you will have to remove all of the hard links to that file.

Symbolic Links

A symbolic link or *symlink* is a special file that stores a pathname to another file. When a symlink is accessed, the system automatically reads the pathname stored in the symlink and accesses the file corresponding to that pathname, thus a symlink can point to any file on the system. The pathname stored in a symlink can be an absolute or relative pathname. If a relative pathname is stored, it is relative to the directory where the link is located rather than the current working directory.

The `ls -l` output for a symbolic link looks similar to the following:

```
lrwxrwxrwx   1 root     root            9 Oct 23 13:58 /bin/ -> ./usr/bin/
```

In this example, the first character `l` specifies that the file is a symlink. The output also indicates that the file `/bin` is a link to the file `./usr/bin`, which is located in the directory `/`.

Symlinks are created by using the `-s` option of `ln`. The syntax is as follows:

```
ln -s src target
```

Here *src* is the pathname that the pathname *target* should point to. For example, if you want to create the symlink `citrus` that points to the file `lime`, you can use the following command:

```
ln -s lime citrus
```

If there is a problem creating the symlink, `ln` displays an error message; otherwise, it displays no output.

If a symlink is created using a relative path, then it may not work properly when moved from the directory in which it was created to another directory. For example:

```
$ echo Persimmons are bitter until they ripen > persimmon
$ ln -s persimmon bitter
$ cat bitter
Persimmons are bitter until they ripen
$ mv bitter ..
$ cat ../bitter
cat: ../bitter: No such file or directory
$ ls -l ../bitter
lrwxrwxrwt  1 root  wheel  9 Jan 13 00:16 ../bitter@ -> persimmon
```

As you can see from the output, the link `bitter` correctly pointed to the file `persimmon` while the two files were located in the same directory. When `bitter` was moved, the link stopped working because a file named `persimmon` did not exist in `bitter`'s new directory. This problem can be avoided by using absolute paths when creating symlinks.

When a symlink is removed the file it points to is not affected. When the file that a symlink points to is removed or moved to a different location the symlink will cease to function properly. For example:

```
$ echo Plums were plentiful this year > plums
$ ln -s plums plentiful
$ cat plentiful
Plums were plentiful this year
$ rm plums
$ cat plentiful
cat: plentiful: No such file or directory
$ ls -l plentiful
lrwxr-xr-x  1 ranga  wheel  5 Jan 13 00:25 plentiful@ -> plums
```

As you can see from the output, the link `plentiful` points to the file `plums` even after that file has been removed. This causes the error message from `cat`.

Common Errors

Two common errors encountered when creating links occur when

- `target` already exists.
- `target` is a directory.

If `target` is a file, `ln` will not create the requested link. For example, if the file `.exrc` exists in the current directory, the following command:

```
$ ln -s /etc/exrc .exrc
```

produces the following error message:

```
ln: cannot create .exrc: File exists
```

If `target` is a directory, `ln` creates the link in that directory with the same filename as `src`. For example, if the directory `pub` exists in the current directory, the following command:

```
$ ln -s /home/ftp/pub/ranga pub
```

creates the link `pub/ranga` rather than complaining that the destination is a directory. Forgetting about this behavior is a common source of problems in shell scripts.

Device Files

In UNIX, devices, such as hard drives, keyboards, and printers, are accessed via *device files*. There are two types of device files: *character special files* and *block special files*.

Device files are normally located in the `/dev` directory.

Character Special Files

Character special files provide a mechanism for communicating with a device one character at a time. Usually character devices represent a "raw" device. The output of `ls -l` on a character special file looks like the following:

```
crw-------   1 ranga    users     4,   0 Feb  7 13:47 /dev/tty0
```

The first letter in the output, `c`, indicates that this is a character special file. The two extra numbers before the date are known as the *major* and *minor* device numbers. UNIX uses these two numbers to identify the device driver that is connected to the character special file.

Block Special Files

Block special files provide a mechanism for communicating with devices by transferring large blocks of data rather than single characters. Block special files are typically used to access hard drives and removable media. The output of `ls -l` on a block special file looks like the following:

```
brw-rw----    1 root     disk        8,   0 Feb  7 13:47 /dev/sda
```

The first letter in the output, `b`, indicates that this file is a block special file. The major and minor numbers for the file identify the device driver that is connected to the block special file.

Named Pipes

An important feature of UNIX is that you can redirect the output of one program to the input of another program with very little work. For example, the following command:

```
$ who | grep ranga
```

takes the output of the `who` command and makes it the input to the `grep` command. On the command line, temporary anonymous pipes are used, but sometimes a program needs more control over the communication channel. *Named pipes* are files that act just like temporary anonymous pipes on the command line.

Named pipes can be created using the `mkfifo` command. Its syntax is as follows:

```
mkfifo file
```

Here *`file`* is the filename that you want to give the pipe. For example, the following command creates a named pipe with the filename `mypipe`:

```
$ mkfifo mypipe
```

The `ls -l` output for this named pipe will be similar to the following:

```
prw-r--r--  1 ranga  wheel  0 Nov 22 17:39 mypipe
```

The first character, `p`, indicates that this file is a named pipe.

Owners, Groups, and Permissions

6

File permissions and file ownership are important components of UNIX because they provide a secure method for storing files. Every file in UNIX has the following attributes:

- Owner permissions
- Group permissions
- Other (world) permissions

The owner's permissions determine which actions the owner of the file can perform on the file. The group's permissions determine which actions a user, who is a member of the group that a file belongs to, can perform on the file. The permissions for others indicate which action all other users can perform on the file.

The actions that can be performed on a file are *read*, *write,* and *execute*. If a user has read permissions, that user can view the contents of a file. A user with write permissions can change the contents of a file, whereas a user with execute permissions can execute that file.

Viewing Permissions

The `ls -l` command displays the permissions of a file. For example, the following command:

```
$ ls -l .profile
```

produces the following output:

```
-rwxr-xr-x   1 ranga    users        2368 Jul 11 15:57 .profile
```

From the output, you can tell that this is a regular file. The characters that appear after the first dash (`-`) indicate the permissions for the file. After the permissions, the owner and the group are listed. For this file, the owner is `ranga` and the group is `users`.

The first three characters indicate the permissions for the owner of the file, the next three characters indicate the permissions for the group of the file, and the last three characters indicate the permissions for all other users. The significance of the individual characters is explained in Table 6.2.

TABLE 6.2 Basic Permissions

Letter	*Permission*	*Definition*
`r`	Read	The user can view the contents of the file.
`w`	Write	The user can alter the contents of the file.
`x`	Execute	The user can run the file, which is likely a program. For directories, the execute permission must be set in order for users to access the directory.

The permissions for the file in the previous example indicates that the user has read, write, and execute permissions, whereas members of the group `users` and all other users have only read and execute permissions.

Directory Permissions

The `x` bit on a directory grants access to the directory. The read and write permissions have no effect if the access bit is not set. The read permission on a directory enables users to use the `ls` command to view files and their attributes that are located in the directory. The write permission on a directory allows users to add and remove files from the directory. A directory that grants a user only execute permission will not enable the user to view the contents of the directory or add or delete any files from the directory, but it will let the user run executable files located in the directory.

> To ensure that your files are secure, check both the file permissions and the permissions of the directory where the file is located.
>
> If a file has write permission for owner, group, and other, the file is insecure. If a file is in a directory that has write and execute permissions for owner, group, and other, all files located in the directory are insecure, no matter what the permissions are on the files themselves.

SUID and SGID File Permission

Often when a command is executed, it will have to be executed with special privileges in order to accomplish its task. As an example, when you change your password with the `passwd` command, your password is stored in the file `/etc/shadow`. As a regular user, you do not have read or write access to this file for security reasons, but when you change your password, you need to have write permission to this file. This means that the `passwd` program has to give you additional permissions so that you can write to the file `/etc/shadow`.

Additional permissions are given to programs via a mechanism known as the *Set User ID* (*SUID*) and *Set Group ID* (*SGID*) bits. When you execute a program that has the SUID bit enabled, you inherit the permissions of that program's owner. Programs that do not have the SUID bit set are run with the permissions of the user who started the program. When a program is executed, it normally executes with the group permissions of the user. A file that has the SGID bit set will be executed using those group permissions.

As an example, the `passwd` command used to change your password is owned by the root and has the set SUID bit enabled. When you execute it, you effectively become the root while the command runs.

The SUID and SGID bits appear as the letter `s` if SUID or SGID permission has been enabled on that file. The SUID `s` bit is located in the permission bits where the owners who execute permission would normally reside. For example, the following command:

```
$ ls -l /usr/bin/passwd
```

produces the following output:

```
-r-sr-xr-x   1 root     bin         19031 Feb  7 13:47 /usr/bin/passwd*
```

6

which shows that the SUID bit is set and that the root owns the command. If a capital letter `S` appears instead of the lowercase `s` it indicates that the execute bit is not set.

The *SUID bit* or *sticky bit* imposes extra file removal permissions on a directory. A directory with write permissions enabled for a user enables that user to add and delete any files from this directory. If the sticky bit is enabled on the directory, files can be removed only if you are one of the following users:

- The owner of the sticky directory
- The owner the file being removed
- The super user, root

You should consider enabling the sticky bit for any directories to which non-privileged users can write. Examples of such directories include temporary directories and public file upload sites.

Directories can also take advantage of the SGID bit. If a directory has the SGID bit set, any new files added to the directory automatically inherit that directory's group, instead of the group of the user writing the file.

Changing File and Directory Permissions

The `chmod` command changes the permissions on a file or directory. Its syntax is as follows:

```
chmod expression  files
```

Here, *`expression`* is a statement that indicates how the permissions are to be changed. There are two types of *`expressions`*: symbolic and octal. The symbolic expression method uses letters to alter the permissions, and the octal expression method uses numbers. The numbers in the octal method are base-8 (octal) numbers ranging from 0 to 7.

Symbolic Method

A symbolic *`expression`* uses syntax of the form:

```
(who)(action)(permissions)
```

Table 6.3 shows the possible values for *`who`*, Table 6.4 shows the possible *`actions`*, and Table 6.5 shows the possible *`permissions`* settings. Using these three reference tables, you can build *`expressions`*.

TABLE 6.3 `who`

Letter	*Represents*
u	Owner
g	Group
o	Other
a	All

TABLE 6.4 `actions`

Symbol	*Represents*
+	Adding permissions to the file
-	Removing permissions from the file
=	Explicitly set the file permissions

TABLE 6.5 `permissions`

Letter	*Represents*
r	Read
w	Write
x	Execute
t	Sticky bit
s	SUID or SGID

Now let's look at a few examples of using `chmod`. To give the "world" read access to all files in a directory, you can use one of the following commands:

```
$ chmod a=r *
$ chmod guo=r *
```


If the command is successful, there is no output.

To stop anyone except the owner of the file `.profile` from writing to it, try this:

```
$ chmod go-w .profile
```

To deny access to the files in your home directory, you can try one of the following commands:

```
$ cd ; chmod go= *
$ cd ; chmod go-rwx *
```

When specifying the user's part or the permission's part, the order in which you give the letters is irrelevant. Thus these commands are equivalent:

```
$ chmod guo+rx *
$ chmod uog+xr *
```

If you need to apply more than one set of permission changes to a file or files, you can use a comma-separated list. For example:

```
$ chmod go-w,a+x a.out
```

removes the groups and "world" write permission on `a.out` and adds the execute permission for everyone.

To set the SUID and SGID bits for your home directory, try the following:

```
$ cd ; chmod ug+s .
```

So far, the examples you have examined involve changing the permissions for files in a directory. However, `chmod` also enables you to change the permissions for every file in a directory (including the files in subdirectories) by using the `-R` option.

For example, if the directory `pub` contains the following directories:

```
$ ls pub
./        ../       README    faqs/     src/
```

you can change the permission read permissions of the file `README` along with the files contained in the directories `faqs` and `src` with the following command:

```
$ chmod -R o+r pub
```

Octal Method

By changing permissions with an octal expression, you can only explicitly set file permissions. This method uses a single number to assign the desired permission to each of the three categories of users (owner, group, and other). The values of the individual permissions are the following:

- Read permission has a value of 4
- Write permission has a value of 2
- Execute permission has a value of 1

Adding the value of the permissions that you want to grant will give you a number between 0 and 7. This number will be used to specify the permissions for the owner, group, and finally the other category.

Setting SUID and SGID using the octal method places these bits out in front of the standard permissions. The permissions SUID and SGID take on the values 4 and 2, respectively.

Let's look at some of the examples to get an idea of how to use the octal method of changing permissions. In order to set the "world" read access to all files in a directory, do the following:

```
chmod 0444 *
```

To stop anyone except the owner of the file `.profile` from writing to it, do this:

```
chmod 0600 .profile
```

Common Errors

Many new users find the octal specification of file permissions confusing. The most important point to keep in mind is that the octal method sets or assigns permissions to a file, but it does not add or delete them. This means that the octal mode does not have an equivalent to

```
chmod u+rw .profile
```

The closest possible octal version is

```
chmod 0600 .profile
```

But this removes permissions for everyone except the user. It can also reduce the user's permissions by removing that user's execute permission.

Changing Owners and Groups

The `chown` (short for change owner) changes the ownership of a file, whereas the `chgrp` (short for change group) changes the group membership of a file. The `chgrp` command is not available on some older systems, thus the `chown` command must be used in its place. This section shows how to use both `chown` and `chgrp` to change the group of a file.

Changing Ownership

6

The `chown` command changes the ownership of a file. The basic syntax is as follows:

```
chown user:group files
```

Here, *`user`* is the name of a user on the system or the user ID (uid) of a user on the system, *`group`* is the name of a group on the system or the group ID (GID) of a group on the system, and *`files`* is a list of files to apply the changes to. If *`group`* is omitted, only the owner of the file is changed. If *`user`* is omitted, only the group of the file is changed.

The following example illustrates the use of this command to change the owner of a file:

```
chown ranga: /home/httpd/html/users/ranga
```

This changes the owner of the given directory to the user `ranga`. The following example illustrates the use of `chown` to change just the group of a file:

```
chown :authors /home/ranga/docs/ch5.doc
```

In this case the group of the given file is changed to the group `authors`.

The `chown` command will recursively change the ownership of all files when the `-R` option is included. For example, the command

```
chown -R ranga: /home/httpd/html/users/ranga
```

changes the owner of all the files and subdirectories located under the given directory to be the user `ranga`.

The super user, root, has the unrestricted capability to change the ownership of a file, but some restrictions occur for normal users. Normal users can change only the owner of files they own.

Be careful when using the `chown` command. If you give another user ownership of a file, you cannot regain ownership of that file. Only the new owner of the file or the super user can return the ownership to you.

On some systems, the `chown` command is disabled for normal user use. This generally happens if the system is running disk quotas. Under a disk quota system, users might be allowed to store only 100MB of files, but if they change the ownership of some files, their free available disk space increases, and they still have access to their files.

Changing Group Ownership

The `chgrp` command changes the group membership of a file. The syntax of this command is as follows:

```
chgrp group files
```

Here *`group`* can be either the name of a group or the GID of a group on the system and *`files`* is a list of files to apply the changes to. For example, the command:

```
chgrp authors /home/ranga/docs/ch5.doc
```

changes the group of the given file to be the group `authors`. Just like `chown`, all versions of `chgrp` understand the `-R` option also.

> Some older systems do not include the `chgrp` command. If you are using such a system, you can use the `chown` command in place of the `chgrp` command.
>
> To use `chown` in place of `chgrp`, you can invoke it as follows:
>
> `chown :`*`group files`*
>
> Here *`group`* is either the name of a group or the GID of a group on the system and *`files`* is a list of files to apply the changes to.

Summary

In this chapter, you learned several important topics relating to files and file permissions. Specifically, you examined:

- Determining a file's type
- Changing file and directory permissions using symbolic and octal notation
- Enabling SUID and SGID permissions for files and directories
- Changing the owner of a file or directory
- Changing the group of a file or directory

As you will see in subsequent chapters, each of these tasks is important in shell scripts.

Questions

For these three questions, refer to the following `ls -l` output:

```
crw-r-----    1 bin        sys         188 0x001000 Oct 13 00:31 /dev/
➥rdsk/c0t1d0
-r--r--r--    1 root       sys             418 Oct 13 16:25 /etc/passwd
drwxrwxrwx   10 bin        bin            1024 Oct 15 20:27 /usr/local/
-r-sr-xr-x    1 root       bin           28672 Nov  6  1997 /usr/sbin/ping
```

1. Identify the file type of each of the files given above.
2. Identify the owner and group of each of the files given above.
3. Describe the permissions for the owner, group, and all "other" users for each of the files given above.

Terms

Regular files The most common type of files on UNIX systems and can be used to store any kind of data, including binary data that the system can execute.

Link A file that points to another file on the system.

Hard link A special directory entry that points to another file.

Symbolic link A special file that stores a pathname to another file. A symbolic link is often referred to as a *symlink*.

Character special files Provide a mechanism for communicating with a device one character at a time.

Block special files Provide a mechanism for communicating devices by transferring large blocks of data.

Hour 7

Processes

In UNIX every program runs as a *process*. A process is an instance of running a program. If, for example, three people are running the same program simultaneously, there are three processes there, not just one. In this chapter you will learn about processes and jobs and the different modes in which they can be executed. You will also look at the commands used to list and terminate processes. Specifically the topics you will examine are:

- Starting processes
- Listing running processes
- Killing processes
- Manipulating parent and child processes

Starting a Process

Whenever you issue a command in UNIX, it creates, or *starts*, a new process on your behalf. When you tried out the `ls` command to list directory contents in Chapter 4, "Working with Directories," the system started a process, the `ls` command, for you.

UNIX tracks processes through a five-digit ID number known as the *pid* (short for process identifier). Each process in the system has a unique pid between 1 and 32,767. Pids eventually repeat when all the possible numbers are used. Two processes with the same pid cannot be concurrently executed on the system.

Foreground Processes

By default, every process runs in the foreground. It gets its input from the keyboard and sends its output to the screen. You can see this happen with the `ls` command. For example, when you execute the `ls` command:

```
$ ls
```

It executes and displays the contents of the current directory:

```
Desktop   Downloads Library   Music     Public
Documents Icon?     Movies    Pictures  Sites
```

While the command is running, you cannot run any other commands (start any other processes). You can enter commands, but no prompt appears and nothing happens until this command completes. For the `ls` command, which usually runs very quickly, this is not a problem, but if you have a program that runs for a long time—such as a large compile, database query, program that calculates pi, or a server—the terminal will be tied up.

Fortunately, you do not have to wait for one process to complete before you can start another. UNIX provides facilities for starting processes in the background, suspending foreground processes, and moving processes between the foreground and background.

Background Processes

A background process runs without being connected to your keyboard. If the background process requires any keyboard input, it waits. The advantage of running a process in the background is that you can run other commands; you do not have to wait until it completes to start another!

The simplest way to start a background process is to add an ampersand (`&`) to the end of the command. For example, if you execute `ls` in the background:

```
$ ls &
```

the output will be similar the following:

```
[1] 621
$ Desktop   Downloads Library   Music     Public
Documents Icon?     Movies    Pictures  Sites
```

The first line of output, produced by the shell, tells you that the process is running in the background:

```
[1] 621
```

This line contains two pieces of information about the background process—the *job ID* (short for job identifier) and the pid. The shell assigns a job ID for every command that is executed in the background.

If you execute this command, you might notice that you do not get back a prompt after the last line of the directory listing. That's because the prompt actually appears immediately after the job/pid line, next to `Desktop`. You can enter a command immediately instead of waiting for `ls` to finish. If you press the Enter key now, you will see something similar to the following:

```
[1] +  Done                    ls &
$
```

The first line tells you that the background `ls` job finished successfully. The second is a prompt for another command.

You will see a different completion message if an error occurs. For example, if you try to list the file with the name `no_such_file`, you will get an error:

```
$ ls no_such_file &
[1]     25389
$ no_such_file: No such file or directory
```

The first line is the background process information and the second shows the prompt for the next command and the output from `ls`—the error message. If you press Enter again, the following message appears on your screen:

```
[1] +  Done(2)                 ls no_such_file &
$
```

This shows that the `ls` command exited with nonzero status, in this case, `2`. The dollar sign (`$`) on the next line is the command prompt.

Background Processes That Require Input

If you run a background process that requires input and do not redirect it to read a file instead of the keyboard, the process will stop. Pressing Enter at an empty command prompt or starting a command will return a message to that effect. For example consider the following script:

```
#!/bin/sh
read LINE
echo $LINE
exit $?
```

Call this script `read.sh` and execute it in the background as follows:

```
$ read.sh &
$
```

Because this command does not produce any output until you give it input, all you see is the command prompt. Pressing Enter at the prompt results in a message similar to the following:

```
[1] + Stopped (SIGTTIN)        read.sh &
```

This message informs you that the command `read.sh` is currently stopped due to the signal `SIGTTIN`. This signal (`SIG`) tells you that the program is waiting for terminal (`TT`) input (`IN`). See Chapter 19, "Signals," for more information on signals. In `bash` and `zsh` the information about the signal is not presented.

If you get a message like this, you have two choices. You can kill the process and rerun it with input redirected, or you can bring the process to the foreground, give it the input it needs, and then let it continue as a foreground or background process. This chapter explains how to handle either of these choices.

Moving a Foreground Process to the Background

In addition to running a process in the background using `&`, you can move a foreground process into the background. While a foreground process runs, the shell does not process any new commands. Before you can enter any commands, you have to suspend the foreground process to get a command prompt. The suspend key on most UNIX systems is Ctrl+Z.

You can determine which key performs which function by using the `stty` command. By entering

```
$ stty -a
```

you are shown the following, along with a lot of other information:

```
intr = ^C; quit = ^\; erase = ^H; kill = ^U;
➥ eof = ^D; eol = ^@
eol2 = ^@; start = ^Q; stop = ^S; susp = ^Z;
➥ dsusp = ^Y; reprint = ^R
discard = ^O; werase = ^W; lnext = ^V
```

The entry after `susp` (`^Z` in this example) is the key that suspends a foreground process. The character `^` stands for Ctrl. If Ctrl+Z does not work for you, use the `stty` command as shown previously to determine the key for your system.

When a foreground process is suspended, a command prompt enables you to enter more commands; the original process is still in memory but is not getting any CPU time. To resume the foreground process, you have two choices—background and foreground. The `bg` command enables you to resume the suspended process in the background while the `fg` command returns it to the foreground. This section covers the `bg` command, whereas the `fg` command is covered in the next section.

For example, say you start a long-running process, in this case `long_running_process`:

```
$ long_running_process
```

While it is running, you decide that it should run in the background so your terminal is not tied up. To do that, you press the Ctrl+Z keys and see the following (the `^Z` is your Ctrl+Z keys being echoed):

```
^Z[1] + Stopped (SIGTSTP)        long_running_process
$
```

You are told the job number (`1`) and that the process is `Stopped`, then you get a prompt. The actual message might be different depending on the shell you are using. To resume a job in the background, you enter the `bg` command as follows:

```
$ bg
[1]     long_running_process &
$
```

As a result, the process runs in the background. Note the last character on the second line, the ampersand (`&`). As a reminder, the shell displays the ampersand there to remind you that the job is running in the background. It behaves just like a command where you type the ampersand at the end of the line.

By default, the `bg` command moves the most recently suspended process to the background. You can have multiple processes suspended at one time. To differentiate them, you can use the job number prefixed with a percent sign (`%`) on the command line.

In the following example, you start two long-running processes, suspend both of them, and put the first one into the background. The next few lines show starting and suspending two foreground processes:

```
$ long_running_process
^Z[1] + Stopped (SIGTSTP)        long_running_process
$ long_running_process2
^Z[2] + Stopped (SIGTSTP)        long_running_process2
$
```

To move the first one to the background, you use the following:

```
$ bg %1
[1]     long_running_process &
$
```

The second process is still suspended and can be moved to the background as follows:

```
$ bg %2
[2]     long_running_process2 &
$
```

The capability to specify which job to perform an action on (move to foreground or background for instance) shows the importance of having job numbers assigned to background processes.

Moving a Background Process to the Foreground (fg Command)

When you have a process that is in the background or suspended, you can move it to the foreground with the `fg` command. By default, the process most recently suspended or moved to the background moves to the foreground. You can also specify the job using its job number.

> If you're ever in doubt about which job will be moved to the background or foreground, don't guess. Put the job number on the `bg` or `fg` command, prefixed with a percent sign.

Using the long-running process in the previous section, a foreground process is suspended and moved into the background in the following example:

```
$ long_running_process
^Z[1] + Stopped (SIGTSTP)        long_running_process
$ bg
[1]     long_running_process &
$
```

You can move it back to the foreground as follows:

```
$ fg %1
long_running_process
```

The second line shows you which command you moved back to the foreground. The same thing would happen if the job was moved back to the foreground after being suspended.

Keeping Background Processes Around (nohup Command)

When you log out, the default action is to terminate all the processes that you are running. You can prevent this behavior from occurring on your background processes using the `nohup` (short for no hang up) command. The `nohup` command is simple to use—

just add it before the command you actually want to run. Because nohup is designed to run when there is no terminal attached, it wants you to redirect output to a file. If you do not, nohup redirects it automatically to a file known as nohup.out.

Running a process in the background with nohup looks like the following:

```
$ nohup ls &
[1]     6695
$ Sending output to nohup.out
```

Because you did not redirect the output from nohup, it is automatically redirected for you. If you redirected the output, you would not see the second message. After waiting a few moments and pressing Enter, you would see the following:

```
[1] +  Done                    nohup ls &
$
```

Waiting for Background Processes to Finish (wait Command)

There are two ways to wait for a background process to finish before doing something else. You can press the Enter key every few minutes until you get the completion message, or you can use the wait command.

There are three ways to use the wait command—with no options (the default), with a process ID, or with a job number prefixed with a percent sign. The command will wait for the completion of the job or process you specify.

If you do not specify a job or process (the default setting), the wait command waits for all background jobs to finish. Using wait without any options is useful in a shell script that starts a series of background jobs. When they are all done, it can continue processing.

With the ls command from the previous example running, you can force a wait with the following command:

```
$ wait %1
```

You cannot enter another command until job number 1 finishes. When you use wait, you do not get the completion message.

Listing and Terminating Processes

You can start processes in the foreground and background, suspend them, and move them between the foreground and background, but how do you know which commands are running? There are two commands to help you find out—jobs and ps.

jobs

The jobs command shows you the processes that are suspended and the ones running in the background. Because jobs runs as a foreground process, it cannot show you active foreground processes. In the following example, you have three jobs—the first one (job 3) is running, the second (job 2) is suspended (a foreground process after Ctrl+Z was issued), and the third one (job 1) is stopped in the background waiting for keyboard input:

```
$ jobs
[3] +  Running                  first_one &
[2] - Stopped (SIGTSTP)         second_one
[1]   Stopped (SIGTTIN)         third_one &
```

You can manipulate these jobs with the fg and bg commands. The most recent job is job number 3 (shown with a plus sign); this is the one that bg or fg act on if no job number is supplied. The most recent job before that is job number two (shown with a minus sign).

The reason for the plus and minus symbols on the jobs listing is that job numbers are reassigned when one completes and another starts. In the previous example, if job number 2 finishes and you start another job, it is assigned job number 2 and a plus sign because it is the most recent job.

ps Command

Another command that shows all processes running is the ps (short for process status) command. By default, it shows those processes that you are running. It also accepts many options, a few of which are described here.

The simplest example (with the same three jobs running as the previous example) is the ps command alone:

```
$ ps
   PID TTY       TIME CMD
  6738 pts/6     0:00 first_one
  6739 pts/6     0:00 second_one
  3662 pts/6     0:00 ksh
  8062 pts/6     0:00 ps
  6770 pts/6     0:01 third_one
```

For each running process, this provides four pieces of information: the pid, the TTY (terminal running this process), the time or amount of CPU consumed by this process, and the command name running.Although you are running three jobs, you have five processes. Of course, one of the extra processes is the ps command itself. The remaining process, ksh, is the shell.

If you are using BSD or older versions of Linux, your output will be similar to the following:

```
$ ps
  PID  TT  STAT      TIME COMMAND
13049  q0  Ss     0:00.06 -ksh (ksh)
13108  q0  R+     0:00.01 ps
```

For each running process, this provides you with five pieces of information: the pid, the `TT` (terminal running this process), `STAT` (the state of the job), the `TIME` or amount of CPU consumed by this process, and finally the command name running.

One of the most commonly used flags for `ps` is the `-f` (short for full*)* option, which provides more information as shown in the following example:

```
$ ps -f
     UID   PID  PPID  C    STIME TTY       TIME CMD
 dhorvath 6738  3662  0 10:23:03 pts/6     0:00 first_one
 dhorvath 6739  3662  0 10:22:54 pts/6     0:00 second_one
 dhorvath 3662  3657  0 08:10:53 pts/6     0:00 -ksh
 dhorvath 6892  3662  4 10:51:50 pts/6     0:00 ps -f
 dhorvath 6770  3662  2 10:35:45 pts/6     0:03 third_one
```

Table 7.1 shows the meaning of each of these columns. The BSD or Linux equivalent of the `-f` option is `-ux`. The column heading in BSD and Linux might be slightly different than those described in Table 7.1.

TABLE 7.1 `ps -f` Columns

Heading	*Description*
`UID`	User ID that this process belongs to (the person running it).
`PID`	Process ID.
`PPID`	Parent process ID (the ID of the process that started it).
`C`	CPU utilization of process.
`unlabeled`	Nice value—used in calculating process priority.
`STIME`	Process start time (when it began).
`CMD`	The command that started this process. `CMD` with `-f` is different from `CMD` without it; it shows any command-line options and arguments.

Note that the `PPID` of all the commands is `3662`, which is the pid of the `ksh` instance that is executing. Because all of the processes were started in `ksh`, it is the parent process for all of these processes.

You might be wondering why `TIME` changed for `third_one`. Between the time I entered the `ps` and the `ps -f` commands, `third_one` used some CPU time—two seconds. On larger UNIX servers, a lot of work can be done with very little CPU time. That's why the `ps` command is showing with zero CPU time; it used time, but not enough to round up to one second.

Two more common options are `-e` (short for every) and `-u` (short for user). The `-e` option is handy if you want to see whether the database is running or whether someone is playing Zork (an old text-based computer game). The BSD and Linux equivalent of the `-e` option is the `-a` option. Because so many processes run on a busy system, it is common to pipe the output of `ps -e` or `ps -a` to a text filter like `grep` (see Chapter 15, "Text Filters").

The `-u` option is handy if you want to see what a specific user is doing—are they busy or do they have time to chat; is your boss busy or checking to make sure you're not playing Zork? With `-u`, you specify the user you want to list after the `-u`. The BSD or Linux equivalent of the `-u` option is the `-U` option.

Killing a Process (`kill` Command)

Another handy command to use with jobs and processes is the `kill` command. As the name implies, the `kill` command kills, or terminates, a process. Just like the `fg` and `bg` commands, the job number is prefixed with a percent sign. To kill job number 1 in the earlier example regarding waiting for keyboard input, you can use the following:

```
$ kill %1
[1] - Terminated                 third_one &
$
```

You can also kill a specific process by specifying the pid on the command line without the percent sign used with job numbers. To kill job number 2 (process `6738`) in the earlier example using process ID, you can use the following:

```
$ kill 6739
$
```

Parent and Child Processes

In the `ps -f` example in the `ps` command section, each process has two ID numbers assigned to it: process ID (pid) and parent process ID (ppid). Each user process in the system has a parent process. Most commands that you execute have the shell as their parent. The parent of your shell is usually the operating system or the terminal communications process (for example, `in.telnetd` for telnet connections).

If you examine the output of `ps -ef`, you see that the parent process of all your commands is `3662`, the pid of the login shell (in this `ksh`):

```
$ ps -f
     UID   PID  PPID  C    STIME TTY       TIME CMD
 dhorvath 6738  3662  0 10:23:03 pts/6     0:00 first_one
 dhorvath 6739  3662  0 10:22:54 pts/6     0:00 second_one
 dhorvath 3662  3657  0 08:10:53 pts/6     0:00 -ksh
 dhorvath 6892  3662  4 10:51:50 pts/6     0:00 ps -f
 dhorvath 6770  3662  2 10:35:45 pts/6     0:03 third_one
```

As you can see, the ppid of `ksh` is `3657`. The output on your system, as well as your shell and its process ID, will most likely be different. Using `ps  -ef` (or `ps  -aux` on some systems) and `grep` to find that number, you see the following:

```
$ ps -ef | grep 3657
 dhorvath 9778  3662  4 10:52:50 pts/6     0:00 ps -f
 dhorvath 9779  3662  0 10:52:51 pts/6     0:00 grep 3657
     root 3657   711  0 08:10:53 ?         0:00 in.telnetd
 dhorvath 3657  3662  0 08:10:53 pts/6     0:00 -ksh
```

This tells you that the terminal session is being handled by `in.telnetd` (the telnet daemon), which is the parent of `ksh`. There is a parent-child relationship between processes. `in.telnetd` is the parent of `ksh`, which is the child of `in.telnetd`, but also the parent of `ps` and `grep`.

When a child is *forked*, or created, from its parent, it receives a copy of the parent's environment, including environment variables. The child can change its own environment, but those changes do not reflect in the parent and go away when the child exits.

Subshells

Whenever you run a shell script, in addition to any commands in the script, another copy of the shell interpreter is created. This new shell is known as a *subshell,* just as a directory contained in or under another is known as a subdirectory.

The best way to show this is with an example. For example, consider the following script, which runs ps and exits:

```
#! /bin/ksh
ps -ef | grep dhorvath
exit 0
```

When run, `psit` produces the following:

```
$ psit
 dhorvath 9830  3662  0 13:58:42 pts/6     0:00 ksh psit
 dhorvath 9831  9830 19 14:05:24 pts/6     0:00 ps -ef
 dhorvath 3662  3657  0 08:10:53 pts/6     0:00 -ksh
 dhorvath 9832  9830  0 13:58:42 pts/6     0:00 grep dhorvath
$
```

The subshell running as process 9830 is a child of process 3662, the original ksh shell. ps and grep are the children of process 9830 (ksh psit). When the psit script is done and exits, the subshell exits, and control is returned to the original shell.

You can also start a subshell by entering the shell name (ksh for Korn, sh for Bourne, and csh for C Shell). This feature is handy if you have one login (default) shell and want to use another. Starting out in Korn Shell and starting C Shell would look like the following:

```
$ csh
% ps -f
     UID   PID  PPID  C    STIME TTY       TIME CMD
 dhorvath 3662  3657  0 08:10:53 pts/6     0:00 -ksh
 dhorvath 3266  8848 11 10:50:40 pts/6     0:00 ps -f
 dhorvath 8848  3662  1 10:50:38 pts/6     0:00 csh
%
```

The C shell uses the percent sign as a prompt. After the csh command starts the shell, the prompt becomes the percent sign. The ps command shows csh as a child process and subshell of ksh. To exit csh and return to the parent shell, you can use the exit command.

Process Permissions

By default, a process runs with the permissions of the user running it. In most cases, this makes sense, enabling you to run a command or utility only on your files. There are times, however, when users need to access files that they do not own. A good example of this is the passwd command, which is usually stored as /usr/bin/passwd. It is used to change passwords and modify /etc/passwd and the shadow password file, if the system is so equipped.

It does not make sense for general users to have write access to the password files; they could create users on-the-fly. The program itself has these permissions. If you look at the file using ls, you see the letter s where x normally appears in the owner and group permissions. The owner of /usr/bin/passwd is root, and it belongs to the sys group. No matter who runs it, it has the permissions of the root user.

Overlaying the Current Process (exec Command)

In addition to creating (forking) child processes, you can overlay the current process with another. The exec command replaces the current process with the new one. Use this command only with great caution. If you use exec in your primary (login) shell interpreter, that shell interpreter (ksh with pid 3662 in the previous examples) is replaced with the new process. Using the command exec ls at your login shell prompt gives you a directory listing and then disconnects you from the system, logging you out. Because exec overlays your shell (ksh, for example), there are no programs to handle commands for you when ls finishes and exits.

You can use exec to change your shell interpreter completely without creating a subshell. To convert from ksh to csh, you can use the following:

```
$ exec csh
% ps -f
     UID   PID  PPID  C    STIME TTY       TIME CMD
 dhorvath  3662  3657  0 08:10:53 pts/6     0:00 csh
 dhorvath  3266  3662 11 14:50:40 pts/6     0:00 ps -f
%
```

The prompt changes and ps shows csh instead of ksh but with the original pid and start time.

Summary

In this chapter, you looked at the four major topics involving processes provided with the shell:

- Starting a process
- Listing running processes
- Killing a process (kill command)
- Manipulating parent and child processes

As you write scripts and use the shell, knowing how to work with processes improves your productivity.

Questions

1. How do you run a command in the background?
2. How do you determine which processes you are running?
3. How do you change a foreground process into a background process?

Terms

Background Describes processes usually running at a lower priority and with their input disconnected from the interactive session. Input and output are usually directed to a file or other process.

Background processes Autonomous processes that run under UNIX without requiring user interaction.

Child processes See *subprocesses*.

Child shells See *subshells*.

Parent process identifier Shown in the heading of the `ps` command as `PPID`. This is the process identifier of the parent process. See also *parent processes*.

Parent processes These processes control other processes that are often referred to as child processes or subprocesses. See *processes*.

Parent shell This shell controls other shells, which are often referred to as child shells or subshells. The login shell is typically the parent shell.

Process identifier Shown in the heading of the `ps` command as pid. It is the unique number assigned to every process running in the system.

Processes Discrete, running programs under UNIX. The user's interactive session is a process. A process can invoke (run) and control another program that is then referred to as a subprocess. Ultimately, everything a user does is a subprocess of the operating system.

Subprocesses Run under the control of other processes, which are often referred to as parent processes. See *processes*.

Subshells Run under the control of another shell, which is often referred to as the parent shell. Typically, the login shell is the parent shell.

PART II
Shell Programming

Hour

HOUR 8

Variables

Variables are words that hold a *value*. The value can be any text string. The shell enables you to create, assign, and delete variables. Although the shell manages some variables, it is mostly up to the programmer to manage variables in shell scripts. By using variables, you can make your scripts flexible and maintainable.

In this chapter, we will examine the following topics:

- Creating variables
- Accessing variables
- Array variables
- Deleting variables
- Environment variables

Working with Variables

Two types of variables can be used in shell programming:

- Scalar variables
- Array variables

Scalar variables can hold only one value at a time. Array variables can hold multiple values. This section explores the use of both types of variables.

Scalar Variables

Scalar variables are defined as follows:

```
name=value
```

Here *name* is the name of the variable, and *value* is the value that the variable should hold. For example,

```
FRUIT=peach
```

defines the variable `FRUIT` and assigns it the value `peach`.

Scalar variables are often referred to as *name-value pairs*, because a variable's name and its value can be thought of as a pair.

Variable Names

The name of a variable can only contain letters (`a` to `z` or `A` to `Z`), numbers (`0` to `9`), and the underscore character (_). Furthermore, a variable's name can only start with a letter or an underscore. The following are examples of valid variable names:

```
_FRUIT
FRUIT_BASKET
TRUST_NO_1
TWO_TIMES_2
```

but

```
2_TIMES_2_EQUALS_4
```

is not a valid variable name. To make this a valid name, we would need to add an underscore at the beginning of its name:

```
_2_TIMES_2
```

Variable names that start with numbers, such as `1`, `2`, or `11`, are reserved for use by the shell. You can use the value stored in these variables, but you cannot set the value yourself.

The reason you cannot use other characters such as `!`,`*`, or `-` is that these characters have a special meaning for the shell. If you try to create a variable name with one of these special characters, it confuses the shell. For example, the variable names

```
FRUIT-BASKET
_2*2
TRUST_NO_1!
```

are invalid names. The error message generated for the first variable name will be similar to the following:

```
$ FRUIT-BASKET=apple
/bin/sh: FRUIT-BASKET=apple:  not found.
```

Variable Values

You can store or assign any value you want in a variable. For example,

```
FRUIT=peach
FRUIT=2apples
FRUIT=apple+pear+kiwi
```

A common error with variables is assigning values that contain spaces. For example, the following assignment

```
$ FRUIT=apple orange plum
```

results in this error message:

```
sh: orange:  not found.
```

Values that have spaces in them need to be *quoted*. For example, both of the following are valid assignments:

```
$ FRUIT="apple orange plum"
$ FRUIT='apple orange plum'
```

The difference between these two quoting schemes is covered in Chapter 10, "Quoting."

Accessing Values

You can access the value stored in a variable by prefixing its name with the dollar sign (`$`). When the shell sees a `$`, it performs the following actions:

1. Reads the next word to determine the *name* of the variable.
2. Retrieves the *value* for the variable. If a value isn't found, the shell uses the empty string `""` as the value.
3. Replaces the `$` and the *name* of the variable with the *value* of the variable.

This process, known as *variable substitution*, is covered in greater detail in Chapter 9, "Substitution." The following example demonstrates this process:

```
$ FRUIT=peach
$ echo $FRUIT
peach
```

In this example, the shell first determines that the variable `FRUIT` has been referenced. Next it looks up the value for `FRUIT`. Finally the string `$FRUIT` is replaced with peach, the value of `FRUIT`, which is what the `echo` command prints.

If you do not use the dollar sign ($), variable substitution is not performed and the name of the variable is used directly. For example,

```
$ echo FRUIT
FRUIT
```

simply prints out `FRUIT`, not the value of the variable `FRUIT`.

The dollar sign ($) is used only when accessing a variable's value. It should not be used to define a variable or assign a value to a variable. For example, the assignment

```
$ $FRUIT=apple
```

generates the following error message

```
sh: peach=apple: not found
```

assuming that the value of `FRUIT` was `peach`. If the variable `FRUIT` did not have a value, the error would have been

```
sh: =apple: not found
```

Array Variables

Arrays are a method for grouping a set of variables together using a single name. Instead of creating a new name for each variable you need, you can use a single array variable to stores all the variables.

To understand how arrays work, consider the following example. Say that we are trying to represent the chapters in this book using a set of scalar variables. We could choose the following variable names to represent some of the chapters:

```
CH01
CH02
CH15
CH07
```

Each of these variable names has a specific format: the letters CH followed by the chapter number. This format serves as a way of grouping these variables together. An array variable formalizes this grouping by using an array name in conjunction with a number known as an *index*. The index is used to locate entries or elements in the array.

Arrays are not available in Bourne shell. Arrays first appeared in Korn Shell, ksh, and were adapted by the Z Shell, zsh. Recent versions (2.0 and newer) of the Bourne Again Shell, bash, include support for arrays, but older versions do not. Several Linux distributions still ship with the older version of bash.

If you are using bash, the following command allows you to determine its version:

```
$ echo $BASH_VERSION
```

If the output starts with the string '1.' as follows:

```
1.14.7(1)
```

the version of bash you are using does not support arrays. The examples in this section will not work 1.x versions of bash.

If the output starts with the string '2.' as follows:

```
2.03.0(1)-release
```

the version of bash you are using supports arrays. The examples in this section will work with 2.0 and newer versions of bash.

Creating Array Variables

The simplest method of creating an array variable is to assign a value to one of its indices. This is expressed as follows:

```
name[index]=value
```

Here name is the name of the array, index is the index of the item in the array that you want to set, and value is the value you want to set for that item. In ksh, index must be an integer between 0 and 1,023. No such restriction is present in bash or zsh. The only restriction is that index must be an integer. It cannot be a floating point or decimal number, such as 10.3, or a string, such as apricot.

As an example, the following commands

```
$ FRUIT[0]=apple
$ FRUIT[1]=banana
$ FRUIT[2]=orange
```

set the values of the first three items in the array named `FRUIT`. You could do the same thing with scalar variables as follows:

```
$ FRUIT_0=apple
$ FRUIT_1=banana
$ FRUIT_2=orange
```

Although this works fine for small numbers of items, the array notation is much more efficient for large numbers of items. If you have to write a script using the Bourne shell only, you can use this method for simulating arrays.

In the previous example, the array indices were set in sequence. This is not necessary. For example, the following command sets the value of the item at index `10` in the `FRUIT` array:

```
$ FRUIT[10]=plum
```

The shell does not create a bunch of blank array items to fill in the space between index `2` and index `10`; it just keeps track of those array indices that contain values.

If an array variable with the same name as a scalar variable is defined, the value of the scalar variable becomes the value of the element of the array at index `0`. For example, if the following commands are executed

```
$ FRUIT=apple
$ FRUIT[1]=peach
```

the zeroth element of `FRUIT` has the value `apple`. At this point, any accesses to the scalar variable `FRUIT` are treated as an access to the array item `FRUIT[0]`.

The second form of array initialization can be used to set multiple elements at once. The syntax for this form of initialization differs between `ksh` and `bash`. In `ksh`, the syntax is as follows:

```
set -A name value1 value2 ... valueN
```

In `bash`, the syntax is

```
name=(value1 ... valueN)
```

Either style can be used in `zsh`. Regardless of the style, *`name`* is the name of the array, and *`value1`* to *`valueN`* are the values of the items to be set. When setting multiple elements at once, consecutive array indices, beginning at `0`, are used.

For example the `ksh` command

```
$ set -A band derri terry mike gene
```

or the `bash` command

```
$ band=(derri terry mike gene)
```

is equivalent to the following commands:

```
$ band[0]=derri
$ band[1]=terry
$ band[2]=mike
$ band[3]=gene
```

When setting multiple array elements in bash, you can place an array index before the value:

```
myarray=([0]=derri [3]=gene [2]=mike [1]=terry)
```

The array indices don't have to be in order.

Accessing Array Values

An array variable can be accessed as follows:

```
${name[index]}
```

Here `name` is the name of the array, and `index` is the index of the desired element. For example, if the array `FRUIT` was initialized as in previous examples, the command

```
$ echo ${FRUIT[2]}
```

produces the following output:

```
orange
```

You can access all the items in an array in one of the following methods:

```
${name[*]}
${name[@]}
```

Here *name* is the name of the array you are interested in. If the `FRUIT` array is initialized as in previous examples, the command

```
$ echo ${FRUIT[*]}
```

produces the following output:

```
apple banana orange
```

If values of any of the array items contain spaces, this form of array access will not work; you will need to use the second form. The second form quotes all the array entries so that embedded spaces are preserved. For example, define the following array item:

```
FRUIT[3]="passion fruit"
```

Assuming that `FRUIT` is defined as in previous examples, accessing the entire array using the following command

```
$ echo ${FRUIT[*]}
```

results in five items, not four:

```
apple banana orange passion fruit
```

Commands accessing `FRUIT` using this form of array access get five values, with `passion` and `fruit` treated as separate items. To get only four items, you have to use the following form:

```
$ echo ${FRUIT[@]}
```

The output from this command looks similar to the previous commands:

```
apple banana orange passion fruit
```

but commands will see only four items because the shell quotes the last item, `passion fruit`, so it is treated as a single item.

Read-Only Variables

A *read-only variable* is a variable whose value cannot be changed after it is defined. Once a variable is specified as read-only, there is no way to get rid of it or to modify its value; it and its value persist until the shell exits.

Variables can be marked read-only using the `readonly` command. Consider the following set of commands:

```
$ FRUIT=kiwi
$ readonly FRUIT
$ echo $FRUIT
kiwi
$ FRUIT=cantaloupe
```

The last command results in an error message similar to the following:

```
/bin/sh: FRUIT: This variable is read only.
```

As you can see, we can read the value of the variable `FRUIT`, but we cannot overwrite the value stored in it.

This feature is often used in scripts to make sure that critical variables are not overwritten accidentally.

In `ksh`, `bash`, and `zsh`, `readonly` can be used to mark both array and scalar variables as read-only:

```
$ FRUITBASKET=(apple orange pear)
$ readonly FRUITBASKET
```

```
$ echo ${FRUITBASKET[1]}
orange
$ FRUITBASKET[1]=kiwi
```

The last command results in an error message similar to the following:

```
sh: FRUITBASKET[1]: is read only
```

This example used the `bash` style array assignment; if you are using `ksh` you will need to change the first command to the following:

```
$ set -A FRUITBASKET apple orange pear
```

Unsetting Variables

Unsetting a variable tells the shell to remove the variable from the list of variables that it tracks. This is like asking the shell to forget a piece of information because it is no longer required.

Both scalar and array variables can be unset using the `unset` command:

```
unset name
```

Here `name` is the name of the variable to unset. For example, the following command unsets the variable `FRUIT`:

```
unset FRUIT
```

The `unset` command cannot be used to unset variables that have been marked read-only via `readonly`. There is no way to unset a read-only variable; it persists until the shell exits.

Environment and Shell Variables

When the shell starts a program, it passes that program a set of variables called the *environment*. The environment is usually a small subset of the variables defined in the shell. Each variable in the environment is called an *environment variable*.

The variables we have examined thus far have been local variables. *Local variables* are variables whose value is restricted to a single shell. Local variables are not passed to programs started by the shell.

In addition to local variables and environment variables, there is a third category of variables called *shell variables*. These are special variables set by the shell that are required for proper operation of the shell. Some shell variables are environment variables, whereas others are local variables.

Table 8.1 compares these three categories of variables.

TABLE 8.1 A Comparison of Local, Environment, and Shell Variables

Attribute	*Local*	*Environment*	*Shell*
Accessible by child processes	No	Yes	Yes
Set by users	Yes	Yes	No
Set by the shell	No	No	Yes
User modifiable	Yes	Yes	No
Required by the shell	No	No	Yes

Exporting Environment Variables

Environment variables are just local variables that have been placed into the environment via the `export` command:

```
export name
```

The variable specified by *name* is placed in the environment. The process of placing variables into the environment is often referred to as *exporting* the variable. The standard shell idiom for exporting variables is

```
name=value ; export name
```

An example of this is

```
PATH=/sbin:/bin ; export PATH
```

Here a value is assigned to `PATH`, and then `PATH` is exported. Often, the assignment statement of an environment variable and the corresponding export statement are written on one line to clarify that the variable is an environment variable. This helps the next programmer, who has to maintain the script, quickly grasp the use of certain variables.

A single `export` command can be used to export more than one variable. For example, the command

```
export PATH HOME UID
```

exports the variables `PATH`, `HOME`, and `UID` to the environment.

Exporting Variables in ksh, bash, and zsh

An alternative form for exporting variables is available in `ksh`, `bash`, and `zsh`:

```
export name=value
```

In this form, the variable specified by *name* is assigned the specified *value* and then that variable is marked for export. In this form command,

```
export PATH=/sbin:/bin
```

is equivalent to

```
PATH=/sbin:/bin ; export PATH
```

In this form, any combination of *name* or *name=value* pairs can be given to the `export` command. For example, the command

```
export FMHOME=/usr/frame CLEARHOME=/usr/atria PATH
```

assigns the specified values to the variables `FMHOME` and `CLEARHOME` and then exports the variables `FMHOME`, `CLEARHOME`, and `PATH`.

Shell Variables

Shell variables are variables that the shell sets during initialization and uses internally. Table 8.2 gives a list of the most common shell variables. Some other shell variables are covered in the section "Variable Substitution" in Chapter 9.

TABLE 8.2 Shell Variables

Variable	*Description*
`PWD`	Indicates the current working directory as set by the `cd` command.
`UID`	Expands to the numeric user ID of the current user, initialized at shell startup.
`SHLVL`	Increments by one each time an instance of `bash` is started. This variable is useful for determining whether the built-in `exit` command ends the current session.
`REPLY`	Expands to the last input line read by the `read` built-in command when it is given no arguments. This variable is not available in Bourne shell.
`RANDOM`	Generates a random integer between 0 and 32,767 each time it is referenced. You can initialize the sequence of random numbers by assigning a value to `$RANDOM`. If `$RANDOM` is unset, it loses its special properties, even if it is subsequently reset. This variable is not available in Bourne shell.
`SECONDS`	Each time this parameter is referenced, it returns the number of seconds since shell invocation. If a value is assigned to `$SECONDS`, the value returned on subsequent references is the number of seconds since the assignment plus the value assigned. If `$SECONDS` is unset, it loses its special properties, even if it is subsequently reset. This variable is not available in Bourne shell.
`IFS`	Indicates the Internal Field Separator that is used by the parser for word splitting after expansion. `$IFS` is also used to split lines into words with the `read` built-in command. The default value is the string, ` \t\n`, where is the space character, `\t` is the tab character, and `\n` is the new-line character.

TABLE 8.2 continued

Variable	*Description*
PATH	Indicates the search path for commands. It is a colon-separated list of directories in which the shell looks for commands. A common value is `PATH=/bin:/sbin:/usr/bin:/usr/sbin:/usr/local/bin:/usr/ucb`
HOME	Indicates the home directory of the current user: the default argument for the `cd` built-in command.

Summary

This chapter covered using variables for shell script programming. You saw how scalar and array variables were defined, accessed, and unset. We also looked at a special category of variables known as environment variables. In subsequent chapters, we will look at how variables are used to achieve a greater degree of flexibility and clarity in shell scripts.

Questions

1. Which of the following are valid variable names?
   a. `_FRUIT_BASKET`
   b. `1_APPLE_A_DAY`
   c. `FOUR-SCORE&7YEARS_AGO`
   d. `Variable`
2. Is the following sequence of array assignments valid in `sh`, `ksh`, and `bash`?
```
$ adams[0]=hitchhikers_guide
$ adams[1]=restaurant
$ adams[3]=thanks_for_all_the_fish
$ adams[42]=life_universe_everything
$ adams[5]=mostly_harmless
```
3. Given the preceding array assignments, how would you access the array item at index `5` in the array `adams`? How would you access every item in the array?
4. What is the difference between an environment variable and a local variable?

Terms

Array Variable An array variable is a variable that groups multiple scalar variables together using a single name. Each of the individual scalar variables is accessed via an index.

Environment The environment is a set of variables that the shell passes to every program it starts.

Environment Variable An environment variable is a variable that is a member of the environment.

Exporting The process of placing a variable in the environment is called exporting.

Local Variable A local variable is a variable that is present within the current instance of the shell. It is not available to programs that are started by the shell.

Read-Only Variable A read-only variable is a variable whose value cannot be changed.

Scalar Variable A scalar variable can hold only one value at a time.

Shell Variable A shell variable is a variable that is set by the shell and is required by the shell to function correctly.

Unsetting Unsetting a variable removes it from the list of variables tracked by the shell.

Variable A variable is a word that holds a value. The value can be any text string.

Variable Substitution Variable substitution is the process by which the shell replaces the name of a variable with its value.

HOUR 9

Substitution

When the shell encounters an expression that contains one or more *meta-characters,* it performs *substitutions* on that expression. Meta-characters are characters that have a special meaning in the shell. Substitution is the process by which the shell converts a string containing meta-characters into a different string that is the result of interpreting the meta-characters. In the last chapter, you saw how the $ meta-character can be used to access a variable's value in a process known as *variable substitution.* In addition to variable substitution, the shell can also perform several other types of substitutions. This chapter looks at each of these types of substitution and their associated meta-characters in detail. Specifically the topics covered are

- Filename substitution
- Value-based variable substitution
- Command substitution
- Arithmetic substitution

Filename Substitution (Globbing)

The most common type of substitution is *filename substitution* or *globbing*. Globbing is the method by which the shell expands a string containing globbing meta-characters or *wildcards* into a list of filenames. Table 9.1 lists the wildcards used in globbing.

TABLE 9.1 Globbing Meta-Characters (Wildcards)

Wildcard	*Description*
*	Matches zero or more occurrences of any character
?	Matches one occurrence of any character
[*characters*]	Matches one occurrence of any of the given *characters*

Any command or script that operates on files can take advantage of globbing. The examples in this section use the `ls` command because its output clearly illustrates the results of globbing.

The * Meta-Character

The simplest form of filename substitution is the asterisk or star, `*`, meta-character. The `*` matches zero or more occurrences of any character in a filename.

When given by itself, the `*` matches all visible filenames in the current directory. For example, the command

```
$ ls *
```

lists every file and the contents of every directory in the current directory. Invisible files or directories are not listed.

Although the `*` is sometimes used by itself, its main use is in matching file prefixes and suffixes.

Matching a Prefix

To match a file prefix, the `*` can be used as follows:

```
cmd prefix*
```

Here *`cmd`* is the name of a command, such as `ls`, and *`prefix`* is the filename prefix you want to match. For example, the following command lists all the files and directories in the current directory that start with the letters `CGI`:

```
$ ls CGI*
CGI.java CGIGet.java CGIGetTest.java CGIPost.java CGIPostTest.java
```

By varying the prefix slightly, you can alter the list of files that are matched. For example, the command

```
$ ls CGIG*
```

generates the following list of files:

```
CGIGet.java     CGIGetTest.java
```

Varying the suffix allows you to manipulate the list of the matched filenames until the list contains just the filenames you are interested in.

Matching a Suffix

To match a file suffix, the `*` can be used as follows:

```
cmd *suffix
```

Here *cmd* is the name of a command, such as `ls`, and *suffix* is the filename suffix you want to match. For example, the following command lists all the files and directories in the current directory that end with the letters `java`:

```
$ ls *java
CGI.java CGIGet.java CGIGetTest.java CGIPost.java CGIPostTest.java
```

By varying the suffix slightly, you can alter the list of files that are matched. To list just the files that end with `Test.java`, you can adjust the command as follows:

```
$ ls *Test.java
CGIGetTest.java  CGIPostTest.java
```

Varying the suffix also allows you to manipulate the list of the matched filenames in order to obtain a list of the filenames that interest you.

Matching Prefixes and Suffixes

You can match both the prefix and the suffix by using the `*` character as follows:

```
cmd prefix*suffix
```

Here *cmd* is the name of a command, such as `ls`, *prefix* is the filename prefix, and *suffix* is the filename suffix. For example, the following command lists all the files and directories in the current directory with the prefix `CGIG` and the suffix `java`:

```
$ ls CGIG*java
CGIGet.java     CGIGetTest.java
```

It is also possible to use multiple `*` in a filename subsitution expression. For example, if you needed to list only those files with the prefix `CGI`, the suffix `java`, and that contain the characters `st`, you could use the following command:

```
$ ls CGI*st*java
```

The output is as follows:

```
CGIGetTest.java  CGIPost.java     CGIPostTest.java
```

Globbing is Case Sensitive

When using the `*`, it is important to specify the correct case for the prefix and suffix. For example, the command `ls CGI*` produces the following output:

```
CGI.java CGIGet.java CGIGetTest.java CGIPost.java CGIPostTest.java
```

whereas the command `$ ls cgi*` does not produce the same list of files.

The ? Meta-Character

One of the limitations of the `*` is that it matches zero or more characters. Consider a situation where you need to list all files that have names of the form `ch0X.doc`, where *X* is a single number or letter. At first glance it seems like the command

```
$ ls ch0*.doc
```

would produce the appropriate list, but inspecting the output shows otherwise:

```
ch01.doc ch01-1.doc ch01-2.doc ch02.doc ch02-1.doc ch02-2.doc
ch03.doc ch03-1.doc ch03-2.doc
```

In order to match only one character, you need to use the question meta-character. The `?` matches exactly one instance of a character. Rewriting the previous example using the `?` yields:

```
$ ls ch0?.doc
```

Now the output contains only those files you were interested in:

```
ch01.doc  ch02.doc  ch03.doc
```

Say that you need to look for all files that have names of the form `chXY`, where *X* and *Y* are any number or character. You can use two `?` meta-characters in order to obtain the desired list of files:

```
$ ls ch??.doc
ch01.doc  ch02.doc  ch03.doc
```

Common Errors

If the shell cannot find any files that match an expression containing a `?`, the shell treats the `?` as a regular character. Because most filenames do not include a `?`, this usually produces an error message. For example, the following command:

```
$ ls ch?.doc
```

produces the error message:

```
ls: ch?.doc: No such file or directory
```

For this reason, a shell script needs to validate the existence of files that are specified as arguments. The procedure for performing such checks is discussed in Chapter 11, "Flow Control."

Matching Sets of Characters

Two potential problems with the `?` and `*` wildcards are

- Any character, including special characters such as hyphens (`-`) or underscores (_), is matched by these characters.
- There is no way to match only letters or only numbers.

Sometimes you need more control over the characters to be matched. Consider the situation where you need to match filenames of the form `ch0X`, where *X* is a number between 0 and 9. Neither the `*` nor the `?` operator is appropriate for this task.

In order to match sets of characters, you need to use the `[` and `]` meta-characters. The syntax for using these meta-characters is as follows:

```
cmd [chars]
```

Here *cmd* is the name of a command, such as `ls`, and *chars* is the set of characters to match. For example, the following command fulfills these requirements:

```
$ ls ch0[0123456789].doc
ch01.doc  ch02.doc  ch03.doc
```

Character Ranges

In the previous example, the set contained an explicit list of all the characters that you wanted to match. This can be cumbersome if you need to deal with large sets of characters. You can simplify this by specifying a *character range* with the - meta-character. A character range is a method for specifying a set of characters by providing the first and last character in the set. For example, the character range 0-9 specifies all the numbers between zero and nine, inclusive.

Using the range 0-9, you can rewrite the previous example as follows:

```
$ ls ch0[0-9].doc
ch01.doc  ch02.doc  ch03.doc
```

Character ranges are most useful when trying to match sets of letters. For example,

```
$ ls [a-z]*
```

lists all the files starting with a lowercase letter. To match all the files starting with uppercase letters, use the following:

```
$ ls [A-Z]*
```

You can also combine multiple character ranges in a single set. For example,

```
$ ls [a-zA-Z]*
```

matches all files that start with a letter, whereas the command

```
$ ls *[a-zA-Z0-9]
```

matches all files ending with a letter or a number.

Coupling sets with other meta-characters gives you the maximum amount of flexibility in filename substitution.

Negating a Set

Consider a situation where you need a list of all files except those that contain a particular letter, for example, the letter a. You can solve this problem in two ways:

- Specify all the characters you want a filename to contain.
- Specify that the filename not include the letter a.

If you choose the first approach, you need to construct a set of all the characters that your filename can contain. You can start with:

```
[b-zA-Z0-9]
```

This set does not include the special characters that are allowed in filenames. Attempting to include all these characters creates a cumbersome set with complicated quoting:

```
[b-zA-Z0-9\-_\+\=\\\'\"\{\[\}\]
```

Compared to this, the second approach seems much simpler, because all you need to do is specify the set of characters to exclude. This is accomplished using the `!` operator. When `!` is the first character in a set, the shell matches only those filenames that do not include the characters in the set that follows the `!`. The syntax for this operator is:

```
cmd [!chars]
```

Here, *cmd* is the name of a command, such as `ls`, and *chars* is the set of characters that should not be matched.

As an example, you can list all files except those starting with the letter a using the command

```
$ ls [!a]*
```

Variable Substitution

In the previous chapter, you learned about a basic form of variable substitution, namely how to retrieve the value of a variable using the $ meta-character. In addition to this, the shell provides several other advanced forms of variable substitution that enable shell programs to manipulate the value of a variable based on its state.

There are two broad categories of advanced variable substitution:

- Actions taken when a variable has a value
- Actions taken when a variable does not have a value

The actions can range from one time value substitution to aborting the script. These categories are broken into four forms of variable substitution. These forms are summarized in Table 9.2.

9

TABLE 9.2 Advanced Variable Substitution

Name	*Syntax*	*Description*
Default Value Substitution	`${param:-word}`	If *param* is null or unset, *word* is substituted for *param*. The value of *param* does not change.
Default Value Assignment	`${param:=word}`	If *param* is null or unset, *param* is set to the value of *word*.
Null Value Error	`${param:?msg}`	If *param* is null or unset, *msg* is printed to STDERR and the shell exits.
Substitute When Set	`${param:+word}`	If *param* is set, *word* is used instead of the value of *param*. The value of *param* does not change.

Default Value Substitution

The first form of advanced variable substitution allows a default value to be substituted when the variable's value is null. The syntax is as follows:

```
${param:-word}
```

Here *param* is the name of the variable and *word* is the default value. Substitution is performed only when *param* is unset. Furthermore, *word* is not assigned to *param*; the shell just replaces the expression with *word*. The following example illustrates the behavior:

```
$ unset MYFRUIT
$ FRUIT=${MYFRUIT:-APPLE}
$ echo MYFRUIT is $MYFRUIT, FRUIT is $FRUIT
MYFRUIT is , FRUIT is APPLE
```

Default Value Assignment

The second form of advanced variable substitution assigns a value to a variable when the variable's value is null. The syntax is as follows:

```
${param:=word}
```

Here *param* is the name of the variable and *word* is the value to assign if the variable's value is null. The following example illustrates the behavior:

```
$ unset FRUIT
$ echo FRUIT is $FRUIT
FRUIT is
$ echo FRUIT is ${FRUIT:=APPLE}
FRUIT is APPLE
```

Null Value Error

Sometimes substituting or assigning default values can hide problems in a shell script. In order to spot such problems in critical parts of a shell script, you can use the third form of variable substitution that outputs a message to STDERR when a variable is unset. The syntax is as follows:

```
${param:?msg}
```

Here, *param* is the name of the variable and *msg* is the message to be printed to STDERR.

If a shell script or shell function requires a certain variable to be set for proper execution, this form of variable substitution can be used. For example, the following expression causes the shell to exit if the variable `$HOME` is unset:

```
: ${HOME:?"Your home directory is undefined."}
```

In addition to using the variable substitution form described previously, this example makes use of the `no-op` (short for no operation) command, :. This command performs no work; it just evaluates the arguments passed to it.

Substitute When Set

The final form of variable substitution is used to substitute a value when a variable is set. The syntax is as follows:

```
${param:+word}
```

Here *param* is the name of the variable and *word* is the value to substitute if the variable is set. If *param* is unset, then nothing is substituted. This form does not alter the value of the variable. It is commonly used by scripts to indicate that the script is running in debug mode:

```
echo ${DEBUG:+"Debug is active."}
```

Command and Arithmetic Substitution

Two additional forms of substitution are *command* and *arithmetic substitution*. Command substitution enables you to capture the output of a command, whereas arithmetic substitution enables you to perform basic integer math using the shell.

Command Substitution

9

Command substitution is the mechanism by which the shell performs a given set of commands and then substitutes their output in the place of the commands. Command substitution is performed when a command is given as

```
`command`
```

Here *command* can be a simple command, a pipeline, or a list.

> Make sure that you are using the backquote character, not the single quote character, when performing command substitution. Command substitution is performed by the shell only when the backquote, or backtick, character, `, is given. Using the single quote instead of the back quote is a common error and leads to hard-to-find bugs.

Command substitution is generally used to assign the output of a command to a variable as the following examples demonstrate:

```
DATE=`date`
USERS=`who | wc -l`
UP=`date ; uptime`
```

In the first example, the output of the `date` command becomes the value for the variable `DATE`. In the second example, the output of the pipeline becomes the value of the variable `USERS`. In the last example, the output of the list becomes the value of the variable `UP`.

You can also use command substitution to provide arguments for other commands. For example,

```
grep `id -un` /etc/passwd
```

looks through the file `/etc/passwd` for the output of the command:

```
id -un
```

The output of this command will be the entry in `/etc/passwd` corresponding to the current user, for example:

```
ranga:*:500:500:Sriranga Veeraraghavan:/home/ranga:/bin/ksh
```

Some system administrators have special scripts that track and report users who access the password file, `/etc/passwd`. Before you execute commands that access this file, please check with your system administrator to ensure that you are not violating site policy.

Arithmetic Substitution

Arithmetic substitution allows you to perform simple integer math using the shell. It was first introduced in `ksh` and has been incorporated into `bash` and `zsh`. It is not available in the Bourne shell. Scripts that use the Bourne shell have to use an external program such as `expr` or `bc` (covered in Chapter 18, "Other Tools") to perform basic interger math.

Arithmetic substitution is performed when an expression of the following form is encountered:

```
$((exp))
```

Here *exp* is a mathematical expression constructed using the operators given in Table 9.3. Standard precedence rules are used for evaluating *exp*.

TABLE 9.3 Arithmetic Substitution Operators

Operator	*Description*
/	The division operator. Divides two numbers and returns the result.
*	The multiplication operator. Multiples two numbers and returns the result.
-	The subtraction operator. Subtracts two numbers and returns the result.
+	The addition operator. Adds two numbers and returns the result.
()	The parentheses clarify which expressions should be evaluated before others.

If *exp* does not evaluate to an integer (whole number), the value of *exp* is truncated. As an illustration, consider the following command:

```
$ echo $(( 5/2 ))
2
```

The result of the division is 2.5, but in integer math the .5 is ignored and the truncated result, 2, is returned. The result isn't rounded; everything that follows the decimal point is discarded.

Precedence Example

The following example illustrates the rules of precedence:

```
$ echo $(( ((5 + 3*2) - 4) / 2 ))
3
```

If you are having trouble understanding the output, just break down the operations starting with the sub-expression contained in the innermost parenthesis:

1. (5 + 3*2). Because * has higher precedence than +, this sub-expression evaluates to 11.
2. Substituting the result from Step 1 yields the sub-expression (11 – 4). This evaluates to 7.
3. Substituting the result from Step 2 yields the sub-expression 7 / 2. This evaluates to 3.5, which is truncated to 3.

Common Errors

A common error in arithmetic substitution is inserting spaces between the parentheses. There should be no spaces between the first or last set of parentheses. The correct syntax is as follows:

```
$(( exp ))
```

If a space is inserted between the parentheses, as follows:

```
$(( exp ) )
$( ( exp ) )
$(( exp ) )
```

the shell will generate an error message. The exact error message depends on *exp*. For example, all the following commands:

```
$ echo $(( 5/2 ) )
$ echo $( ( 5/2 ) )
$ echo $( ( 5/2 ))
```

will produce an error message similar to the following:

```
sh: command not found: 5
```

On some systems the error message is

```
sh: no such file or directory: 5
```

Summary

In this chapter, you looked at four forms of substitution available in the shell:

- Filename substitution
- Variable substitution
- Command substitution
- Arithmetic substitution

As you write scripts and use the shell to solve problems, these types of substitution will be of immense utility.

Questions

1. What combination of wildcards should you use to list all the files in the current directory that end in the form `hw`*XYZ*.*ABC*?

   Here *X* and *Y* can be any number; *Z* is a number between 2 and 6; and *A*, *B*, and *C* are characters.

2. What action is performed by the following line, if the variable `MYPATH` is unset:

   ```
   : ${MYPATH:=/usr/bin:/usr/sbin:/usr/ucb}
   ```

3. What is the difference between the actions performed by the command given in the previous problem and the action performed by the following command:

   ```
   : ${MYPATH:-/usr/bin:/usr/sbin:/usr/ucb}
   ```

4. What is the output of the following command (figure it out by yourself before typing it into the shell):

   ```
   echo $(( 3 * 2 + ( 4 - 3 / 4) ))
   ```

Terms

Character range A method for specifying a set of characters by giving the first and last character in the set.

Globbing The process used by the shell to produce a list of files that match a particular expression. Also known as filename substitution.

Meta-characters Characters that have a special meaning in the shell.

Substitution The process by which the shell converts a string containing meta-characters into a different string that is the result of interpreting the meta-characters.

Wildcards Meta-characters used in globbing. The two main wildcards are `*` and `?`.

HOUR 10

Quoting

In the preceding chapter, you looked at substitution, which occurs automatically whenever you enter a command containing a meta-character or a $. The way the shell interprets these and other special characters is generally useful, but sometimes it is necessary to turn off shell substitution and let each character stand for itself. Turning off the special meaning of a character is called *quoting*, and it can be done in three ways:

- Using the backslash (\)
- Using the single quote (')
- Using the double quote (")

Quoting can be a very complex issue, even for experienced UNIX programmers. In this chapter, you look at each of these forms of quoting and learn how to use them. You learn a series of simple rules to help you understand when quoting is needed and how to do it correctly.

Quoting with Backslashes

To start out, let's use `echo` to get a better idea about how the shell treats special characters. For example,

```
$ echo Hello world
```

displays the following message on your screen:

```
Hello world
```

Watch what happens if you add the semicolon (`;`) meta-character in between `Hello` and `world`:

```
$ echo Hello; world
Hello
sh: world: Command not found
```

The semicolon (`;`) character tells the shell that it has reached the end of one command and what follows is a new command. This character enables multiple commands on one line. Because `world` is not a valid command, you get an error message (the error message on your system might be slightly different).

In order to display a meta-character, you need to *quote* it. When a character is quoted, its special meaning is disabled. In the shell, characters are quoted using the backslash (`\`) character. As an example, you can resolve the problem in the previous example by quoting the semicolon as follows:

```
$ echo Hello\; world
Hello; world
```

As you can see, the quoting character (`\`) is not displayed in the output. The shell preprocesses the command line, performing variable substitution, command substitution, and filename substitution, unless the special character that would normally invoke substitution is quoted. The backslash is then removed from the command arguments, so the command being run never sees the quoting character.

The technique of quoting a meta-character with the backslash is frequently referred to as *escaping*. The terms quoting and escaping are often used interchangeably.

You might also see the backslash referred to as the escape character.

Here is another example where escaping is needed:

```
$ echo You owe $1250
You owe 250
```

This seems like a simple `echo` statement, but notice that the output is not what was expected because the shell treats the `$1` in `$1250` as the shell variable `$1`. The `$` meta-character must be quoted in order to avoid variable substitution:

```
$ echo You owe \$1250
```

Now you get the desired output:

```
You owe $1250
```

Now let's say you need to print a message that contains a backslash:

```
$ echo A:\ is my floppy drive
A: is my floppy drive
```

As you can see, the backslash is not present in the output. This is because a single backslash is always used to quote the next character, in this case a space. In order to obtain a backslash, you need to quote it with a backslash as follows:

```
$ echo A:\\ is my floppy drive
A:\ is my floppy drive
```

10

Meta-Characters and Escape Sequences

The previous examples covered three of the meta-characters that need to be quoted. The complete set of meta-characters that need to be quoted follows:

```
* ? [ ] ' " \ $ ; & ( ) | ^ ! # newline tab
```

Frequently you will see newline and tab expressed as `\n` and `\t` respectively. When the backslash precedes a normal character, such as *n* or *t*, the resulting string, called an *escape sequence*, takes on a special meaning. As you learned in Chapter 5, "Input and Output," escape sequences make it possible to embed special characters such as newlines and tabs in messages output by scripts.

Using Single Quotes

Here is an `echo` command that must be modified because it contains many special shell characters:

```
$ echo <-$1250.**>; (update?) [y|n]
```

You could quote the entire string by putting a backslash in front of each special character, but this is tedious and makes the resulting command difficult to read and understand:

```
$ echo \<-\$1250.\*\*\>\; \(update\?\) \[y\|n\]
```

An alternative technique for quoting a large group of characters is to put a single quote (') at the beginning and end of the string. When a string is quoted using the single quote, all the meta-characters within the string lose their special meaning and are treated literally. For example, the following command is equivalent to the previous example:

```
$ echo '<-$1250.**>; (update?) [y|n]'
```

Quoting regular characters is harmless, because regular characters are treated the same whether or not they are quoted. This is true for the backslash, single quotes, and double quotes.

In the previous example, you put single quotes around a whole string, quoting both the special characters and the regular letters and digits that do not require quoting. Strictly speaking, you did not have to do this; you could have just quoted those parts of the string that contained meta-characters. Quoting everything is simply easier, both to write and maintain, and incurs no performance penalty.

If a single quote appears within a string to be output, you should not put the whole string within single quotes:

```
$ echo 'It's Friday'
```

This fails and only outputs the following character, while the cursor waits for more input:

```
>
```

The > sign is the secondary shell prompt (as stored in the `PS2` shell variable), and it indicates that you have entered a multiple-line command—what you have typed so far is incomplete. Single quotes must be entered in pairs, and their effect is to quote all characters that occur between them. In case you are wondering, you cannot get around this by putting a backslash before an embedded single quote. To correct the problem you need to quote just the single quote in the word *It's* as follows:

```
$ echo It\'s Friday
```

Using Double Quotes

In many cases, you will need to quote some meta-characters but allow others to be evaluated by the shell. For example, the following `echo` command contains some meta-characters that must be quoted and others that should not:

```
$ echo '$USER owes <-$1250.**>; [ as of (`date +%m/%d`) ]'
```

Because the string is single quoted, the output is easy to predict—what you see is what you get:

```
$USER owes <-$1250.**>; [ as of (`date +%m/%d`) ]
```

As you can imagine, this is not exactly what you wanted; the single quotes have prevented variable substitution and command substitution from occurring, thus the variable `$USER`, which contains the username of the current user, was not replaced with the appropriate value and the `date` command was not executed. So now the problem is to quote most of the meta-characters, such as `*` and `;`, but to allow some meta-characters, such as `$` and `` ` ``, to be evaluated.

Double quotes are the solution to this problem. Double quotes disable all of the meta-characters except for `$` and `` ` ``, thus allowing variable and command substitution to be performed in a quoted string. Watch what happens if you replace the single quotes with double quotes as follows:

```
$ echo "$USER owes <-$1250.**>; [ as of (`date +%m/%d`) ]"
Fred owes <-250.**>; [ as of (12/21) ]
```

10

As you can see, double quotes permit you to display many meta-characters literally while still enabling variable and command substitutions. However, as you might have noticed, the amount of money owed is incorrect because `$1` is substituted. To correct this, you need to use a backslash to escape the `$`:

```
$ echo "$USER owes <-\$1250.**>; [ as of (`date +%m/%d`) ]"
```

The escaped dollar sign is no longer a special character, so the dollar amount appears correctly in the output now:

```
ranga owes <-$1250.**>;  [ as of (12/21) ]
```

If you need to print a double quote inside a double-quoted string, you need to quote it with a backslash (`\"`) as follows:

```
$ echo "He said \"Hello my dear\""
He said "Hello my dear"
```

Quoting Rules and Situations

Now that you know the basics about quoting, let's look at some additional rules that will help you use quoting effectively.

Quoting Ignores Word Boundaries

In English, you are used to quoting whole words or sentences. In shell programming, the special characters must be quoted, but it does not matter whether the regular characters are quoted in the same word, as follows:

```
$ echo "Hello; world"
Hello; world
```

You can move the quotes off word boundaries as long as any special characters remain quoted. This command produces the same output as the preceding one:

```
$ echo Hel"lo; w"orld
```

Of course, it is easier to read the line if the quotes are on word boundaries. This simple example illustrates the manner in which quoting can be used. Quoting off of word boundaries will be useful in some of the more complex quoting situations you will encounter.

Combining Quoting in Commands

You can freely switch from one type of quoting to another within the same command. For example, the following command contains single quotes, a backslash, and double quotes:

```
$ echo The '$USER' variable contains this value \> "|$USER|"
The $USER variable contains this value > |ranga|
```

As you can see from the output, you can intermix multiple forms of quoting in the same command.

Embedding Spaces in a Single Argument

To the shell, one or more spaces or tabs form a single command-line argument separator. For example, the output from the following command:

```
$ echo Name            Address
```

does not preserve the spacing:

```
Name Address
```

Even though you put multiple spaces between `Name` and `Address`, the shell regards them as special characters forming one separator. The `echo` command simply displays the arguments it has received separated by a single space. You can quote the spaces to achieve the desired result:

```
$ echo "Name            Address"
```

Now the multiple spaces are preserved in the output:

```
Name            Address
```

Spaces must be quoted to embed them in a single command-line argument:

```
$ mail -s Meeting tomorrow fred jane < meeting.notice
```

The `mail` command enables you to send mail to a list of users. The `-s` option enables the following argument to be used as the subject of the mail. Although the word `tomorrow` is part of the subject (`Meeting tomorrow`), it is taken as one of the users to receive the message, which results in an error. You can solve this by quoting the embedded space within the subject using any of the three types of quoting:

```
mail -s Meeting\ tomorrow fred jane < meeting.notice
mail -s 'Meeting tomorrow' fred jane < meeting.notice
mail -s "Meeting tomorrow" fred jane < meeting.notice
```

Unless the users `fred` and `jane` exist on your system, the `mail` commands in the previous examples will most likely fail to deliver mail and will result in the creation of a file named `dead.letter` in your home directory.

Quoting Newlines to Continue on the Next Line

The newline character is found at the end of each line of a UNIX shell script; it is a special character that tells the shell that it has encountered the end of a line. When a script is being created, the newline character is inserted each time you press Enter or Return at the end of a line.

Normally you can't see the newline characters in your script, but if you are using the `vi` editor, the `vi` command

```
:set list
```

marks each newline character with a dollar sign. This allows you to see where the newlines are in your scripts.

You can quote the newline character to enable a long command to extend to another line as follows:

```
$ cp file1 file2 file3 file4 file5 file6 file7 \
> file8 file9 /tmp
```

Notice the last character in the first line is a backslash. This backslash quotes the newline character at the end of the line. The shell recognizes this and displays > (the PS2 prompt) as confirmation that you are entering a continuation line or multiple-line command. For this to work properly, you must not have any characters, including spaces, after the final backslash on the first line.

A quoted newline also acts as an argument separator just like a space or tab. For example:

```
$ echo 'Line 1
> Line 2'
```

The newline at the end of the first line of the command is quoted because it is between a pair of single quotes. The output from this command is

```
Line 1
Line 2
```

Quoting to Access Filenames Containing Special Characters

In the previous chapter, you saw that any word that contains the characters `*`, `?`, `[`, and `]` is automatically expanded to a list of files that match the specified pattern. For example, the command:

```
$ rm ch1*
```

removes all files in the current directory whose names start with the prefix `ch1`. In this case, the `*` character is a special character. Most of the time, this is exactly what you want, but there is a case where you need to use quoting to remove this character's special meaning. Assume you have these files in a directory:

```
ch1     ch1*     ch1a     ch15
```

Notice that the filename `ch1*` contains the `*` character. Although this is certainly not recommended, sometimes you encounter files whose names contain strange characters (usually such files are created by accident). If you only want to delete the file `ch1*`, the following command is overkill:

```
$ rm ch1*
```

because it deletes all of the files that start with `ch1`. To delete just the file named `ch1*` you need to quote the `*`. You can use the backslash, the single quote, or the double quote for this purpose:

```
$ rm ch1\*
$ rm 'ch1*'
$ rm "ch1*"
```

Quoting the special character takes away its wildcard meaning and enables you to delete the desired file.

Avoid using special characters in filenames because you have to quote the special character each time you access that file.

Also take extra care when dealing with files that include a filename expansion meta-character in their filenames. If such a filename is supplied to the `mv` or `rm` commands without proper quoting, you might lose many files before you find the mistake.

Quoting Regular Expression Wildcards

In Chapter 16, "Filtering Text with Regular Expressions," you learn about another type of expression known as regular expressions. Regular expressions use some of the same wildcard characters as filename substitution, as you can see in this `grep` command (which is covered in Chapter 15, "Filtering Text"):

```
grep '[0-9][0-9]*$' report2 report7
```

The quoted string `[0-9][0-9]*$` is a regular expression that `grep` searches for within the contents of files `report2` and `report7`. Wildcards in the `grep` pattern must be quoted to prevent the shell from erroneously replacing that pattern with a list of filenames that match the pattern.

You should always quote your regular expressions to protect them from shell filename expansion, but sometimes they work even if you don't quote them. The shell only expands the pattern if it finds existing files whose names match the pattern. If you happen to be in a directory where no matching files are found, the pattern is left alone, and `grep` works fine. Move to another directory, though, and the same command might fail.

Quoting the Backslash to Enable `echo` Escape Sequences

In Chapter 5, you saw that `echo` enables you to use escape sequences, such as `\n`, in your output. For example,

```
$ printf "Line 1\nLine 2\n"
```

displays the following:

```
Line 1
Line 2
```

You might be wondering how the quoting rules apply here. If the backslash takes away the special meaning of its following character, shouldn't you just see `n` in the output?

A backslash within double quotes is special only if it precedes one of these four characters:

- `$`
- `` ` ``
- `"`
- `\`

The `\n` within double quotes is treated as two normal characters that are passed to the `echo` command as arguments. The `printf` command enables its own set of special characters, which are indicated by a preceding backslash. The `\n` passed to `printf` tells `printf` to display a newline. In this example, the `\n` has to be quoted so that the backslash can be passed to `printf` and not removed before `printf` can see it. Watch what happens when you don't quote the backslash:

```
$ printf Line 1\nLine 2\n
```

This displays:

```
Line 1nLine 2n
```

The `\n` is not quoted, so the shell removed the backslash before `printf` sees the arguments. Because `printf` sees `n`, not `\n`, it simply displays `n`, not a newline as desired.

Quoting Wildcards for `cpio` and `find`

There are other commands like `printf` that have their own special characters that must be quoted for the shell to pass them unaltered. The `cpio` is a command that saves and restores files. It allows you to use the filename expansion meta-characters to select the files to restore. In order for `cpio` to receive these meta-characters in tact, they must be quoted as in the following example:

```
$ cpio -icvdum 'usr2/*' < /dev/rmt0
```

`-icvdum` includes options to `cpio` to specify how it should restore files from the tape device `/dev/rmt0`. The string `usr2/*` says to restore all files from directory `usr2` on tape. Again, this command sometimes works correctly even if the wildcards aren't quoted because shell expansion doesn't occur if matching files aren't found in the current path (in this case, if there is no `usr2` subdirectory in the current directory). It is best to quote these `cpio` wildcards so you can be sure the command works properly every time.

> Before using the `cpio` command to restore files from a tape device such as `/dev/rmt0`, please consult your system administrator to ensure that you have sufficient permissions to use such devices.

The `find` command covered in Chapter 18, "Other Tools," supports its own wildcards as well. For example, in the following command

```
find / -name 'ch*.doc' -print
```

`ch*.doc` is a wildcard pattern that tells `find` to display all filenames that start with `ch` and end with a `.doc` suffix. Unlike shell filename expansion, this `find` command checks all directories on the system for a match. However, the wildcard must be quoted using single quotes, double quotes, or a backslash, so the wildcard is passed to `find` and not expanded by the shell.

Summary

In this chapter, you looked at three types of quoting and when to use them:

- Backslash
- Single quote
- Double quote

In addition, you learned several quoting rules:

- A backslash takes away the special meaning of the character that follows it.
- The character doing the quoting is removed before command execution.
- Single quotes remove the special meaning of all enclosed characters.
- Quoting regular characters is harmless.
- A single quote cannot be inserted within a single quoted string.
- Double quotes remove the special meaning of most enclosed characters.
- Quoting can ignore word boundaries.
- Different types of quoting can be combined in one command.
- Quote spaces to embed them in a single argument.
- Quote the newline to continue a command on the next line.
- Use quoting to access filenames that contain special characters.
- Quote regular expression wildcards.
- Quote the backslash to enable `echo` escape sequences.

Questions

1. Give an echo command to display this message:

```
It's <party> time!
```

2. Give an echo command to display one line containing the following fields:
   - The contents of variable $USER
   - A single space
   - The word "owes"
   - Five spaces
   - A dollar sign ($)
   - The contents of the variable $DEBT (this variable contains only digits)
   - Sample output:

```
fred owes     $25
```

Terms

Escaping Escaping a character means to put a backslash (\) just before that character. Escaping can either remove the special meaning of a character in a shell command, or it can add special meaning as you saw with \n in the echo command. The character following the backslash is called an escaped character.

Literal characters These characters have no special meaning and cause no extra action to be taken. Quoting causes the shell to treat a wildcard as a literal character.

Meta-characters A character that has an extra meaning or causes some action to be taken by the shell or other UNIX commands.

Newline This is literally the linefeed character whose ASCII value is 10. In general, the newline character is a special shell character that indicates a complete command line has been entered and can now be executed.

Quoting Literally encloses selected text within some type of quotation marks. When applied to shell commands, quoting disables shell interpretation of special characters by enclosing the characters within single or double quotes or by escaping the characters.

HOUR 11

Flow Control

The order in which commands execute in a shell script is called the *flow* of the script. In the scripts that you have looked at so far, the flow is always the same because the same set of commands executes every time. Most scripts, however, need to change their flow depending on one or more conditions. Commands that allow the flow of a script to be conditionally changed are called *conditional flow control commands,* or just *flow control commands*.

The two main flow control statements available in the shell are:

- The `if` statement
- The `case` statement

The `if` statement is normally used for the conditional execution of commands, whereas the `case` statement enables any number of command sequences to be executed depending on which one of several patterns matches a variable first.

In this hour, you will learn about flow control and two conditional statements.

The `if` Statement

The `if` statement performs actions depending on whether a given condition is true or false. The `if` statement uses the return code of a command to determine whether a condition is true or false. A return code of zero is treated as true, whereas a non-zero return code is treated as false. The syntax of the `if` statement is as follows:

```
if list1
then
   list2
elif list3
then
   list4
else
   list5
fi
```

Both the `elif` and the `else` statements are optional. If you have an `elif` statement, you don't need an `else` statement and vice versa. An `if` statement can be written with any number of `elif` statements.

Because the `if` statement is treated as a list, it can be also written on a single line:

```
if list1 ; then list2 ; elif list3 ; then list4 ; else list5 ; fi ;
```

Usually this form is used only for short `if` statements.

The execution of the `if` statement is as follows:

1. *`list1`* is executed.
2. If the exit code of *`list1`* is `0` (true), *`list2`* is executed and the `if` statement terminates.
3. Otherwise, *`list3`* is executed.
4. If the exit code of *`list3`* is `0` (true), *`list4`* is executed and the `if` statement terminates.
5. If the exit code of *`list3`* is non-zero, *`list5`* is executed.

An `if` Statement Example

The following example illustrates the use of the `if` statement:

```
if uuencode cherry.gif cherry.gif > cherry.uu ; then
   echo "Encoded cherry.gif to cherry.uu"
else
   echo "Error encoding cherry.gif"
fi
```

Look at the flow of control through this statement:

1. First, the command

   ```
   uuencode cherry.gif cherry.gif > cherry.uu
   ```

   is executed.
2. If this command is successful, the command

   ```
   echo "Encoded cherry.gif to cherry.uu"
   ```

   is executed and the `if` statement exits.
3. Otherwise the command

   ```
   echo "Error encoding cherry.gif"
   ```

   is executed, and the `if` statement exits.

You might have noticed that both the `if` and `then` statements appear on the same line in this example. Most shell programmers prefer to write `if` statements this way in order to make the statement more concise and readable.

Common Errors

Four common errors that can occur when using the `if` statement are

- Omitting the semicolon (`;`) before the `then` statement in the single line form.
- Using `else if` or `elsif` instead of `elif`.
- Omitting the `then` statement when an `elif` statement is used.
- Writing `if` instead of `fi` at the end of an `if` statement.

The error message generated in each of these cases varies from system to system. In the following examples, a typical error message is displayed; the actual error message on your system may use slightly different wording.

The following example illustrates the first type of error:

```
if uuencode cherry.gif cberry.gif > cherry.uu then
   echo "Encoded cherry.gif to cherry.uu"
else
   echo "Error encoding cherry.gif"
fi
```

This example is the same as the previous example, except that the semicolon, `;`, preceding the `then` statement has been omitted. This `if` statement generates an error message similar to the following:

```
sh: syntax error near unexpected token `else'
```

If you encounter an error message like this, make sure that a semicolon precedes the `then` statement.

The second type of error can be illustrated by modifying the following example:

```
if uuencode cherry.gif cherry.gif > cherry.uu ; then
   echo "Encoded cherry.gif to cherry.uu"
elif rm cherry.uu ; then
   echo "Encoding failed, temporary files removed."
else
   echo "An error occured."
fi
```

Here you have an `elif` statement that removes the intermediate file `cherry.uu`, if `uuencode` fails. If `elif` is changed to an `else if` as follows

```
if uuencode cherry.gif cherry.gif > cherry.uu ; then
   echo "Encoded cherry.gif to cherry.uu"
else if rm cherry.uu ; then
   echo "Encoding failed, temporary files removed."
else
   echo "An error occured."
fi
```

an error message similar to the following is generated:

```
sh: syntax error: unexpected end of file
```

If `elif` is changed to `elsif` as follows

```
if uuencode cherry.gif cherry.gif > cherry.uu ; then
   echo "Encoded cherry.gif to cherry.uu"
elsif rm cherry.uu ; then
   echo "Encoding failed, temporary files removed."
else
   echo "An error occured."
fi
```

an error message similar to the following is generated:

```
sh: syntax error near unexpected token 'then'
```

The following example illustrates the third type of error:

```
if uuencode cherry.gif cherry.gif > cherry.uu ; then
   echo "Encoded cherry.gif to cherry.uu"
elif rm cherry.uu
   echo "Encoding failed, temporary files removed."
else
   echo "An error occured."
fi
```

Here the `then` statement following the `elif` statement has been omitted. This generates an error message similar to the following:

```
sh: syntax error near unexpected token 'else'
```

The following example illustrates the fourth type of error:

```
if uuencode cherry.gif cberry.gif > cherry.uu ; then
   echo "Encoded cherry.gif to cherry.uu"
else
   echo "Error encoding cherry.gif"
if
```

Here the final `fi` statement is written as `if`. This generates an error message similar to the following:

```
sh: syntax error: unexpected end of file
```

This error indicates that the `if` statement was not closed with a `fi` statement.

Using test

Usually the list given to an `if` statement is one or more `test` commands. A `test` command has the following syntax:

```
test expr
```

Here *`expr`* is constructed using one of the options understood by `test`. After evaluating *`expr`*, `test` returns either `0` (true) or `1` (false). The open bracket, `[`, is often used as a shorthand for `test`:

```
[ expression ]
```

Here *`expr`* is any valid expression understood by `test`. The close bracket, `]`, the space after the open bracket, `[`, and the space before the close bracket are required. Without the spaces and the close bracket, the shell cannot tell where *`expr`* begins and ends.

There are three main types of expressions understood by `test`:

- File tests
- String comparisons
- Numerical comparisons

File Tests

File test expressions test whether a file fits a particular criteria. The general syntax for a file test is

```
test option file
```

or

```
[ option file ]
```

Here *option* is one of the options given in Table 11.1 and *file* is the name of a file or directory.

TABLE 11.1 File Test Options for `test`

Option	*Description*
`-b` *file*	True if *file* exists and is a block special file.
`-c` *file*	True if *file* exists and is a character special file.
`-d` *pathname*	True if *pathname* exists and is a directory.
`-e` *pathname*	True if the file or directory specified by *pathname* exists.
`-f` *file*	True if *file* exists and is a regular file.
`-g` *pathname*	True if the file or directory specified by *pathname* exists and has its SGID bit set.
`-h` *file*	True if *file* exists and is a symbolic link. This option is not available on some older systems.
`-k` *pathname*	True if the file or directory specified by *pathname* exists and has its "sticky" bit set.
`-p` *file*	True if *file* exists and is a named pipe.
`-r` *pathname*	True if the file or directory specified by *pathname* exists and is readable.
`-s` *file*	True if *file* exists and has a size greater than zero.
`-u` *pathname*	True if the file or directory specified by *pathname* exists and has its SUID bit set.
`-w` *pathname*	True if the file or directory specified by *pathname* exists and is writeable.
`-x` *pathname*	True if the file or directory specified by *pathname* exists and is executable. A directory must be executable in order for its contents to be accessed.
`-O` *pathname*	True if the file or directory specified by *pathname* exists and is owned by the effective user ID of the current process.

> The `-w` and `-x` options only test a file's permission flags. They do not take into account the state of the underlying disk. For example, files on read-only disks such as CD-ROMs or DVDs can have the writeable bit set, but they cannot be written to because the underlying media is read-only.

The next few examples, taken from OpenBSD's system startup script `/etc/rc`, illustrate the use of file tests. This section doesn't go over every option listed in Table 11.1; just enough to give you a general idea about how file test operators are used in the real world.

The first example illustrates the use of the `-d` option to test for the existence of a directory:

```
# /var/crash should be a directory if core dumps
# are to be saved.
if [ -d /var/crash ]; then
   savecore /var/crash
fi
```

Here the script determines whether the directory `/var/crash` exists. If the directory exists, `savecore` is executed. If the directory does not exist, the `if` statement performs no actions.

11

The second example illustrates the use of the `-f` option to test for the existence of a regular file:

```
if [ -f /var/account/acct ]; then
   echo 'turning on accounting'; accton /var/account/acct ;
fi
```

Here the script determines whether the file `/var/account/acct` exists. If the file exists, the script outputs the message:

```
turning on accounting
```

and executes `accton`. If the file does not exist, the `if` statement performs no actions.

The third example illustrates the use of the `-x` option to determine whether a file is executable:

```
if [ -x /usr/libexec/vi.recover ]; then
   echo 'preserving editor files'; /usr/libexec/vi.recover
fi
```

Here the script determines whether the file `/usr/libexec/vi.recover` is executable. If the file is executable, the script outputs the message:

```
preserving editor files
```

and executes `/usr/libexec/vi.recover`. If the file is not executable, the `if` statement performs no actions.

String Comparisons

The test and [commands allow for simple string comparisons. They can be used to determine whether a string is empty and whether two strings are identical or equal. The options relating to string comparisons are listed in Table 11.2.

TABLE 11.2 String Comparison Options for the test Command

Option	*Description*
-z *str*	True if *str* has zero length.
-n *str*	True if *str* has nonzero length.
str1 = *str2*	True if *str1* and *str2* are equal.
str1 != *str2*	True if *str1* and *str2* are not equal.

Checking Whether a String Is Empty

There are several ways to determine whether a string is empty. The most common method is to use the -z option as follows:

```
test -z str
```

or

```
[ -z str ]
```

Here *str* is the string you want to check. As an example, consider the following if statement:

```
if [ -z "$FRUIT_BASKET" ] ; then
    echo "Your fruit basket is empty"
else
    echo "Your fruit basket contains: $FRUIT_BASKET"
fi
```

If the variable $FRUIT_BASKET does not have a value, the message:

```
Your fruit basket is empty
```

is produced. Otherwise a message that contains the value of $FRUIT_BASKET is produced.

If you were to use the -n option instead of the -z option, the example would change as follows:

```
if [ -n "$FRUIT_BASKET" ] ; then
    echo "Your fruit basket has the following fruit: $FRUIT_BASKET"
else
    echo "Your fruit basket is empty"
fi
```

You might have noticed that the variable `$FRUIT_BASKET` was quoted in the previous examples. Quoting handles the case when `$FRUIT_BASKET` is unset or null. If `$FRUIT_BASKET` was unset and you did not quote it, an error message similar to the following would be displayed:

```
test: argument expected
```

Without quotes, after the shell performs variable substitution, the statement looks like the following:

```
[ -z ]
```

The `test` command complains that a required argument is missing, because the *`str`* argument to `-z` is missing. When quoting is used, the same statement looks like the following after variable substitution:

```
[ -z "" ]
```

Here *`str`* is `""`, so `test` works correctly.

When `bash` is presented with a variable that does not have a value, it automatically uses the value `""`. Thus you do not have to quote your variables in `bash`.

Although the quoting is not required in `bash`, you should still include it in your script for the sake of clarity and maintainability.

11

Equality of Strings

The `test` and `[` commands enable you to determine whether two strings are equal. Two strings are considered equal if they contain the identical sequence of characters. For example, the following strings are considered equal:

```
"There are more things in heaven and earth"
"There are more things in heaven and earth"
```

Whereas the following strings are not considered equal because of differences in capitalization:

```
"than are dreamt of in your philosophy"
"Than are dreamt of in your Philosophy"
```

The syntax for checking whether two strings are equal is

```
test str1 = str2
```

or

```
[ str1 = str2 ]
```

Here *str1* and *str2* are the two strings being compared. If these two strings are equal, the test succeeds and returns true (0). If the two strings are not equal, the test fails and returns false (1).

The following example, slightly modified from OpenBSD's /etc/rc, illustrates a common use of string comparisons:

```
# if $portmap == YES, the portmapper is started.
if [ "$portmap" = "YES" ]; then
   echo -n ' portmap'; portmap
fi
```

Here *str1* is the value of `$portmap` and *str2* is the string `YES`. The `if` statement uses the = operator to determine whether the value stored in `$portmap` is equal to `YES`. If `$portmap` is equal to `YES`, a message is issued and the program `portmap` is executed.

Note that `$portmap` is quoted in this example. Just like in previous examples, quoting is used to prevent problems resulting from variable substitution when `$portmap` happens to be is unset or null. If `$portmap` was not quoted and it happened to be null, an error message similar to the following would be produced:

```
test: argument expected
```

An alternative technique to quoting is sometimes used to avoid these types of errors. Basically it involves prefixing *str1* and *str2* with an extra character, usually `X`. The syntax for this technique is

```
test Xstr1 = Xstr2
```

or

```
[ Xstr1 = Xstr2 ]
```

If either *str1* or *str2* is null, the string `X` is used instead of null. Rewriting the previous example using this technique yields:

```
# if $portmap == YES, the portmapper is started.
if [ X$portmap = X"YES" ]; then
   echo -n ' portmap'; portmap
fi
```

If `$portmap` is null then the strings `X` and `XYES` are compared; because these strings do not match, the test fails. If `$portmap` is `YES` then the strings `XYES` and `XYES` are compared; because these strings match, the test succeeds.

Inequality of Strings

You can determine whether two strings are not equal using the `!=` operator. The syntax for this operator is similar to that of the = operator:

```
test str1 != str2
```

or

```
[ str1 != str2 ]
```

Here *str1* and *str2* are the two strings being compared. If these two strings are not equal, the test succeeds and returns `0` (true). If the two strings are equal, the test fails and returns `1` (false).

The following example, slightly modified from OpenBSD's `/etc/rc`, illustrates the use of the `!=` operator:

```
if [ "$lpd_flags" != "NO" ]; then
   echo -n ' printer'; lpd $lpd_flags
fi
```

Here *str1* is the value of the variable `$lpd_flags` and *str2* is the string `NO`. You can determine whether the value of `$lpd_flags` is not `NO`. If the value is something other than `NO`, the program issues a message and executes `lpd` with the value of `$lpd_flags` as its argument.

11

Just as in previous examples, quoting was used in order to handle the case when `$lpd_flags` is unset or null. An alternate technique that is sometimes used involves prefixing *str1* and *str2* with an extra character, usually `X`. The syntax for this technique is

```
test Xstr1 != Xstr2
```

or

```
[ Xstr1 != Xstr2 ]
```

If either *str1* or *str2* is null, the string `X` is used instead of null. Rewriting the previous example using this technique yields:

```
if [ X$lpd_flags != X"NO" ]; then
   echo -n ' printer'; lpd $lpd_flags
fi
```

If `$lpd_flags` is null, the strings `X` and `XNO` are compared; because these strings do not match, the test succeeds. If `$lpd_flags` is `NO` then the strings `XNO` and `XNO` are compared; because these strings match, the test fails.

Numerical Comparisons

The `test` and `[` commands can also be used to compare integers. The basic syntax is

```
test int1 op int2
```

or

```
[ int1 op int2 ]
```

Here *`int1`* and *`int2`* can be any positive or negative integer and *op* is one of the operators listed in Table 11.3. If either *`int1`* or *`int2`* is a string, not an integer, it is treated as `0`.

TABLE 11.3 Numerical Comparison Operators for the `test` Command

Operator	*Description*
`int1` `-eq` *`int2`*	True if *`int1`* equals *`int2`*.
`int1` `-ne` *`int2`*	True if *`int1`* is not equal to *`int2`*.
`int1` `-lt` *`int2`*	True if *`int1`* is less than *`int2`*.
`int1` `-le` *`int2`*	True if *`int1`* is less than or equal to *`int2`*.
`int1` `-gt` *`int2`*	True if *`int1`* is greater than *`int2`*.
`int1` `-ge` *`int2`*	True if *`int1`* is greater than or equal to *`int2`*.

A common task in a shell script is checking the exit code from a program. The numerical comparison operators allow you to easily check the exit status of a command and perform different actions depending on whether a command executed correctly. For example, consider the following command:

```
ln -s /usr/local/bin/bash /usr/bin
```

If you execute this command on the command line, you can see any error messages and intervene to fix the problem. In a shell script, error messages are ignored and the script continues to execute. In most cases it is a mistake to ignore errors.

The exit status of the last command is stored in the variable `$?`, so you can use this variable to check whether a command was successful as follows:

```
if [ $? -eq 0 ] ; then
    echo "Command was successful." ;
else
    echo "An error was encountered."
    exit
fi
```

Recall that an exit code of `0` indicates success and a non-zero exit code indicates failure. If the command exits with an exit code of `0`, the "success" message is issued; otherwise, an error message is issued and `exit` is called.

> In some scripts you may see the = operator used in place of the -eq operator. Some extremely old versions of the shell did not include the -eq operator, thus shell programmers were forced to use the = operator instead. All modern shells, including Bourne shell, ksh, bash and zsh support the -eq operator.

By using the -ne operator, you can simplify the previous example as follows:

```
if [ $? -ne 0 ] ; then
    echo "An error was encountered."
    exit
fi
echo "Command was successful."
```

Here you check to see whether the command failed. If so, you issue an error message and exit; otherwise, you continue with the rest of the program (in this case you just issue the "success" message). This version is slightly more efficient than the previous example that uses an `else` clause.

> In some scripts, you might see the != operator used in place of the -ne operator. Some older versions of the shell did not include the -ne operator, thus shell programmers were forced to use the != operator instead. All modern shells, including the Bourne shell, ksh, bash, and zsh, support the -ne operator.

11

Compound Expressions

So far you have dealt with individual expressions, but many times you need to combine expressions in order to test for a particular condition. When two or more expressions are combined, the result is called a *compound* expression.

You can create compound expressions by using `test` and `[`'s built-in operators, or by using the conditional execution operators, `&&` and `||`. Another way to create a compound expression is to use the negation operator, `!`, which negates an expression. Table 11.4 summarizes these operators..

TABLE 11.4 Operators for Creating Compound Expressions

Operator	*Description*
`! expr`	True if *expr* is false.
`expr1 -a expr2`	True if both *expr1* and *expr2* are true.
`expr1 -o expr2`	True if either *expr1* or *expr2* is true.

The syntax for creating compound expressions using the built-in operators is

```
test expr1 op expr2
```

or

```
[ expr1 op expr2 ]
```

Here *expr1* and *expr2* are any valid test expressions, and *op* is `-a` (short for and) or `-o` (short for or). If the `-a` operator is used, both *expr1* and *expr2* must be true in order for the compound expression to be true. If the `-o` operator is used, either *expr1* or *expr2* must be true in order for the compound expression to be true.

The syntax for creating compound expressions using the conditional operators is

```
test expr1 op test expr2
```

or

```
[ expr1 ] op [ expr2 ]
```

Here *expr1* and *expr2* are any valid test expressions, and *op* is `&&` (and) or `||` (or). If the `&&` operator is used, both *expr1* and *expr2* must be true in order for the compound expression to be true. If the `||` operator is used, either *expr1* or *expr2* must be true in order for the compound expression to be true.

The following `if` statement, taken from OpenBSD's `/etc/rc`, illustrates a compound expression constructed using the built-in operator `-a`:

```
if [ -f /sbin/kbd -a -f /etc/kbdtype ]; then
   kbd `cat /etc/kbdtype`
fi
```

This `if` statement is executed as follows:

1. First the test

   ```
   -f /sbin/kbd
   ```

   is performed. If the file `/sbin/kbd` exists then the test returns true (`0`), otherwise the test returns false and the `if` statement performs no actions.
2. If `/sbin/kbd` exists, the second test

   ```
   -f /etc/kbdtype
   ```

   is performed. If the file `/etc/kbdtype` exists then the test returns true (`0`), otherwise the test returns false and the `if` statement performs no actions. If the first test failed, this test is not performed.

3. If both files exist, the command

   ```
   kbd `cat /etc/kbdtype`
   ```

   is executed.

As an illustration of how the conditional operators are used, the previous example can be rewritten to use conditional operators as follows:

```
if [ -f /sbin/kbd ] && [ -f /etc/kbdtype ]; then
   kbd `cat /etc/kbdtype`
fi
```

You just replaced the `-a` operator with `] && [`. The execution of this version is similar to that of the previous example:

1. First the expression

   ```
   [ -f /sbin/kbd ]
   ```

   is evaluated. If the file `/sbin/kbd` exists then the expression returns true (`0`), otherwise the test returns false and the `if` statement performs no actions.
2. If `/sbin/kbd` exists, the expression

   ```
   [ -f /etc/kbdtype ]
   ```

   is evaluated. If the file `/etc/kbdtype` exists then the test returns true (0), otherwise the test return false and the `if` statement performs no actions. If the first test failed, this test is not performed.
3. If both files exist, the command

   ```
   kbd `cat /etc/kbdtype`
   ```

   is executed.

The difference between the two versions is that in the first version *`list1`* is a single command, whereas in the second version *`list1`* is a compound command.

Some programmers prefer the version that uses the conditional operators because the individual tests are isolated. Other programmers prefer the second form because it invokes the `[` command only once and thus might be marginally more efficient for large numbers of tests. If your shell scripts need to be portable, you should use the conditional operators.

> In the previous examples you used only two expressions in your compound expressions. You are not limited to two expressions. You can combine any number of expressions into one compound expression.

Negating an Expression

Negation reverses the result of a test expression. An expression that would have been true is treated as false and vice versa. The basic syntax of the negation operator is

```
test ! expr
```

or

```
[ ! expr ]
```

Here *expr* is any valid `test` expression.

The following example, taken from OpenBSD's `/etc/rc` startup script, illustrates the use of the `!` operator:

```
if [ ! -f /etc/motd ]; then
   install -c -o root -g wheel -m 664 /dev/null /etc/motd
fi
```

This example creates the file `/etc/motd` (the message of the day on UNIX systems) using the `install` command if it does not exist or is not a regular file. The execution is as follows:

1. First the test

   ```
   -f /etc/motd
   ```

   is performed.
2. The result of the test is negated because of the `!` operator. If the file `/etc/motd` exists and is a regular file, the compound expression returns false (`1`); otherwise, it returns true.
3. If the result of the previous step is true, the file `/etc/motd` is created; otherwise, the `if` statement performs no actions.

This example can also be written as either of the following commands:

```
test ! -f /etc/motd && install -c -o root -g wheel -m 664
➥ /dev/null /etc/motd[ -f /etc/motd ] && install -c -o root -g
➥ wheel -m 664 /dev/null /etc/motd
```

This achieves the same result because `install` is executed only if the `test` or `[` commands return true.

The case Statement

The case statement is the second form of flow control available in the shell. Its syntax is as follows:

```
case word in
    pattern1)
            list1
            ;;
    pattern2)
            list2
            ;;
...
    patternN)
            listN
            ;;
esac
```

Here the string *word* is compared to each of the patterns from *pattern1* to *pattern*. When a matching pattern is found, the list following the matching pattern is then executed.

When a list finishes executing, the special command ;; indicates that flow should jump to the end of the case statement. The ;; is similar to the break command in the C programming language. If no matches are found, the case statement does not perform any actions. The minimum number of patterns is one. There is no limit on the maximum number of patterns.

Some programmers prefer to use a more concise form of the case statement, written as follows:

```
case word in
   pattern1) list1 ;;
...
   patternN) listN ;;
esac
```

This form should be used only if the list of commands to be executed is short.

A case Statement Example

The following example illustrates the use of the case statement:

```
FRUIT=kiwi
case "$FRUIT" in
    apple) echo "Apple pie is quite tasty." ;;
    banana) echo "I like banana nut bread." ;;
    kiwi) echo "New Zealand is famous for kiwi." ;;
esac
```

The execution of the case statement is as follows:

1. The string contained in the variable FRUIT is expanded to kiwi.
2. The string kiwi is compared against the first pattern, apple. Because they don't match, the program goes on to the next pattern.
3. The string kiwi is compared against the next pattern, banana. Because they don't match, the program goes on to the next pattern.
4. The string kiwi is compared against the final pattern, kiwi. Because they match, the following message is produced:

   ```
   New Zealand is famous for kiwi.
   ```

Common Errors

Two common errors that are encountered while using the case statement are as follows:

- Ommitting the ;; at the end of a list.
- Writing case instead of esac at the end of the case statement.

To illustrate the first type of error, the previous example is modified so that the ;; is missing after the first list:

```
FRUIT=kiwi
case "$FRUIT" in
    apple) echo "Apple pie is quite tasty."
    banana) echo "I like banana nut bread." ;;
    kiwi) echo "New Zealand is famous for kiwi." ;;
esac
```

This ommission produces an error message similar to the following:

```
bash: syntax error near unexpected token `banana)'
```

What this error message means is that while the shell was trying to execute the list for the pattern apple, it saw the start of the pattern banana. Because this pattern started before the shell encountered the end of the list for the pattern apple, an error message was produced. To illustrate the second type of error, the ending esac is changed to case:

```
FRUIT=kiwi
case "$FRUIT" in
    apple) echo "Apple pie is quite tasty." ;;
    banana) echo "I like banana nut bread." ;;
    kiwi) echo "New Zealand is famous for kiwi." ;;
case
```

This change produces an error message similar to the following:

```
bash: syntax error near unexpected token `case'
```

What this error message means is that the shell did not see the appropriate closing `esac` for the `case` statement.

Using Patterns

In the previous example, you used fixed strings as the pattern. When used in this fashion, the `case` statement is basically an `if` statement. For example, the `if` statement corresponding to the `case` statement in previous example is

```
if [ "$FRUIT" = apple ] ; then
    echo "Apple pie is quite tasty."
elif [ "$FRUIT" = banana ] ; then
    echo "I like banana nut bread."
elif [ "$FRUIT" = kiwi ] ; then
    echo "New Zealand is famous for kiwi."
fi
```

Although the `case` statement is more concise and readable, the real power of the `case` statement does not lie in enhancing the readability of your scripts; its power lies in the fact that it uses *patterns* rather than fixed strings to perform matching. A pattern is a string that consists of regular characters and special *wildcard* characters. The pattern determines whether a match is present. The `case` statement patterns use the same special characters as patterns for pathname expansion covered in Chapter 9, "Substitution." The patterns can also include the OR operator, `|`.

11

An example of a simple `case` statement that uses patterns is as follows:

```
case $- in
    *i*) # an interactive shell
        PS1="`uname -n`$ "
        PATH="$PATH:$HOME/bin"
        export PS1 PATH ;;
esac
```

The special variable `$-` contains a list of the shell options. In this case, you determine whether that list contains the letter `i`, which indicates that the shell is interactive. Checking if `$-` contains the letter `i` is the most portable method for determining whether the shell is running in interactive mode or in non-interactive mode. In this example, you set up the prompt, `PS1`, and the command search path, `PATH`, if the shell is running in interactive mode; otherwise, no actions are performed.

Summary

In this chapter, you examined the two main flow control mechanisms available in the shell: `if` and `case`. You also looked at the `test` command and its use in `if` statements. Specifically, the chapter covered the following topics:

- Performing file tests
- Performing string comparisons
- Performing numerical comparisons
- Using compound expressions

In the next chapter, you will examine loops, which are complementary to flow control statements.

Questions

1. What is the difference between the following commands?

   ```
   if [ -e /usr/local/bin/bash ] ; then /usr/local/bin/bash ; fi
   if [ -x /usr/local/bin/bash ] ; then /usr/local/bin/bash ; fi
   ```

2. Given the following variable declarations,

   ```
   HOME=/home/ranga
   BINDIR=/home/ranga/bin
   ```

   what is the output of the following `if` statement?

   ```
   if [ $HOME/bin = $BINDIR ] ; then
       echo "Your binaries are stored in your home directory."
   fi
   ```

3. Write a `test` command that can be used to test if `/usr/bin` is a directory or a symbolic link.

4. Given the following `if` statement, write an equivalent `case` statement:

   ```
   if [ "$ANS" = "Yes" -o "$ANS" = "yes" -o "$ANS" = "y" -o "$ANS" = "Y" ] ;
   then
       ANS="y"
   else
       ANS="n"
   fi
   ```

Terms

Conditional flow control commands Commands that allow the flow of a script to be conditionally changed. Also called flow control commands.

Compound expression When two or more expressions are combined, the result is called a compound expression.

Flow control commands See conditional flow control commands.

Negating expressions Reverses the result of a test expression. An expression that would have been true is treated as false and vice versa.

HOUR 12

Loops

Loops enable you to execute a series of commands multiple times. The two main types of loops are the `while` loop and the `for` loop. In addition to these two types of loops, `ksh`, `bash`, and `zsh` support an additional type of loop called the `select` loop. It can be used to present a menu of choices to a shell scripts user. In this chapter, you will examine loops in detail. Specifically, this chapter covers the following topics:

- The `while` loop
- The `for` loop
- The `select` loop
- Loop control

The while Loop

The `while` loop enables you to execute a set of commands repeatedly until some condition occurs. It is normally used when you need to manipulate the value of a variable repeatedly. The basic syntax of the `while` loop is

```
while cmd
do
    list
done
```

Here, *cmd* is a single command, whereas *list* is a list of one or more commands. Although *command* can be any valid UNIX command, it is usually a test expression of the type covered in Chapter 11, "Flow Control." The list called *list* is commonly referred to as the *body* of the while loop. The do and done keywords are not considered part of the body of the loop because the shell uses them only for determining where the while loop begins and ends.

The execution of a while loop proceeds according to the following steps:

1. Execute *cmd*.
2. If the exit status of *cmd* is nonzero, exit from the while loop.
3. If the exit status of *cmd* is zero, execute *list*.
4. When *list* finishes executing, return to Step 1.

If both *cmd* and *list* are short, the while loop can be written on a single line as follows:

```
while cmd ; do list ; done
```

Here is a simple example that uses the while loop to display the numbers from zero to nine:

```
x=0
while [ $x -lt 10 ]
do
    echo $x
     x=`expr $x + 1`
done
```

Its output looks like this:

```
0
1
2
3
4
5
6
7
8
9
```

Each time this loop executes, the variable x is checked to see whether it has a value that is less than 10. If the value of x is less than 10, this test expression has an exit status of 0. In this case, the current value of x is displayed and then x is incremented by 1. If x is equal to 10 or greater than 10, the test expression returns 1, causing the while loop to exit.

The previous example uses the `expr` command to increment and decrement the variable `$x`. If you are not familiar with the `expr` command, don't worry, it is covered in Chapter 18, "Other Tools."

Nesting `while` Loops

It is possible to use a `while` loop as part of the body of another `while` loop as follows:

```
while cmd1 ; # this is loop1, the outer loop
do
    list1
    while cmd2 ; # this is loop2, the inner loop
    do
       list2
    done
    list3
done
```

Here *`cmd1`* and *`cmd2`* are single commands, whereas *`list1`*, *`list2`*, and *`list3`* are sets of one or more commands. Both *`list1`* and *`list3`* are optional.

In situations in which there are two `while` loops, *`loop1`* and *`loop2`*, *`loop1`* is referred to as the *main loop* or *outer loop*, and *`loop2`* is referred to as the *inner loop*. When describing the inner loop, *`loop2`*, many programmers say that it is *nested* one level deep. The term *nested* refers to the fact that *`loop2`* is located in the body of *`loop1`*. If you had a *`loop3`* located in the body of *`loop2`*, it would be nested two levels deep. The level of nesting is relative to the outermost loop. There are no restrictions on how deeply nested loops can be, but you should try to avoid nesting loops more deeply than four or five levels to avoid difficulties in finding and fixing problems in your scripts.

12

As an illustration of loop nesting, let's add another countdown loop inside the loop that you used to count to nine:

```
x=0
while [ "$x" -lt 10 ] ; # this is loop1
do
    y="$x"
    while [ "$y" -ge 0 ] ; # this is loop2
    do
        printf "$y "
        y=`expr $y - 1`
    done
    echo
    x=`expr $x + 1`
done
```

The main change introduced is the variable `y`. It is set to the value of `x-1` before *`loop2`* executes. Because of this, each time `loop2` executes, it displays all the numbers greater than 0 and less than `x` in reverse order. The output looks like the following:

```
0
1 0
2 1 0
3 2 1 0
4 3 2 1 0
5 4 3 2 1 0
6 5 4 3 2 1 0
7 6 5 4 3 2 1 0
8 7 6 5 4 3 2 1 0
9 8 7 6 5 4 3 2 1 0
```

Validating User Input with `while`

Say that you need to write a script that needs to ask the user for the name of a directory. You could use the following steps to get information from the users:

1. Ask the user a question.
2. Read the user's response.
3. Determine whether the user responded with the name of a directory.

But what should you do when the user gives you a response that is not a directory?

The simplest choice would be to do nothing, but this is not very user friendly. Your script can be much more user friendly by informing the user of the error and asking for the name of a directory again. The `while` loop is perfect for doing this. In fact, a common use for the `while` loop is to determine whether user input has been gathered correctly. Usually a strategy similar to the following is employed:

1. Set a variable's value to null.
2. Start a `while` loop that exits when the variable's value is not null.
3. In the `while` loop, ask the user a question and read in the users response.
4. Validate the response.
5. If the response is invalid the variable's value is set to null. This enables the `while` loop to repeat.
6. If the response is valid, the variable's value is not changed. It continues to hold the user's response. Because the variable's value is not null, the `while` loop exits.

A `while` loop that implements this is

```
RESPONSE=
while [ -z "$RESPONSE" ] ;
do
```

```
    echo "Enter the name of a directory where your files are
    ➥located:\c "
    read RESPONSE
    if [ ! -d "$RESPONSE" ] ; then
        echo "ERROR: Please enter a directory pathname."
        RESPONSE=
    fi
done
```

Here, you store the user's response in the variable `RESPONSE`. Initially this variable is set to null, enabling the `while` loop to begin executing. When the `while` loop first executes, the user is prompted as follows:

```
Enter the name of a directory where your files are located:
```

The user can type the name of a directory at this prompt. When the user finishes typing and presses Enter, `read` stores the input into the variable `RESPONSE`. You then check to make sure the input is a directory. If the input is not a directory, you issue an error message and repeat. An error message is produced so that the user knows what was wrong with the input. If the user does not enter any value, the variable `RESPONSE` is still set to null. In this case the value stored in the variable `RESPONSE` is not a directory, thus the error message is produced.

Input Redirection and `while`

The `while` loop can also be combined with input redirection and `read` in order to read a file one line at a time. The basic syntax is

```
while read LINE
do
: # manipulate file here
done < file
```

In the body of the `while` loop, you can manipulate each line of the specified *`file`*. A simple example of this is

```
while read LINE
do
   case $LINE in
   *root*) echo $LINE ;;
esac
done < /etc/passwd
```

Here only the lines that contain the string `root` in the file `/etc/passwd` are displayed. The output will be similar to the following:

```
root:x:0:1:Super-User:/:/sbin/sh
```

`while` and Subshells

A problem with the loop used in the previous example is that it is executed in a subshell in Bourne shell and older versions of `ksh`. This means that any changes to the script environment, such as exporting variables and changing the current working directory, might not be present after the `while` loop completes. As an example, consider the following script:

```
#!/bin/sh
if [ -f "$1" ] ; then
    i=0
    while read LINE
    do
        i=`expr $i + 1`
    done < "$1"
    echo $i
fi
```

This script tries to count the number of lines in the file specified to it as an argument. Executing this script on the file

```
$ cat dirs.txt
/tmp
/usr/local
/opt/bin
/var
```

can produce the following incorrect result:

```
0
```

Although you are incrementing the value of `$i` using the command

```
i=`expr $i + 1`
```

when the `while` loop completes, the value of `$i` is not preserved. In this case, you need to change a variable's value inside the `while` loop and then use that value outside the loop. One way to solve this problem is to redirect STDIN prior to entering the loop and then restore STDIN after the loop completes. The basic syntax is

```
exec n<&0 < file
while read LINE
do
: # manipulate file here
done
exec 0<&n n<&-
```

Here, *n* is an integer greater than 2, and *file* is the name of the file you want to read. Usually *n* is chosen as a small number such as 3, 4, or 5. This allows you to construct a shell version of the `cat` command as follows:

```
#!/bin/sh
if [ $# -ge 1 ] ; then
    for FILE in $@
    do
        exec 4<&0 < "$FILE"
        while read LINE ; do echo $LINE ; done
        exec 0<&4 4<&-
    done
fi
```

The `until` Loop

The `while` loop is perfect for a situation where you need to execute a set of commands while some condition is true, but sometimes you need to execute a set of commands until a condition is true. The `until` loop, available in `ksh`, `bash` and `zsh`, provides this functionality. Its syntax is

```
until cmd
do
    list
done
```

Here *cmd* is a single command, whereas *list* is a set of one or more commands. Although *cmd* can be any valid UNIX command, it is usually a `test` expression of the type covered in Chapter 11, "Flow Control."

12

The execution of an `until` loop is similar to that of the `while` loop:

1. Execute *cmd*.
2. If the exit status of *cmd* is nonzero, exit from the `until` loop.
3. If the exit status of *cmd* is zero, execute *list*.
4. When *list* finishes executing, return to Step 1.

If both *cmd* and *list* are short, the `until` loop can be written on a single line as follows:

```
until cmd ; do list ; done
```

In most cases an `until` loop is identical to a `while` loop with *cmd* negated using the `!` operator. For example, the following `while` loop

```
x=1
while [ ! $x -ge 10 ]
do
    echo $x
    x=`expr $x + 1`
done
```

is equivalent to the following `until` loop:

```
x=1;
until [ $x -ge 10 ]
do
    echo $x
    x=`expr $x + 1`
done
```

The `until` loop offers no advantages over the equivalent `while` loop. Because it isn't supported by the Bourne shell, most programmers do not favor it. It is covered here for the sake of completeness.

The `for` and `select` Loops

Unlike the `while` loop, which exits when a certain condition is false, the `for` and `select` loops operate on lists of items. This section covers these two loops in detail.

The `for` Loop

The `for` loop enables you to execute a set of commands repeatedly for each item in a list. One of its most common uses is in performing the same set of commands for a large number of files. The basic syntax is

```
for name in word1 word2 ... wordN
do
    list
done
```

Here *name* is the name of a variable and *word1* to *wordN* are sequences of characters separated by spaces (words). Each time the `for` loop executes, the value of the variable *name* is set to the next word in the list of words, *word1* to *wordN*. The first time, *name* is set to *word1*; the second time, it's set to *word2*; and so on. This means that the number of times a `for` loop executes depends on the number of words that are specified. For example, if the following words were specified to a `for` loop

```
there comes a time
```

the loop would execute four times. In each iteration of the `for` loop, the commands specified in *list* are executed.

A `for` loop can be written on a single line as follows:

```
for name in word1 word2 ... wordN ; do list ; done
```

If *list* and the number of words are short, the single line form is often chosen; otherwise, the multiple-line form is preferred.

A simple `for` loop example is

```
for i in 0 1 2 3 4 5 6 7 8 9
do
    echo $i
done
```

This loop counts to nine as follows:

```
0
1
2
3
4
5
6
7
8
9
```

Note that although the output is identical to the `while` loop, the `for` loop does something altogether different. In each iteration, `$i` is set to the next item in the list. When the list is finished, the loop exits. In this example, you chose the list to be the numbers from 0 to 9. In the `while` loop, the next number to display was being computed, and it was not part of a predetermined list.

If you change the list slightly, notice how the output changes:

```
for i in 0 1 2 4 3 5 8 7 9
do
    echo $i
done
```

```
0
1
2
4
3
5
8
7
9
```

12

Manipulating a Set of Files

Say that you need to copy a bunch of files from one directory to another and change the permissions on the copy. You could do this by copying each file and changing the permissions manually.

A better solution is to determine the commands you need to execute in order to copy a file and change its permissions, and then have the computer do this for every file you were interested in. In fact this is one of the most common uses of the `for` loop—iterating over a set of filenames and performing some operations on those files.

The procedure to do this follows:

1. Create a `for` loop with a variable named `file` or `FILE`. Other favored names include `i`, `j`, and `k`. The name of the variable is usually singular.
2. Create a list of files to manipulate. This is frequently accomplished using the filename substitution technique discussed in Chapter 9, "Substitution."
3. Manipulate the files in the body of the loop.

An example of this is the following `for` loop:

```
for FILE in $HOME/.bash*
do
    cp $FILE ${HOME}/public_html
    chmod a+r ${HOME}/public_html/${FILE}
done
```

In this loop, you use filename substitution to obtain a list of files in your home directory that start with `.bash*`. In the body of the loop, each of these files is copied to the directory `public_html` and made readable by everyone.

The `select` Loop

The `select` loop provides an easy way to create a numbered menu from which users can select options. It is useful when you need to ask the user to choose one or more items from a list of choices. The `select` loop was introduced in `ksh` and has been adapted by `bash` and `zsh`. It is not available in the Bourne shell.

The basic syntax of the `select` loop is

```
select name in word1 word2 ... wordN
do
    list
done
```

Here *`name`* is the name of a variable and *`word1`* to *`wordN`* are sequences of characters separated by spaces (words). The set of commands to execute after the user has made a selection is specified by *`list`*.

The execution process of a `select` loop is as follows:

1. Each item in *`list1`* is displayed along with a number.
2. A prompt, usually `#?`, is displayed.
3. When the user enters a value, `$REPLY` is set to that value.

4. If `$REPLY` contains a number of a displayed item, the variable specified by *`name`* is set to the item in *`list1`* that was selected. Otherwise, the items in *`list1`* are displayed again.
5. When a valid selection is made, *`list2`* executes.
6. If *`list2`* does not exit from the `select` loop using one of the loop control mechanisms such as `break`, the process starts over at Step 1.

If the user enters more than one valid value, `$REPLY` contains all the user's choices. In this case, the variable specified by *`name`* is not set.

An Example of the `select` Loop

One common use of the `select` loop is in scripts that configure software. The following example is a simplified version of one such script. The actual configuration commands have been omitted because they are not relevant in this discussion.

```
select COMPONENT in comp1 comp2 comp3 all none
do
    case $COMPONENT in
        comp1|comp2|comp3) CompConf $COMPONENT ;;
        all) CompConf comp1
             CompConf comp2
             CompConf comp3
             ;;
        none) break ;;
        *) echo "ERROR: Invalid selection, $REPLY." ;;
    esac
done
```


The menu presented by the `select` loop looks like the following:

```
1) comp1
2) comp2
3) comp3
4) all
5) none
#?
```

As you can see, each of the items in the list

```
comp1 comp2 comp3 all none
```

are displayed with a number preceding them. The user can enter one of these numbers to select a particular component. If a valid selection is made, the `select` loop executes a `case` statement contained in its body. This `case` statement performs the correct action based on the user's input. Here the correct action is either calling a command named `CompConf`, exiting the loop, or displaying an error message.

If you are using `zsh`, the output from the previous example will be slightly different than shown above. In `zsh` the menu items are listed on a single line rather than being listed on separate lines:

```
1) comp1    2) comp2    3) comp3    4) all      5) none
?#
```

As you can see, the prompt is still listed on a separate line.

Changing the Prompt

You can change the prompt displayed by the `select` loop by altering the variable `PS3`. If `PS3` is not set, the default prompt, `#?`, is displayed. For example, the commands

```
$ PS3="Please make a selection => " ; export PS3
```

change the menu displayed in the previous example to the following:

```
1) comp1
2) comp2
3) comp3
4) all
5) none
Please make a selection =>
```

Notice that the value of `PS3` used has a space as its last character. This ensures that user input does not run into the prompt and thus makes the menu user friendly.

Versions of `bash` prior to 2.0 do not always use the value stored in `PS3` for the prompt of the select loop. This problem is not present in `ksh` or `zsh`.

Loop Control

So far you have looked at creating loops and working with loops to accomplish different tasks. Sometimes you will need to stop a loop or skip iterations of the loop. In this section you'll examine the `break` and `continue` commands that are used to control the execution of loops.

Infinite Loops and the `break` Command

Recall that the `while` loop terminated when a particular condition was met. This happened when the task of the `while` loop completed. If you make a mistake in specifying the termination condition of a `while` loop, it can continue forever. For example, say you forgot to specify the `$` before the `x` in the test expression:

```
x=0
while [ x -lt 10 ]
do
    echo $x
     x=`expr $x + 1`
done
```

This loop would continue to display numbers forever. A loop that executes forever without terminating executes an infinite number of times. For this reason, such loops are called *infinite* loops.

In most cases infinite looping is not desired and stems from programming errors, but in certain instances they can be useful. For example, say that you need to wait for a particular event, such as someone logging on to a system. You can use an infinite loop to check every few seconds whether the event has occurred. Because you don't know how many times you need to execute the loop, you need to exit the infinite loop using the `break` command. The `break` command terminates or breaks a loop.

You can create infinite loops using the `while` loop by specifying *`cmd`* as either `:` or `/bin/true`. The basic syntax of the infinite `while` loop is

```
while :
do
    list
done
```

In most infinite loops, the `while` loop usually exits from within *`list`* via a `break` command.

Consider the following interactive script that reads and executes commands:

```
while :
do
    read CMD
    case $CMD in
        [qQ]|[qQ][uU][iI][tT]) break ;;
        *) $CMD ;;
     esac
done
```

In this loop a command is read at the beginning of each iteration. If that command is either `q` or `Quit`, the loop exits; otherwise, the loop tries to process the command.

12

Breaking Out of Nested Loops

The `break` command also accepts as an argument an integer, greater than or equal to 1, indicating the number of levels to break out of. This feature is useful in nested loops. Consider the following nested `for` loops:

```
for i in 1 2 3 4 5
do
    mkdir -p /mnt/backup/docs/ch0${i}
    if [ $? -eq 0 ] ; then
        for j in doc c h m pl sh
        do
            cp $HOME/docs/ch0${i}/*.${j} /mnt/backup/docs/ch0${i}
            if [ $? -ne 0 ] ; then break 2 ; fi
        done
    else
        echo "Could not make backup directory."
    fi
done
```

In this loop, you are making a backup of several important files to a backup directory. The outer loop takes care of creating the backup directory, whereas the inner loop copies the important files based on the extension. In the inner loop, you use a `break` command with the argument `2`. This indicates that if an error occurs while copying, both loops should be terminated, rather than just the inner loop.

> The previous example makes copies of several files in your home directory `$HOME` and places them in a directory under `/mnt`. Please ensure that you are permitted (by your system administrator) to copy files from your home directory to `/mnt` before executing this example.

The `continue` Command

The `continue` command is similar to the `break` command, except that it causes only the current iteration of the loop to exit, rather than the entire loop. This command is useful when an error has occurred but you want to try to execute the next iteration of the loop. As an example, the following loop doesn't exit if one of the input files is bad:

```
for FILE in $FILES ;
do
    if [ ! -f "$FILE" ] ; then
        echo "ERROR: $FILE is not a file."
        continue
    fi
    # process the file
done
```

If one of the filenames in `$FILES` is not a file, this loop skips it, rather than exiting.

Summary

Loops allow you to execute sets of commands repeatedly. In this chapter, you have examined the following types of loops:

- `while`
- `until`
- `for`
- `select`

You have also examined the concept of nested loops, infinite loops, and loop control. The next chapter introduces the concept of parameters, which require extensive use of loops.

Questions

1. What changes are required to the following `while` loop

```
x=0
while [ $x -lt 10 ]
do
    echo "$x \c"
    y=$(($x-1))
    x=$(($x+1))
    while [ $y -ge 0 ] ; do
        y=$(($y-1))
       echo "$y \c"
    done
    echo
done
```

so that the output looks like the following:

```
0
0 1
0 1 2
0 1 2 3
0 1 2 3 4
0 1 2 3 4 5
0 1 2 3 4 5 6
0 1 2 3 4 5 6 7
0 1 2 3 4 5 6 7 8
0 1 2 3 4 5 6 7 8 9
```

2. Write a `select` loop that lists each file in the current directory and enables the user to view the file by selecting its number. In addition to listing each file, use the string `Exit Program` as the key to exit the loop. If the user selects an item that is not a regular file, the program should identify the problem. If no input is given, the menu should be redisplayed.

Terms

Body The set of commands executed by a loop.

Infinite loops Loops that execute forever without terminating. See *loops.*

Iteration A single execution of the body of a loop.

Loops Enable you to execute a series of commands multiple times. Two main types of loops are the `while` and `for` loops.

Nested loops When a loop is located inside the body of another loop, it is said to be nested within another loop.

HOUR 13

Parameters

As you saw in previous chapters, the general format for the invocation of programs in UNIX is

```
cmd opts files
```

Here *cmd* is the command name, *opts* is any option that you need to specify, and *files* is an optional list of files on which the command should operate. Consider the following example:

```
$ ls -l *.doc
```

Here `ls` is the command, `-l` is the only option, and `*.doc` is the list of files for `ls` to operate on.

Because most UNIX users are familiar with this interface, it is best to use this format in shell scripts. This means that scripts that can have options must be able to read and interpret them correctly.

This chapter examines the following topics related to the handling of options passed to a shell script:

- Special variables related to option parsing and command execution
- Handling options manually using a `case` statement
- Handling options using the `getopts` command

For scripts that support only one or two options, the first method is easy to implement and works quite well, but many scripts allow any combination of several options to be given. For such scripts, the `getopts` command is very useful because it affords the maximum flexibility in parsing options.

Special Variables

The shell defines several special variables that are relevant to option parsing and command execution. Table 13.1 describes all of these special variables.

TABLE 13.1 Special Shell Variables

Variable	*Description*
`$0`	The name of the command being executed. For shell scripts, this is the path which invoked it.
`$`*n*	These variables correspond to the arguments with which a script was invoked. Here *n* is a positive decimal number corresponding to the position of an argument (the first argument is `$1`, the second argument is `$2`, and so on).
`$#`	The number of arguments supplied to a script.
`$*`	All the arguments are double quoted. If a script receives two arguments, `$*` is equivalent to `$1 $2`.
`$@`	All the arguments are individually double quoted. If a script receives two arguments, `$@` is equivalent to `$1 $2`.
`$?`	The exit status of the last command executed.
`$$`	The process number of the current shell. For shell scripts, this is the process ID under which they are executing.
`$!`	The process number of the last background command.

Using `$0`

Let's start by looking at `$0`. This variable is commonly used to determine the behavior of scripts that can be invoked with more than one name. Consider the following script:

```
#!/bin/sh
case $0 in
    *listtar) TARGS="-tvf $1" ;;
    *maketar) TARGS="-cvf $1.tar $1" ;;
esac
tar $TARGS
```

You can use this script to list the contents of a tar file (short for tape archive, a common format for distributing files in UNIX) or to create a tar file based on the name with which the script is invoked. The tar file to read or create is specified as the first argument, `$1`, to the script.

Let's call this script `mytar` and make two symbolic links to it, called `listtar` and `maketar`, as follows:

```
$ ln -s mytar listtar
$ ln -s mytar maketar
```

If the script is invoked with the name `maketar` and is given a directory or filename, it creates a tar file with the contents of that directory or file. Say you have a directory called `fruits` with the following contents:

```
$ ls fruits
apple   banana  mango   peach   pear
```

You can invoke the script as `maketar` to obtain a `tar` file called `fruit.tar` containing this directory, by issuing the following command:

```
$ ./maketar fruits
```

If you want to list the contents of the tar file this command creates, you can invoke the script as follows:

```
$ ./listtar fruits.tar
rwxr-xr-x 500/100        0 Nov 17 08:48 1998 fruits/
rw-r--r-- 500/100        0 Nov 17 08:48 1998 fruits/apple
rw-r--r-- 500/100        0 Nov 17 08:48 1998 fruits/banana
rw-r--r-- 500/100        0 Nov 17 08:48 1998 fruits/mango
rw-r--r-- 500/100        0 Nov 17 08:48 1998 fruits/pear
rw-r--r-- 500/100        0 Nov 17 08:48 1998 fruits/peach
```

The exact output depends on the version of `tar` on your system. Some versions include more detailed output than is shown here.

Usage Statements

Another common use for `$0` is in the *usage statement* of a script. The usage statement is a short message that a script outputs in order to inform a user of the proper invocation syntax for the script. All scripts used by more than one user should include usage statements.

In general, the usage statement is something like the following:

```
echo "Usage: $0 [options][files]"
```

Returning to the `mytar` script, adding a usage statement would be a helpful, especially if the script is executed with a name other than `listtar` or `maketar`. You can implement this change as follows:

```
case $0 in
    *listtar) TARGS="-tvf $1" ;;
    *maketar) TARGS="-cvf $1.tar $1" ;;
    *) echo "Usage: $0 [file|directory]"
       exit 0
       ;;
esac
```

Now if the script is invoked as say, `mytar`, it will output the following message:

```
Usage: mytar [file|directory]
```

Although this message describes the usage of the script correctly, it does not inform you that the script's name was given incorrectly. There are two possible methods for rectifying this:

- Hard coding the valid names in the usage statement
- Changing the script to use its arguments to decide in which mode it should run

To demonstrate the use of options, the next section uses the latter method.

Options and Arguments

Options are given on the command line to change the behavior of a script or program. For example, the `-a` option of the `ls` command changes the behavior of the `ls` command from listing all visible files to listing all files (as explained in Chapter 3). This section shows you how to use options to change the behavior of scripts.

Often you will see or hear options called *arguments*. The difference between the two is subtle. A command's arguments are all of the separate strings or words that appear on the command line after the command name, whereas *options* are only those arguments that change the behavior of the command.

For example, in the following example:

```
$ ls -aF fruit
```

the command is `ls`, and its arguments are `-aF` and `fruit`. The options to the `ls` command are `-aF`.

Dealing with Arguments

To illustrate the use of options, let's change the `mytar` script to use its first argument, `$1`, as the mode argument and `$2` as the tar file to read or create. You can implement this change as follows:

```
USAGE="Usage: $0 [-c|-t] [file|directory]"
case "$1" in
    -t) TARGS="-tvf $2" ;;
    -c) TARGS="-cvf $2.tar $2" ;;
    *) echo "$USAGE"
       exit 0
       ;;
esac
```

The three main changes are as follows:

- All references to `$1` have been changed to `$2` because the second argument is now the filename.
- `listtar` has been replaced by `-t`.
- `maketar` has been replaced by `-c`.

Now running `mytar` produces the following output:

```
Usage: ./mytar [-c|-t] [file|directory]
```

To create a tar file of the directory `fruits` with this version, use the command

```
$ ./mytar -c fruits
```

To list the contents of the resulting tar file, `fruits.tar`, use the command

```
$ ./mytar -t fruits
```

Using `basename`

13

Currently, the usage statement of `mytar` outputs the entire path with which the script was invoked. What it should really output is just the name of the script. You can correct this by using the `basename` command.

The `basename` command takes an absolute or relative pathname to a file or directory and returns just the file or directory name from that path. The basic syntax is as follows:

```
basename file
```

For example,

```
$ basename /usr/bin/sh
```

prints the following:

```
sh
```

Using basename, you can change the variable $USAGE in the mytar script as follows:

```
USAGE="Usage: `basename $0` [-c|-t] [file|directory]"
```

so that the usage statement produces the desired output:

```
Usage: mytar [-c|-t] [file|directory]
```

You can also use the basename command in the first version of the mytar script to avoid using the * wildcard character in the case statement:

```
#!/bin/sh
case `basename $0` in
    listtar) TARGS="-tvf $1" ;;
    maketar) TARGS="-cvf $1.tar $1" ;;
    *) echo "Usage: $0 [file|directory]"
       exit 0
       ;;
esac
tar $TARGS
```

In this version, basename allows you to match the exact names with which scripts can be called. As an illustration of a potential problem with the original version, you can see that if the script is called

```
$ ./makelisttar
```

the original version would use the first case statement, even though it was incorrect, but the new version would fall through and report an error.

Emulating basename

Some older Linux and BSD systems do not include the basename command. If you are using such a system, you can emulate this command by creating a shell script that provides the equivalent functionality. A shell script version of basename might look like the following:

```
#!/bin/sh

if [ -n "$1" ] ; then
   echo "$1" | sed -e 's/^.*\///'
else
   echo "Usage: basename [file]" 1>&2
   exit 1
fi

exit 0
```

Don't worry if you don't understand how the sed command works. You'll read more about it in Chapter 16, "Filtering Text with Regular Expressions."

Common Argument Handling Problems

Now that the `mytar` script uses options to set the mode in which the script will run, you need to solve another problem. Namely, what should you do if the second argument, `$2`, is not provided? You don't have to worry about what happens if the first argument, `$1`, is not provided because the `case` statement deals with this situation via the default case, `*`.

The simplest method for checking the necessary number of arguments is to see whether the number arguments, `$#`, match the number of required arguments. You can add this check to the script as follows:

```
#!/bin/sh

USAGE="Usage: `basename $0` [-c|-t] [file|directory]"

if [ $# -lt 2 ] ; then
    echo "$USAGE"
    exit 1
fi

case "$1" in
    -t) TARGS="-tvf $2" ;;
    -c) TARGS="-cvf $2.tar $2" ;;
     *) echo "$USAGE"
        exit 0
        ;;
esac

tar $TARGS
```

Handling Additional Files

The `mytar` script is mostly finished, but you can still make a few improvements. For example, it only deals with the first file that is given as an argument, and it does not determine whether this argument is really a file.

You can add the processing of all file arguments by using the special shell variable `$@`. Let's start by modifying the `-t` option to work with this variable:

```
case "$1" in
    -t) TARGS="-tvf"
        for i in "$@"
        do
            if [ -f "$i" ] ; then
               tar $TARGS "$i"
            fi
        done
        ;;
    -c) TARGS="-cvf $2.tar $2" ;
```

```
            tar $TARGS
            ;;
        *) echo "$USAGE" ;
            exit 0
            ;;
esac
```

The main changes are

- The -t case now includes a for loop that processes the arguments.
- There is an if statement in the for loop that determines whether the argument is a file. If an argument is a file, tar is executed on that file.

$* and $@

The arguments specified to a shell script are stored in two special variables, $* and $@. The main difference between these two special variables is how they store arguments: $* stores each argument without preserving quoting, whereas $@ stores each argument by preserving quoting.

The behavior of $* can sometimes cause a problem. For example, if your script has a filename containing spaces as an argument:

```
mytar -t "my tar file.tar"
```

using $* instead of $@ would create a problem because the for loop would be executed three times for files named my, tar, and file.tar, instead of just once for the file you requested, my tar file.tar. By using $@, you avoid this problem because each argument is stored as it was quoted on the command line.

A Few Minor Issues

There are two minor issues in mytar that you should deal with:

- mytar treats all its arguments, including the first argument, $1, as files. Because you are using the first argument to indicate the mode in which the script runs you should not consider it as a file. This will reduce the number of times the for loop is executed, and will prevent the script from trying to run tar on a file with the name -t.
- Another issue involves what the script should do when an operation fails. In the case of the list operation, if tar cannot list the contents of a file, you should skip the file and print an error.

You can solve the first issue by using `shift` to remove the first argument. You can solve the second issue by using the variable `$?` to check the exit status of `tar`. If you implement these changes, your script becomes:

```
#!/bin/sh

USAGE="Usage: `basename $0` [-c|-t] [files|directories]"

if [ $# -lt 2 ] ; then
    echo "$USAGE" ;
    exit 1 ;
fi

case "$1" in
    -t) shift
        TARGS="-tvf" ;
        for i in "$@" ;
        do
            if [ -f "$i" ] ; then
                FILES=`tar $TARGS "$i" 2>/dev/null`
                if [ $? -eq 0 ] ; then
                    echo ; echo "$i" ; echo "$FILES"
                else
                    echo "ERROR: $i not a tar file."
                fi
            else
                echo "ERROR: $i not a file."
            fi
        done
        ;;
    -c) shift
        TARGS="-cvf" ;
        tar $TARGS archive.tar "$@"
        ;;
     *) echo "$USAGE"
        exit 0
        ;;
esac
exit $?
```

13

Option Parsing in Shell Scripts

In the previous example, you manually handled the options passed to your script. In this second example, you will explore a second method, using the `getopts` command. The syntax of the `getopts` command is as follows:

```
getopts option-string var
```

Here *option-string* is a string consisting of all the single character options getopts should consider and *var* is the name of the variable that the option should be set to. Usually *var* is a variable named OPTION.

The process by which getopts parses the options given on the command line is as follows:

1. getopts examines all the command-line arguments, looking for arguments starting with the - character.
2. When an argument starting with the - character is found, it compares the characters following the - to the characters given in the *option-string*.
3. If a match is found, the specified *var* is set to the option; otherwise, *var* is set to the ? character.
4. Steps 1 through 3 are repeated until all the options have been considered.
5. When parsing has finished, getopts returns a nonzero exit code. This allows it to be easily used in loops. Also, when getopts has finished, it sets the variable OPTIND to the index of the last argument.

Another feature of getopts is its capability to indicate options requiring an additional parameter. This can be accomplished by following the option with a colon, :, character. In this case, after an option is parsed, the additional parameter is set to the value of the variable named OPTARG.

Some early versions of bash (1.x) did not completely support the getopts command. If you are using an older version of bash, you might encounter some errors when executing the examples in this section. If possible, you should upgrade to bash 2.0 or newer or use an alternate shell such as ksh or zsh when executing these examples.

Using getopts

To get a feeling for how getopts works and how to deal with options, you will write a script that simplifies the process of uuencoding a file.

For readers who are not familiar with uuencode, it is a program that was originally used to encode binary files (executable files) into ASCII text so that they could be e-mailed or transferred via FTP. Today, MIME encoding has taken the place of uuencoding for e-mail attachments, but it is still used for posting binaries to newsgroups and transferring binaries via modem.

You'll first examine the interface of this script, which makes it easier to understand the implementation. Your script should be able to accept the following options:

- `-f` to indicate the input filename
- `-o` to indicate the output filename
- `-v` to indicate the script should be verbose

The `getopts` command to implement these requirements is

```
getopts e:o:v OPTION
```

This indicates that all the options except for `-v` require an additional parameter. The support variables that are required are

- `VERBOSE`, which stores the value of the verbose flag. By default, the value of this variable is `false`.
- `INFILE`, which stores the name of the input file.
- `OUTFILE`, which stores the name of the output filename. If this value is unset, `uudecode` uses the same name as the input file and appends the `.uu` extension to it.

The following loop implements these requirements:

```
VERBOSE=false
while getopts f:o:v OPTION ;
do
    case "$OPTION" in
        f) INFILE="$OPTARG" ;;
        o) OUTFILE="$OPTARG" ;;
        v) VERBOSE=true ;;
       \?) echo "$USAGE" ;
           exit 1
           ;;
    esac
done
```

13

Now that you have dealt with option parsing, you need to deal with error conditions. For example, what should your script do if the input file is not specified? The simplest behavior would be to exit with an error, but with a little more work, you can make the script much more user friendly.

By using the fact that `getopts` sets the variable `OPTIND` to the value of the last option that was scanned, you can have the script assume that the first argument after this is the input filename. If no additional arguments remain, you should exit. Your error checking can be implemented as follows:

```
shift `echo "$OPTIND - 1" | bc`
if [ -z "$1" -a -z "$INFILE" ] ; then
```

```
    echo "ERROR: Input file was not specified."
    exit 1
fi

if [ -z "$INFILE" ] ; then
   INFILE="$1"
fi
```

Here you use the `shift` command to discard the arguments given to the script by one minus the last argument processed by `getopts`. The exact number of arguments to shift is calculated by the `bc` command, which is a command-line calculator. Its usage is explained in detail in Chapter 18. Strictly speaking, you do not have to shift the arguments; it just simplifies the `if` statement.

After shifting the arguments, you need to check whether the new `$1` contains a value. If it does not contain a value, you output an error message and exit; otherwise, you set `INFILE` to the filename specified by `$1`.

You also need to set the output filename, in case the `-o` option was not specified. You can use variable substitution to accomplish this

```
: ${OUTFILE:=${INFILE}.uu}
```

Here you set the name of the output file to the input file plus the `.uu` extension, if an output file is not given. You use the `:` command to prevent the shell from trying to execute the result of the variable substitution.

After you have made sure that all the inputs are correct, the actual work is quite simple. The `uuencode` command that you use is as follows:

```
uuencode $INFILE $INFILE > $OUTFILE ;
```

You should also check whether the input file is really a file before doing this command, so the actual body of your program is:

```
if [ -f "$INFILE" ] ; then
   uuencode "$INFILE" "$INFILE" > "$OUTFILE" ;
fi
```

At this point the script is fully functional, but you still need to add support for verbose reporting. This changes the preceding `if` statement to the following:

```
if [ -f "$INFILE" ] ; then
    if [ "$VERBOSE" = "true" ] ; then
        echo "uuencoding $INFILE to $OUTFILE... \c"
    fi
    uuencode "$INFILE" "$INFILE" > "$OUTFILE"
    RET=$?
    if [ "$VERBOSE" = "true" ] ; then
```

```
        MSG="Failed"
        if [ $RET -eq 0 ] ; then
           MSG="Done."
        fi
        echo $MSG
    fi
fi
```

You could simplify the verbose reporting to print a statement after the uuencode completes, but issuing two statements, one before the operation starts and one after the operation completes, is much more user-friendly. This method clearly indicates that the operation is being performed.

The complete script is as follows:

```
#!/bin/sh

USAGE="Usage: `basename $0` [-v] [-f] [filename] [-o] [filename]";
VERBOSE=false

while getopts f:o:v OPTION ;
do
    case "$OPTION" in
        f) INFILE="$OPTARG" ;;
        o) OUTFILE="$OPTARG" ;;
        v) VERBOSE=true ;;
       \?) echo "$USAGE"
           exit 1
           ;;
    esac
done

shift `echo "$OPTIND - 1" | bc`

if [ -z "$1" ] && [ -z "$INFILE" ] ; then
    echo "ERROR: Input file was not specified."
    exit 1
fi
if [ -z "$INFILE" ] ; then
   INFILE="$1"
fi

: ${OUTFILE:=${INFILE}.uu}

if [ -f "$INFILE" ] ; then
    if [ "$VERBOSE" = "true" ] ; then
        echo "uuencoding $INFILE to $OUTFILE... \c"
    fi
    uuencode $INFILE $INFILE > $OUTFILE
    RET=$?
```

```
    if [ "$VERBOSE" = "true" ] ; then
        MSG="Failed"
        if [ $RET -eq 0 ] ; then
           MSG="Done."
        fi
        echo $MSG
    fi
fi
exit 0
```

Assuming this script is called `uu`, you can use it to `uuencode` files in all of the following ways:

```
uu ch13.doc
uu -f ch13.doc
uu -f ch13.doc -o ch13.uu
```

In each of the preceding commands, file `ch13.doc` is uuencoded. The last command places the result into the file `ch13.uu` instead of the default `ch13.doc.uu`; this might be required if the document needs to be used on a DOS or Windows system.

Because this script uses `getopts`, any of the commands given previously can run in verbose mode by simply specifying the `-v` option.

Summary

In this chapter, you examined how to deal with arguments and options in shell script. Specifically you looked at the following methods:

- Manually handling arguments and options using a `case` statement
- Handling options using `getopts`

You worked through two examples that illustrate the implementation and rationale behind each method. In addition, you saw several special variables that pertain to arguments and command execution.

As you will see in later chapters, using options greatly increases the flexibility and the reusability of your shell scripts.

Questions

1. Add `tar` file extraction to the `mytar` script.

   Assume that the `-x` option indicates that the user wants to extract `tar` files and that the correct value of `TARGS` for extracting `tar` files is `-xvf`.

2. Add the extract option to the `uu` script. Assume that the `-x` option indicates that the file should be extracted, and that the command

```
uudecode $INFILE
```

is used to extract a uuencoded file.

Terms

Usage statement A short message that a script outputs in order to inform a user of the proper invocation syntax for the script.

HOUR 14

Functions

Shell functions provide a way of mapping a name to a list of commands. Functions are similar to subroutines and procedures in other programming languages. You can also think of them as miniature shell scripts, complete with exit codes and arguments. The main difference between a script and a function is that a new instance of the shell is started for a shell script, whereas functions run in the current instance of the shell.

This chapter is divided into the following two sections:

- Using functions
- Understanding scope, recursion, return codes, and data sharing

The first section introduces the syntax for defining functions and illustrates their use, whereas the second section covers more advanced topics relating to the interaction of scripts and functions.

Using Functions

Functions are defined as follows:

```
name () { list ; }
```

Here, *name* is the name of the function and *list* is a list of commands. The list of commands, *list*, is referred to as the body of the function. The parentheses, (and), that follow *name* are required.

The job of a function is to bind *name* to *list*, so that whenever *name* is specified *list* is executed. When a function is defined, *list* is not executed; the shell parses *list* to ensure that there are no syntax errors and stores *name* in its list of commands. The following example illustrates a basic function definition:

```
lsl() { ls -l ; }
```

Here you define the function `lsl` and specify *list* as `ls -l`.

An alternative form of function definition is available in `ksh`, `bash`, and `zsh`:

```
function name { list ; }
```

Here, *name* is the name of the function and *list* is the list of commands to be executed. This form of function definition is not available in the Bourne shell. Scripts that need to be ported to older systems should not use this form for function definition.

Executing Functions

You can execute or call a function that has been defined by specifying its *name*. For example, you can execute the function `lsl`, defined in the previous example, as follows:

```
$ lsl
```

This causes the shell to execute the body of the function, in this case the command `ls -l`, and output the result. The output will be similar to the following:

```
total 6
drwxrwxrwt   3 root  wheel  512 Oct 29 08:59 ./
drwxr-xr-x  25 root  wheel  512 Oct 29 00:02 ../
drwxrwxrwt   2 root  wheel  512 Nov  3 17:49 vi.recover/
```

Functions are normally defined on the command line or within a script. Once defined, the function acts as a valid command in all the sub-shells started by that shell or script. For example, if you enter the command:

```
$ lsl() { ls -l ; }
```

The function `lsl` becomes a valid command name that can be accessed by specifying `lsl`. It is accessible in sub-shells as well:

```
$ ( lsl )
total 6
drwxrwxrwt   3 root  wheel  512 Oct 29 08:59 ./
```

```
drwxr-xr-x  25 root  wheel  512 Oct 29 00:02 ../
drwxrwxrwt   2 root  wheel  512 Nov  3 17:49 vi.recover/
```

A function defined in a script is accessible within that script and any sub-shells started by that script. For example, consider the following script:

```
#!/bin/sh
lsl() { ls -l ; }
cd "$1" && lsl
```

The function `lsl` is only available in that script.

Arguments

Just as you can execute commands with arguments, you can also execute functions with arguments. The general syntax for invoking a function is as follows:

```
name arg1 … argN
```

Here, *name* is the name of the function and *arg1 … argN* are the arguments to the function. The arguments specified to a function are accessed in the same way as arguments specified to a shell script; the individual arguments are available as `$1`, `$2`, and so on, whereas the set of all the arguments is available as `$@`.

The following function illustrates the use of individual arguments:

```
printMsg () { echo "$1: $2" ; }
```

This function uses `echo` to print a message with a colon, :, which separates the first two arguments when it's executed as follows:

```
printMsg Error Failed
```

the output is

```
Error: Failed
```

As defined, this function can handle only two arguments; it ignores all the others. In order to make the function a bit more useful, it needs to be able to handle an arbitrary number of arguments. Because all of the arguments specified to a function are available in the variable `$@`, you can use it as follows:

```
printMsg() {
   PREFIX="$1"
   shift
   echo "$PREFIX: $@"
}
```

14

Here, you have redefined the function `printMsg`. It saves its first argument in `$PREFIX` and then uses `echo` to print the message in the desired format. You use `shift` to remove the first argument from `$@` before calling `echo`. Now you can execute the function with any number of arguments and the message will be printed properly. For example, if `printMsg` is executed as follows:

```
printMsg Info All Quiet on the Western Front
```

the output is

```
Info: All Quiet on the Western Front
```

Function Chaining

Function chaining is the process of calling a function from another function. The following script illustrates function chaining:

```
#!/bin/sh

orange () {
   echo "Now in orange"
   banana                        # call func2()
}

banana () {
   echo "Now in banana"
}

orange
```

This script defines two functions, `orange` and `banana`, and then executes `orange`. The first function, `orange`, outputs a message and then calls the function `banana`. The second function, `banana`, just outputs a message. The output from this script is

```
Now in orange
Now in banana
```

Common Errors

Two common errors with declaring and using functions are

- Omitting the parentheses, `()`, in a function definition.
- Specifying the parentheses, `()`, in a function invocation.

The following example illustrates the first type of error:

```
lsl { ls -l ; }
```

Here, the parentheses are missing after `lsl`. This is an invalid function definition and will result in an error message similar to the following:

```
sh: syntax error: '}' unexpected
```

The following command illustrates the second type of error:

```
$ lsl()
```

Here, the function `lsl` is executed along with the parentheses, `()`. This will not work because the shell interprets it as a redefinition of the function with the name `lsl`. Usually such an invocation results in a prompt similar to the following:

```
>
```

This is a prompt produced by the shell when it expects you to provide more input. The input it expects is the body of the function `lsl`.

Aliases Versus Functions

An *alias* is an abbreviation or an alternative name, usually mnemonic, for a command. Aliases were first introduced in `csh` and were later adopted by `ksh`, `bash`, and `zsh`. They are not supported in the Bourne shell.

Aliases are defined using the `alias` command:

```
alias name="cmd"
```

Here *`name`* is the name of the alias and *`cmd`* is the command to execute when *`name`* is specified. Aliases are similar to functions in that they associate a command with a name. Two key differences are

- In an alias, *`cmd`* cannot be a compound command or a list.
- In an alias, there is no way to manipulate the argument list (`$@`).

Due to their limited capabilities, aliases are not commonly used in shell programs. They are discussed here for the sake of completeness.

As an example, the following command defines the alias `lsl` and specifies that the command `ls -l` should be executed when the command `lsl` is specified:

```
alias lsl="ls -l"
```

This alias is equivalent to the function:

```
lsl () { ls -l "$@" ; }
```

A common use for aliases is to specify a default set of options to a command. For example, say you have the following alias:

```
alias ls="ls -a"
```

When the `ls` command is given, the shell executes `ls -a` instead of plain `ls` without options. It is possible to mimic this behavior with a function such as:

```
name () { path "$@" ; }
```

Here, *name* is the name of the command to be "aliased" and *path* is the fully qualified path to the command. For example, the following function is equivalent to the alias given in the previous example:

```
ls () { /bin/ls -a "$@" ; }
```

Unalias

Once an alias has been defined, it can be unset using the `unalias` command:

```
unalias name
```

Here, *name* is the name of the alias to be unset. For example, the following command unsets the alias `lsl`:

```
unalias lsl
```

Unsetting Functions

Once a function has been defined, it can be undefined via the `unset` command:

```
unset name
```

Here, *name* is the name of the function you want to unset. For example, the following command unsets the previously defined function `lsl()`:

```
unset lsl
```

After a function has been unset it cannot be executed.

Understanding Scope, Recursion, Return Codes, and Data Sharing

Now that you have a basic understanding of the use and operation of functions in shell scripts, let's look at more advanced topics such as scope, recursion, return codes, and data sharing.

Scope

The term *scope* refers to the region within a program where a variable's value can be accessed. There are two types of scope:

- *Global scope* If a variable has global scope, its value can be accessed from anywhere within a script. Variables with global scope are referred to as *global variables*.
- *Local scope* If a variable has local scope, its value can only be accessed within the function in which it is declared. Variables with local scope are referred to as *local variables*.

By default all variables, except for the special variables associated with function arguments, have global scope. In ksh, bash, and zsh, variables with local scope can be declared using the typeset command. The typeset command is discussed later in this chapter. This command is not supported in the Bourne shell, so it is not possible to have programmer-defined local variables in scripts that rely strictly on the Bourne shell.

Global Variables

The following script illustrates the behavior of global variables:

```
#!/bin/sh

pearFunc () {
   pear=2;                                  # set $pear
   echo "In pearFunc(): pear is $pear"      # print out its value
}

pearFunc                                    # call pearFunc
echo "Outside of pearFunc(): pear is $pear" # print out $pear
```

First the script defines a function, pearFunc, that sets the value of the global variable $pear (all variables are global by default) and outputs that value. Then the script executes pearFunc. Finally, the script prints the value of $pear outside of the function. The output is

```
In pearFunc(): pear is 2
Outside of pearFunc(): pear is 2
```

As you can see from the output, the value assigned to the variable $pear in the function pearFunc is accessible outside of pearFunc.

A common use for global variables is to communicate information from a function to the main script, as illustrated in the following script:

```
#!/bin/sh

readPass () {
    PASS=""                         # clear password
    echo -n "Enter Password: "      # print the prompt
    stty -echo                      # turn off terminal echo to prevent peeping!
    read PASS                       # read the password
    stty echo                       # restore terminal echo
    echo                            # printout a new line to make output nice
}

readPass
echo Password is $PASS
```

This script uses the `readPass` function to read in a password from the user. The `readPass` function reads the password and stores it in the global variable `PASS`. The script then accesses the password using the variable `PASS`.

The `readPass` function is quite simple. It function starts by undefining `PASS`. Then it issues a prompt for the password and deactivates terminal echo using the `stty -echo` command. Terminal echo is deactivated because you don't want someone other than the user to inadvertently see the password. Next, you read the password and store its value in `PASS` by using the `read` command. Finally, you restore terminal echo using the `stty echo` command and echo a new line.

Local Variables

Local variables are defined using `typeset` command:

```
typeset var1[=val1] ... varN[=valN]
```

Here, *`var1`* ... *`varN`* are variable names and *`val1`* ... *`valN`* are values to assign to the variables. The values are optional as the following example illustrates:

```
typeset fruit1 fruit2=banana
```

This command declares two local variables, `fruit1` and `fruit2`, and assigns the value `banana` to the variable `fruit2`.

The following script illustrates the behavior of local variables:

```
#!/bin/sh

pearFunc () {
   typeset pear=2;                            # set $pear
   echo "In pearFunc(): pear is $pear"        # print out its value
}

pearFunc                                      # call pearFunc
echo "Outside of pearFunc(): pear is $pear" # print out $pear
```

First, the script defines a function, `pearFunc`, which sets the value of a local variable `$pear` and outputs that value. Then the script executes `pearFunc`. Finally, the script prints the value of `$pear` outside of the function. The output is

```
In pearFunc(): pear is 2
Outside of pearFunc(): pear is
```

From the output, you can see that when the value of `$pear` is accessed within the `pearFunc` it has the value `2`, but when the value of `$pear` is accessed outside the function, it has no value.

Recursion

In the previous section, you learned about the concept of function chaining, where one function calls another function. *Recursion* is a special instance of function chaining in which a function calls itself. The following example illustrates the use of recursion:

```
reverse() {
   if [ $# -gt 0  ] ; then
      typeset arg="$1"
      shift
      reverse "$@"
      echo "$arg "
   fi
}

reverse "$@"
```

This script prints its arguments in reverse order. It does so by calling the function `reverse` with `$@` as the arguments. The reverse function is really simple; it determines whether there are any arguments. If there are no arguments, the function does nothing. Otherwise, it saves the first argument, removes it from the argument list using `shift` and calls itself. Once this call returns, the function just prints the argument it saved.

If you name the script `reverse.sh` and execute it with the arguments `a b c`, as follows:

```
#!/bin/sh

readPass () {
    PASS=""                           # clear password
    echo -n "Enter Password: "        # print the prompt
    stty -echo                        # turn off terminal echo to prevent peeping!
    read PASS                         # read the password
    stty echo                         # restore terminal echo
    echo                              # printout a new line to make output nice
}

readPass
echo Password is $PASS
```

The output is

```
c
b
a
```

In the previous example, you executed the script using `/bin/sh`. This will not work on Solaris and SunOS systems. On those systems, you need to execute the script using `/bin/ksh` rather than `/bin/sh` as `/bin/sh` on Solaris does not support the `typeset` command.

The execution of this script proceeds as follows:

1. The script executes `reverse "$@"` (effectively it calls `reverse a b c`).
2. The function `reverse` determines whether `$#` (the number of arguments) is greater than 0. In this case, `$#` will be equal to `3` (`a b c`).
3. Because `$#` is greater than `0`, `reverse` saves the first argument, `$1` (in this case `a`) in the local variable `$arg`, and then calls `shift` to remove it from `$@`. Now, `$@` holds two arguments, `b c`.
4. The function `reverse` calls itself with the shortened `$@`.
5. The function `reverse` determines whether `$#` (the number of arguments) is greater than `0`. In this case, `$#` will be equal to `2` (`b c`).
6. Because `$#` is greater than `0`, `reverse` saves the first argument, `$1` (in this case `b`) in the local variable `$arg`, and then calls `shift` to remove it from `$@`. Now, `$@` holds just one argument, `c`.
7. The function `reverse` calls itself with the shortened `$@`.
8. The function `reverse` determines whether `$#` (the number of arguments) is greater than `0`. In this case, `$#` will be equal to `1`.
9. Because `$#` is greater than 0, `reverse` saves the first argument, `$1` (in this case `c`) in the local variable `$arg`, and then calls `shift` to remove it from `$@`. Now, `$@` holds no arguments.
10. The function `reverse` calls itself with the shortened `$@`.
11. The function `reverse` determines whether `$#` (the number of arguments) is greater than `0`. Because there are no arguments in `$@`, this check fails and the function returns.
12. After the call to `reverse` returns, you output the value of the local variable `$arg`, in this case `c`, and return.
13. After the call to `reverse` returns, you output the value of the local variable `$arg`, in this case `b`, and return.
14. After the call to `reverse` returns, you output the value of the local variable `$arg`, in this case `a`, and return.

Divide and Conquer

Recursion is normally used to solve problems using a technique known as *divide and conquer*. Basically, divide and conquer means that a problem is divided into smaller and smaller instances until an instance that is small enough to solve directly is found. Each instance that is too big to solve directly is solved recursively, and the solutions are combined to produce a solution to the original problem.

> You used divide and conquer in the previous example; the function `reverse` kept calling itself with smaller and smaller parts of the argument list `$@` until all the arguments were exhausted, and then it just printed each argument.

Return Codes

When a shell script completes, it can use the `exit` command to return exit status via an exit code. The function analogue to `exit` is the `return` command. This command allows function to return exit status. The exit status from a function is called its *return code*. The convention for return codes is the same as for exit codes; a `0` equals success and a nonzero equals failure.

The syntax of the `return` command is

```
return rc
```

Here *`rc`* is the return code. The following function illustrates the use of `return`:

```
isInteractive () {
   case $- in             # $- holds the invocation options
      *i*) return 0;;     # if $- contains i, the shell is interactive
   esac
   return 1
}
```

You can use this function to detect whether a particular shell is interactive as follows:

```
if isInteractive ; then
   echo "Interactive shell"
else
   echo "Non-interactive shell"
fi
```

Data Sharing

The functions you have seen thus far are mostly independent, but in most shell scripts functions either depend on or share data with other functions. In this section, you will look at an example in which three functions work together and share data.

Moving Around the File System

The C shell, `csh`, introduced three commands for quickly moving around in the UNIX directory tree:

14

- `popd`
- `pushd`
- `dirs`

These commands maintain a stack of directories internally and enable the user to add and remove directories from the stack and list the contents of the stack.

> **Understanding Stacks**
>
> For those readers who are not familiar with the programming concept of a *stack*, you can think of it as a stack of plates: you can add or remove a plate only at the top of the stack. You can access only the top plate, not any of the middle plates in the stack. A stack in programming terms is similar. You can add or remove an item only at the top of the stack.

These commands are not available in Bourne shell or `ksh`. Newer versions of `bash` and `zsh` have introduced these commands. In this section, you will implement each of these commands as shell functions so that they can be used with any Bourne-like shell.

In `csh`, the directory stack used by these commands is maintained within the shell; in this implementation you will maintain the stack as an global exported environment variable, called `_DIR_STACK`. The entries in `_DIR_STACK` are separated by colons, `:`, just like entries in `PATH` or `MANPATH`. This allows you to handle almost any directory name.

Implementing `dirs`

First let's look at the simplest of the three functions, `dirs`. This function just lists the entries in the directory stack:

```
dirs() {

   OLDIFS="$IFS"             # save IFS (internal field separator)
   IFS=:                     # set  IFS to :, so that we can process
                             # each entry in _DIR_STACK easily

   for i in $_DIR_STACK      # print out each entry in _DIR_STACK
   do
      echo "$i \c"
   done

   echo                      # print out new line (makes output pretty)

    IFS="$OLDIFS"            # restore IFS
}
```

First, you save the current value of `IFS` in `OLDIFS` and then you set `IFS` to `:`. Because `IFS` is the Internal Field Separator for the shell, modifying it allows you to use the `for` loop to cycle through the individual entries in `_DIR_STACK`. When you are finished with all the entries, you restore the value of `IFS`.

> The shell uses the value of the variable `IFS` to split up a string into separate words. The default setting for `IFS` is the space and tab characters. This enables the shell to determine the number of words that are in most strings. Normally, the shell uses the default value of `IFS` to determine how many options are supplied to a command, script, or shell function along with how many items are specified to a `for` loop.
>
> In the previous example, you manipulated the value of IFS in order to simplify the processing of the entries in _DIR_STACK.

Implementing `pushd`

The `pushd` function is a bit more complicated than the `dirs` function. In addition to listing the directories in the stack, it must also change to a requested directory and then add that directory to the top of the stack. The requested directory is the first argument to the function. If an argument is not specified, the current directory (`.`) is used.

This example implements `pushd` as follows:

```
pushd() {

   # set REQ to the first argument (if given, otherwise use .)

   REQ="${1:-.}"

   # if $REQ is not a directory, print an error and return

   if [ ! -d "$REQ" ] ; then
      echo "ERROR: $REQ is not a directory." 1>&2
      return 1
   fi

   # if we can cd to $REQ, update _DIR_STACK and print it out
   # otherwise print an error and return

   if cd "$REQ" > /dev/null 2>&1 ; then
      _DIR_STACK="`pwd`:$_DIR_STACK" ; export _DIR_STACK ;
      dirs
   else
      echo "ERROR: Cannot change to directory $REQ." >&2
      return 1
   fi

   unset REQ
}
```


This function starts by determining the directory to push onto the stack. It uses the default value substitution form of variable substitution, covered in Chapter 9, “Substitution,” to obtain this value. Then, the function determines whether the requested directory is really a directory. If it is not a directory, you print an error and return 1 to indicate failure. Otherwise, you change to that directory and then update the directory stack with the full path of the new directory. You have to use the full path rather than value in `$REQ`, because the value stored in `$REQ` might be a relative path. After the directory stack has been updated, you call `dirs` to output the directories stored on the stack.

Implementing popd

The `popd()` function is much more complicated than the other two functions. Let's look at the operations it performs:

1. Removes the first entry from the directory stack
2. Updates the directory stack to reflect the removal
3. Changes to the directory indicated by the entry that was removed from the stack
4. Displays the full path of the current directory

To simplify the first and second operations, you can implement a helper function for `popd()` called `_popd_helper()`. This function performs all the work; `popd()` is simply a wrapper around it. Often you need to write functions in this manner: one function that provides a simple interface and another that performs the actual work.

Implementing _popd_helper

Let's first look at the function `_popd_helper` to see how the directory stack is manipulated:

```
_popd_helper() {

    # set the directory to pop to the first argument, if
    # this directory is empty, issue an error and return 1
    # otherwise get rid of POPD from the arguments

    POPD="$1"
    if [ -z "$POPD" ] ; then
        echo "ERROR: The directory stack is empty." >&2
        return 1
    fi
    shift

    # if any more arguments remain, reinitalize the directory
    # stack, and then update it with the remaining items,
    # otherwise set the directory stack to null

    if [ -n "$1" ] ; then
        _DIR_STACK="$1" ;
        shift ;
```

```
        for i in $@ ; do _DIR_STACK="$_DIR_STACK:$i" ; done
    else
        _DIR_STACK=
    fi

    # if POPD is a directory cd to it, otherwise issue
    # an error message

    if [ -d "$POPD" ] ; then
        cd "$POPD" > /dev/null 2>&1
        if [ $? -ne 0 ] ; then
            echo "ERROR: Could not cd to $POPD." >&2
        fi
        pwd
    else
        echo "ERROR: $POPD is not a directory." >&2
    fi

    export _DIR_STACK
    unset POPD
}
```

This function expects each of the directories in the directory stack to be given to it as arguments, so the first thing that it checks is whether `$1`, the first argument, has any value. You do this by setting `$POPD` equal to `$1` and then checking if `$POPD` has a value. If the directory stack is empty, you issue an error message and return; otherwise, you shorten the stack using `shift`. At this point, you have taken care of the first operation.

Next, you determine whether the directory stack became empty after you removed an entry from it. Because the individual items in the stack are the arguments to this function, you need to check whether `$1`, the new first argument, has a value. If it does, you reinitialize the directory stack with this value and proceed to add all the remaining values back onto the stack; otherwise, you set the value of the directory stack to null. At this point, you have taken care of the second operation.

The final `if` statement takes care of the third and fourth operations. Here, you determine whether the path stored in `$POPD` is a directory. This check is required because the path might have been removed from the system after it was added to the directory stack. If the path is a directory, you try to `cd` to that directory. If the change is successful, you print the full path to the directory, otherwise you print an error message.

The Wrapper Function

Now that you know how the helper function works, you can write an appropriate wrapper function to translate the value of `_DIR_STACK` into separate arguments. This is fairly easy, thanks to `IFS`.

The `popd()` function is

```
popd() {
    OLDIFS="$IFS"
    IFS=:
    _popd_helper $_DIR_STACK
    IFS="$OLDIFS"
}
```

In this function, you first save the old value of `IFS`. Then you set `IFS` to `:` and call `_popd_helper` with the directory stack specified as arguments. After `_popd_helper` returns, you restore the value of `IFS`.

Summary

In this chapter, you learned how to use functions in shell scripts. Some of the important topics you learned about are

- Creating functions
- Invoking functions
- Using variable scope
- Function chaining and recursion
- Return codes from functions
- Data sharing between functions

In Chapter 21, "Problem Solving with Functions," you will revisit functions and learn how to create a set of functions that can be used in multiple scripts. In the next chapter, you will explore the topic of text filtering.

Questions

1. Write a function that determines whether a command is located in one of the directories in `$PATH`. The command will be supplied as the first argument. If the command is located in one of the directories in `$PATH`, your function should print the full path to the command and return 0. Otherwise your function should return `1` and optionally print an error message.
2. Write a function to make a directory (and all of its parents) change to that directory and then print the full path of that directory. Please include error checking at all levels. Make sure that your function generates all of the error messages, rather than the commands that it executes.

3. Rewrite the function you wrote in Question 2 without using `mkdir -p`.
4. Enhance the `readPass` function given in this chapter so that it reads the password twice and confirms that both the passwords are the same.
5. Chapter 5, "Input and Output," introduced the concept of prompting the user from a shell script. Write a function that can be used to prompt the user for a response. This function should take a single argument that is the prompt, and it should place the user's response in the variable `RESPONSE`. Be sure to include error checking at all levels.

Terms

Alias An abbreviation or an alternative name, usually mnemonic, for a command.

Function chaining The process of calling a function from another function.

Functions Provide a way of mapping a name to a list of commands. Functions are similar to subroutines and procedures in other programming languages.

Global scope If a variable has global scope, its value can be accessed from anywhere within a script.

Global variables Variables with global scope are referred to as global variables.

Local scope If a variable has local scope, its value can only be accessed within the function in which it is declared.

Local variables Variables with local scope are referred to as local variables.

Recursion A special instance of function chaining in which a function calls itself.

Return code The exit status from a function is called its return code. The convention for return codes is the same as for exit codes; `0` equals success and nonzero equals failure.

Scope Refers to the region within a program where a variable's value can be accessed.

HOUR 15

Text Filters

Shell scripts are often called on to manipulate and reformat the output from commands. Sometimes this task is as simple as displaying only part of the output by filtering out certain lines, but in most instances, the processing required is much more sophisticated.

In this chapter, you will look at several commands that can be used for filtering text. These commands are

- `head`
- `tail`
- `grep`
- `sort`
- `uniq`
- `tr`

The `head` and `tail` Commands

In Chapter 3, "Working with Files," you looked at viewing the contents of a file using the `cat` command. This command enables you to view an entire file, but often you need more control over lines that are displayed. The `head` and `tail` commands provide some of this control.

The `head` Command

The `head` command is used to display the first few lines of a file. Its basic syntax is

```
head [-n lines] files
```

Here *`files`* is the list of the files you want the `head` command to process. Without the `-n` *`lines`* option, the `head` command shows the first 10 lines of its standard input. When this option is specified, `head` shows the number of lines specified by *`lines`* instead.

On some versions of Linux the output from the `-n` *`lines`* option might include one line less than the number of lines you specified. For example, the command:

```
$ head -n 5 file
```

may produce only four lines of output rather than the expected five.

Although this command is useful for viewing the tops of large `README` files, its real power happens in daily applications. Consider the following problem: you need to generate a list of the five most recently accessed files in a directory. You can devise a solution to this problem by breaking the problem down. First, you can generate a list of the files in the directory using the `ls -1` command. For example, if you are interested in the files in the directory `/home/ranga/public_html`, you can use the following command:

```
$ ls -1 /home/ranga/public_html
```

In this case, the following list of files and directories is generated:

```
RCS
cgi-bin
downloads
humor
images
index.html
misc
projects
school
```

Next, you need to sort the list by the date of the last access. This can be accomplished by specifying the `-ut` (sort by last accessed time) option of the `ls` command:

```
$ ls -1ut /home/ranga/public_html
```

The output now changes as follows:

```
RCS
humor
misc
downloads
images
resume
projects
school
cgi-bin
index.html
```

To retrieve a list of the five most recently accessed files, you can pipe the output of this `ls` command into a `head` command as follows:

```
$ ls -1ut /home/ranga/public_html | head -5
```

This produces the following list:

```
index.html
RCS
humor
misc
downloads
```

The `tail` Command

The `tail` command is used to display the last few lines of a file. Its basic syntax is similar to that of the `head` command:

```
tail [-n lines] files
```

Here *`files`* is the list of the files the `tail` command should process. Without the `-n` *`lines`* option, the `tail` command shows the last 10 lines of its standard input. When this option is specified, `tail` shows the number of lines specified by *`lines`* instead.

To illustrate the use of the `tail` command, consider the problem of generating a list of the five oldest mail spools located in `/var/spool/mail`. You can start with `ls -1` command again, but this time you'll use just the `-t` (sort by last modified time) option:

```
$ ls -1t /var/spool/mail
```

To get the bottom five, you can use `tail` as follows:

```
$ ls -1t /var/spool/mail | tail -5
```

The output will be similar to the following:

```
anna
root
amma
vathsa
ranga
```

In this list, the files are listed from newest to oldest. To reverse the order, you can specify the `-r` option of the `ls` command as follows:

```
ls -1rt /var/spool/mail | tail -5
```

This changes the output as follows:

```
ranga
vathsa
amma
root
anna
```

The `follow` Option

An extremely useful feature of the `tail` command is the `-f` (short for follow) option:

```
tail -f file
```

Specifying the `-f` option enables you to examine the specified *`file`* while programs are writing to it.

If you have to look at the log files generated by a program that you are debugging, but don't want to wait for the program to finish, you can start the program and then use `tail -f` to view its log file. Some Web administrators use a command similar to the following to watch the HTTP requests made for their system:

```
$ tail -f /var/log/httpd/access_log
```

> If you use `tail -f`, make sure that you do not leave it running for extended periods of time. This command can cause an undue burden on the resources of a heavily loaded machine.

Using `grep`

The `grep` command lets you locate the lines in a file that contain a particular word or a phrase. The word grep is short for globally regular expression print. The command is derived from a feature of the original UNIX text editor, `ed`. To find a word in `ed`, the following command was used:

```
g/word/p
```

Here *`word`* is a regular expression. For those readers who are not familiar with regular expressions, Chapter 16, "Filtering Text Using Regular Expressions," discusses them in detail. This particular `ed` command was used widely in shell scripts, thus it was factored into its own command called `grep`. In this section, you will look at the `grep` command along with some of its most commonly used options.

15

Looking for Words

The basic syntax of the grep command is

```
grep word file
```

Here *file* is the name of a file in which you want to search for the word specified by *word*. Every line in *file* that contains *word* is displayed. When you specify more than one file, grep precedes each of the output lines with the name of the file that contains that line.

As an example, the following command locates all the occurrences of the word pipe in file ch15.doc (this chapter):

```
$ grep pipe ch15.doc
I've broken the command into two lines, with the pipe character
➥as the
the right thing and use the next line as the command to pipe to. It's
The first few lines look like (ten actually, I piped the output to
```

If you specify more than one file, the output changes as follows:

```
$ grep pipe ch15.doc ch15-01.doc
ch15.doc:I've broken the command into two lines, with the pipe
➥character as the
ch15.doc:the right thing and use the next line as the command to
➥pipe to. It's
ch15.doc:The first few lines look like (ten actually, I piped the
➥output to
ch15-01.doc:I've broken the command into two lines, with the pipe
➥character as the
ch15-01.doc:the right thing and use the next line as the command to
➥pipe to.  It's
ch15-01.doc:The first few lines look like (ten actually, I piped
➥the output to
```

As you can see, the name of the file precedes each line that contains the word pipe.

If grep cannot find a line in any of the specified files that contain the requested word, no output is produced. For example,

```
$ grep utilities ch15.doc
```

produces no output because the word utilities does not appear in the file ch15.doc.

Case-Independent Matching

One of the features of grep is that it is case sensitive; grep matches only those words that are identical to *word* in terms of content and case. For example, grep treats the words Apple1' and apple1 as different words. For example, the command

```
$ grep unix ch15.doc
```

produces the output:

```
all unix users.  The GNU versions of these commands support all the
unix has several additional pieces of information associated with it.
unix counterparts, but implement a few nice options which makes their
unix files names, but they are, and handling them correctly is
```

On the other hand, the command

```
$ grep UNIX ch15.doc
```

produces different output:

```
GNU stands for GNU's not UNIX and is the name of a UNIX-compatible
Project utilities are the GNU implementation of familiar UNIX programs
```

Sometimes you will want to match words regardless of the case that you specify. This is accomplished using the `-i` option. You can get a sum of the output from the two previous examples using the `-i` option as follows:

```
$ grep -i unix ch15.doc
GNU stands for GNU's not UNIX and is the name of a UNIX-compatible
Project utilities are the GNU implementation of familiar UNIX
➥programs
all unix users.  The GNU versions of these commands support all the
unix has several additional pieces of information associated with it.
unix counterparts, but implement a few nice options which makes their
unix files names, but they are, and handling them correctly is
```

Reading From STDIN

When no files are specified, `grep` looks for matches on the lines that are entered on STDIN. This makes `grep` perfect for use with pipes. For example, the following command looks for all users named `ranga` in the output of the `who` command:

```
$ who | grep ranga
ranga    tty1     Aug 26 14:12
ranga    ttyp2    Nov 23 14:15 (rishi.bosland.u)
```

The -v Option

Most of the time you use `grep` to search through a file looking for a particular word, but sometimes you want to acquire a list of all the lines that do not match a particular word. Using `grep`, this is simple—specify the `-v` option. For example, the following command produces a list of all the lines in `/etc/hosts` that do not contain the # character:

```
$ grep -v '#' /etc/hosts
```

The output will be similar to the following:

```
10.32.43.51 scotch scotch.CSUA scotch.CSUA.Berkeley.EDU
10.32.43.52 internal internal.soda.CSUA.Berkeley.EDU
10.32.43.139 mkv mkv.csua.berkeley.edu
```

One common use of the -v option is to parse the output of the ps command. For example, if you were looking for all instances of bash that were running on a system, you could use the following command:

```
$ /bin/ps -ef | grep bash
```

Normally the output contains just the information for bash, but sometimes the output looks like the following:

```
ranga  3277  3276  2 13:41:45 pts/t0    0:02 -bash
ranga  3463  3277  4 18:38:26 pts/t0    0:00 grep bash
```

The second process in this list is the grep command that you just ran. Because it is not really an instance of bash, you want to remove it from the output. You can do this using the -v option as follows:

```
$ /bin/ps -ef | grep bash | grep -v grep
```

This removes the extraneous output:

```
ranga  3277  3276  0 13:41:45 pts/t0    0:02 -bash
```

Line Numbers

As grep looks through a file for a given word, it keeps track of the line numbers that it has examined. You can have grep list the line numbers along with the matching lines by specifying the -n option. When this option is specified, grep's output format is as follows:

```
file:line number:line
```

Here *file* is the name of the file in which the match occurs, *line number* is the line number in the file on which the matching line occurs, and *line* is the complete line that contains the specified word. For example, the command

```
$ grep -n pipe ch15.doc ch15-01.doc
```

produces the following output:

```
ch15.doc:969:I've broken the command into two lines, with the pipe
➥character as the
ch15.doc:971:the right thing and use the next line as the command
➥to pipe to.  It's
ch15.doc:1014:The first few lines look like (ten actually, I piped
➥the output to
ch15-01.doc:964:I've broken the command into two lines, with the
➥pipe character as the
ch15-01.doc:966:the right thing and use the next line as the command
➥to pipe to.  It's
ch15-01.doc:1009:The first few lines look like (ten actually, I
➥piped the output to
```

As you can see, the lines might be the same in both files, but the line numbers are different.

Listing Filenames Only

Sometimes you don't really care about the actual lines in a file that match a particular word. You just want a list of all the files that contain that word. For example, the following command looks for the word `delete` in all the files in the `projects` directory:

```
$ grep delete projects/*
```

In this case, it produces the following output:

```
pqops.c:/* Function to delete a node from the heap. Adapted from
➥Introduction
pqops.c:void heap_delete(binary_heap *a,int i) {
pqops.c:  node deleted;
pqops.c:  /* return with an error if the input is invalid, ie trying
➥to delete
pqops.c:   sprintf(messages,"heap_delete(): %d, no such element.",i);
pqops.c:  /* switch the item to be deleted with the last item, and
➥then
pqops.c:  deleted = a->elements[i];
pqops.c:  /* (compare_priority(a->elements[i],deleted)) ? heap_
➥up(a,i) : heap_down(a,i); */
pqops.h:extern void        heap_delete(binary_heap *a,int i);
scheduler.c:    /* if the requested id is in the heap, delete it */
scheduler.c:    heap_delete(&my_heap,node_num);
```

As you look at the output, you see that only three files—`pqops.c`, `pqops.h`, and `scheduler.c`—contain the word `delete`. Here you had to generate a list of matching lines and then manually look at the filenames in which those lines were contained. By using the `-l` option of the `grep` command, you can reach this conclusion much faster. For example, the following command

```
$ grep -l delete projects/*
pqops.c
pqops.h
scheduler.c
```

produces the list you wanted.

Counting Words

Counting words is an essential capability in shell scripts. There are many ways to do it, with the easiest being the `wc` command. Unfortunately, it displays only the number of characters, words, or lines. What about when you need to count the number of occurrences of a particular word in a file? The `wc` command falls short. In this section, you will solve this problem using the following commands:

- `tr`

- sort
- uniq

The tr command (short for transliterate) changes all the characters in one set into characters in a second set, whereas the sort command sorts the lines in an input file. The uniq command (short for unique) prints all the unique lines in a file.

The text of this chapter, ch15.doc, is used as the input file for the examples in this section.

The tr Command

The first step in solving this problem is to eliminate all the punctuation and delimiters in the input file. You need to do this because the string 'end.' and the string 'end' are both the same word, end. You can accomplish this task using the tr command. The basic syntax for this command is

```
tr 'set1' 'set2'
```

Here all the characters in *set1* are transliterated into the characters in *set2*. Usually, the characters themselves are used, but escape sequences covered in previous chapters can also be used.

To accomplish your first task, you can use the following command:

```
$ tr '!?":;\[\]{}(),.' ' ' < ch15.doc
```

Here you specified *set2* as the space character because words separated by the characters in *set1* need to remain separate after the punctuation is removed.

Notice that the characters [and] are given as \[and \]. As you will see later in this chapter, these two characters have a special meaning in tr and need to be escaped using the backslash character (\) in order to be handled correctly.

The tr command on some versions of Linux does not handle the \[escape sequence properly, used in the previous example, and might generate an error message similar to the following:

```
tr: invalid backslash escape '\['
```

You can work around this problem by using the punctuation class described later in this chapter.

At this point most of the words are separated by spaces, but some words might still be separated with tabs and newlines. To get an accurate count, all the words need to be separated by spaces, so you need to convert all tabs and newlines to spaces as follows:

```
$ tr '!?":;\[\]{}(),.\t\n' ' ' < ch15.doc
```

The next step is to transliterate all capitalized versions of words to the lowercase version because words such as `To` and `to` and `The` and `the` are really the same word. You can do this by using `tr` to change all the capital characters `'A-Z'` into lowercase characters `'a-z'` as follows:

```
$ tr '!?":;\[\]{}(),.\t\n' ' ' < ch15.doc | tr 'A-Z' 'a-z'
```

Here you pipe the output of the first `tr` command into a second `tr` command. The input to the first `tr` command is the file `ch15.doc`, whereas the input to the second `tr` command is the output of the first `tr` command.

> **Differences Between tr Versions**
>
> In this example, you are using a single space for *set2*. Most versions of `tr` interpret this to mean transliterating all the characters in *set1* to a space. Some versions of `tr` do not do this.
>
> You can determine whether your version of `tr` works correctly using the following test:
>
> ```
> $ echo 'Hello, my dear!' | tr ',!' ' '
> ```
>
> Most versions of `tr` produce the following output:
>
> ```
> Hello  my dear
> ```
>
> Some versions produce the following output instead:
>
> ```
> Hello  my dear!
> ```
>
> To obtain the desired behavior from these versions of `tr`, make sure that *set1* and *set2* have the same number of characters. In this case, *set2* needs to contain two spaces:
>
> ```
> $ echo 'Hello, my dear!' | tr ',!' '  '
> ```
>
> In the case of the example, *set2* would need to contain 15 spaces.

Squeezing Out Spaces

At this point, several of the lines have multiple spaces separating the words. You need to reduce or squeeze these multiple spaces into single spaces to avoid problems generating counts later. To do this, you need to use the -s (short for squeeze) option of the `tr` command. The basic syntax is

```
tr -s 'set1'
```

When `tr` encounters multiple consecutive occurrences of a character in *set1*, it replaces these with only one occurrence of the character. For example,

```
$ echo "feed me" | tr -s 'e'
```

produces the output

```
fed me
```

The two *e*'s in `feed` were reduced to a single *e*.

If you specify more than one character in *`set1`*, the replacement is character specific. For example:

```
$ echo "Shell Programming" | tr -s 'lm'
```

produces the following output:

```
Shel Programing
```

As you can see the two *l*'s in `Shell` were reduced to a single *l*. Also, the two *m*'s in `Programming` were reduced to a single *m*.

Using this option you can squeeze multiple spaces in the output of the second `tr` command into a single space:

```
$ tr '!?":;\[\]{}(),.\t\n' ' ' < ch15.doc | tr 'A-Z' 'a-z' |  tr -s ' '
```

The `sort` Command

To get a count of how many times each word is used, you need to sort the file using the `sort` command. In its simplest form, the `sort` command sorts each of its input lines. In this example, you need to modify the output of `tr` so that it lists one word per line. You can do this changing all the spaces into new lines as follows:

```
$ tr '!?":;\[\]{}(),.\t\n' ' ' < ch15.doc | tr 'A-Z' 'a-z' | tr -s ' '  |
tr ' ' '\n'
```

Now you can sort the output, by adding the `sort` command as follows:

```
$ tr '!?":;\[\]{}(),.\t\n' ' ' < ch15.doc | tr 'A-Z' 'a-z' | tr -s ' '  |
tr ' ' '\n' | sort
```

The `uniq` Command

At this point you have all the information required to determine the number of times a particular word occurs in the file. You just need a command that will compute this information for you. This command is `uniq`.

By default, the `uniq` command discards all but one of the repeated lines. For example, the commands

```
$ echo '
peach
peach
peach
apple
```

```
apple
orange
' > ./fruits.txt
$ uniq fruits.txt
```

produce the output

```
peach
apple
orange
```

As you can see, uniq discarded all but one of the repeated lines.

The uniq command produces a list of the uniq items in a file by comparing consecutive lines. To function properly, its input needs to be sorted. For example, if you change fruits.txt as follows

```
$ echo '
peach
peach
orange
apple
apple
peach
' > ./fruits.txt
$ uniq fruits.txt
```

the output from uniq will be incorrect for your purposes:

```
peach
orange
apple
peach
```

Returning to the original problem, you need uniq to print not only a list of the unique words, but also the number of times a word occurs. You can do this by specifying the -c (short for count) option of the uniq command:

```
$ tr '!?":;\[\]{}(),.\t\n' ' ' < ch15.doc | tr 'A-Z' 'a-z' | tr -s ' ' |
tr ' ' '\n' | sort | uniq -c
```

Sorting Numbers

At this point the output is sorted alphabetically. Although this is useful, it is much easier to determine the most frequently used words if the list is sorted by the number of times a word occurs. To obtain such a list, you need sort to sort by numeric value instead of string comparison. It would also be nice if the largest values were printed first. By default, sort prints the largest values last. To satisfy both of these requirements, you need to use the -n (short for numeric) and -r (short for reverse) options of the sort command:

```
$ tr '!?":;\[\]{}(),.\t\n' ' ' < ch15.doc | tr 'A-Z' 'a-z' | tr -s ' ' |
tr ' ' '\n' | sort | uniq -c | sort -rn
```

By piping the output to head, you can get an idea of the ten most repeated words:

```
$ tr '!?":;\[\]{}(),.\t\n' ' ' < ch15.doc | tr 'A-Z' 'a-z' | tr -s ' ' |
tr ' ' '\n' | sort | uniq -c | sort -rn | head
389 the
164 to
127 of
115 is
115 and
111 a
 80 files
 70 file
 69 in
 65 '
```

Sorting Numbers in a Different Column

In the preceding output, you used the sort -rn command to sort the output by numbers because the numbers occurred in the first column instead of the second. If the numbers occurred in any other column, this would not be possible. Suppose the output looked like the following:

```
$ cat switched.txt
files 80
file 70
is 115
and 115
a 111
in 69
' 65
the 389
to 164
of 127
```

Now you need to tell sort to sort on the second column; you cannot simply use the -r and -n options. You need to use the -k (short for key) option.

The sort command constructs a "key" for each line in the file, and then it arranges these keys into sorted order. By default, the key spans the entire line. The -k option gives you the flexibility of telling sort where the key should begin and where it should end, in terms of columns. The number of columns in a line is the number of individual *words* (alphanumeric strings separated by a tab or space) on that line. For example, the following line contains three columns:

```
files 80 100
```

The basic syntax of the -k option is

```
sort -k start,end files
```

Here *start* is the starting column for the key, and *end* is the ending column for the key. The first column is 1, the second column is 2, and so on. For switched.txt, *start* and *end* are both 2 because there are only two columns and you want to sort on the second one. The command you could use is

```
$ sort -rn -k 2,2 switched.txt
 403 the
 121 command
 120 to
 120 of
  88 '
  84 tr
  84 in
  79 a
  78 grep
  73 is
```

Using Character Classes with tr

If you look at the output of the previous command you might have noticed that the fifth most common word in this chapter is the single quote character. You are correct in wondering what's going on because we said the very first tr command took care of dealing with punctuation. Well, the problem is that you took care of all the characters that would fit between single quotes, and a single quote won't fit. You can't backslash escape the single quote because some versions of the shell can't handle an escaped single quote.

So what is the solution?

The solution is to use the predefined character sets in tr. The tr command knows several character classes, and the punctuation class is one of them. Table 15.1 gives a complete list of the character class names.

Table 15.1 Character Classes Understood by the tr Command

Class	*Description*
alnum	Letters and digits
alpha	Letters
blank	Horizontal whitespace
cntrl	Control characters
digit	Digits
graph	Printable characters, not including spaces
lower	Lowercase letters
print	Printable characters, including spaces

TABLE 15.1 Continued

Class	*Description*
`punct`	Punctuation
`space`	Horizontal or vertical whitespace
`upper`	Uppercase letters
`xdigit`	Hexadecimal digits

The syntax to invoke `tr` with one of these character classes is as follows:

```
tr '[:classname:]' 'set2'
```

Here *`classname`* is the name of one of the classes given in Table 15.1, and *`set2`* is the set of characters you want the characters in *`classname`* to be transliterated to. For example, you can get rid of punctuation and spaces in the problem by using the `punct` and `space` classes as follows:

```
$ tr '[:punct:]' ' ' < ch15.doc | tr '[:space:]' ' ' | tr 'A-Z' 'a-z' |
tr -s ' '  | tr ' ' '\n' | sort | uniq -c | sort -rn | head
```

The output now becomes:

```
 411 the
 182 command
 159 i
 123 to
 122 of
 105 a
  93 tr
  90 grep
  89 in
  73 is
```

You could also have replaced `'A-Z'` and `'a-z'` with the `upper` and `lower` classes, but there is no real advantage to using the classes in this case.

Summary

In this chapter you looked at some of the commands that are heavily used for filtering text in scripts. These commands include:

- `head`
- `tail`
- `grep`

- `sort`
- `uniq`
- `tr`

You also learned how to combine these commands to solve problems such as counting the number of times a word is repeated in a text file. In Chapter 16, you will learn about two more text filtering commands, `awk` and `sed`, that provide much more control over editing lines and printing specific lines and columns of output.

Questions

1. Given the following shell function

   ```
   lspids() { /bin/ps -ef | grep "$1"| grep -v grep ; }
   ```

   make the necessary changes so that when the function is executed as follows

   ```
   $ lspid -h ssh
   ```

   the output looks like this:

   ```
   UID    PID  PPID  C    STIME TTY          TIME COMMAND
   root  2121     1  0  Nov 16  ?             0:14 /opt/bin/sshd
   ```

   Also, when the function executes as

   ```
   $ lspid ssh
   ```

   the output looks like this:

   ```
   root  2121     1  0  Nov 16  ?             0:14 /opt/bin/sshd
   ```

   Here you are using `ssh` as the *`word`* specified to `grep`, but your function should be able to use any *`word`* as an argument.

   Also, validate that you have enough arguments before executing the `ps` command.

   If you are using a Linux or BSD-based system, please use the following version of the function `lspids` as a starting point instead of the version given previously:

   ```
   lspids() { /bin/ps -auwx 2> /dev/null | grep "$1"| grep -v
   ➥grep ; }
   ```

   (HINT: The header that is the first line in the output from the `/bin/ps` command.)

2. Take the function you wrote in question 1 and add an `-s` option that sorts the output of the `ps` command by process ID. The process IDs, or pids, do not have to be arranged from largest to smallest.

   If you are using a Linux or BSD system, you need to sort on column 1. On other systems you need to sort on column 2.

Terms

grep A command that lets you locate the lines in a file that contain a particular word or a phrase. The term *grep* is short for globally regular expression print.

head A command used to display the first few lines of a file.

tail A command used to display the last few lines of a file.

Hour 16

Filtering Text with Regular Expressions

The most powerful text filtering tools in UNIX are a pair of oddly named programs, awk and sed. These programs allow shell programmers to easily edit text files and filter the output of commands using regular expressions. A *regular expression* is compact notation for describing sets of strings.

The stream editor, sed, was created as an editor for use with shell programs. As its name implies, sed is stream oriented; input is read, modified internally, and the modified version is printed out. The input file is not changed. This chapter covers the use of sed in shell scripts. Specifically we will examine the following topics:

- Regular expressions
- Using sed

Chapter 17, "Filtering Text with awk," covers the details of awk programming; however, some of similarities between awk and sed are discussed at the beginning of this chapter.

The Basics of awk and sed

Many similarities exist between awk and sed:

- Both have similar invocation syntax.
- Both execute a set of programmer specified instructions on every line in their input files.
- Both use regular expressions to find string and matching lines.

For those of you who are not familiar with regular expressions, they will be explained shortly.

Invocation Syntax

The invocation syntax for awk and sed is as follows:

```
cmd 'script' files
```

Here *cmd* is either awk or sed, *script* is a list of commands understood by awk or sed, and *files* is a list of files that *cmd* acts on.

The single quotes around *script* are required to prevent the shell from accidentally performing substitutions. The actual contents of *script* differ greatly between awk and sed. The command set for sed is covered later in this chapter, whereas awk's command set is covered in the next chapter.

If filenames are not given, both awk and sed read input from STDIN. This enables them to be used as output filters on other commands.

Basic Operation

When an awk or sed command runs, it performs the following operations:

1. Reads a line from an input file
2. Makes a copy of the line
3. Executes *script* on the line
4. Goes to the next line and repeats step 1

These operations illustrate the main feature of awk and sed—they provide a method of acting on every *record* or line in a file using a single script. When every record has been read, the input file is closed. If the input file is the last file specified in *filenames*, the command exits.

16

Script Structure and Execution

The `script` usually consists of one or more lines of the following form:

```
/pattern/ action
```

Here *`pattern`* is a regular expression, and *`action`* is the action that either `awk` or `sed` should take when *`pattern`* is encountered. The slash characters (`/`) that surround *`pattern`* act as delimiters and indicate where *`pattern`* starts and ends. Multiple *`pattern`* and *`action`* pairs can be specified.

When *`script`* is executing, it uses the following procedure on each record:

1. Each *`pattern`* is sequentially searched until a match is found.
2. When a match is found, the corresponding *`action`* is performed on the record.
3. When the *`action`* is complete, the next *`pattern`* is selected and step 1 is repeated.
4. When all the *`pattern`*s have been exhausted, the next line is read and step 1 is repeated.

Just before step 4 is performed, `sed` automatically outputs the modified record. In order to obtain this behavior with `awk`, the modified record must be manually output.

The actions taken in `awk` and `sed` are quite different. In `sed`, the actions consist of commands that edit single letters, whereas in `awk` the action is usually a set of programming statements.

Regular Expressions

A *regular expression* is a compact notation for describing sets of strings. Regular expressions are constructed similar to arithmetic expressions; various operators are used to combine smaller expressions. The basic building blocks of a regular expression are

- Ordinary characters
- Meta-characters

Ordinary characters are

- Uppercase and lowercase letters such as *A* or *b*
- Numerals such as *1* or *2*
- Characters such as a space or an underscore

Meta-characters are characters that have a special meaning inside a regular expression; they are expanded to match ordinary characters. By using meta-characters, you need not explicitly specify all the different combinations of ordinary characters that you want to match. The basic set of meta-characters understood by both sed and awk is given in Table 16.1.

TABLE 16.1 Meta-characters

Character	*Description*
.	Matches any single character except a new-line.
*	Matches zero or more occurrences of the character immediately preceding it.
[*chars*]	Matches any one of the characters given in *chars*, where *chars* is a sequence of characters. You can use the - character to indicate a range of characters. If the ^ character is the first character in *chars*, one occurrence of any character that is not specified by *chars* is matched.
^	Matches the beginning of a line.
$	Matches the end of a line.
\	Treats the character that immediately follows the \ literally. This is used to *escape* (remove the special meaning) a meta-character.

Regular expressions are referred to by several names—of which the most common are *regex* and *patterns*. Meta-characters are sometimes referred to as *wildcards*. These terms are often used interchangeably.

Regular Expression Examples

The simplest regular expression is one that exactly represents the sequence of characters that needs to be matched. For example, the following regular expression

```
/peach/
```

matches the string peach exactly. If this expression was used in awk or sed, any line that contains the string peach will be selected, including lines similar to the following:

```
We have a peach tree in the backyard
I prefer peaches to plums
```

Matching Characters

Now let's look at a slightly more complicated example. The following expression

```
/a.c/
```

matches lines that contain strings such as a+c, a-c, abc, match, and a3c, whereas the expression

```
/a*c/
```

matches those same strings along with strings such as `ace`, `yacc`, and `arctic`. It also matches the following line

```
close the window
```

although the letter `a` does not appear in this sentence. This is because of the `*`: It matches zero or more occurrences of the character immediately preceding it.

Another important thing to note about the `*` is that it tries to make the longest possible match. For example, consider the expression

```
/a*a/
```

and the following line

```
able was I, ere I saw elba
```

Here you have asked to match lines that contain a string that starts and ends with the letter *a*. In the sample line, there are several possibilities:

```
able wa
able was I, ere I sa
able was I, ere I saw elba
```

The `*` always matches the longest possible match; in this case, the last one is selected.

The `.` and the `*` can be combined to obtain behavior equivalent to the `*` filename expansion wildcard covered in Chapter 8, "Variables." For example, the following expression

```
/ch.*doc/
```

matches the strings `ch01.doc`, `ch02.doc`, and `chdoc`. The shell's `*` wildcard matches files of the same names.

Sets of Characters

One of the major limitations with the `.` operator is that it does not enable you to specify which characters you want to match; it matches all characters. To specify a particular set of characters in a regular expression, we need to use the bracket characters, (`[` and `]`), as follows:

```
/[chars]/
```

Here a single character in the set given by `chars` is matched. The use of sets in a regular expression is almost identical to the use of sets in filename substitution. Table 16.2 shows some frequently used sets of characters.

As an example of using sets, the following expression matches the string `The` and `the`:

```
/[tT]he/
```

Table 16.2 Common Sets

Set	*Description*
`[a-z]`	Matches a single lowercase letter
`[A-Z]`	Matches a single uppercase letter
`[a-zA-Z]`	Matches a single letter
`[0-9]`	Matches a single number
`[a-zA-Z0-9]`	Matches a single letter or number

Sometimes it is hard to determine the exact set of characters that you need to match. Say that you needed to match every character except the letter *T*. Constructing a set of characters that includes every character except the letter *T* is error prone; you might forget a space or a punctuation character. To solve this problem, you can use the negation operator, `^`. For example, the set that matches all characters except *T* is

```
[^T]
```

When `^` is the first character in the set, any character not given in the set is matched. This is called *reversing*. Any set, including those given in Table 16.2, can be reversed or negated by specifying `^` as the first character. For example, the following expression

```
/ch[^0-9]/
```

matches the beginnings of the strings `chapter` and `chocolate`, but not the strings `ch01` or `ch02`.

You can combine sets with the `*` character to extend their functionality. For example, the following expression

```
/ch0[0-9]*doc/
```

matches the strings `ch01.doc` and `ch02.doc` but not the strings `chdoc` or `changedoc`.

Anchoring Expressions

Let's say that we need to find lines that start with the word *the*. For example,

```
the plains were rich with crops
```

We might be tempted to use the following simple expression:

```
/the/
```

Although this expression will match lines that start with *the*, it also matches the following lines:

```
there were many orchards of fruit tree
in the dark it was like summer lightning
```

The two main problems with the simple expression are

- Only the word *the* should be matched. Lines starting with words such as *there* should not be matched.
- The word *the* should be at the beginning of the line.

To solve the first problem, we can add a space as follows:

```
/the /
```


To solve the second problem, you need the ^ meta-character, which matches the beginning of a line. In regular expressions, ^ *anchors* the expression to the beginning of the line: Only lines that start with the expression are matched. Normally, any line that contains an expression is matched.

By adding the ^ as follows,

```
/^the /
```

you have an expression that matches only those lines that start with the word *the*.

Expressions can also be anchored to the end of the line using the $. For example, the following expression

```
/friend$/
```

matches the line

```
I have been and always will be your friend
```

But it doesn't match the line

```
What are friends for
```

You can combine ^ and $ along with sets and other meta-characters to match lines according to an expression. For example, the following expression

```
/^Chapter [1-9]*[0-9]$/
```

matches lines such as

```
Chapter 1
Chapter 20
```

but it does not match lines such as

```
Chapter 00 Introduction
Chapter 101
```

> Because the ^ and $ meta-characters anchor the expression to the beginning and end of a line, an empty line is matched by the expression /^$/.

Escaping Meta-Characters

Sometimes we will need to match meta-characters in strings. Suppose that we need to match lines that contain prices:

```
Peaches $0.89/lbs
Oil $15.10/barrel
```

A price contains two meta-characters, `$` and `.`, whereas the strings contain a third meta-characters, `/`. An expression such as the following

```
/$[0-9].[0-9][0-9]/[a-zA-Z]*/
```

will not match either of the previous strings because of the following problems:

- The first character in the expression is the `$` character. Because the `$` matches the end of the line, the expression tries to look for characters after the end of the line, which is an impossible expression to match.
- Because the `.` matches a single occurrence of any character, this expression might produce false positives; strings such as `0x00` and `1234` will be matched in addition to strings of the desired format.
- The expression contains three slashes, which constitutes a garbled or invalid expression. The first two slashes are used as the delimiters for the expression.

We can solve these problems by *escaping* the meta-characters using the backslash meta-character (`\`). When a backslash is present in a regular expression, the character immediately following the backslash is always treated literally. For example,

```
$
```

matches the end of a line, but

```
\$
```

matches a dollar sign (`$`). When an ordinary character is preceded by a backslash, the backslash has no effect. For example, `\a` and `a` are both treated as a lowercase *a*.

Rewriting our earlier expression with escaping gives us the following:

```
/\$[0-9]*\.[0-9][0-9]\/[a-zA-Z]*/
```

This expression matches the prices correctly.

> In order to match \, you can escape it using itself: \\.

Useful Regular Expressions

Table 16.3 provides some useful regular expressions.

TABLE 16.3 Some Useful Regular Expressions

String Type	*Expression*
Blank lines	`/^$/`
An entire line	`/^.*$/`
One or more spaces	`/  */`
HTML (or XML) tag sets	`/<[^>][^>]*>/`
Valid URLs	`/[a-zA-Z][a-zA-Z]*:\/\/[a-zA-Z0-9][a-zA-Z0-9\.]*.*/`
Formatted dollar amounts	`/\$[0-9]*\.[0-9][0-9]/`

Using sed

`sed` is a stream editor that performs a set of actions on every line of its input. This allows `sed` to be used as a filter. The basic syntax of a `sed` command is

```
sed 'script' files
```

Here *`files`* is a list of one or more files, and *`script`* is one or more commands of the form

```
/pattern/ action
```

where *`pattern`* is a regular expression and *`action`* is one of the commands given in Table 16.4. If *`pattern`* is omitted, `action` is performed for every line of input.

TABLE 16.4 Some of the Actions Available in `sed`

Action	*Description*
`p`	Prints the line (p as in print)
`d`	Deletes the line (d as in delete)
`s`	Substitutes one expression with another (s as in substitute)

Printing Lines

Let's start with the simplest feature available in sed—printing a line that matches an expression.

The following is a price list for a small fruit market:

```
$ cat fruit_prices.txt
Fruit           Price/lbs
Banana          0.89
Paech           0.79
Kiwi            1.50
Pineapple       1.29
Apple           0.99
Mango           2.20
```

This file lists the name of a fruit and its price per pound. Most of the following examples assume that this list is stored in the file `fruit_prices.txt`.

To start with, let's print out a list of those fruits that cost less than $1 per pound. We will need to use the sed command p:

```
/pattern/p
```

Here *pattern* is a regular expression.

Let's try the following sed command:

```
$ sed '/ 0\.[0-9][0-9]$/p' fruit_prices.txt
```

This will print all the lines that match the expression:

```
/ 0\.[0-9][0-9]$/
```

This expression specifies that only lines ending in prices such as 0.89 and 0.99 should be printed. The leading 0 ensures that lines ending in prices such as 2.20 or 10.10 are not printed.

Looking at the output,

```
Fruit           Price/lbs
Banana          0.89
Banana          0.89
Paech           0.79
Paech           0.79
Kiwi            1.50
Pineapple       1.29
Apple           0.99
Apple           0.99
Mango           2.20
```

we find that the lines for fruit with prices less than a dollar are printed twice, whereas lines for fruit with prices greater than a dollar are printed only once. This demonstrates the default behavior of sed—it prints every input line to the output. To avoid this behavior, we can specify the -n option to sed as follows:

```
$ sed -n '/ 0\.[0-9][0-9]$/p' fruit_prices.txt
```

This changes the output as follows:

```
Banana          0.89
Paech           0.79
Apple           0.99
```


Deleting Lines

Say that we run out of mangos and thus need to delete them from the list. To accomplish this task, we can use the sed command d:

```
/pattern/d
```

Here *pattern* is a regular expression.

We can use the following sed command:

```
$ sed '/^[Mm]ango/d' fruit_prices.txt
```

This command deletes lines that start with the words mango or Mango. The output is as follows:

```
Fruit           Price/lbs
Banana          0.89
Paech           0.79
Kiwi            1.50
Pineapple       1.29
Apple           0.99
```

Notice that you did not have to specify the -n option to sed to get the correct output. The p command tells sed to produce additional output, whereas the d command tells sed to modify the regular output.

Although you have modified the output and have verified that it is correct, the file still needs to be updated. You can do this with the help of the shell:

```
$ mv fruit_prices.txt fruit_prices.txt.$$
$ sed '/^[Mm]ango/d' fruit_prices.txt.$$ > fruit_prices.txt
$ cat fruit_prices.txt
```

First, we rename the file fruit_prices.txt to fruit_prices.txt.$$. Recall that the value of the variable $$ is the process ID of the current shell. Appending the value of $$ to the end of a file is a commonly used method for creating temporary files with unique names.

Next, we use `sed` to delete the lines starting with `Mango` or `mango` from the temporary file. Then the output of the `sed` command is redirected into the file `fruit_prices.txt`.

We used `cat` to show us that the update was successful:

```
Fruit           Price/lbs
Banana          0.89
Paech           0.79
Kiwi            1.50
Pineapple       1.29
Apple           0.99
```

Now that we know that the update happened correctly, we can remove the temporary file as follows:

```
$ rm fruit_prices.txt.$$
```

Performing Substitutions

By now you might have noticed that `Peach` is misspelled as `Paech` in our file. We can fix this by substituting `Paech` with the correct spelling using the `sed` command `s`:

/pattern1/s/pattern2/pattern3/

Here *pattern1*, *pattern2,* and *pattern3* are regular expressions. The `s` command replaces *pattern2* with *pattern3* on any line that matches *pattern1*.

Frequently *pattern1* is omitted, so you see the `s` command used as follows:

`s/`*pattern2*`/`*pattern3*`/`

If *pattern1* is omitted, the `s` command is executed for every input line.

To fix the spelling of `Paech`, you can use the following `sed` command:

```
$ sed 's/Paech/Peach/' fruit_prices.txt
```

Now the output resembles the following:

```
Fruit           Price/lbs
Banana          0.89
Peach           0.79
Kiwi            1.50
Pineapple       1.29
Apple           0.99
```

You did not have to specify the `-n` option to `sed` to obtain the desired output. The `s` command is similar to the `d` command in that it tells `sed` to modify its normal output.

Common Errors

A common error with the s command is forgetting one or more of the / characters. For example, say that you were to issue the following command:

```
$ sed 's/Paech/Peach' fruit_prices.txt
```

An error message similar to the following is produced:

```
sed: command garbled: s/Paech/Peach
```


This error message illustrates the standard style for sed error messages:

```
sed: command garbled: command
```

sed just repeats the command and states that it could not understand it. No additional error messages or information are produced, so you have to determine what went wrong yourself.

Performing Global Substitutions

In the last example, you just needed to fix a single misspelling on a single line. Sometime you might need to perform multiple corrections. As an example, take a look at the following file:

```
$ cat nash.txt
things that are eqal to the same thing are eqal to each other
```

In this file, the word equal is misspelled as eqal. You can try to fix this using the s command as follows:

```
$ sed 's/eqal/equal/' nash.txt
things that are equal to the same thing are eqal to each other
```

As you can see, the first misspelling was fixed, but the second one was not. This is the default behavior of the s command: It only performs one substitution on a line. To perform more than one substitution, we need to use the g (g as in global) operator:

```
/pattern1/s/pattern1/pattern2/g
```

The g operator tells the s command to substitute every occurrence of *pattern2* with *pattern3* on lines matching *pattern1*. If *pattern1* is omitted, every line of input is operated on.

In this case, we need to use the g operator as follows:

```
$ sed 's/eqal/equal/g' nash.txt
things that are equal to the same thing are equal to each other
```

Reusing an Expressions Value

Returning to the price list of fruits, say that we want to change the list to reflect that the prices are in dollars by appending the $ character in front of each of the prices. By using the following expression, we can match all the lines that end with a price:

```
/ *[0-9][0-9]*\.[0-9][0-9]$/
```

The problem is replacing the existing price with a price that is preceded by the $ character. It seems as though we would need to write a separate s command for each line in the file. Fortunately, the s command provides the & operator, which enables us to reuse the matched string from *pattern2* in *pattern3*.

We can reuse the price that was matched as follows:

```
$ sed 's/ *[0-9][0-9]*\.[0-9][0-9]$/\$&/' fruit_prices.txt
Fruit           Price/lbs
Banana          $0.89
Paech           $0.79
Kiwi            $1.50
Pineapple       $1.29
Apple           $0.99
```

Using Multiple sed Commands

As you can see from the last example, we were able to update the prices, but Peach remains misspelled as Paech. In order to perform both changes, you will have to perform more than one sed command on the file. This can be accomplished in one of two ways:

- Perform the first change and then update the file. Perform the second change command and then update the file.
- Perform both changes using a single sed command and then update the file.

As you can guess, the second method is much more efficient and less prone to error because the file is updated only once. You can perform both changes using a single sed command as follows:

```
sed -e 'cmd1'... -e 'cmdN' files
```

Here *cmd1 ... cmdN* are sed commands of the type discussed previously. Each command is applied to every line in each of the files specified by *files*.

We can perform both updates using either of the following commands:

```
$ sed -e 's/Paech/Peach/' -e 's/ *[0-9][0-9]*\.[0-9][0-9]$/\$&/'
➥fruit_prices.txt
$ sed -e 's/ *[0-9][0-9]*\.[0-9][0-9]$/\$&/' -e 's/Paech/Peach/'
➥fruit_prices.txt
```

Both commands produce the same output:

```
Fruit           Price/lbs
Banana          $0.89
Peach           $0.79
Kiwi            $1.50
Pineapple       $1.29
Apple           $0.99
```

To update the file, we can use the following procedure:

```
$ mv fruit_pieces.txt fruit_pieces.txt.$$
$ sed -e 's/Paech/Peach/' -e 's/ *[0-9][0-9]*\.[0-9][0-9]$/\$&/'
➥fruit_prices.txt.$$ > fruit_pieces.txt
$ cat fruit_pieces.txt
Fruit           Price/lbs
Banana          $0.89
Peach           $0.79
Kiwi            $1.50
Pineapple       $1.29
Apple           $0.99
```

16

Using sed in a Pipeline

If a list of files is not specified, `sed` reads lines from STDIN, making it useful in pipelines.

As an example of using `sed` in a pipeline, we will use it to determine a user's numeric user ID (uid). On most systems, the `/usr/bin/id` command prints out the current user's uid and gid information. The output of `id` resembles the following:

```
$ /usr/bin/id
uid=500(ranga) gid=100(users)
```

As you can see from the output, the numeric uid for the user `ranga` is `500`. Let's modify this output so that only the numeric value is printed. First we need to eliminate everything following the first parenthesis. We can do that as follows:

```
$ /usr/bin/id | sed 's/(.*$//'
```

Now the output looks like the following:

```
uid=500
```

If we eliminate the `uid=` portion at the beginning of the line, we are finished. This can be accomplished as follows:

```
$ /usr/bin/id | sed -e 's/(.*$//' -e 's/^uid=//'
```

Now the output is

```
500
```

which is what we want. Notice that when we added the second s command, we changed from the single command form for sed to the multiple command form that uses the -e option.

Summary

In this chapter, we looked at filtering text using regular expressions. Some of the major topics covered were

- Matching characters
- Specifying sets of characters
- Anchoring expressions
- Escaping meta-characters

We also looked at the similarities between awk and sed and covered the use of sed in detail.

In the next chapter, I will introduce the awk command and its programming language. Using the material covered in this chapter, you will be able to use awk to perform difficult text manipulations.

Questions

1. Using sed, write a shell function that searches for a word or simple expression in a list of files, printing out a list of matches.

   You do not have to support all possible sed expressions. Your function should take the word to look for as its first argument. It should treat its other arguments as a list of files.

   HINT: Use double quotes (") instead of single quotes (') to surround your sed script.

2. Write a sed command that takes as its input the output of the uptime command and prints only the load averages. The uptime command's output resembles the following:

   ```
   $ uptime
   6:34pm  up 2 day(s), 49 min(s),  1 user,  load average:
   ➥0.00, 0.00, 0.02
   ```

   Your output should resemble the following:

   ```
   load average: 0.05, 0.01, 0.03
   ```

3. Write a `sed` command that takes as its input the output of the command `df -k` and prints only those lines that start with a `/`. The output of the `df -k` command resembles the following:

```
Filesystem           kbytes    used   avail capacity  Mounted on
/dev/dsk/c0t3d0s0    739262  455143  224979    67%    /
/proc                     0       0       0     0%    /proc
fd                        0       0       0     0%    /dev/fd
/dev/dsk/c0t3d0s1    123455    4813  106297     5%    /var
/dev/dsk/c0t3d0s5    842150  133819  649381    18%    /opt
swap                 366052   15708  350344     5%    /tmp
kanchi:/home        1190014  660165  468363    59%    /users
```

On HP-UX, use the command `df -b` instead of `df -k`.

4. Write a `sed` command that takes as its input the output of the `ls -l` command and prints the permissions and the filename for regular files. Directories, links, and special files should not appear in the output. The output of `ls -l` will be similar to the following:

```
-rw-r--r--   1 ranga users  85 Nov 27 15:34 fruit_prices.txt
-rw-r--r--   1 ranga users  80 Nov 27 13:53 fruit_prices.txt.7880
lrwxrwxrwx   1 ranga users   8 Nov 27 19:01 nash -> nash.txt
-rw-r--r--   1 ranga users  62 Nov 27 16:06 nash.txt
lrwxrwxrwx   1 ranga users   8 Nov 27 19:01 urls -> urls.txt
-rw-r--r--   1 ranga users 180 Nov 27 12:34 urls.txt
```

Your output should resemble the following:

```
-rw-r--r-- fruit_prices.txt
-rw-r--r-- fruit_prices.txt.7880
-rw-r--r-- nash.txt
-rw-r--r-- urls.txt
```

Terms

Anchoring Anchoring a regular expression limits matches to lines that begin or end with the expression.

Escaping Preceding a meta-character with a \ is called escaping. An escaped meta-character is treated literally.

Meta-Characters Meta-characters are characters that have a special meaning inside a regular expression; they are expanded to match ordinary characters.

Regular Expression A regular expression is compact notation for describing sets of strings.

16

Hour 17

Filtering Text with awk

In Chapter 16, "Filtering Text with Regular Expressions," you learned how to use regular expressions with `sed` to filter text. In this chapter, you will look at another powerful text filtering program called `awk`.

`awk` is a program and a complete programming language that enables you to search many files for patterns and to conditionally modify files without having to worry about opening files, reading lines, or closing files. It's found on all UNIX systems and is quite fast, easy to learn, and extremely flexible. This chapter concentrates on the `awk` elements that are most commonly used in shell scripts, specifically:

- Field editing
- Variables
- Flow control statements

What Is awk?

`awk` is a program and a programming language that enable you to search through files and modify records in these files based on patterns. The name *awk* comes from the last names of its creators Alfred Aho, Peter Weinberger, and Brian Kernighan. awk was added to UNIX Version 7 in 1978 and has been an indispensable part of it ever since.

There are three versions of awk:

- Original awk
- New nawk
- The POSIX/GNU version gawk

Original awk has remained almost the same since its first introduction to UNIX in 1978. It was intended to be a small programming language for filtering text and producing reports. By the mid-1980s, people were using awk for large programs, so its authors decided to extend it. This version, called nawk (short for new awk), was released to the public in 1987 and became a part of SunOS 4.1.*x*. nawk was supposed to replace awk, but this has not yet happened. Most commercial UNIX versions such as HP-UX and Solaris still ship with both awk and nawk. BSD systems also ship with awk rather than nawk.

In 1992 the Institute of Electrical and Electronics Engineers (IEEE) standardized awk as part of its Portable Operating Systems Interface standard (POSIX). gawk, the GNU version of awk, is based on the POSIX standard. All Linux systems ship with gawk.

The examples in this chapter work with any version of awk.

Basic Syntax

The basic syntax of an awk command is

```
awk 'script' files
```

Here, *files* is a list of one or more files, and *script* is one or more commands of the form:

```
/pattern/ { actions }
```

Here *pattern* is a regular expression, and *actions* are one or more of the commands covered later in this chapter. If *pattern* is omitted, awk performs the *actions* for each input line.

Let's get started by looking at a simple task: printing the lines in a file. In order to print the file fruit_prices.txt (from the previous chapter), you can use the following command:

```
$ awk '{ print ; }' fruit_prices.txt
Fruit           Price/lbs       Quantity
Banana          $0.89           100
```

```
Peach           $0.79           65
Kiwi            $1.50           22
Pineapple       $1.29           35
Apple           $0.99           78
```

Here the awk command print is used to print each line of the input. When the print command is given without arguments, it prints an input line exactly as it was read. Notice that there is a semicolon (;) after the print command. This semicolon indicates to awk where the end of a command is. Although some older versions of awk do not require the semicolon, it is good practice to include it.

Field Editing

One of the nicest features available in awk is that it automatically divides input lines into *fields*. A field is a set of characters separated by one or more *field separator characters*. The default field separator characters are tab and space.

When a line is read, awk places the fields that it has parsed into the variable 1 for the first field, 2 for the second field, and so on. The value of a field is accessed using the field operator, $. For example, the first field is $1.

The use of the $ in awk is slightly different than in the shell. The $ is required only when accessing the value of a field variable; it is not required when accessing the values of other variables. Creating and using variables in awk is explained in depth later in this chapter.

To demonstrate the use of fields, let's see how you can use them to print only the name of a fruit and its quantity from the file:

```
$ awk '{ print $1 $3 ; }' fruit_prices.txt
```

Here you use awk to print two fields from every input line:

- The first field, which contains the fruit name
- The third field, which contains the quantity

The output looks like the following:

```
FruitQuantity
Banana100
Peach65
Kiwi22
Pineapple35
Apple78
```

Notice that in the output there is no separation between the fields. This is the default behavior of the `print` command. To print a space between each field you need to use the comma operator as follows:

```
$ awk '{ print $1 , $3 ; }' fruit_prices.txt
Fruit Quantity
Banana 100
Peach 65
Kiwi 22
Pineapple 35
Apple 78
```

You can format the output by using the `awk printf` command instead of the `print` command as follows:

```
$ awk '{ printf "%-15s %s\n" , $1 , $3 ; }' fruit_prices.txt
Fruit           Quantity
Banana          100
Peach           65
Kiwi            22
Pineapple       35
Apple           78
```

All the features of the `printf` command discussed in Chapter 5, "Input and Output," are available in the `awk` command `printf`.

The order in which the fields are output is not restricted to the order in which they are present in the input.

In the previous examples, the output order of the fields `$1` and `$3` preserved the input order: `$1` was output before `$3`. There was no requirement to preserve the input order; you could easily have output `$3` before `$1` without any problems (aside from having a confusing table):

```
awk '{ printf "%s %-15s\n" , $3 , $1 ; }' fruit_prices.txt
```

Taking Pattern-Specific Actions

Let's say that you want to highlight those fruits that cost more than a dollar by printing a trailing `*` after those fruits. In order to accomplish this, you need to perform different actions depending on the pattern that was matched to the price of the fruit. You start with the following script:

```
#!/bin/sh
awk '
    / *\$[1-9][0-9]*\.[0-9][0-9] */ { print $1,$2,$3,"*"; }
    / *\$0\.[0-9][0-9] */ { print ; }
' fruit_prices.txt
```

Here you have two patterns: The first one looks for fruit priced higher than a dollar, and the second one looks for fruit priced lower than a dollar. When a fruit priced higher than a dollar is encountered, the three fields are output with a `*` at the end of the line. For all other fruit, the line is printed exactly as it was read.

Assuming that this script is called `fruit_prices.sh` and is located in the current directory, it can be invoked as follows:

```
$ ./fruit_prices.sh
```

The output looks like the following:

```
Banana          $0.89           100
Peach           $0.79           65
Kiwi $1.50 22 *
Pineapple $1.29 35 *
Apple           $0.99           78
```


One problem here is that the lines you wanted to flag with the `*` in are no longer formatted in the same manner as the other lines. You could solve this problem using `printf`, but a much simpler solution is to use the `$0` field. The variable `0` is used by `awk` to store the entire input line as it was read.

Let's change the script as follows:

```
#!/bin/sh
awk '
    / *\$[1-9][0-9]*\.[0-9][0-9] */ { print $0,"*"; }
    / *\$0\.[0-9][0-9] */ { print ; }
' fruit_prices.txt
```

This changes the output so that all the lines are formatted correctly:

```
$ ./fruit_prices.sh
Banana          $0.89           100
Peach           $0.79           65
Kiwi            $1.50           22 *
Pineapple       $1.29           35 *
Apple           $0.99           78
```

Comparison Operators

Now say that you have to flag all the fruit whose quantity is less than 75 for reorder by appending the string `REORDER`. In this case you have to check whether the third field, which holds the quantity, is less than or equal to 75.

To solve this problem, you need to use a comparison operator. In `awk`, comparison operators compare the values of numbers and strings. Their behavior is similar to operators found in the C language or the shell. When a comparison operator is used, the syntax of an awk command changes to the following:

```
expression { actions; }
```

Here *expression* is constructed using one of the comparison operators given in Table 17.1.

TABLE 17.1 Comparison Operators in awk

Operator	*Description*
<	Less than
>	Greater than
<=	Less than or equal to
>=	Greater than or equal to
==	Equal to
!=	Not equal to
`value ~ /pattern/`	True if `value` matches pattern
`value !~ /pattern/`	True if `value` does not match pattern

You can solve your problem using the following script:

```
#!/bin/sh
awk '
    $3 <= 75 { printf "%s\t%s\n",$0,"REORDER" ; }
    $3 >  75 { print $0 ; }
' fruit_prices.txt
```

Here you determine whether the third field contains a value less than or equal to 75. If it does, you print the input line followed by the string `REORDER`. Next, you determine whether the third field contains a value greater than 75 and, if it does, you print the input line unchanged.

Assuming that this script is called `reorder.sh` and is located in the current directory, it can be invoked as follows:

```
$ ./reorder.sh
```

The output from this scripts looks like the following:

```
Fruit           Price/lbs       Quantity
Banana          $0.89           100
Peach           $0.79           65          REORDER
Kiwi            $1.50           22          REORDER
Pineapple       $1.29           35          REORDER
Apple           $0.99           78
```

Compound Expressions

Often, you need to combine two or more expressions to check for a particular condition. When you combine two or more expressions, the result is called a *compound expression*. Compound expressions are constructed by using either the `&&` (and) or the `||` (or) compound operators. The syntax is

```
(expr1) && (expr2)
(expr2) || (expr2)
```

Here *expr1* and *expr2* are expressions constructed using the conditional operators given in Table 17.1. The parentheses surrounding *expr1* and *expr2* are required. When the `&&` operator is used, both *expr1* and *expr2* must be true for the compound expression to be true. When the `||` operator is used, the compound expression is true if either *expr1* or *expr2* is true.

17

As an example of using a compound expression, you can use the compound operators to obtain a list of all the fruits that cost more than a dollar and of which there are less than 75:

```
#!/bin/sh

awk '
    ($2 ~ /^\$[1-9][0-9]*\.[0-9][0-9]$/) && ($3 < 75) {
        printf "%s\t%s\t%s\n",$0,"*","REORDER" ;
    }
' fruit_prices.txt ;
```

If this script is called `reorder_expensive.sh` and is located in the current directory, it can be invoked as follows:

```
$ ./ reorder_expensive.sh
```

The output looks like the following

```
Kiwi            $1.50           22      *       REORDER
Pineapple       $1.29           35      *       REORDER
```

> **The Compound Expression Operators**
>
> The `&&` operator is often called the *and–and operator* because it consists of two ampersands (*and* characters). Similarly, the `||` operator is referred to as the *or-or operator*.

The `next` Command

Let's reconsider the "reorder" script:

```
#!/bin/sh
awk '
    $3 <= 75 { printf "%s\t%s\n",$0,"REORDER" ; }
```

```
    $3 > 75 { print $0 ; }
' fruit_prices.txt
```

Clearly it is performing more work than it needs to. For example, when the input line is

```
Kiwi            $1.50           22
```

the execution of the script is as follows:

1. Checks whether the value of the third column, 22, is less than 75. Because the value is less than 75, the script proceeds to step 2.
2. Prints the input line followed by `REORDER`.
3. Checks whether the value of the third column, 22, is greater than 75. Because the value is not greater than 75, the script reads the next line.

There is no real need to execute step 3 because step 2 has already printed a line. To prevent step 3 from executing, you can use the `next` command. The `next` command tells `awk` to skip all the remaining patterns and expressions and instead read the next input line and start from the first pattern or expression.

Let's change the script to use the `next` command:

```
#!/bin/sh
awk '
    $3 <= 75 { printf "%s\t%s\n",$0,"REORDER" ; next ; }
    $3 > 75 { print $0 ; }
' fruit_prices.txt ;
```

Now when the line:

```
Kiwi            $1.50           22
```

is encountered, the execution of the script is as follows:

1. Checks whether the value of the third column, 22, is less than 75. Because the value is less than 75, the script proceeds to step 2.
2. Prints the input line followed by `REORDER`.
3. Reads the next input line and starts over with the first pattern.

As you can see, the second comparison (`$3 > 75`) is never performed for this input line.

Using STDIN as Input

Recall that the basic form of an `awk` command is

```
awk 'script' files
```

If the list of files (*files*) is omitted, awk reads its input from STDIN. This enables you to use awk to filter the output of other commands. For example, the command

```
$ ls -l
```

produces output formatted similar to the following:

```
total 64
-rw-r--r--    1 ranga    users    635 Nov 29 11:10 awkfruit.sh
-rw-r--r--    1 ranga    users    115 Nov 28 14:07 fruit_prices.txt
-rw-r--r--    1 ranga    users     80 Nov 27 13:53 fruit_prices.txt.7880
lrwxrwxrwx    1 ranga    users      8 Nov 27 19:01 nash -> nash.txt
-rw-r--r--    1 ranga    users     62 Nov 27 16:06 nash.txt
-rw-r--r--    1 ranga    users     11 Nov 29 10:38 nums.txt
lrwxrwxrwx    1 ranga    users      8 Nov 27 19:01 urls -> urls.txt
-rw-r--r--    1 ranga    users    180 Nov 27 12:34 urls.txt
```

17

Let's use awk to manipulate the output of the `ls -l` command so that only the name of a file and its size are printed. The values you are interested in are stored in fields 9 and 5: the name of the file is in field 9 and its size is in field 5. The following command prints the name of each file along with its size:

```
$ ls -l | awk '$1 !~ /total/ { printf "%-32s %s\n",$9,$5 ; }'
```

The output looks like the following:

```
awkfruit.sh                      635
fruit_prices.txt                 115
fruit_prices.txt.7880            80
nash                             8
nash.txt                         62
nums.txt                         11
urls                             8
urls.txt                         180
```

Using awk Features

So far you have learned about the basics of using awk, now you will look at some of its more powerful features:

- Variables
- Flow control
- Loops

Variables

Variables in awk are similar to variables in the shell; they are words that hold a value. The basic syntax of defining a variable is

```
name=value
```

Here *name* is the name of the variable and *value* is the value of that variable. For example, the following awk command

```
fruit="peach"
```

creates the variable `fruit` and assigns it the value `peach`. There is no need to initialize a variable; the first time you use it, it is automatically initialized.

Like the shell, the name of a variable can contain only letters, numbers, and underscores. A variable's name cannot start with a number.

You can assign both numeric and string values to a variable in the same script. For example, consider the following awk commands:

```
fruit="peach"
fruit=100
```

The first command assigns the value `peach` to the variable `fruit`. The second command assigns the value `100` to the variable `fruit`.

The value that you assign a variable can also be the value of another variable or a field. For example, the following awk commands

```
fruit=peach
fruity=fruit
```

set the value of the variables `fruit` and `fruity` to `peach`. First the value of the variable `fruit` is set to `peach`, next the value of `fruity` is set to the value of the variable fruit, which is `peach`.

In order to set the value of a variable to one of the fields parsed by awk, you need to use the standard field access operator. For example, the following awk command

```
fruit=$1
```

sets the value of the variable `fruit` to the first field of the input line.

Using Numeric Expressions

You can also assign a variable the value of a *numeric expression*. Numeric expressions are commands that add, subtract, multiply, and divide two numbers and are of the form

```
num1 operator num2
```

Here *num1* and *num2* can be constants, such as 1 or 2, or variable names. *operator* is one of the numeric operators listed in Table 17.2. The action specified by *operator* is performed on *num1* and *num2*, and the answer is returned. For example, the following awk commands

```
a=1
b=a+1
```

assign the value 2 to the variable b.

TABLE 17.2 Numeric Operators in awk

Operator	*Description*
+	Add
-	Subtract
*	Multiply
/	Divide
%	Modulo (Remainder)
^	Exponentiation

If *num1* or *num2* is the name of a variable whose value is a string rather than a number, awk uses the value 0 rather than the string.

If a variable that has not yet been created is used, awk creates the variable and assigns it a value of 0.

As an example of using numeric expressions, let's look at a script that counts the number of blank lines in a file:

```
#!/bin/sh
for i in $@ ;
do
    if [ -f $i ] ; then
        echo $i
        awk ' /^ *$/ { x=x+1 ; print x ; }' $i
    else
        echo "ERROR: $i not a file." >&2
    fi
done
```

In the awk command, you increment the variable x and print it each time a blank line is encountered. Because a new instance of the awk command runs for each file, the count is unique for each file.

Consider the file `urls.txt`, which contains four blank lines:

```
$ cat urls.txt
http://www.cusa.berkeley.edu/~ranga

http://www.cisco.com

ftp://prep.ai.mit.edu/pub/gnu/
ftp://ftp.redhat.com/

http://www.yahoo.com/index.html
ranga@kanchi:/home/ranga/pub

ranga@soda:/home/ranga/docs/book/ch01.doc
```

If the script is named `urls.sh` and is located in the current directory, it can be used to count the blank lines in the file `urls.txt` by invoking it as follows:

```
$ ./urls.sh urls.txt
```

The output looks like the following:

```
urls.txt
1
2
3
4
```

The Assignment Operators

In the previous example, the `awk` command:

```
awk ' /^ *$/ { x=x+1 ; print x ; }' $i
```

Uses the assignment:

```
x=x+1
```

In `awk` this can be written in a more concise fashion using the addition assignment operator:

```
x += 1
```

Here, the assignment operator `+=` takes the value of `x`, adds `1` to it, and then assigns the result to `x`.

In general the assignment operators have the syntax

```
name operator num
```

Here *`name`* is the name of a variable, *`operator`* is one of the operators specified in Table 17.3, and *`num`* is either the name of a variable or a numeric constant such as `1` or `2`.

TABLE 17.3 Assignment Operators in awk

Operator	*Description*
`+=`	Add
`-=`	Subtract
`*=`	Multiply
`/=`	Divide
`%=`	Modulo (Remainder)
`^=`	Exponentiation

Using an assignment operator is shorthand for writing a numeric expression of the form:

```
name=name operator num
```

Many programmers prefer using the assignment operators because they are slightly more concise than a regular numeric expression.

The Special Patterns: BEGIN and END

In the previous example, the awk command

```
awk ' /^ *$/ { x=x+1 ; print x ; }' $i
```

prints the value of x each time it is incremented. It would be much nicer if you could print the total number of empty lines. In order to accomplish this, you need to use the special patterns BEGIN and END.

Recall that the general syntax of a command in an awk script is

```
/pattern/ { actions }
```

Usually *pattern* is a regular expression, but you can also use two special patterns, BEGIN and END. Taking these patterns into account, the general form of an awk command is

```
awk '
    BEGIN { actions }
    /pattern/ { actions }
    /pattern/ { actions }
    END { actions }
' files
```

When the BEGIN pattern is specified, awk executes its *actions* before reading any input. When the END pattern is specified, awk executes its *actions* before it exits. When these patterns are given the execution of an awk, the script is as follows:

1. If a BEGIN pattern is present, it executes the *actions* it specifies.
2. Reads an input line and parses it into fields.

3. Compares each of the specified *patterns* against the input line, until it finds a match. When it does find a match, the script executes the *actions* specified for that *pattern*. This step is repeated for all available *patterns*.
4. Repeats steps 2 and 3 while input lines are present.
5. After the script reads all the input lines, if the `END` pattern is present, it executes the *actions* that the pattern specifies.

The `BEGIN` pattern must be the first pattern that is specified, and the `END` pattern must be the last pattern that is specified. Between the `BEGIN` and `END` patterns you can have any number of `awk` commands of the form:

```
/pattern/ { action ; }
```

Both `BEGIN` and `END` are optional. If a program consists of only a `BEGIN` pattern, `awk` does not read *files*.

To solve this problem, you can use the `END` pattern to print the value of `x`. The modified `urls.sh` script is as follows:

```
#!/bin/sh
for i in $@ ;
do
    if [ -f "$i" ] ; then
        echo "$i\c"
        awk '
            /^ *$/ { x+=1 ; next; }
            END { printf " %s\n",x; }
        ' "$i"
    else
        echo "ERROR: $i not a file." >&2
    fi
done
```

Now the output looks like

```
$ ./urls.sh urls.txt
urls.txt 4
```

If the output on your system looks like the following:

```
urls.txt\c
4
```

instead of as shown, you will need to replace the following line in the script:

```
echo "$i\c"
```

with the line:

```
echo -n "$1"
```

Built-in Variables

In addition to the variables that you can define, awk predefines several variables. The complete list of these variables is given in Table 17.4.

TABLE 17.4 Built-in Variables in awk

Variables	*Description*
FILENAME	The name of the current input file. You should not change the value of this variable.
NR	The number of the current input line or record in the input file. You should not change the value of this variable.
NF	The number of fields in the current line or record. You should not change the value of this variable.
OFS	The output field separator (default is space).
FS	The input field separator (default is space and tab).
OFMT	The output format for numbers (default is %.6g).
ORS	The output record separator (default is newline).
RS	The input record separator (default is newline) .

Using FILENAME and NR

In the previous example, you used the shell to print the name of the input file. By using the variable FILENAME in conjunction with the BEGIN statement, you can do this all in awk. While you are at it, you can change the previous script to print the percentage of lines in the file that were blank using the following expression in the END pattern:

```
100*(x/NR)
```

Here you are using the variable NR, which stores the current record or line number. In the END pattern, the value of NR is the line number of the last line that was processed, which is the same as the total number of lines processed.

With these changes, the script is

```
#!/bin/sh
for i in $@ ;
do
    if [ -f "$i" ] ; then
        awk '
            /^ *$/ {file=FILENAME; x+=1 ; next ; }
            END { printf "%s %s %3.1f\n",file,x,(100*(x/NR)); }
        ' "$i"
    else
```

```
        echo "ERROR: $i not a file." >&2
    fi
done
```

The new output looks like

```
$ ./urls.sh urls.txt
urls.txt        4       36.4
```

Notice that the percentage is given as a decimal or floating point value. awk treats all numbers as floating point values and returns floating point values from all of its computations.

Changing the Input Field Separator

The input field separator, FS, controls how awk breaks up fields in an input line. The default value for FS is the string " \t" (a space followed by a tab). Because most commands, such as ls or ps, use spaces or tabs to separate columns, this default value enables you to easily manipulate their output using awk.

You can manually set FS to any other characters in order to influence how awk breaks up an input line. Usually, this character is changed when you look through system databases, such as /etc/passwd. The two methods available for changing FS are

- Manually resetting FS in a BEGIN pattern
- Specifying the -F option to awk

As an example, let's set FS to a colon (:) using the following BEGIN pattern:

```
BEGIN { FS=":" ; }
```

The following awk invocation is equivalent to the BEGIN pattern:

```
awk -F: '{ ... }'
```

The major difference between these two methods is that the -F option enables you to use a shell variable to specify the field separator dynamically as follows:

```
$ MYFS=: ; export MYFS ; awk -F${MYFS} '{ ... }'
```

whereas the BEGIN block forces you to hard code the value of the field separator.

A simple example that demonstrates the use of changing FS is the following:

```
$ awk 'BEGIN { FS=":" ; } { print $1 , $6 ; }' /etc/passwd
```

This command prints each user's username and home directory. It can also be written as follows:

```
$ awk -F: '{ print $1, $6 ; }' /etc/passwd
```

The output is similar to the following:

```
root /
daemon /
bin /usr/bin
sys /
adm /var/adm
ranga /home/ranga
```

Allowing awk to Use Shell Variables

Most versions of awk have no direct way of accessing the values of environment variables set by the shell. In order for awk to use these variables, you have to convert them to awk variables on the command line as follows:

```
awk 'script' awkvar1=value awkvar2=value ... files
```

Here, *script* is the awk script that you want to execute. The variables *awkvar1*, *awkvar2*, and so on are the names of awk variables that you want to set. As usual, *files* is a list of files.

Let's say that you want to generate a list of all the fruits in fruit_prices.txt that are less than or equal to some number x, where x is supplied by the user. In order to make this possible, you need to forward the value of x given by the user to awk. Assuming that the user-supplied value of x is available in the shell variable $1, the script is

```
#!/bin/sh
NUMFRUIT="$1"
if [ -z "$NUMFRUIT" ] ; then NUMFRUIT=75 ; fi

awk '
    $3 <= numfruit  { print ; }
' numfruit="$NUMFRUIT" fruit_prices.txt
```

Only those lines that have less than the specified number of fruit are printed.

Assuming this script is called reorder_user.sh and is located in the current directory, it can be executed as follows:

```
$ ./reorder_user.sh 25
```

This produces the output

```
Kiwi            $1.50           22
```

Flow Control

There are three main forms for flow control in awk:

- The if statement
- The while statement
- The for statement

The `if` and `while` statements are similar to those found in the shell; whereas the `for` statement is much closer to the version found in the C programming language.

The `if` Statement

The `if` statement enables you to make tests before executing some `awk` command. The pattern matching and expressions that you have used in the previous examples are essentially `if` statements that affect the overall execution of the `awk` program.

The basic syntax of the `if` statement is

```
if (expr1) {
    action1
} else if (expr2) {
    action2
} else {
    action3
}
```

Here *`expr1`* and *`expr2`* are expressions created using the conditional operators. The parentheses surrounding *`expr1`* and *`expr2`* are required. The actions—*`action1`*, *`action2`*, and *`action3`*—can be any sequence of valid `awk` commands. The braces surrounding these actions are required only when an action contains more than one statement, but most programmers always include them for the sake of clarity and maintainability.

Both the `else if` and the `else` statements are optional. There is no limit on the number of `else if` statements that can be given.

The execution is as follows:

1. Evaluate *`expr1`* (`if`).
2. If *`expr1`* is true, execute *`action1`* and exit the `if` statement.
3. If *`expr1`* is false, evaluate *`expr2`* (`else if`).
4. If *`expr2`* is true, execute *`action2`* and exit the `if` statement.
5. If *`expr2`* is false, execute *`action3`* and exit the `if` statement (`else`).

As a simple example, let's write a script that prints a list of fruits in `fruit_prices.txt` highlighting the following conditions:

- Whether an item costs more than a dollar
- Whether you need to reorder the item

As you did in previous examples, you will use the `*` character and the string `REORDER` for highlighting these conditions.

Using the if statement, the script is

```
#!/bin/sh

awk '{
    printf "%s\t",$0;

    if ( $2 ~ /\$[1-9][0-9]*\.[0-9][0-9]/ ) {

        printf " * ";
        if ( $3 <= 75 ) {
            printf "REORDER\n" ;
        } else {
            printf "\n" ;
        }

    } else {

        if ( $3 < 75 ) {
            printf "   REORDER\n" ;
        } else {
            printf "\n" ;
        }

    }
}' fruit_prices.txt ;
```

If the script is called reorder_expensive.sh and is located in the current directory, it can be invoked as follows:

```
$ ./reorder_expensive.sh
```

The output looks like the following

```
Fruit           Price/lbs       Quantity
Banana          $0.89           100
Peach           $0.79           65           REORDER
Kiwi            $1.50           22         * REORDER
Pineapple       $1.29           35         * REORDER
Apple           $0.99           78
```

The while Statement

The while statement executes awk commands while an expression is true. The basic syntax is

```
while (expr) {
    actions
}
```

17

Here *expr* is an expression created using the conditional operators. The parentheses surrounding *expr* are required. The actions that should be performed, *actions*, are any sequence of valid awk commands. The braces surrounding the *actions* are required only for actions that contain more than one statement, but most programmers always include them for the sake of clarity and maintainability.

The following example uses a while loop to print the fields of the file fruit_prices.txt in reverse order:

```
#!/bin/sh
awk '{ x=NF ;
       while (x>0) {
         printf("%16s ",$x);
         x-=1;
       }
       print "" ;
}' fruit_prices.txt
```

Here, you use NF to access the number of fields in the current record. You also use the field access operator, $, in conjunction with the variable x to access the value of a particular field.

If this script is called reverse_fruit.sh and is located in the current directory, it can be invoked as follows:

```
$ ./reverse_fruit.sh
```

The output is similar to the following:

```
        Quantity        Price/lbs            Fruit
             100            $0.89           Banana
              65            $0.79            Peach
              22            $1.50             Kiwi
              35            $1.29        Pineapple
              78            $0.99            Apple
```

The do Statement

A variation on the while statement is the do statement. It also performs some actions while an expression is true. The main difference between while and do is that the do statement executes at least once. The basic syntax is

```
do {
    actions
} while (expr)
```

Here *expr* is an expression created using the conditional operators. The parentheses surrounding *expression* are required. The actions that should be performed, *actions*, are any sequence of valid awk commands. The braces surrounding the *actions* are required only for actions that contain more than one statement, but most programmers include them for the sake of clarity and maintainability.

As an example, you can rewrite the `while` loop in the previous example using a `do` loop:

```
#!/bin/sh
awk '{
        x=NF;
        do {
                printf("%16s ",$x);
                x-=1;
        } while(x>0);
        print "";
}' fruit_prices.txt
```

The behavior of the do statement varies among nawk, gawk, and awk. If you want to use the statement, you should stick to nawk or gawk because older versions of awk might have trouble with it. If you are concerned with portability to older versions of UNIX, you should avoid using the do statement.

The `for` Statement

The `for` statement enables you to repeat commands a certain number of times. The `for` loop in `awk` is similar to the `for` loop in the C language. The `for` loop has a counter that is initialized before the loop starts executing. At the beginning of every iteration, the value of the counter is compared to a predefined value. The loop executes when the comparison is true. If the comparison is false, the loop terminates. Every time the loop executes, the counter is incremented. This is quite different from the `for` loop in the shell, which executes a set of commands for each item in a list.

The basic syntax of the `for` loop is

```
for (init_cntr; test_cntr; incr_cntr) {
    action
}
```

Here *`init_cntr`* initializes the counter variable, *`test_cntr`* is an expression that tests the counter variable's value, and *`incr_cntr`* increments the value of the counter. The parentheses surrounding the expression used by the `for` loop are required. The actions that should be performed, *`action`*, are any sequence of valid `awk` commands. The braces surrounding the *`action`* are required only for actions that contain more than one statement, but most programmers always include them for the sake of clarity and maintainability.

A common use of the `for` loop is to iterate through the fields in a record and output them, possibly modifying each record in the process. The following `for` loop prints each field in a record separated by two spaces:

```
#!/bin/sh
awk '{
    for (x=1;x<=NF;x+=1) {
        printf "%s  ",$x ;
    }
    printf "\n" ;
}' fruit_prices.txt
```

Summary

This chapter introduced `awk` programming. `awk` is one of the most powerful text-filtering tools available in UNIX. By using `awk`, it is possible to modify and transform text in ways that are difficult or impossible using only the shell.

Some of the important topics covered in this chapter include:

- Field editing
- Pattern specific actions
- Using STDIN as input
- Variables
- Numeric and assignment expressions
- Using flow control

In addition to these topics, `awk` offers features such as multiple–line editing, arrays, and functions. If you are interested in learning more about these topics, consult one of the following sources:

The UNIX Programming Environment by Brian Kernighan and Rob Pike (Prentice-Hall, 1984)

The AWK Programming Language by Alfred Aho, Peter Weinberger, and Brian Kernighan (Addison-Wesley, 1984)

Effective AWK Programming by Arnold Robbins and Michael Brennan (O'Reilly & Associates, 2001)

sed & awk by Arnold Robbins and Dale Dougherty (O'Reilly & Associates, 1997)

The GNU `awk` *User's Guide* by Arnold Robbins (SCC, 1996)

Questions

1. Using the `for` statement, write an `awk` script that prints each of the fields in a record in reverse order.

2. Write an `awk` script that balances a checking account. Your program needs to print the balance in the account every time the user makes a transaction.

   The transactions are stored in a file. Each line or record in the file has the following format:

   `command:date:comment:amount`

   Here *`date`* is the date on which the transaction was made, *`comment`* is a string (including embedded spaces) describing the transaction, and *`amount`* is the amount of the transaction. The *`command`* determines what should be done to the balance with *`amount`*. The valid *`commands`* are

   - `B` indicates balance. When this command is encountered, the balance in the account should be set to the transaction *`amount`*.
   - `D` indicates a deposit. When this command is encountered, the transaction *`amount`* should be added to the balance.
   - `C` indicates a check. When this command is encountered, the transaction *`amount`* should be subtracted from the balance.
   - `W` indicates a withdrawal. When this command is encountered, the transaction *`amount`* should be subtracted from the balance.

   The main difference between the `C` (check) and the `W` (withdrawal) commands is that the `C` (check) command adds an extra field to its records:

   `command:date:comment:check number:amount`

   In addition, the `B` (balance) command uses only two fields:

   `B:`*`amount`*

   Here *`amount`* is the balance amount in the account.

   For the purposes of this problem, you need to be concerned with the first field, which contains the command; the second field, which contains the transaction date; and the last field, which contains the transaction amount.

   The sample input file looks like the following:

```
$ cat account.txt
account.txt
B:0
D:10/24/97:inital deposit:1000
C:10/25/97:credit card:101:100
W:10/30/97:gas:21.43
```

17

```
W:10/30/97:lunch:11.34
C:11/02/97:toner:41.45
C:11/04/97:car payment:347.23
D:11/06/97:dividend:687.34
W:11/10/97:emergency cash:200
```

Your output should look like the following:

```
10/24/97     1000.00
10/25/97      900.00
10/30/97      878.57
10/30/97      867.23
11/02/97      825.78
11/04/97      478.55
11/06/97     1165.89
11/10/97      965.89
```

3. Modify the program you wrote for question 2, to print the ending (total) balance after all input records have been considered. Your output should now look like the following:

```
10/24/97     1000.00
10/25/97      900.00
10/30/97      878.57
10/30/97      867.23
11/02/97      825.78
11/04/97      478.55
11/06/97     1165.89
11/10/97      965.89
-
Total         965.89
```

(HINT: Use the `END` pattern)

4. Modify the program you wrote in question 3 to support a new command:
   - `M` indicates the minimum balance. When the balance drops below this minimum balance, a warning should be printed at the end of the output line.

The `M` (minimum balance) command uses only two fields:

`M:`*`amount`*

Here *`amount`* is the balance amount in the account.

The input file changes as follows:

```
$ cat account.txt h
B:0
M:500
D:10/24/97:inital deposit:1000
C:10/25/97:credit card:101:100
W:10/30/97:gas:21.43
W:10/30/97:lunch:11.34
```

```
C:11/02/97:toner:41.45
C:11/04/97:car payment:347.23
D:11/06/97:dividend:687.34
W:11/10/97:emergency cash:200
```

Your output should be similar to the following:

```
10/24/97     1000.00
10/25/97      900.00
10/30/97      878.57
10/30/97      867.23
11/02/97      825.78
11/04/97      478.55 * Below Min. Balance
11/06/97     1165.89
11/10/97      965.89
-
Total         965.89
```


Terms

Field A set of characters that are separated by one or more field separator characters. The default field separator characters are tab and space.

Field Separator Controls the manner in which an input line is broken into fields. In the shell, the field separator is stored in the variable `IFS`. In `awk`, the field separator is stored in the `awk` variable `FS`. Both the shell and `awk` use the default value of space and tab for the field separator.

Hour 18

Other Tools

In this chapter, you will look at several useful UNIX commands that are often encountered in shell scripts and that you can use in your own programs. The specific set of commands covered in this chapter includes:

- `eval`
- `:`
- `type`
- `sleep`
- `find`
- `xargs`
- `bc`
- `expr`

The Built-In Commands

The first set of commands examined in this chapter are *built-in* commands. A built-in command is part of the shell itself; it is not stored in a separate file on disk. Built-in commands are slightly more efficient than external programs because there is no overhead associated with reading and loading them from a file on disk. Unless you are looping thousands of times, it usually does not matter whether the command you use is built in or external. The built-in commands you will examine are `eval`, `:`, and `type`.

The `eval` Command

The `eval` command is used when you want the shell to execute a command after performing substitution. The basic syntax is

```
eval cmd
```

Here *cmd* is any valid shell command. The `eval` command is normally used when shell special characters are inserted via variable substitution or command substitution (refer to Chapter 9, "Substitution"). For example,

```
$ OUTPUT="> out.txt"
$ echo hello $OUTPUT
```

The variable `OUTPUT` contains the > sign to redirect standard output to a file called `out.file`. However, if you try to use the `OUTPUT` variable in the `echo` statement, you'll find that the output goes to the screen rather than the file `out.txt`:

```
hello > out.txt
```

The output went to the screen rather than the file because the output redirection operator, >, was not present when the shell first looked for redirection operators. You can solve this problem by inserting `eval` at the start of the command as follows:

```
$ eval echo hello $OUTPUT
```

When this command is executed, the prompt is returned and no text is displayed on the screen. The output is correctly redirected to the file `out.txt`. If you were to change the value of `OUTPUT` as follows:

```
OUTPUT=" >> out.txt"
```

The output will be appended to `out.txt` instead of overwriting it.

The : Command

The : command, referred to as the *no-op* (short for no-operation) command, does nothing other than exit with an exit code of zero. Three common uses for the : command are as follows:

- `if` statements
- `while` loops
- Variable substitution

: and `if`

The : command is sometimes used as the command following the `then` in the `if` statement. For example:

```
if [ -x $CMD ] ; then
   :
else
   echo Error: $CMD is not executable >&2
fi
```

The shell flags a syntax error if a command does not follow the `then`, so you can insert the : command as a temporary no-op command that can be replaced by other code later.

: and `while`

Because the : always returns a successful result, it is used to create an infinite loop as follows:

```
while :
do
   list
done
```


This type of loop will continue forever or until a `break` is executed within the loop. Infinite loops are useful for eliciting valid input from users. For example:

```
while :
do
   echo -n "Do you want to play a game (y/n)? "
   read RESPONSE
   case "$RESPONSE" in
      [nN]|no|No|NO)
         RESPONSE="n" ; break ;;
      [yY]|yes|Yes|YES)
         RESPONSE="y" ; break ;;
   esac
   echo "Error: Invalid response: '$RESPONSE'"
done
```

This loop prompts the users for a response to the question:

```
Do you want to play a game (y/n)?
```

It then reads the users' responses, stores them in the variable `RESPONSE`, and validates the responses to make sure that they are in some form of yes or no. If an incorrect response was given, an error message is displayed and the loop executes again. Otherwise the loop breaks and the user's response is stored in the variable `RESPONSE`.

Some programmers use `true` in place of `:` when creating infinite loops. Using the `:` is more efficient because it is a shell built-in command, whereas `true` is an external command and must be read from disk.

: and Variable Substitution

Another use of the : command takes advantage of the fact that the shell evaluates arguments to it. This is a useful way to invoke variable substitution. For example:

```
: ${LINES:=24} ${TERM:?"TERM not set"}
```

The : is a no-op, but the shell still evaluates its arguments. Thus `LINES` is set to `24` if `LINES` is empty or undefined. If `TERM` is empty or undefined, the whole script aborts with the error message `"TERM not set"`.

: and the C shell

You might sometimes find the : used as the first line of a older shell scripts. Some early versions of the C shell contained a bug that automatically assumes that any script whose first character is # is a C shell script. For this reason Bourne shell scripts had to start with something other than a # sign; the : was often used for this purpose.

Current versions of the C shell do not contain this bug, but some older Bourne shell scripts still use : as the first line.

The type Command

The `type` command tells you the full pathname of a command if the shell can find that command in the search path, `$PATH`. The basic syntax is

```
type cmd1 ... cmdN
```

Here *cmd1...cmdN* are command names. If a command is not an external command that exists on disk, `type` tells you whether it is one of the following:

- A shell built-in command
- A shell keyword or reserved word
- An alias

If the given command is an alias for another command, `type` also gives the command that is actually invoked when you run the alias. For example,

```
$ type true vi case ulimit history
true is /bin/true
vi is /usr/bin/vi
```

```
case is a keyword
ulimit is a shell builtin
history is an exported alias for fc -l
```

If a single command is specified, `type`'s exit code can be used to determine if that command can be found in the search path `$PATH`. If a command can be found, `type` exits with an exit code of `0` indicating success or `1` indicating failure. For example, the following function allows you to determine whether particular commands exist on the system:

```
haveCMD () {
   type "$1" > /dev/null 2>&1
   return $?
}
```

The `sleep` Command

The `sleep` command pauses for a given number of seconds. The basic syntax is

```
sleep n
```

where *n* is the number of seconds to sleep or pause. Some types of UNIX enable other time units to be specified. It is usually recommended that *n* not exceed 65,534.

18

The `sleep` command can be used to give a user time to read an output message before clearing the screen. It can also be used when you want to give a series of beeps:

```
echo -e "A value must be input!\a"
sleep 1
echo -ne "\a"
sleep 1
echo -ne "\a"
```

`\a` causes `echo` to output an audible beep. The `-e` option is required on some UNIX systems for `\a` to sound a beep. The `-n` option suppresses the newline that `echo` normally prints. The `sleep` command is used in the previous example to give a sequence of beeps, spaced one second apart.

`sleep` can be used in a loop to repeat a job periodically:

```
while :
do
   date
   who
   sleep 300
done >> logfile
```

This code enables a list of users logged into the system to be appended to `logfile` every five minutes (300 seconds). If you want to leave this code running all the time, you must clear `logfile` periodically so that it does not eat up all your disk space.

The `find` Command

The `find` command is a very powerful, very flexible way to create a list of files that match given criteria. The basic syntax is

```
find dir options actions
```

where *`dir`* is the name of a directory and *`options`* and *`actions`* are discussed in this section.

Here is a simple `find` example:

```
$ find / -name alpha -print
```

This example looks for all files named `alpha` and displays the full pathname to the screen (standard output). It is a useful command to know about when you are sure you have a file named `alpha` but can't remember what directory it is in or want to know whether it exists in more than one directory. Here is some possible output from that command:

```
/reports/1998/alpha
/reports/1998/region2/alpha
/tmp/alpha
```

If you specify the starting directory to find as `/`, UNIX will search every directory on your system. Because many directories will be inaccessible, this will produce many error messages. You can redirect the error messages to `/dev/null` using output redirection as follows: `find` *`dir options action`* `2> /dev/null`.

You will shortly learn about the elements of the `find` command in detail. Files can be selected not only by name but also by size, last modification date, last access date, and so on. First let's examine this more complex example with a brief explanation of each part of the example, so you get a sense of what options and actions look like:

```
$ find /reports/1998 -name alpha -type f -print -exec lp {} \;
```

Table 18.1 provides a breakdown of these elements.

TABLE 18.1 A Sample `find` Command

Command Element	*Description*
`/reports/1998`	The starting directory. `find` looks only in this directory and its subdirectories for files that match the following criteria.
`-name alpha`	An option that says you are looking only for files whose name is `alpha`—`/reports/1998/region2/alpha`, for example. The `find` command does not check any words in the directory portion of a filename for `alpha`. It checks only the filename itself.

TABLE 18.1 Continued

Command Element	*Description*
`-type f`	An option that says you are looking only for files of type `f`, which means regular or normal files, and not directories, device files, and so on. Any files selected must match both conditions: they must have the name `alpha` and must be regular files.
`-print`	An action that says to display to standard output the pathname for any files that match the criteria given by the options.
`-exec lp {} \;`	An action that says to use the `lp` command to print a hard copy of any files that match the criteria. Multiple actions can be specified.

`find`: Starting Directory

Because most systems contain a huge number of files, `find` can take several minutes or more to complete. For this reason, `find` enables you to specify a starting directory to narrow down the number of files it has to search. Only files in this directory and all its subdirectories are checked. The starting directory can be either an absolute or relative pathname. If you specify an absolute pathname such as `/reports`,


```
$ find /reports -name alpha -print
```

then all the files found are specified as absolute pathnames, as in this sample output:

```
/reports/1998/alpha
/reports/1998/region2/alpha
```

If you specify a relative pathname to `find`,

```
$ cd /reports
$ find ./1998 -name alpha -print
```

all the files are displayed relative to the starting directory. For example,

```
./1998/alpha
./1998/region2/alpha
```

To search the whole system, you can specify `/` as the starting directory. For example, the following `find` command displays all files on the system that have the file `alpha`:

```
find / -name alpha -print
```

To search the entire system and still display the filenames as relative pathnames, you can do the following:

```
$ cd / && find . -name alpha -print
```

In this case, you first `cd` to `/` and then tell `find` to search all the directories, starting with the current directory (`/`) for files with the name `alpha`.

Sample output:

```
./reports/1998/alpha
./reports/1998/region2/alpha
```

This point about relative versus absolute pathnames is important if you are using `find` to generate a list of files to be backed up. It is better to back up using relative pathnames that enable the files to be restored to a temporary directory.

find: -name Option

The `-name` option enables you to specify either an exact or partial filename for `find` to match. You have already seen examples of how to specify a full filename. In order to specify a partial pathname, you need to use the filename substitution meta-characters from Chapter 9. For instance,

```
find / -name '*alpha*' -print
```

This displays all files that contain `alpha` anywhere within the filename. Here is some sample output:

```
/reports/1998/alpha
/reports/1998/alpha2
/reports/1998/old-alpha
/reports/1998/region2/alpha
/tmp/alpha
/usr/fredp/ralphadams
```

All the wildcards covered in Chapter 9 can be used:

```
* ? [characters] [!characters]
```

You must enclose the filename containing these wildcards within single quotes (see Chapter 9); otherwise, your `find` command will not always give you the desired results.

find: -type Option

The `-type` option enables you to specify the type of file to search for, as in this example:

```
find / -type d -print
```

`-type d` indicates directories, so only files that are directories are displayed. In this example, all directories in the whole system are displayed. Notice that no `-name` option has been given, so you display all directories regardless of their names. Table 18.2 lists other types.

TABLE 18.2 Types Available for the `find` Command

Type	*Description*
`f`	Regular or normal file
`d`	Directory
`b`	Block special device file
`c`	Character special device file (raw)
`l`	Symbolic link
`p`	Named pipe

find: `-mtime`, `-atime`, `-ctime`

The `find` command has three options that allow you to find files based on their last modified, accessed, or changed times:

`-mtime`	Finds files last modified more than, exactly, or fewer than *n* days ago.
`-atime`	Finds files last accessed more than, exactly, or fewer than *n* days ago.
`-ctime`	Finds files that were last changed more than, exactly, or fewer than *n* days ago.

A file is considered to have changed when it is first created and also later if the owner, group, or permissions are changed.

Each of these options must be specified with an additional integer argument, *n*, which is measured in days:

+*n*	Finds files last modified, accessed, or changed more than *n* days ago.
n	Finds files last modified, accessed, or changed exactly *n* days ago.
-*n*	Finds files last modified, accessed, or changed fewer than *n* days ago.

Let's look at a few examples that illustrate how these options work. The following `find` command locates files that were last modified fewer than five days ago:

```
find / -mtime -5 -print
```

A command of this sort is useful when you are sure you modified a file recently but can't remember its name or directory. To find files that have not been modified in the last *n* days, you need to look for files that were last modified more than *n* days ago:

```
find / -mtime +90 -print
```

This shows all files that were last modified more than 90 days ago—that is, files that have not been modified in the last 90 days.

`-atime` Is Often Defeated by Nightly Backups

In theory, `find`'s `-atime` option is useful if you are short of disk space and want to find files that have not been accessed in a long time so that you can archive and delete them. However some backup programs, such as `tar`, prevent `-atime` from being useful because all files are accessed nightly during the system backup.

`find`: `-size` Option

The `-size` option enables you to locate files based on the size of a file. It is useful when you want to find the largest files that are consuming disk space. Following `-size`, you must specify an integer number:

+*n*	Finds files that contain more than *n* blocks.
n	Finds files that contain exactly *n* blocks.
-n	Finds files that contain fewer than n blocks.

For example, the following command prints the name of all the files that are larger than 2,000 blocks:

```
find / -size +2000 -print
```

It is a very rare occasion when you need to search for files that contain an exact number of blocks. Usually you look for files that contain more than *n* blocks or fewer than *n* blocks. A common error is to forget the plus or minus sign for these types of `find` options and then wonder why `find` did not locate the expected files.

What Is a Block?

A *block* is the smallest unit of the disk that can be allocated to a file. Although the size of the data in the file might be much less than the size of the block, it still takes up exactly one block on the disk.

The size of a block varies between systems. On BSD and Solaris systems the block size is usually 512 bytes. On Linux it is usually 1024 bytes.

`find`: Combining Options

If you specify more than one option, the file must match all options to be displayed:

```
find / -name alpha -size +50 -mtime -3 -print
```

Here `find` displays files only when all the following are true:

- The name is `alpha`
- The size is greater than 50 blocks
- The file was last modified fewer than three days ago

You can specify a logical "or" condition using `-o`:

```
find / \( -size +50 -o -mtime -3 \) -print
```

Notice the use of the escaped parentheses to group the "either" and "or" options. This finds files that either have size greater than 50 blocks or were last modified fewer than three days ago.

`find`: Negating Options

You can use the `!` sign to select files that do not match the given option:

```
find /dev ! \( -type b -o -type c -o type d \) -print
```

This locates all files in the `/dev` directory and its subdirectories that are not blocked special device files, character special device files, or directories. This is a useful command to locate device names that users have misspelled, which leaves a regular file in `/dev` that can waste a large amount of disk space. The parentheses in this example are escaped so that the shell does not try to interpret them.

18

`find`: `-print` Action

The `-print` action tells `find` to display the pathnames of all files that match the options given before `-print`. If you put the `-print` action before other options in the command line, those options are not used in the selection process:

```
find / -size -20 -print -mtime +30
```

This command prints all files that contain fewer than 20 blocks. The `-mtime` option is ignored because it comes after the `-print` action on the command line.

If no action is specified on the command line, `-print` is performed by default on Linux and BSD systems. On other versions of UNIX, you must include `-print` specifically; otherwise output will not be generated.

`find`: `-exec` Action

The `-exec` action allows you to specify a command to execute on each of the files that match the options given. The syntax for the `-exec` option is

```
-exec cmd \;
```

Here *cmd* is the name of the command you want to execute. The string `\;` must terminate the command, otherwise `find` will display a syntax error similar to the following:

```
find: -exec: no terminating ";"
```

If you need to access the filename in *cmd*, you can use the string `{}`. For example, the following command:

```
$ find / -name alpha -exec chmod a+r {} \;
```

executes `chmod` on every file named `alpha` so that everyone can read the file. Another example,

```
$ find / -name core -exec rm -f {} \;
```

finds all files on the system named `core` and executes the `rm` command to delete them. The `-f` option to `rm` is specified so that `rm` does not ask for confirmation if you don't own the file and don't have write permission to the file. This is a useful command for root to run periodically because, if a process aborts, it might leave a debugging file named `core` in the current directory. After a while, these `core` files, which are not small, can collectively consume an unreasonable amount of disk space. This `find` command restores that disk space by finding and deleting those `core` files.

xargs

`xargs` is a command that accepts a list of words from standard input and provides those words as arguments to a given command:

```
cat filelist | xargs rm
```

You cannot pipe the output of `cat` directly to `rm` because `rm` does not look for filenames on standard input. `xargs` reads the files being passed by `cat` and builds up a command line beginning with `rm` and ending with the filenames. If there are a large number of files, `xargs` runs the `rm` command multiple times, deleting some of the files each time. You can specify how many arguments from standard input to build up on the command line with the `-n` option:

```
cat filelist | xargs -n 20 rm
```

`-n 20` says to put only 20 arguments on each command line, so you delete only 20 files at a time. Here is a different example to give you more insight into how `xargs` works:

```
$ ls
acme
report16
report3
report34
```

```
report527
$ ls | xargs -n 2 echo '==>'
==> acme report16
==> report3 report34
==> report527
```

The first `ls` command shows you that there are only five files in the current directory. (These five can be regular files or directories; it does not matter for this example.) Next you pipe the output of `ls` to `xargs`, which composes and executes this command (the first of several):

```
echo ==> acme report16
```

The command begins with `echo ==>` because these are the arguments given to the `xargs` command. The command then contains two filenames read from standard input because the `-n 2` tells `xargs` to add only two words from standard input to each `echo` command. The ==> was added as the first `echo` argument so you can visually find the output from each separate `echo` command. You can see that `xargs` called `echo` three times to process all the files specified on the standard input.

In some cases the file list produced by filename expansion can be too long for the shell to process. For example, consider the following error message:


```
$ rm abc*
rm: arg list too long
```

The current directory contained too many filenames starting with `abc`, so an error message was printed, and none of the files were deleted. You can use `xargs` to solve this problem as follows:

```
ls | grep '^abc' | xargs -n 20 rm
```

Here you use `grep` (covered in Chapter 15, "Text Filters") and regular expressions (covered in Chapter 16, "Filtering Text with Regular Expressions") to filter the output of `ls` passing only filenames that begin with `abc`. You then use `xargs` to invoke `rm` to operate on those files and delete them. This will work no matter how many files there are in the current directory that start with the string `abc`.

If you have thousands of files to process using `find`, `xargs` is more efficient than `-exec`. Because `xargs` invokes the command only as required, it uses fewer system resources and executes faster. For example, the command

```
$ find / -name core -print | xargs rm -f
```

is much more efficient than

```
$ find / -name core -exec rm -f {} \;
```

The expr Command

The `expr` command can be used to perform simple integer arithmetic. The general syntax of an `expr` command is

```
expr int1 op int2
```

Here, *int1* and *int2* are integers and *op* is one of the operators given in Table 18.3. The spaces separating *op* from *int1* and *int2* are required.

TABLE 18.3 expr Operands

Operand	*Description*
+	Addition
-	Subtraction
*	Multiplication
/	Integer division (any fraction in the result is dropped)
%	Remainder from a division operation (also called the modulus function)

Let's look at a few examples that illustrate the use of `expr`. The first example illustrates multiplication:

```
$ expr 3 \* 5
15
```

Notice that the `*` sign must be escaped in order to prevent the shell from viewing it as a filename expansion meta-character. The second example illustrates integer division:

```
$ expr 8 / 3
2
```

Notice that the fractional result is ignored and only the integer part is returned. The third example illustrates the remainder or modulus function:

```
$ expr 19 % 7
5
```

The remainder or modulus is what remains after a division operation. The modulus function is often called *mod* for short. In this example, 7 goes into 19 two times with a remainder of 5. You can say that 19 mod 7 equals 5.

Frequently `expr` is used within backquotes in shell programming to increment a variable:

```
CNT=`expr $CNT + 1`
```

In this example, `expr` adds 1 to the current value in variable `CNT`. Command substitution allows you to assign the new value back to the variable `CNT`.

expr and Regular Expressions

The expr command—in ksh, zsh and newer versions of bash (2.x and later)—can also return the number of characters matched by a regular expression. The syntax for this is

```
expr str : regex
```

Here, *str* is the string and *regex* is a regular expression of the characters to count. For example:

```
$ ABC=1234abc
$ expr $ABC : '.*'
7
```

Here, .* is a regular expression pattern indicating all characters, so all characters of variable $ABC are counted. In this case, expr shows that it contains seven characters. In the following example

```
$ expr $ABC : '[0-9]*'
4
```

the regular expression [0-9]* matches any group of digits. In this example, expr counts the number of digits that occur at the start of the string.

If part of the regular expression, *regex*, is grouped in escaped parentheses, expr returns the portion of the pattern indicated by the parentheses:

```
$ expr abcdef : '..\(..\)..'
cd
$
```

Each period is a regular expression wildcard that represents one character of the given string. The middle two periods are enclosed in escaped parentheses, so those two characters, cd, are output. This example also illustrates that the string following expr can be a literal string of characters, but it is more common in scripts for the string to be generated by variable or command substitution.

The bc Command

The bc command is an arithmetic utility not limited to integers:

```
$ bc
scale=4
8/3
2.6666
2.5 * 4.1/6.9
1.4855
quit
$
```

In this example, you invoke bc and set scale to 4, meaning that you want it to calculate any fraction to four decimal places. You ask it to calculate 8/3, which gives 2.6666 and then a more complex calculation. Note that spaces are optional. Finally you enter **quit** to return to the shell prompt. bc can handle addition (+), subtraction (-), multiplication (*), division (/), remainder or modulo (%), and integer exponentiation (^). It can accurately compute numbers of any size

```
9238472938742937 * 29384729347298472
271470026887302339647844620892264
```

and can be used in shell variable assignment to assign calculated values to variables:

```
AVERAGE=`echo "scale=4; $PRICE/$UNITS" | bc`
```

The echo command is used here to print directives that are piped to bc. The first directive sets the scale to 4; the second directive is a division operation. These directives are piped to bc, which does the calculations and returns the result. The backquotes allow the result from bc to be stored in the variable AVERAGE.

You can also convert between different number bases using bc:

```
$ bc
obase=16
ibase=8
400
100
77
3f
10*3
18
quit
$
```

obase=16 sets the output base to hexadecimal; ibase=8 sets the input base to octal. It is important to set the output base first. First you enter **400**. It shows an octal 400 is a hex 100. Next you enter **77**. It shows an octal 77 is a hex 3f. Then you multiply 10 and 3, which equals 24 because 10 octal is 8 in decimal and 8*3 is 24. However, because the output base is hex, bc converts 24 in decimal to hex, which gives 18 as the reported result.

Summary

In this chapter, you learned about several miscellaneous tools:

- eval
- :
- type

- `sleep`
- `find`
- `xargs`
- `expr`
- `bc`
- `remsh/rsh/rcmd/remote`

A large part of this chapter discussed the basics of the `find` command. Peruse the man page on `find`, and you can see other useful `find` options for your scripts that were not covered here.

Questions

1. You are about to run a custom command called `process2`, but you would first like to determine where that command resides. Give a UNIX command to do this.
2. How can you determine all directories under `/data` that contain a file called `process2`, allowing any possible prefix or suffix to also be displayed (for example, you want to find names such as `process2-doc`)?
3. How can you increase the numeric value in variable `PRICE` to be 3.5 times its current amount? Allow two digits to the right of the decimal point.

Terms

Built-in Command A command whose code is part of the shell as opposed to a utility that exists in a separate disk file and which must be read into memory before it is executed.

Modulus See *remainder*.

no-op A command that does nothing and thus can be used as a dummy command or placeholder where syntax requires a command.

Remainder The remainder of a division operation, which is the amount that is left over when the amounts are not evenly divisible.

PART III

Advanced Topics

Hour

HOUR 19

Signals

Signals are software interrupts sent to a program indicating that an important event has occurred. The events can vary from user requests to illegal memory access errors. Some signals, such as the interrupt signal, indicate that a user has asked the program to do something that is not in the usual flow of control.

Because signals can arrive at any time during the execution of a script, they add an extra level of complexity to shell scripts. Scripts must account for this and include extra code that can determine the appropriate response to a signal, regardless of what the script was doing when the signal was received.

This chapter looks at the following signal-related topics:

- The different types of signals encountered in shell programming
- How to deliver signals using the `kill` command
- Handling signals
- How to use signals within your script

How Are Signals Represented?

In UNIX, every type of event that can occur is represented by a separate signal. Every signal is a small positive integer. The signals most commonly encountered in shell script programming are given in Table 19.1. The signals are available on all versions of UNIX.

TABLE 19.1 Important Signals for Shell Scripts

Name	*Value*	*Description*
SIGHUP	1	Hangup detected on controlling terminal or death of controlling process
SIGINT	2	Interrupt from keyboard
SIGQUIT	3	Quit from keyboard
SIGKILL	9	Kill signal
SIGALRM	14	Alarm Clock signal (used for timers)
SIGTERM	15	Termination signal

In addition to the signals listed in Table 19.1, you might see a reference to signal 0. This signal is more of a shell convention than a real signal. When a shell script exits either by using the `exit` command or by executing the last command in the script, the shell sends itself a signal 0 to indicate that the script is complete and should terminate.

Getting a List of Signals

All the signals understood by your system are listed in the C language header file `/usr/include/sys/signal.h`. Some vendors provide a `man` page for this file, which you can view as follows:

```
$ man signal
```

Another way to obtain a list of signals supported by your system is to use the `-l` option of the `kill` command. On a Solaris system, the output is

```
$ kill -l
1) SIGHUP        2) SIGINT        3) SIGQUIT       4) SIGILL
 5) SIGTRAP       6) SIGABRT       7) SIGEMT        8) SIGFPE
 9) SIGKILL      10) SIGBUS       11) SIGSEGV      12) SIGSYS
13) SIGPIPE      14) SIGALRM      15) SIGTERM      16) SIGUSR1
17) SIGUSR2      18) SIGCHLD      19) SIGPWR       20) SIGWINCH
21) SIGURG       22) SIGIO        23) SIGSTOP      24) SIGTSTP
25) SIGCONT      26) SIGTTIN      27) SIGTTOU      28) SIGVTALRM
29) SIGPROF      30) SIGXCPU      31) SIGXFSZ      32) SIGWAITING
33) SIGLWP       34) SIGFREEZE    35) SIGTHAW      36) SIGCANCEL
37) SIGLOST
```

The actual set of signals depends on your version of UNIX.

Default Actions

Every signal, including those listed in Table 19.1, has a default action associated with it. A *default action* is the action that the system takes on behalf of the program in the absence of a signal handler. A *signal handler* is a function provided by a program that defines the actions to take when a signal is received. Signal handlers are covered later in this chapter.

Some common default actions are

- Terminate the process.
- Ignore the signal.
- Dump core. This creates a file called `core` containing the memory image of the process when it received the signal.
- Stop the process.
- Continue a stopped process.

The signals that are of interest to us all have the same default action: Terminate the process.

Delivering Signals

There are several methods of delivering signals to programs. The most common method is for a user to press Ctrl+C while a program is executing, causing a `SIGINT` to be sent to the program. Upon receipt of `SIGINT`, the default behavior of a program is to terminate.

19

Another method for delivering signals is the `kill` command:

```
kill -signal pid
```

Here *`signal`* is either the number or name of the signal to deliver, and *`pid`* is the PID that the signal should be delivered to. Recall from Chapter 7, "Processes," that a PID (Process ID) is a number assigned to a program by the kernel while it is executing.

SIGTERM

In previous chapters, we looked at using `kill` without specifying a *`signal`*. When *`signal`* is omitted, `kill` sends a `SIGTERM` (terminate) to the process specified by *`pid`*. Thus both of the following commands are equivalent:

```
kill pid
kill -s SIGTERM pid
```

SIGHUP

The following command

```
$ kill -s SIGHUP 1001
```

sends the HUP (hang-up) signal to the program that is running with PID 1001. You can also use the numeric value of the signal as follows:

```
$ kill -1 1001
```

This command also sends the hang-up signal to the program that is running with PID 1001. Although the default action for this signal is to terminate the process, many UNIX programs use this signal as an indication that they should reinitialize themselves. For this reason, you should use a different signal if you are trying to terminate or kill a process.

SIGQUIT and SIGINT

In some cases, SIGTERM will not be sufficient to terminate a process. In such cases, you can try to send the process either a SIGQUIT (quit) or a SIGINT (interrupt):

```
$ kill -s SIGQUIT 1001
```

or

```
$ kill -s SIGINT 1001
```

One of these signals should terminate a process, either by asking it to quit (the QUIT signal) or by asking it to interrupt its processing (the INT signal).

SIGKILL

To terminate a truly pernicious program that refuses to die, you can resort to using SIGKILL. This signal is usually referred to by its integer value, 9. SIGKILL has the special property that it cannot be caught; any process receiving it terminates immediately.

The following command sends a SIGKILL to the program running with PID 1001:

```
$ kill -9 1001
```

The downside to using SIGKILL is that the process receiving it is never given a chance to properly clean up and therefore might leave data files it was using in a corrupted state. For this reason, you should only use this signal when all other signals fail to terminate a process.

Dealing with Signals

A program can deal with a signal in three ways:

- Do nothing and let the default action occur. This is the simplest method for a program to deal with a signal because it requires no extra code.
- Ignore the signal and continue executing. This method is not the same as doing nothing because ignoring a signal requires the program to have some code that explicitly ignores the signal.

- Catch the signal and perform some signal-specific commands. This method requires the program to define a function that is executed when a signal is received. This is the most complex and powerful method of dealing with a signal.

The first method is the default behavior for all shell scripts. All the scripts that you have looked at thus far handle signals using this method. This section illustrates scripts that use the second and third methods.

The `trap` Command

The `trap` command sets and unsets the action taken when a signal is received. Its syntax is

```
trap name sigs
```

Here `name` is either a list of commands or the name of a shell function to execute and `sigs` is a list of signals. When a signal listed in *`sigs`* is received by the script, the commands specified by *`name`* are executed. If `name` is omitted, `trap` resets the action for the given *`sigs`* to the default action.

Some common uses for `trap` are

- Clean up temporary files
- Always ignore signals
- Ignore signals only during critical operations

We will look at a fourth use, setting up a timer, later in this chapter.

Cleaning Up Temporary Files

If a script creates temporary files, it is common practice to remove these files before the script exits. Most scripts perform this type of cleanup correctly during normal execution, but few scripts perform the appropriate cleanup actions when signals occur. Consider the following script:

```
#!/bin/sh
TMPF=".arch"
uname -m > "$TMPF"
read ARCH < "$TMPF"
rm -f "$TMPF"
echo $ARCH
exit 0
```

This script creates a temporary file, `.arch`, which is removed before exiting. Under normal circumstances, the temporary file will not be present after the script exits. However, if a signal is received, the temporary file might not be deleted. In order to solve this problem, we can use `trap` as follows:

```
trap "rm -f $TMPF; exit 2" 1 2 3 15
```

When `SIGHUP`, `SIGINT`, `SIGQUIT`, or `SIGTERM` signal is received, the temporary file is removed and `exit` is called with a return code of `2`, indicating that the script exited under abnormal circumstances. Usually when a script exits normally, its exit code is `0`. If anything abnormal happens, the exit code should be a nonzero.

Sometimes more complicated cleanup is required. In such cases, a shell function, or signal handler, should be used. For example, we can modify the `uu` script (described in Chapter 13, "Parameters") signal safe, we could add something similar to the following:

```
CleanUp() {
    if [ -f "$OUTFILE" ] ; then
        printf "Cleaning Up... ";
        rm -f "$OUTFILE" 2> /dev/null ;
        echo "Done." ;
    fi
}

trap CleanUp 1 2 3 15
```

The function `CleanUp` will be invoked whenever the script receives a `SIGHUP`, `SIGINT`, `SIGQUIT`, or `SIGTERM` signal. This function removes the output file of the script, if that file exists. By cleaning up when a signal is received, partially encoded files are not left around to confuse users.

Multiple Signal Handlers

In the previous example, a single signal handler was used for all the signals. This is not a strict requirement and frequently different signals have different handlers. For example, the following `trap` commands are completely valid:

```
trap CleanUp 2 15
trap Init 1
```

Here the script calls a cleanup routine when a `SIGINT` or `SIGTERM` is received, and it calls its initialization routine when a `SIGHUP` is received. Declarations such as these are common in scripts that run as daemons.

The following script, which can be used to keep a process "alive," behaves differently depending on the signal that it receives:

```
#!/bin/sh

PROG="$1"
if [ "$PROG" = "" ] ; then
```

```
    echo "Usage: $0 cmd."
    exit 1
fi

Init() {
    if [ "$!" != "" -a "$!" != "0" ] ; then
        if kill -0 "$!" > /dev/null 2>&1 ; then
            kill "$!" > /dev/null 2>&1 || return
        fi
    fi
    $PROG &
}

CleanUp() {
     if [ "$!" != "" -a "$!" != "0" ] ; then
        kill -9 "$!" > /dev/null 2>&1
     fi
     exit 2
}

trap CleanUp 2 3 15
trap Init 1

while : ;
do
   if [ "$!" != "" -a "$!" != "0" ] ; then
        wait "$!"
   fi
   $PROG &
done

exit 0
```


This script launches a program, specified as the first argument, in the background and waits for that program to terminate. If the program terminates, it is launched again. The script exits when it receives a `SIGINT`, `SIGQUIT` or `SIGTERM`. If the script receives a `SIGHUP`, it attempts to restart the program.

Ignoring Signals

In some instances, there is no easy way to clean up if a signal is received. In such cases, it is better to ignore signals than to deal with them. There are two methods of ignoring signals:

```
trap '' sigs
trap : sigs
```

Here, `sigs` is the list of signals to ignore. The first form passes a null (`''`) argument to `trap`, which interprets this as ignore. The second form specifies the command to execute as :, which is the no-op command as you might recall. Because both forms produce the same result, feel free to use either one.

As an example, we can update the uu script from Chapter 12 to ignore all signals by adding the following line at the beginning of the script:

```
trap '' 1 2 3 15
```

Ignoring Signals During Critical Operations

If you specify a trap command such as

```
trap '' 1 2 3 15
```

at the beginning of your script, the script will ignore all signals until it completes. From a programmer's perspective, this seems like a good idea, but from the user's perspective, it is not. The ideal method is to ignore signals during only the most critical sections of the script. This allows users to terminate the script while ensuring that critical operations are performed without interruption by signals.

Let's say we have a shell script with a shell function called `DoImportantStuff()` that should not be interrupted by a signal. In order to ensure that this function isn't interrupted, you can install the signal handler before the function is called and reset it after the call finishes:

```
trap '' 1 2 3 15
DoImportantStuff
trap 1 2 3 15
```

The second call to `trap` has only signal arguments. This causes `trap` to reset the handler for each of the signals to the default handler.

Setting Up a Timer

In many scripts, there are critical sections where commands that require a large amount of time to complete are executed. On rare occasions, these commands might not finish processing. In order to deal with this situation, you need to set up a timer within the script. When the timer expires, the script should terminate and inform the user about the problem. In this section, you will look at a simple script that demonstrates the major aspects of setting up a timer using `SIGALARM` in conjunction with a signal handler.

The main body of our script performs the following actions:

1. Sets a handler for `SIGALARM`.
2. Sets the timer.
3. Executes the program.
4. Waits for the program to finish executing.
5. Unsets the timer.

If the timer expires before the program finishes executing, the handler for SIGALARM should terminate the program.

The main body resembles the following:

```
# main()

trap AlarmHandler 14

SetTimer 15

$PROG &
CHPROCIDS="$CHPROCIDS $!"
wait $!

UnsetTimer

echo "All Done."
exit 0
```

The only thing in the main body that was not mentioned previously is the CHPROCIDS variable. This variable maintains a list of the PIDs of the processes started by the script so that the signal handler for SIGALARM can terminate these processes.

AlarmHandler

Now let's look at the signal handler for SIGALARM, AlarmHandler:

```
AlarmHandler() {
    echo "Got SIGALARM, cmd took too long."
    KillSubProcs
    exit 14
}
```


This is a simple function that prints a message to the screen, calls the function KillSubProcs, and exits with an exit code of 14. This exit code is used to indicate that the alarm was triggered.

The KillSubProcs function kills all the child processes of the script, which are stored in the variable CHPROCIDS:

```
KillSubProcs() {
    kill ${CHPROCIDS:-$!}
    if [ $? -eq 0 ] ; then
        echo "Sub-processes killed." ;
    fi
}
```

This is a simple function that prints a message to the screen, calls the function KillSubProcs, and exits with an exit code of 14. This exit code is used to indicate that the alarm was triggered.

The `KillSubProcs` function kills all the child processes of the script, which are stored in the variable `CHPROCIDS`:

```
KillSubProcs() {
    kill ${CHPROCIDS:-$!}
    if [ $? -eq 0 ] ; then
        echo "Sub-processes killed." ;
    fi
}
```

SetTimer

Once the signal handler for SIGALARM is in place, we need a function that sets up the timer. The function we are using is `SetTimer`:

```
SetTimer() {
    DEF_TOUT=${1:-10};
    if [ $DEF_TOUT -ne 0 ] ; then
        sleep $DEF_TOUT && kill -s 14 $$ &
        CHPROCIDS="$CHPROCIDS $!"
        TIMERPROC=$!
    fi
}
```

This function takes a single argument that indicates the number of seconds the timer should be set. The default is 10 seconds.

The timer itself is fairly trivial; it is just the command

```
sleep $DEF_TOUT && kill -s 14 $$
```

executing in the background. This command uses `sleep` to wait for some period of time (stored in `$DEF_TOUT`); after which, it uses `kill` to send the script `SIGALARM` (recall that the PID of the script is stored in $$).

Because the timer runs in the background, we need to update the list of child processes, `$CHPROCIDS`, with its PID. We also save the PID of the timer in `$TIMERPROC` so that we can use it later when we need to unset the timer.

UnsetTimer

Finally, we need a function to unset the timer started by `SetTimer`. The `UnsetTimer` function does this by using `kill` to terminate the timer (`SetTimer` saved the PID of the timer in `$TIMERPROC`):

```
UnsetTimer() {
    kill $TIMERPROC
}
```

The Complete Timer Script

The complete timer script follows:

```
#! /bin/sh

AlarmHandler() {
    echo "Got SIGALARM, cmd took too long."
    KillSubProcs
    exit 14
}

KillSubProcs() {
    kill ${CHPROCIDS:-$!}
    if [ $? -eq 0 ] ; then
        echo "Sub-processes killed." ;
    fi
}

SetTimer() {
    DEF_TOUT=${1:-10};
    if [ $DEF_TOUT -ne 0 ] ; then
        sleep $DEF_TOUT && kill -s 14 $$ &
        CHPROCIDS="$CHPROCIDS $!"
        TIMERPROC=$!
    fi
}

UnsetTimer() {
    kill $TIMERPROC
}

# main()

trap AlarmHandler 14

SetTimer 15
$PROG &
CHPROCIDS="$CHPROCIDS $!"
wait $!
UnsetTimer
echo "All Done."
exit 0
```

Summary

This chapter covered the concept of signals. Signals inform a program that an important event has occurred.

First we examined the most common signals encountered in shell programming. This was followed by a discussion of the methods for obtaining a list of the signals supported on your system. This section also covered the concept of delivering signals and the default actions associated with a signal.

The second section demonstrated two methods of signal handling. The first method is to catch signals and handle them using a signal handler. The second method is to ignore signals. Finally, we explored the use of signals to set up a timer.

Questions

1. The following is the main body of the "live" script presented earlier in this chapter. Change the script such that `SIGQUIT` causes it to exit after the `wait` command returns.

```
# main()

trap CleanUp 2 3 15
trap Init 1

PROG=$1
Init

while : ;
do
    wait $!
    $PROG &
done
```

2. Add a signal handler to the timer script to handle `SIGINT`.

Terms

Signal A signal is a software interrupt sent to a program to indicate that an important event has occurred.

Default Action The default action is the action that the system takes on behalf of the program in the absence of a signal handler.

Signal Handler A signal handler is a function provided by a program that defines the actions to take when a signal is received.

HOUR 20

Debugging

Most of the scripts you have looked at have been quite short, thus the issue of debugging has boiled down to examining the output to ensure it is correct. For larger shell scripts, especially scripts used to change system configurations, trying to deduce the source of a problem based on just output is insufficient. By the time you get the output it might be too late—the script could have made incorrect and possibly destructive modifications.

Fortunately, the shell provides several built-in commands for enabling different modes of debugging support. The built-in debugging support can be very helpful when you need to add features to a large script that someone else developed; it can help you ensure that your changes don't affect the rest of the script.

This chapter covers several techniques for debugging shell scripts, with a concentration on the following:

- Syntax checking
- Shell tracing

Enabling Debugging

By now, you are quite familiar with the basic syntax for executing a shell script:

```
$ script arg1 arg2 ... argN
```

Here *script* is the name of the script and *arg1* through *argN* are the arguments to the script.

An alternative method to execute a shell script is

```
$ /bin/sh opt script arg1 arg2 ... argN
```

This invokes the shell, in this case `/bin/sh`, with the debugging option specified by *opt* and instructs the shell to execute *script*. Table 20.1 lists the various debugging options.

A second way to enable debugging is to change the first line of *script*. Usually, the first line of a script is

```
#!/bin/sh
```

UNIX uses this line to determine the shell you can use to execute a script. This indicates that the shell `/bin/sh` should be used to execute the script. You can modify this line, as follows, in order to specify a debugging option:

```
#!/bin/sh opt
```

These methods for enabling debugging modes take effect when a script is invoked, so they are sometimes referred to as *invocation activated* debugging modes.

TABLE 20.1 Debugging Options for Shell Scripts

Name	*Option*	*Description*
No Exec	`-n`	Reads all commands, but does not execute them.
Verbose	`-v`	Displays all lines as they are read.
Execution Trace	`-x`	Displays commands and their arguments as they are executed. Often referred to as *shell tracing.*

Debugging and $-

When one of the debugging options is activated, a letter corresponding to that option is added to the variable `$-`. For example, if the `-v` (verbose) option is used, the letter `v` is added to `$-`. Similarly when the `-x` is used, the letter `x` is added to `$-`.

You can detect if one of these options is active by using a case statement similar to the following:

```
case $- in
   *v*) : # verbose mode
```

```
        ;;
    *x*) : # shell tracing mode
        ;;
esacdebugging modes
```

Using the set command

In the invocation activated debugging modes, the debugging mode takes effect at the start of the script and remains in effect until the script exits. Most of the time you need to debug just one function or a small section of your script. In these cases, enabling debugging for the entire script is overkill.

As you will see later in this chapter, the debugging output is quite extensive, and it is often hard to sort out the real errors from the noise. You can address this problem by using the `set` command to enable the debugging modes just in the parts of the script where you need debugging information.

Enabling Debugging Using set

The basic syntax of the `set` command is

```
set opt
```

Here *`opt`* is one of the options listed in Table 20.1.

The `set` command can be used anywhere in a shell script, and many scripts use it to change the debugging flags as part of the normal execution of the script. Because these debugging modes are activated only when the shell script programmer uses the `set` command, they are sometimes referred to as *programmer activated* modes.

Consider the following excerpt from a shell script (the line numbers are provided for your reference):

```
1  #!/bin/sh
2  set -x
3  if [ -z "$1" ] ; then
4      echo "ERROR: Insufficient Args."
5      exit 1
6  fi
```


This script enables shell tracing (the `-x` option) on line 2:

```
set -x
```

Because this command occurs before the `if` statement (lines 3 through 6), shell tracing will be active while the `if` statement executes. Unless explicitly disabled later in the script, shell tracing will remain in effect until the script exits. You will look at the effect of shell tracing on the output of a script in the "Shell Tracing" section of this chapter.

Disabling Debugging Using `set`

You can use the `set` command to disable a debugging mode as follows:

```
set +opt
```

Here *opt* is a letter corresponding to one of the options given in Table 20.1. For example, the following command disables shell tracing:

```
$ set +x
```

To deactivate any and all the debugging modes that have been enabled, you can use the command:

```
$ set -
```

Enabling Debugging for a Single Function

One of the most common uses of the `set` command is to enable a particular debugging mode before a function executes and then disable debugging when the function finishes.

For example, say you have a problematic function named `BuggyFunction()` and you want to enable shell tracing only while that function executes. You could use the following command:

```
set -x ; BuggyFunction; set +x ;
```

Here the debugging mode is enabled just before the function is called and is disabled after the function completes. This method is favored over explicitly using the `set` command inside a function to enable debugging because it enables the implementation of the function to remain unchanged.

Using Syntax Checking

When dealing with any shell script, it is a good idea to check the syntax of the script before trying to execute it. This will help you find and fix most problems.

To enable syntax checking, use the `-n` option as follows:

```
/bin/sh -n script arg1 arg2 ... argN
```

Here *script* is the name of a script and *arg1* through *argN* are the arguments for that script. If there are syntax errors in *script*, the shell generates an error message that indicates the source of the error.

Check the syntax of the following script (the line numbers are included for your reference) and see if you can spot the error:

```
1  #!/bin/sh
2
3  YN=y
4  if [ $YN = "yes" ]
5       echo "yes"
6  fi
```

If this script is stored in the file `buggy1.sh`, you can check its syntax as follows:

```
$ /bin/sh -n ./buggy1.sh
```

The output looks like the following:

```
./buggy1.sh: syntax error at line 7: 'fi' unexpected
```

This tells you that when the shell tried to read line 7, it found that the `fi` statement on line 6 was unexpected. By now you have probably figured out that the reason the shell was trying to read line 7 is that the `if` statement on line 4 is not properly terminated with a `then` statement:

```
if [ $YN = "y" ]
```

This line should read as:

```
if [ $YN = "y" ] ; then
```

By making this change, you will find that the command

```
$ /bin/sh -n buggy1.sh
```

produces no output, indicating that there are no syntax errors in the script.

Why Syntax Checking Is Important

After looking at the shell script in the previous example, you might be wondering why you couldn't just execute the shell script to determine the problem. After all, the output of the command:

```
$ /bin/sh ./buggy1.sh
buggy1.sh: syntax error at line 7: 'fi' unexpected
```

is identical to the output of the command:

```
$ /bin/sh -n ./buggy1.sh
```

In this particular instance, it does not make a difference, but this is not always the case. As an example, consider the following script (the line numbers are included for your reference):

```
1  #!/bin/sh
2
3  Failed() {
4      if [ $1 -ne 0 ] ; then
5          echo "Failed. Exiting." ; exit 1 ;
6      fi
7      echo "Done."
8  }
9
10 echo "Deleting old backups, please wait... \c"
11 rm -r backup > /dev/null 2>&1
12 Failed $?
13
14 echo "Make backup (y/n)? \c"
15 read RESPONSE
16 case $RESPONSE in
17     [yY]|[Yy][Ee][Ss]|*)
18         echo "Making backup, please wait... \c"
19         cp -r docs backup
20         Failed
21     [nN]|[Nn][Oo])
22         echo "Backup Skipped." ;;
23 esac
```

There are at least three errors in this script. See if you can find them.

You should not try to run this script until you have found and fixed the bugs it contains.

If this script is in a file called buggy2.sh, executing it produces the following output:

```
Deleting old backups, please wait... Done.
Make backup (y/n)?
```

Entering y at the prompt produces the following error:

```
./buggy3.sh: syntax error at line 21: ')' unexpected
```

Due to a bug in the script, you can't make a backup, and you have already lost your previous backup. As you can imagine, this is a very bad situation.

The reason the script doesn't detect the error earlier is due to the manner in which the shell reads and executes scripts; it reads and executes each line of a shell script individually, just like it does on the command line. In this case the shell reads and executes lines until it encounters a problem.

When the `-n` option is specified, the shell does not execute the script. It just checks the syntax of each line. In the previous example using this option would have avoided the situation encountered by running the script.

Using Verbose Mode

Now that you know why syntax checking should be employed, let's track down the source of the problem by looking at line 21 of `buggy2.sh`:

```
21        [nN]|[Nn][Oo])
```

does not provide sufficient context to determine the source of the problem. Sometimes knowing where a syntax error occurs is not enough—you have to know the context in which the error occurs. In order to determine the context of the problem, you can use the `-v` (*v* as in *verbose*) debugging mode. When this option is specified, the shell prints each line of a script as it is read.

If the `-v` option is specified by itself, the shell executes every line in the script. Because you want to just check the syntax, you need to combine the `-n` and `-v` options as follows:

```
$ /bin/sh -nv script arg1 arg2 ... argN
```

If you execute `buggy2.sh` with these debugging options

```
$ /bin/sh -nv ./buggy2.sh
```

the output looks like the following (the line numbers are provided for your reference):

```
 1  #!/bin/sh
 2
 3  Failed() {
 4      if [ $1 -ne 0 ] ; then
 5          echo "Failed. Exiting." ; exit 1 ;
 6      fi
 7      echo "Done."
 8  }
 9
10  echo "Deleting old backups, please wait... \c"
11  rm -r backup > /dev/null 2>&1
12  Failed $?
13
14  echo "Make backup (y/n)? \c"
15  read RESPONSE
16  case $RESPONSE in
17      [yY]|[Yy][Ee][Ss])
18          echo "Making backup, please wait... \c"
```

```
    19            cp -r docs backup
    20            Failed
    21        [nN]|[Nn][Oo])
➥./buggy2.sh: syntax error at line 21: ')' unexpected
```

Based on this output, the problem is apparent: Line 20 does not terminate the first pattern of the `case` statement with `;;`. You can make either of the following changes to fix the script:

```
Failed ;;
```

or

```
Failed
;;
```

After making either of these change, you find that the command

```
$ /bin/sh -n buggy2.sh
```

does not produce an error message. As you will see in the next section, this does not necessarily mean that the script is bug free.

Shell Tracing

There are many instances when syntax checking will give your script a clean bill of health, even though bugs are still lurking within it. Running syntax checking on a shell script is similar to running a spelling checker on a text document—it might find most of the misspellings, but it can't fix problems like *read* spelled *red*. In order to find and fix these types of errors in a text document, you need to proofread it. Shell tracing is proofreading your shell script.

In shell tracing mode each command is printed in the exact form that it is executed. For this reason, shell tracing mode is often referred to as *execution tracing mode*. Shell tracing is enabled by the `-x` option (*x* as in *execution*). The following command enables tracing for an entire script:

```
$ /bin/sh -x script arg1 arg2 ... argN
```

Tracing can also be enabled using the `set` command:

```
set -x
```

To get an idea of what the output of shell tracing looks like, try the following command:

```
$ set -x ; ls *.sh ; set +x
```

The output will be similar to the following:

```
+ ls buggy.sh buggy1.sh buggy2.sh buggy3.sh buggy4.sh
buggy.sh   buggy1.sh  buggy2.sh  buggy3.sh  buggy4.sh
+ set +x
```

In the output, the lines preceded by the plus (+) character are the commands that the shell executes. The other lines are output from those commands. As you can see from the output, the shell prints the exact `ls` command it executes. This is extremely useful in debugging because it enables you to determine whether all the substitutions were performed correctly.

Finding Syntax Bugs Using Shell Tracing

In the preceding example, you used the script `buggy2.sh`. One of the problems with this script is that it deleted the old backup before asking whether you wanted to make a new backup. To solve this problem, the script is rewritten as follows:

```
#!/bin/sh

Failed() {
    if [ $1 -ne 0 ] ; then
        echo "Failed. Exiting." ; exit 1 ;
    fi
    echo "Done."
}

YesNo() {
    echo "$1 (y/n)? \c"
    read RESPONSE
    case $RESPONSE in
        [yY]|[Yy][Ee][Ss]) RESPONSE=y ;;
        [nN]|[Nn][Oo]) RESPONSE=n ;;
    esac
}

YesNo "Make backup"
if [ $RESPONSE = "y" ] ; then

    echo "Deleting old backups, please wait... \c"
    rm -fr backup > /dev/null 2>&1
    Failed $?

    echo "Making new backups, please wait... \c"
    cp -r docs backup
    Failed

fi
```


There are at least three syntax bugs in this script and at least one logical oversight. See if you can find them.

Assuming that the script is called `buggy3.sh`, first check its syntax as follows:

```
$ /bin/sh -n ./buggy3.sh
```

Because there is no output, you can execute it:

```
$ /bin/sh ./buggy3.sh
```

The script first prompts you as follows:

```
Make backup (y/n)?
```

Answering y to this prompt produces output similar to the following:

```
Deleting old backups, please wait... Done.
Making new backups, please wait... buggy3.sh: test: argument expected
```

Now you know there is a problem with the script, but the error message doesn't tell you where it is, so you need to track it down manually. From the output you know that the old backup was deleted successfully; therefore, the error is probably in the following part of the script:

```
    echo "Making new backups, please wait... \c"
    cp -r docs backup
    Failed
```

Let's just enable shell tracing for this section:

```
    set -x
    echo "Making new backups, please wait... \c"
    cp -r docs backup
    Failed
    set +x
```

The output changes as follows (assuming you answer y to the question):

```
Make backup (y/n)? y
Deleting old backups, please wait... Done.
+ echo Making new backups, please wait... \c
Making new backups, please wait... + cp -r docs backup
+ Failed
+ [ -ne 0 ]
buggy3.sh: test: argument expected
```

From this output you can see that the problem occurred in the following statement:

```
[ -ne 0 ]
```

From Chapter 11, "Flow Control," you know that the form of a numerical test command is

```
[ num1 operator num2 ]
```

Here it looks like *num1* does not exist. Also from the trace you can tell that this error occurred after executing the `Failed` function:

```
Failed() {
    if [ $1 -ne 0 ] ; then
        echo "Failed. Exiting." ; exit 1 ;
```

```
    fi
    echo "Done."
}
```

There is only one numerical test in this function; the test that compares `$1`, the first argument to the function, to see whether it is equal to `0`. The problem should be obvious now. When `Failed` was invoked, you forgot to give it an argument:

```
    echo "Making new backups, please wait... \c"
    cp -r docs backup
    Failed
```

Therefore, the numeric test failed. There are two possible fixes for this bug. The first is to fix the code that calls the function:

```
    echo "Making new backups, please wait... \c"
    cp -r docs backup
    Failed $?
```

The second is to fix the function itself by quoting the first argument, `"$1"`:

```
Failed() {
    if [ "$1" -ne 0 ] ; then
        echo "Failed. Exiting." ; exit 1 ;
    fi
    echo "Done."
}
```

By quoting the first argument, `"$1"`, the shell uses the null or empty string when the function is called without any arguments. In this case the numeric test will not fail because both *num1* and *num2* have a value.

The best idea is to perform both fixes. After these fixes are applied, the shell tracing output is similar to the following:

```
Make backup (y/n)? y
Deleting old backups, please wait... Done.
+ echo Making new backups, please wait... \c
Making new backups, please wait... + cp -r docs backup
+ Failed
+ [  -ne 0 ]
+ echo Done.
Done.
+ set +x
```

20

Finding Logical Bugs Using Shell Tracing

As mentioned before, there is at least one logical bug in this script. With the help of shell tracing, you can locate and fix this bug.

Consider the prompt produced by this script:

```
Make backup (y/n)?
```

If you do not type a response but simply press Enter or Return, the script reports an error similar to the following:

```
./buggy3.sh: [: =: unary operator expected
```

To determine where this error occurs, it is probably best to run the entire script in shell tracing mode:

```
$ /bin/sh -x ./buggy3.sh
```

The output is similar to the following:

```
+ YesNo Make backup
+ echo Make backup (y/n)? \c
+ /bin/echo Make backup (y/n)? \c
Make backup (y/n)? + read RESPONSE

+ [ = y ]
./buggy3.sh: [: =: unary operator expected
```

The blank line is the result of pressing Enter or Return without typing a response to the prompt. The next line that the shell executes is the source of the error message:

```
[ = y ]
```

Which is part of the `if` statement:

```
if [ $RESPONSE = "y" ] ; then
```

Although this problem can be fixed by just quoting `$RESPONSE`,

```
if [ "$RESPONSE" = "y" ] ; then
```

the better fix is to determine why it is not set and change that code so that it always sets `$RESPONSE`. Looking at the script, you find that this variable is set by the function `YesNo`:

```
YesNo() {
    echo "$1 (y/n)? \c"
    read RESPONSE
    case $RESPONSE in
        [yY]|[Yy][Ee][Ss]) RESPONSE=y ;;
        [nN]|[Nn][Oo]) RESPONSE=n ;;
    esac
}
```

There are two problems here. The first one is that the `read` command

```
read RESPONSE
```

will not set a value for `$RESPONSE` if the user just presses Enter or Return. Because you can't change the `read` command, you need to find a different method to solving the problem. Basically you have a logical problem—the `case` statement needs to validate the user input, which it is currently not doing. A simple fix for the problem is to change `YesNo` as follows:

```
YesNo() {
    echo "$1 (y/n)? \c"
    read RESPONSE
    case "$RESPONSE" in
        [yY]|[Yy][Ee][Ss]) RESPONSE=y ;;
        *) RESPONSE=n ;;
    esac
}
```

Now you treat all responses other than `"yes"` as negative responses. This includes null responses generated when the user simply types Enter or Return.

Using Debugging Hooks

In the previous examples, you were able to deduce the location of a bug using shell tracing. In order to enable tracing for a particular part of the script, you have to edit the script and insert the `debug` command:

```
set -x
```

For larger scripts, a better practice is to embed *debugging hooks*. Debugging hooks are functions that enable shell tracing in critical code sections. Debugging hooks are normally activated in one of two ways:

- The script is run with a command-line option (commonly `-d` or `-x`).
- The script is run with an environment variable set to true (commonly `DEBUG=true` or `TRACE=true`).

The following function enables you to activate and deactivate debugging by setting `$DEBUG` to `true`:

```
Debug() {
    if [ "$DEBUG" = "true" ] ; then
        if [ "$1" = "on"  -o "$1" = "ON" ] ; then
            set -x
        else
            set +x
        fi
    fi
}
```

To activate debugging, you can use the following:

```
Debug on
```

20

To deactivate debugging, you can use either of the following:

```
Debug
Debug off
```

Actually, passing any argument to this function other than `on` or `ON` deactivates debugging.

The normal practice, with regard to debugging, is to activate it only when necessary. By default, debugging should be off.

To demonstrate the use of this function, you can modify the functions in the script `buggy3.sh` to have debugging automatically enabled if the variable `DEBUG` is set. The modified version of `buggy3.sh` is as follows:

```
#!/bin/sh

Debug() {
    if [ "$DEBUG" = "true" ] ; then
        if [ "$1" = "on"  -o "$1" = "ON" ] ; then
            set -x
        else
            set +x
        fi
    fi
}

Failed() {
    Debug on
    if [ "$1" -ne 0 ] ; then
        echo "Failed. Exiting." ; exit 1 ;
    fi
    echo "Done."
    Debug off
}

YesNo() {
    Debug on
    echo "$1 (y/n)? \c"
    read RESPONSE
    case "$RESPONSE" in
        [yY]|[Yy][Ee][Ss]) RESPONSE=y ;;
        *) RESPONSE=n ;;
    esac
    Debug off
}

YesNo "Make backup"
if [ "$RESPONSE" = "y" ] ; then
```

```
    echo "Deleting old backups, please wait... \c"
    rm -r backup > /dev/null 2>&1
    Failed $?

    echo "Making new backups, please wait... \c"
    cp -r docs backup
    Failed $?
fi
```

There is no change in the output if the script is executed in either of the following ways:

```
$ /bin/sh ./buggy3.sh
$ ./buggy3.sh
```

The output includes shell tracing if the same script is executed in either of the following ways:

```
$ DEBUG=true /bin/sh ./buggy3.sh
$ DEBUG=true ./buggy3.sh
```

Summary

In the process of developing or maintaining large shell scripts, you will need to find and fix bugs in them. This chapter looked at how to use the shell to facilitate this task. Some of the topics covered include:

- Enabling debugging
- Syntax checking using `sh -n` and `sh -nv`
- Using shell tracing to find syntax and logic bugs
- Embedding debugging hooks in your shell scripts

By learning the techniques used in debugging shell scripts, you can fix your own scripts as well as maintain scripts written by other programmers.

Questions

1. What are the three main forms of enabling debugging in a shell script?
2. Enhance the `Debug()` function given in this chapter so that the programmer has to press Enter or Return after debugging is deactivated.

   When you debug scripts that have several dozen functions, this feature enables you to study the debugging output from a particular function before executing the next function.

Terms

Debugging Hooks Functions that enable shell tracing in critical code sections.

Execution Tracing See shell tracing.

Invocation Activated Methods for enabling debugging modes that take effect when a script is invoked.

Programmer Activated Debugging modes activated only when the shell script programmer uses the `set` command.

Shell Tracing Each command is printed in the exact form that it is executed.

Syntax Checking The process of verifying a script's syntax without executing it.

Hour 21

Problem Solving with Functions

In previous chapters, you wrote short shell scripts that performed specific tasks. Many of these scripts performed common operations such as displaying error and warning messages and prompting the users for input. To easily repeat these tasks, you created reusable functions for your scripts.

In this chapter, you take this a step farther and create a *library* of functions that can be readily reused in shell scripts. A library is a repository of functions that can be accessed by shell scripts. The specific topics related to libraries that you will examine are

- Library basics
- Creating a library

Library Basics

In many of the scripts in this book, you created utility functions that display error message and prompt the users for input. When two scripts needed the same function, you just copied the function from one script to the other. This method works fine when you are dealing with one or two scripts, but it breaks down with many scripts. Say you have a dozen scripts that share a function and you located a bug in that function. You can image how hard it would be to fix every one of those scripts. A repository or library of common functions would reduce the complexity of developing and maintaining these shell scripts.

What Is a Library?

Creating a library of functions is exactly like creating a shell script. The only difference between a script and a library is that a library contains only function definitions, whereas a script can contain both function definitions and *executable code*. The executable code in a script consists of all the commands in the script outside of the function definitions. In the following shell script, lines 1, 2, and 4 are executable code:

```
1  #!/bin/sh
2  MSG="hello"
3  echo_error() { echo "ERROR:" $@ 1>&2 ; }
4  echo_error $MSG
```

Line 3, which contains a function definition, is not executable code.

A library does not contain any executable code; it contains only function definitions. For example, the following is a library:

```
#!/bin/sh
echo_error() { echo "ERROR:" $@ 1>&2 ; }
echo_warning() { echo "WARNING:" $@ 1>&2 ; }
```

Strictly speaking, nothing prevents a library from containing executable code; the distinction between a script and a library is purely a conceptual one.

Using a Library

You can access the functions defined as a library in your scripts using the `.` command. Its syntax is

```
. file
```

Here, `file` is the pathname to the library. When a library is accessed via the `.` command, it is referred to as *sourced* or *loaded*. If `file` is not a valid pathname or not a script, the shell will display an error message and then exit. For this reason, most scripts load all of their libraries before executing any commands.

For example, if the functions given in the previous example are stored in a file called `messages.sh`, the following command can be used to load them:

```
. messages.sh
```

You can rewrite the script

```
#!/bin/sh
MSG="hello"
echo_error() { echo "ERROR:" $@ >&2 ; }
echo_error $MSG
```

to use the library `messages.sh` as follows:

```
#!/bin/sh
. $HOME/lib/sh/messages.sh
MSG="hello"
echo_error $MSG
```

This example assumes that the file `messages.sh` is stored in the directory `$HOME/lib/sh`. If this directory did not contain `messages.sh` or `messages.sh` was not a script, an error message similar to the following would be produced before the shell exits:

```
sh: /home/ranga/lib/sh/messages.sh: No such file or directory
```

When you include a file using the `.` command, make sure that the file does not contain the `exit` command as this will cause the current instance of the shell to exit.

If you use the `.` command to include a file in your login session, your session will be terminated and you will have to log in again.

Creating a Library

Now that you have learned the basics about creating and using a library, you can create a library of utility functions designed to facilitate scripting tasks. In this section, you will learn about several of the functions from the library. The "Questions" section at the end of this chapter asks you to develop five additional functions for this library. The entire library, including sample implementations of the functions you will be asked to develop, is listed in Appendix D, "Shell Function Library."

Naming the Library

For the purposes of this discussion, assume that the library is located in the file `$HOME/lib/sh/libTYSP2.sh`. The name of this library was derived as follows:

- The `lib` in `libTYSP2.sh` indicates that this file is a library. This is similar to the convention used in the C language.
- The `.sh` in `libTYSP2.sh` indicates that this file contains Bourne-like shell code.

- The directory `$HOME/lib` indicates that this file is a library because it resides in the `lib` (short for library) directory.
- The directory `$HOME/lib/sh` indicates that the file is a shell library because it resides in the `sh` directory under the `lib` directory.

To use this library in your scripts, you need to load it using the command:

```
. $HOME/lib/sh/libTYSP2.sh
```

There is no requirement that the library be stored in `$HOME/lib/sh/libTYSP2.sh`; you can place the library in any location.

If you place the library in an alternate location, your scripts would need to load it using its absolute pathname. For example, if you place the library in `/usr/local/lib/sh`, your scripts would have to load it as follows:

```
. /usr/local/lib/sh/libTYSP2.sh
```

You would also have to use this alternate path in the examples covered later in this chapter.

Naming the Functions

For each function or group of functions in the library, this section presents a brief description followed by the implementation and a discussion of the implementation. These functions use the following naming scheme:

- `print`*`String`* for functions that display a message, described by *`String`*.
- `prompt`*`String`* for functions that prompt the user for input. Here *`String`* is the name of the global variable set by the function after reading input from the user.
- `is`*`String`* for functions that determine whether a particular condition, described by *`String`*, is true or false and return an appropriate value (`0` for true, `1` for false).
- `get`*`String`* for functions that retrieve some type of data, described by *`String`*.

Some of these functions need to be modified to work properly on all versions of UNIX. In this chapter, you will just see the differences. In Chapter 23, "Scripting for Portability," you will see how these functions can be modified to account for the differences between versions of UNIX.

Displaying Error and Warning Messages

The first two functions in this library, `printError` and `printWarning`, facilitate the display of error and warning messages from scripts. An error message is normally displayed when an unexpected event that is difficult to recover from, such as a command failure, occurs. A warning message is normally displayed when an unexpected but recoverable event occurs.

```
# Name: printError
# Desc: prints an message to STDERR
# Args: $@ -> message to print

printError () {
    echo "ERROR:   $@" 1>&2
}

# Name: printWarning
# Desc: prints an message to STDERR
# Args: $@ -> message to print

printWarning () {
    echo "WARNING: $@" 1>&2
}
```

Because both of these functions display messages indicating that an erroneous condition was encountered, they use output redirection to display their messages on STDERR, which is reserved for error reporting.

Asking Questions

In interactive shell scripts, you often need to obtain input from the users. The input might be a simple yes or no response to a question, or it might be much more complicated. The next two functions in this library are designed to aid in the process of obtaining user input in response to questions.

Asking a Yes or No Question

One of the most common questions asked by scripts elicits a yes or no response. The function, `promptYESNO`, provides a reusable method of asking yes or no questions and gathering responses. This implementation stores the user's response—`y` indicating yes or `n` indicating no—in the global variable `YESNO` after the function completes.

```
# Name:    promptYESNO
# Desc:    Asks a yes/no question
# Args:    $1 -> The prompt
#          $2 -> The default answer (optional)
# Globals: YESNO -> set to the users response y for yes, n for no

promptYESNO () {

   YESNO=""
```

```
    if [ $# -lt 1 ] ; then
       return 1
    fi

    _YNPROMPT="$1 (y/n)? "
    _YNDEFANS=""

    case "$2" in
       [yY]|[yY][eE][sS]) _YNDEFANS="y" ;;
       [nN]|[nN][oO])     _YNDEFANS="n" ;;
    esac

    _YNPROMPT="$_YNPROMPT${_YNDEFANS:+[$_YNDEFANS] }"

    while :
    do
       printf "$_YNPROMPT"
       read YESNO
       case "${YESNO:-$_YNDEFANS}" in
          [yY]|[yY][eE][sS])
              YESNO="y"
              break
              ;;
          [nN]|[nN][oO])
              YESNO="n"
              break
              ;;
          *) YESNO="" ;;
       esac
    done

    unset _YNPROMPT _YNDEFANS
    export YESNO
    return 0
}
```

This function can handle two arguments:

- `$1` is treated as the base from which to construct the yes/no question. It is required.
- `$2` is the default answer and is optional.

First the function clears the value of `YESNO`. Then the function determines whether at least one argument was supplied, because you need at least one argument. If no arguments are supplied the function returns `1`, indicating improper usage:

```
if [ $# -lt 1 ] ; then
   return 1
fi
```

Next, the function creates two internal variables, `_YNPROMPT` and `_YNDEFANS`:

```
_YNPROMPT="$1 (y/n)? "
_YNDEFANS=""
```

The variable `_YNPROMPT` holds the question, whereas `_YNDEFANS` holds the default answer. Initially, `_YNDEFANS` is set to null, and then a `case` statement is used to set its value:

```
case "$2" in
      [yY]|[yY][eE][sS]) _YNDEFANS="y" ;;
      [nN]|[nN][oO])     _YNDEFANS="n" ;;
esac
```

This `case` statement determines whether the second argument is in the form of y, n, yes, or no (regardless of case). If it is, `_YNDEFANS` is set appropriately and the prompt, `_YNPROMPT`, is updated to reflect this:

```
_YNPROMPT="$_YNPROMPT${_YNDEFANS:+[$_YNDEFANS] }"
```

After updating the prompt, the function enters an infinite `while` loop that exits when the user provides a valid response to the question stored in `_YNPROMPT`. The `while` loop first prints the prompt and then reads the response into the variable `YESNO`:

```
printf "$_YNPROMPT"
read YESNO
```

Once a response has been read, a `case` statement evaluates the response:

```
case "${YESNO:-$_YNDEFANS}" in
         [yY]|[yY][eE][sS])
             YESNO="y"
             break
             ;;
         [nN]|[nN][oO])
             YESNO="n"
             break
             ;;
         *) YESNO="" ;;
esac
```

If some form of `y`, n, yes or no was entered, `YESNO` is set appropriately and the loop terminates by calling `break`; otherwise, the value of `YESNO` is set to null and the loop executes again. This allows the function to keep prompting the user for a response until a valid response is specified.

Finally, the function unsets the variables that store the prompt and the default answer. The function then exports the variable `YESNO` to the environment in order to ensure that this variable is available to commands executed after the function completes. Finally, the function returns `0`:

```
unset _YNPROMPT _YNDEFANS
export YESNO
return 0
```

Using `promptYESNO`

Now that you know how this function works, take a look at an example of its use:

```
#!/bin/sh

. $HOME/lib/sh/libTYSP2.sh

promptYESNO "Do you want to play a game"
if [ "$YESNO" = "y" ] ; then
    /usr/games/tictactoe
else
   echo "Maybe later."
fi
```

This generates the following prompt:

```
Do you want to play a game (y/n)?
```

If the response is some form of y or yes, the variable `YESNO` is set to `y` and the `if` statement executes the command `/usr/games/tictactoe`. If the response is some form of n or no, the variable `YESNO` is set to `n` and the `if` statement prints the message:

```
Maybe later.
```

If any other response is specified, the prompt will be repeated.

The following example illustrates the use of a default argument as follows:

```
#!/bin/sh

. $HOME/lib/sh/libTYSP2.sh

promptYESNO "Do you want to play a game" "y"
if [ "$YESNO" = "y" ] ; then
    /usr/games/thermonuclearwar
else
   echo "Maybe later."
fi
```

This generates a prompt similar to the following:

```
Do you want to play a game (y/n)? [y]
```

When the default answer is specified, the users can simply press Enter or Return or they can manually specify a response. If the users specify y or yes or choose the default answer, the system will execute a game on the user's behalf.

Prompting for a Response

In some shell scripts, you need to gather more information from the users than a simple yes or no response. For example, an installation script might have to ask for the name of a directory or the location of a file. The `promptRESPONSE` function can elicit this type of information from the user. The function in this example stores the user's response in the global variable `RESPONSE`. Validation of the response should be handled outside the function.

```
# Name:    promptRESPONSE
# Desc:    Asks a question
# Args:    $1 -> The prompt
#          $2 -> The default answer (optional)
# Globals: RESPONSE -> set to the users response

promptRESPONSE () {

   RESPONSE=""

   if [ $# -lt 1 ] ; then
      return 1
   fi

   _RDEFANS="${2:+$2}"
   _RPROMPT="$1? ${_RDEFANS:+[$_RDEFANS] }"

   while :
   do
      printf "$_RPROMPT"
      read RESPONSE
      RESPONSE="${RESPONSE:-$_RDEFANS}"
      if [ -n "$RESPONSE" ] ; then
         break
      fi
      RESPONSE=""
   done

   unset _RDEFANS _RPROMPT
   export RESPONSE
   return 0
}
```


This function can handle two arguments:

- `$1` is treated as the base from which to construct the question. It is required.
- `$2` is the default answer and is optional.

First the function clears the value of RESPONSE. Then the function determines whether at least one argument was supplied, because you need at least one argument. If no arguments are supplied, the function returns 1, indicating improper use:

```
if [ $# -lt 1 ] ; then
   return 1
fi
```

Next, the function creates two internal variables, _RDEFANS and _RPROMPT:

```
_RDEFANS="${2:+$2}"
_RPROMPT="$1? ${_RDEFANS:+[$_RDEFANS] }"
```

The variable _RDEFANS holds the default answer and is set to the value of $2, but only if a second argument was specified. The variable _RPROMPT holds the question and is based on the value of $1 and _RDEFANS.

Next, the function enters an infinite while loop that exits when the user provides a valid response to the question stored in _RPROMPT. The while loop first prints the prompt and then reads the response into the variable RESPONSE:

```
printf "$_RPROMPT"
read RESPONSE
```

Variable substitution then ensures that RESPONSE contains a value or a default value:

```
RESPONSE="${RESPONSE:-$_RDEFANS}"
```

If RESPONSE contains a value, the loop terminates by issuing break; otherwise the loop sets RESPONSE to null and repeats:

```
if [ -n "$RESPONSE" ] ; then
   break
fi
RESPONSE=""
```

The function then unsets the variables that store the prompt and the default answer and exports the variable RESPONSE to the environment in order to ensure that this variable is available to commands executed after the function completes. Finally, the function returns 0:

```
unset _RDEFANS _RPROMPT
export RESPONSE
return 0
```

Using promptRESPONSE

Now that you know how this function works, take a look at an example of its use:

```
#!/bin/sh

. $HOME/lib/sh/libTYSP2.sh

promptRESPONSE "What is your favorite fruit"
echo "Your favorite fruit is $RESPONSE."
```

This generates the following prompt:

```
What is your favorite fruit?
```

The echo statement then displays the response:

```
Your favorite fruit is apple.
```

Checking Disk Space

System administrators often use scripts to keep apprised of the disk usage in certain essential directories. For example, if the incoming mail or news directories were to fill up, users would not be able to obtain new e-mail or news articles. The next two functions in this library ease the process of monitoring disk usage.

Determining Free Space

The free space in a directory can be determined using the `df -k` (k as in kilobytes) command. The output of this command is similar to the following:

```
$ df -k
Filesystem           1024-blocks  Used Available Capacity Mounted on
/dev/hda1               1190014  664661   463867      59%   /
/dev/hdd1               4128240 1578837  2335788      40%   /internal
/dev/hdb1               1521567  682186   760759      47%   /store
/dev/hda3                320086   72521   231034      24%   /tmp
```

When a directory or file is specified as an additional argument, the output just contains information about the partition where that directory or file is located:

```
$ df -k /home/ranga
Filesystem           1024-blocks  Used Available Capacity Mounted on
/dev/hda1               1190014  664661   463867      59%   /
```

As you can see, the output consists of a header followed by information about the partitions on your system. The amount of free space in a given partition is stored in the fourth column. This function uses awk to retrieve this value.

```
# Name: getSpaceFree
# Desc: Outputs the space avail for a directory
# Args: $1 -> The directory to check

getSpaceFree () {
   if [ $# -ge 1 ] ; then
      df -k "$1" 2> /dev/null | awk 'NR != 1 { print $4; }'
      return $?
   fi
   return 1
}
```

21

As you can see, the function is quite simple. It first determines whether it was supplied as an argument. If an argument was supplied, the `df -k` command is executed and its output is modified by `awk`:

```
df -k "$1" 2> /dev/null | awk 'NR != 1 { print $4; }'
```

You use the `awk` expression

```
NR != 1
```

to skip the header in the first line of the output. For more information on `awk`, review Chapter 17, "Filtering Text with `awk`."

The following example illustrates the use of this function:

```
getSpaceFree /usr/local
```

The output of this command is similar to the following (provided the directory `/usr/local` exists on your system):

```
2335788
```

The number returned is in kilobytes, which in this case translates to 2.3GB free in the directory `/usr/local`.

In some cases, you might need to compare the output of this function to some value. For example, the following example determines whether more than 20,000KB are available in the directory `/usr/local`:

```
#!/bin/sh

. $HOME/lib/sh/libTYSP2.sh

if [ "`getSpaceFree /usr/local`" -gt 20000 ] ; then
    echo "Enough space"
fi
```

If you are using HP-UX, the `df -k` command used in the previous functions will not work properly for you. You will need to use an alternate form of the `df` command covered in Chapter 23.

Determining Space Used

Sometimes you need to know how much disk space a directory uses rather than the amount of free space available. For example, a system might have a temporary directory that needs to be cleaned out when it exceeds a certain size.

You can use the du (short for disk usage) command to determine the amount of disk space used by a directory. Because you are interested in the disk usage for the entire directory in kilobytes, you need to use the -s (short for sum) and -k (short for kilobytes) options. The output of the du -sk command looks like the following:

```
$ du -sk /home/ranga/pub
4922    /home/ranga/pub
```

The size of the directory in kilobytes is listed in the first column. This function uses awk to retrieve this number.

```
# Name: getSpaceUsed
# Desc: output the space used for a directory
# Args: $1 -> The directory to check

getSpaceUsed () {
   if [ -d "$1" ] ; then
      du -sk "$1" | awk '{ print $1; }'
      return $?
   fi
   return 1
}
```

This function is almost as simple as getSpaceFree. It first determines whether it was given an argument. If no argument was given, it displays an error message and returns. Otherwise, it determines whether the first argument is a directory. If it is not, an error message is displayed and the function returns.

This function is quite simple; if the first argument, $1, is a directory, it executes du to determine the disk usage and then retrieves that value using awk:

```
du -sk "$1" | awk '{ print $1; }'
```

If the first argument is not a directory; the function returns 1, indicating failure.

The following example illustrates the use of this function:

```
getSpaceUsed /usr/local
```

The output is similar to the following (provided the directory /usr/local exists on your system):

```
15164
```

The number returned is in kilobytes, which in this case translates to about 15.1MB.

Often, you will want to compare the output of this function to some value. For example, the following example determines whether more than 10,000KB is used by the directory `/var/tmp`:

```
#!/bin/sh

. $HOME/lib/sh/libTYSP2.sh

if [ "`getSpaceUsed /var/tmp`" -gt 10000 ] ; then
    printWARNING "You're using to much space!"
fi
```

Obtaining a Process ID by its Process Name

One of the difficulties with the `ps` command is that it is difficult to obtain the process ID (PID) of a command by specifying its process name. This capability is essential in scripts that start and stop processes. The next function in the library provides this capability.

```
# Name: getPID
# Desc: Outputs a list of process id matching $1
# Args: $1 -> the command name to look for

getPID() {

    if [ $# -lt 1 ] ; then
        return 1
    fi

    PSOPTS="-ef"

    /bin/ps $PSOPTS | grep "$1" | grep -v grep | awk '{ print $2; }'
}
```

As you can see, this function is a set of filters for the output of the command `/bin/ps -ef`. The first `grep` command looks for all lines that match the first argument. As an example, executing this on the command line produces output similar to the following:

```
$ /bin/ps -ef | grep sshd
```

Here you are looking for all the lines that contain the word `sshd`. The output might be similar to the following:

```
root  1449     1  8 12:23:06 ?        0:02 /opt/bin/sshd
ranga  1451   944  5 12:23:08 pts/t0    0:00 grep sshd
```

As you can see, the output contains two lines. The first one contains the process ID of the command that you are looking for, but the second contains the process ID of the `grep` command that you executed. In order to ignore such lines, the command `grep -v grep` is used in the pipeline. Finally, `awk` extracts the process ID, which is stored in the second column of the output of ps. If more than one process has the requested name, this function displays each process ID.

Readers who are using Linux or BSD systems have to change this function in order for it to run properly. The value of the variable PSOPTS should be set to -auwx instead of -ef on these systems. In Chapter 23, you will see how to incorporate these changes into the function so that it runs without modification under any version of UNIX.

The following command illustrates the use of getPID:

```
getPID httpd
```

The output of this command is a list of process IDs, similar to the following:

```
330
331
332
333
334
```

Getting a User's Numeric User ID

Some shell scripts need to determine whether a user has sufficient permissions to execute commands. For example, a startup script might need to run as root (UID 0) to modify system files correctly.

A user's ID can be checked by using the id command. The default for this command is to output information about the current user:

```
$ id
uid=500(ranga) gid=100(users) groups=100(users),101(ftpadmin)
```

If a username is supplied as an argument, the id command outputs information for that user:

```
$ id vathsa
uid=501(vathsa) gid=100(users) groups=100(users)
```

This chapter's function supports both modes.

```
# Name: getUID
# Desc: outputs a numeric user id
# Args: $1 -> a user name (optional)

getUID() {
    id $1 | sed -e 's/(.*$//' -e 's/^uid=//'
}
```

This function executes the id command and then uses sed to filter all the unimportant information.

When `getUID` is executed by itself

```
getUID
```

the output is similar to the following:

```
500
```

When the function is called with a username

```
getUID vathsa
```

the output is similar the following:

```
500
```

Usually you need to compare this output to some known UID as follows:

```
#!/bin/sh

. $HOME/lib/sh/libTYSP2.sh

if [ "`getUID`" -gt 100 ] ; then
    printERROR "You do not have sufficient privileges."
    exit 1
fi
```

Here the output of the `getUID` function is checked to see whether it is greater than 100.

Summary

In this chapter you examined libraries of functions. Libraries can simplify your scripts by providing a shared interface for common scripting tasks. You also examined several functions in a library. By using and improving these implementations, you can avoid having to reinvent the wheel when faced with a particular problem.

Questions

1. Write a function named `toLower` that converts its arguments to all lowercase and outputs the converted string to STDOUT. (HINT: Use `tr`.)
2. Write a function named `toUpper` that converts its arguments to all uppercase and outputs the converted string to STDOUT. (HINT: Use `tr`.)
3. Write a function called `isSpaceAvailable` to check whether a directory contains a certain amount of disk space.

   The function should accept two arguments. The first one indicates the directory to check, and the second one indicates the amount of space to check. The function should return `1` if both arguments are not supplied or if the first argument is not a directory.

If sufficient space is present, your function should return `0`. This enables you to use it as follows:

```
if isSpaceAvailable /usr/local 20000 ; then
    : # perform some action
fi
```

(HINT: Use the function `getSpaceFree`.)

4. Modify your `isSpaceAvailable` function to accept an optional third argument that specifies the units of the amount space to check.

   The default should remain in kilobytes, but you should support `m` or `mb` indicating megabytes and `g` or `gb` indicating gigabytes. If some other units are given, assume that the user meant kilobytes.

   (The following conversion factors apply to this problem: 1 megabyte equals 1024 kilobytes, and 1 gigabyte equals to 1024 megabytes.)

   (HINT: Use the `bc` command.)

5. Write a function called `isUserRoot` that determines whether the ID of a user is equal to 0. If no user is given, it should determine whether the ID of the current user is root. (HINT: Use `getUID`.)

Terms

Executable Code The part of the script that consists of all the commands in the script outside of the function definitions.

Library A repository of functions that can be accessed by shell scripts.

HOUR 22

Problem Solving with Shell Scripts

In Chapter 21, "Problem Solving with Functions," you examined several useful functions that can be used in shell scripts. In this chapter, you will learn about two shell scripts that demonstrate how you can use shell scripts to solve everyday problems.

These scripts illustrate how the tools covered in previous chapters can be used to create new re-usable tools. For each script, the chapter first describes the motivations for its development, followed by some design issues. Then it presents the script along with a discussion of the script's flow.

This chapter examines two scripts related to the following topics:

- Startup scripts
- Maintaining an address book

Startup Scripts

A common task for many shell programmers is writing system startup scripts. In this section, you will develop a basic system startup script that can be reused (after a little editing). Before you begin, let's look at a little background into the UNIX system startup and initialization.

System Startup

When a UNIX system starts, the first program to be executed is `init` (usually located in `/sbin`). This program is responsible for system startup and initialization. In early versions of UNIX, `init` was aided in this by the script `/etc/rc`. This script handled all of the nitty-gritty details of system initialization such as checking the disks, starting the networking layers, and enabling console and remote login programs.

When a system administrator wanted to enable additional services at system startup, he or she had to edit `/etc/rc` to include the commands required to start the system. This method had two problems:

- A typo or mistake in `/etc/rc` could render the system unbootable and might require many hours or days to recover.
- An upgrade of the system software might overwrite `/etc/rc`, causing the system administrator to lose all the modifications.

In order to solve these two problems, BSD introduced a secondary startup script, `/etc/rc.local`, that contained all of the system-specific startup commands. This script was never upgraded by updates to the system software and the system would boot correctly even if this script contained errors. Although `rc.local` solved these two problems, there were still other problems:

- There was no easy way to stop all the running programs in a clean way during system shutdown.
- Software vendors could not easily integrate their programs into the system startup or shutdown. If a software vendor provided a program that needed to start up at boot time, they were stuck having to edit the `rc.local` script in their software installation scripts, an error-prone operation.
- There was no way to enforce startup and shutdown dependencies; if program B depended on program A starting up first, the system administrator had to manually sequence the commands in `rc.local` so that this dependency was enforced.
- There was no way to limit the number of programs that were started when the system booted; there was no way to boot the system into a limited maintenance mode.

AT&T System V System Initialization

When AT&T released System V UNIX, they fixed these problems by introducing a new system initialization infrastructure based on *init scripts and run-levels.*

Init scripts were simple scripts, originally stored in `/sbin/init.d`, that were responsible for starting and stopping a single program. Every program that was to be started at boot time had an init script, which made it easy for system administrators to maintain along with providing an easy method for software vendors to integrate their programs into a system's startup process. Because the init scripts were also responsible for stopping programs, they could be used to stop processes cleanly during system shutdown. Later in this section you will be developing an init script.

Run-levels partitioned the system startup into seven levels (zero through six) and provided a method for enforcing startup dependencies and partitioning the startup of system services into the different levels. Each of the run-levels had a specific purpose and made it possible to implement a limited maintenance mode along with a shutdown mode. The different run-levels are described in Table 22.1.

TABLE 22.1 Run-Levels

Run-level	*Name*	*Description*
0	Halt	Used for shutting down a system and powering it off (if supported by the hardware).
1	Single-User	A limited maintenance mode for performing backups, upgrades, and other maintenance activities. Run-level 1 can only be used by the super-user root (uid 0).
2	Multi-User	The system starts all the programs necessary for supporting multiple users along with basic network services.
3	Networked Multi-User	The system starts any additional network programs such as Web servers, FTP servers, and mail servers. Most systems are usually used at this run-level.
4	Unused	This run-level is currently unused except on HP-UX where it is used to launch the windowing environment HP VUE.
5	Graphical Multi-User or Halt	On Linux systems this run-level is used to automatically start the X11 windowing environment. On Solaris and other systems, it is used to halt the system and power it off (if supported by the hardware).
6	Reboot	Used to reboot the system.

> **Run-Level S on Solaris**
>
> In addition to the run-levels covered in Table 22.1, Solaris includes an extra run-level known as run-level S. Run-level S is the Solaris equivalent of run-level 1 and is used to put the system into single-user mode.

How Init Scripts Work

Each run-level has a corresponding directory. The run-level directories are located in `/sbin` and have names of the form `rc`*`lvl`*`.d`, where *`lvl`* is an integer (0-6) corresponding to a particular run-level. Each directory contains specially named links to the init scripts from `/sbin/init.d` appropriate for that run-level. The links are named as follows:

- `S`*`XXname`*—Corresponds to a startup script. Known as start scripts.
- `K`*`YYname`*—Corresponds to a shutdown script. Known as stop scripts.

In both cases, *`XX`* and *`YY`* are numbers from 00 to 99 and *`name`* is the name of the init script that this link corresponds to. The number, *`XX`*, allows startup and shutdown dependencies to be enforced via script names, because scripts with smaller numbers will be executed before scripts with larger numbers. In general, *`YY`* should be equal to 100 – *`XX`*. This allows for programs to be shut down in the reverse order of the startup sequence, thus enforcing shutdown dependencies.

As an example, the start script link in `rc3.d` for the secure shell daemon (SSH) might look like the following:

```
$ ls -l /sbin/rc3.d/S99sshd
lrwxr-xr-x  1 root  wheel  14 Jun  5 18:47 /sbin/rc3.d/S99sshd ->
/sbin/init.d/sshd
```

The corresponding shutdown script in `rc5.d` and `rc6.d` might look like the following:

```
$ ls -l /sbin/rc5.d/K01sshd /sbin/rc6.d/K01sshd
lrwxr-xr-x  1 root  wheel  14 Jun  5 18:47 /sbin/rc5.d/K01sshd ->
/sbin/init.d/sshd
lrwxr-xr-x  1 root  wheel  14 Jun  5 18:47 /sbin/rc6.d/K01sshd ->
/sbin/init.d/sshd
```

When a particular run-level is reached, all of the scripts that start with `K` (stop scripts) are executed with the argument `stop`. Then all of the scripts that start with `S` (start scripts) are executed with the argument `start`. This defines the basic interface for every init script; it must accept and understand the arguments start and stop:

```
script [ start | stop ]
```

When the system first starts, it is at run-level 1. It starts by executing all of the stop scripts in the `/sbin/rc1.d` directory followed by all of the start scripts in that directory. Once all of the scripts in the directory corresponding to run-level 1 have been executed, the scripts in the directory corresponding to run-level 2 are executed with the argument `start` followed by the scripts in run-level 3. When all of the scripts in run-level 3 finish executing, the system is ready for general use.

When the system is shut down and powered off or halted, the scripts in the directory `/sbin/rc5.d` are executed. When the system is rebooted, the scripts in the directory `/sbin/rc6.d` are executed.

Platform Variations

With the exception of BSD, UNIX vendors readily adopted AT&T's initialization infrastructure. BSD still continues to use the system based on the files `/etc/rc` and `/etc/rc.local`.

Hewlett-Packard adopted it in HP-UX 10.0 and uses it with a slight modification. In HP-UX init scripts are still stored in the directory `/sbin/init.d` and the run-level directories are stilled named `/sbin/rc`*`lvl`*`.d`, but the start and stop scripts have three digits, *XXX* or *YYY*, as opposed to just two digits, *XX* or *YY*. Thus on HP-UX *YYY* should be equal to 1000 – *XXX*.

Sun Microsystems adopted it in Solaris 2.0 (SunOS 5.0) and modified it to suit its needs. In Solaris the init scripts are stored in the directory `/etc/init.d` and the run-level directories are named `/etc/rc`*`lvl`*`.d`.

Linux also adopted a modified AT&T style initialization. In Linux the init scripts are stored in `/etc/rc.d/init.d` and the run-level directories are named `/etc/rc.d/rc`*`lvl`*`.d`. Linux has also changed the meaning associated with run-level 5; rather than use this run-level for halting and powering down the system, it is used to start the processes required for the graphical windowing environment (X11). Linux also retains some vestiges of BSD, as it still uses the file `rc.local (relocated to the directory /etc/rc.d)`.

BSD Might Eventually Adopt System V Initialization

Although BSD has avoided adopting System V style initialization for more than a decade, there are rumblings of a change. An initiative known as the NetBSD `rc.d` System was introduced by the NetBSD foundation during the summer of 2001. More information on this initiative can be found in the following paper:

`http://www.cs.rmit.edu.au/~lukem/papers/rc.d.pdf`

Developing an Init Script

As discussed previously, the basic interface for an init script is

```
script [ start | stop ]
```

You will start by creating a script for the secure shell daemon (SSH) that implements this interface and then adds several improvements to enhance the functionality of the script. Once you have the completed script, this section highlights the changes necessary to adapt the script for a different program.

For the purposes of this section, assume that your init script is named `sshd` and is stored in `/sbin/init.d`. The actual location for startup scripts is system-dependent, as discussed previously.

The Basic Script

The following script implements the basic start and stop interface:

```
#!/bin/sh

PGM=/usr/local/sbin/sshd
PGM_OPTS=

case "$1" in
   start) "$PGM" $PGM_OPTS ;;
   stop) /bin/ps -ef | grep "$PGM" | grep -v grep | \
         awk '{ print $2; }' | xargs kill 2> /dev/null
         ;;
esac

exit 0
```

At the beginning of the script, you define two variables, `$PGM` and `$PGM_OPTS`. The variable `$PGM` contains the full path to the program to start (in this case `/usr/local/sbin/sshd`); whereas the variable `$PGM_OPTS` contains any additional options or arguments that might need to be specified to the program.

The `case` statement that follows the variable definitions evaluates the argument supplied to the script. If the argument `starts`, the program stored in `$PGM` is executed as follows:

```
"$PGM" $PGM_OPTS
```

If the argument `stops`, the program stops using the following compound command:

```
/bin/ps -ef | grep "$PGM" | grep -v grep | \
awk '{ print $2; }' | xargs kill 2> /dev/null
```

Basically this command uses `grep` to look through the output of `ps` for all the entries that match the string stored in `$PGM`. It then ignores any entries that contain both `$PGM` and grep. Then it extracts the process IDs for these processes using awk and uses kill to terminate these processes.

Although the basic script is serviceable, there are a few problems that you need to solve in order to make it much more useable:

- The script has no error reporting when the program stored in $PGM does not exist or is not executable.
- The script has no error reporting when the program stored in $PGM is already running.
- No usage information is supplied if an invalid argument (or no arguments) is supplied to the script.

To solve the first and second problems, you can change the start clause of the case statement to the following:

```
start)
      if [ ! -x "$PGM" ] ; then
         echo "Error: Not Executable: $PGM" 1>&2
         exit 1
      fi

      RUNNING=`/bin/ps -ef | grep "$PGM" | \
               grep -v grep | head`
      if [ -n "$RUNNING" ] ; then
         echo "Error: Already running: $PGM" 1>&2
         exit 1
      fi

      "$PGM" $PGM_OPTS
      ;;
```

As you can see, the start clause now includes two if statements that perform the necessary error checking. First, you verify if the program is executable using the -x file test option. If it is not executable (or does not exist), an error message is reported and the script exits. Otherwise, the script proceeds to the next step in the error checking.

In order to check if the program is already running, you use the following compound command:

```
RUNNING=`/bin/ps -ef | grep "$PGM" | grep -v grep | head`
```

If the program is already running, the value of the variable RUNNING will contain the output of ps for at least one instance of the program. Otherwise RUNNING will be null. You use the -z option to check the variable RUNNING; if it is not null an error message is reported.

The final part of the `start` clause is unchanged; you simply execute the program as follows:

```
"$PGM" $PGM_OPTS
```

To solve the third problem, you can simply add a default clause to the `case` statement:

```
*) echo "Usage: $0 [ start | stop ]" ;;
```

By incorporating these changes, the script now looks like the following:

```
#!/bin/sh

PGM=/usr/local/sbin/sshd
PGM_OPTS=

case "$1" in
   start)
      if [ ! -x "$PGM" ] ; then
         echo "Error: Not Executable: $PGM" 1>&2
         exit 1
      fi

      RUNNING=`/bin/ps -ef | grep "$PGM" | \
               grep -v grep | head`
      if [ -n "$RUNNING" ] ; then
         echo "Error: Already running: $PGM" 1>&2
         exit 1
      fi

      "$PGM" $PGM_OPTS
      ;;
   stop) /bin/ps -ef | grep "$PGM" | grep -v grep | \
         awk '{ print $2 ; }' | xargs kill 2> /dev/null
         ;;
   *) echo "Usage: $0 [ start | stop ]"
      exit 1
      ;;
esac

exit 0
```

Problems with ps

One issue with this script resides in the use of the `ps` command. As you might recall from Chapter 7, "Processes," the options understood by `ps` differ among systems. This script used the Solaris style `-ef` options. Linux and BSD systems do not always support these options, so on those systems you need to use the `auwxx` options instead. This script should be able to detect the type of system it is being executed on and adapt appropriately.

You can use the `uname -s` command to detect the system type, and then use a `case` statement to modify the options to the `ps` command:

```
case "`uname -s`" in
   Linux|Darwin|*BSD) PS="/bin/ps auwxx" ;;
   *) PS="/bin/ps -ef" ;;
esac
```

This `case` statement evaluates the output of the `uname -s` command. If the output is Linux, Darwin (MacOS X), or some version of BSD, the variable `ps` is set as follows:

```
PS="/bin/ps auwxx"
```

Otherwise it defaults to a Solaris style value:

```
PS="/bin/ps -ef"
```

> The `uname` command is discussed in detail in the next chapter. For the purposes of this chapter it is sufficient to know that the `uname -s` command outputs the system type.

Now all that remains is to change the `start` and `stop` clauses to use the value of `$PS` rather than calling `ps` directly:

```
start)
      if [ ! -x "$PGM" ] ; then
         echo "Error: Not Executable: $PGM" 1>&2
         exit 1
      fi

      RUNNING=`$PS | grep "$PGM" | grep -v grep | head`
      if [ -n "$RUNNING" ] ; then
         echo "Error: Already running: $PGM" 1>&2
         exit 1
      fi

      "$PGM" $PGM_OPTS
      ;;
   stop) $PS | grep "$PGM" | grep -v grep | \
         awk '{ print $2 ; }' | xargs kill
         ;;
```

The complete script, incorporating all of these changes, is as follows:

```
#!/bin/sh

PGM=/usr/local/sbin/sshd
PGM_OPTS=
```

```
case "`uname -s`" in
   Linux|Darwin|*BSD) PS="/bin/ps auwxx" ;;
   *) PS="/bin/ps -ef" ;;
esac

case "$1" in
   start)
      if [ ! -x "$PGM" ] ; then
         echo "Error: Not Executable: $PGM" 1>&2
         exit 1
      fi

      RUNNING=`$PS | grep "$PGM" | grep -v grep | head`
      if [ -n "$RUNNING" ] ; then
         echo "Error: Already running: $PGM" 1>&2
         exit 1
      fi

      "$PGM" $PGM_OPTS
      ;;
   stop) $PS | grep "$PGM" | grep -v grep | \
         awk '{ print $2 ; }' | xargs kill 2> /dev/null
         ;;
   *) echo "Usage: $0 [ start | stop ]"
      exit 1
      ;;
esac

exit 0
```

Improvements

As it stands, the init script is quite complete and performs all of the necessary actions for starting and stopping the program it controls. There are two usability and functionality improvements you can make:

- Support for multiple arguments. Currently, only the first argument is evaluated. This means that if you want to restart the program you must do the following:

  ```
  # /sbin/init.d/sshd stop ; /sbin/init.d/sshd start ;
  ```

  If the script handled multiple arguments, you can stop and start the program in one command rather than two:

  ```
  # /sbin/init.d/sshd stop start
  ```

  UNIX programmers and administrators regard any modification that reduces typing as a usability improvement.
- Support for enabling and disabling the init script without having to remove its links from the run-level directories or the init file directory.
- Verification that the user invoking the script is root.

In this section, you will implement the first two improvements, and you will be asked to implement the last one as one of the questions at the end of the chapter.

In order to support multiple arguments, you can simply embed the main `case` statement within a `for` loop as follows:

```
for ARG in "$@"
do
   case "$ARG" in
      start)
         if [ ! -x "$PGM" ] ; then
            echo "Error: Not Executable: $PGM" 1>&2
            exit 1
         fi

         RUNNING=`$PS | grep "$PGM" | grep -v grep | head`
         if [ -n "$RUNNING" ] ; then
            echo "Error: Already running: $PGM" 1>&2
            exit 1
         fi

         "$PGM" $PGM_OPTS
         ;;
      stop) $PS | grep "$PGM" | grep -v grep | \
            awk '{ print $2 ; }' | xargs kill
            ;;
      *) echo "Usage: $0 [ start | stop ]"
         exit 1
         ;;
   esac
done
```

The `for` loop loops through all of the arguments stored in `$@`, and the `case` statement evaluates each of these arguments, instead of just evaluating `$1`. There is one problem with this modification: If no arguments are given, the usage message is no longer output. This is because the `for` loop is not executed if `$@` does not contain a value, as is the case when no arguments are given. To rectify this you can simply check for this and output the usage message earlier in the script by using the following `if` statement:

```
USAGE="Usage: $0 [ start | stop ]"
if [ -z "$@" ] ; then
   echo $USAGE
   exit 1
fi
```

The usage message is now stored in a variable because you now need to output it in two places within the script, and it is easier to maintain and update if it is located in a single place within the script.

In order to complete the second task, you need to come up with a method of enabling and disabling the init script without having to deal with the hassle of removing its links from the various run-level directories. A method you can use is as follows:

- If a file named `/etc/.no-`*pgm* is present, where *pgm* is the name of the program, the init script considers itself disabled for the purposes of starting the program. If this file is not present, the init script considers itself enabled.
- Add support in the init script for two additional parameters, enable and disable, that control the creation and deletion of the file `/etc/.no-`*pgm*.

You can extract *pgm*, the name of program, from the variable `$PGM` by using the `sed` command as follows:

```
echo $PGM | sed -e 's/^.*\///'
```

This `sed` command removes all of the directory information from the path stored in `$PGM` and just gives you the name of the program. You can store that in a variable as follows:

```
PGM_NAME="`echo $PGM | sed -e 's/^.*\///'`"
```

To enable the program you just need to remove the file `/etc/.no-`*pgm* using `rm`:

```
rm -f "/etc/.no-$PGM_NAME"
```

Thus the `enable` clause in the `case` statement is

```
enable) rm -f "/etc/.no-$PGM_NAME" ;;
```

Disabling the script is almost as easy. You just need to create the file `/etc/.no-$PGM_NAME` using the `touch` command:

```
touch "/etc/.no-$PGM_NAME"
```

Thus, the `disable` clause in the `case` statement is

```
disable) touch "/etc/.no-$PGM_NAME" ;;
```

The final modification to support enabling and disabling the program is in the `start` clause; you need to modify this clause to check if the program is disabled and refuse to start it if it is. This can be accomplished using the following `if` statement:

```
if [ -e "/etc/.no-$PGM_NAME" ] ; then
   echo "Error: Program disabled: $PGM" 1>&2
   exit 1
fi
```

The final script that incorporates all of these improvements is given in Listing 22.1 The line numbers are provided for your reference.

Listing 22.1 Complete Listing of the sshd Init Script

```
#!/bin/sh

USAGE="Usage: $0 [ start | stop | enable | disable ] "

# print out an usage message if no arguments are specified

if [ -z "$@" ] ; then
   echo "$USAGE"
   exit 1
fi

# variables that hold the location of the program, any options
# that might be required and the name of the program itself

PGM=/usr/local/sbin/sshd
PGM_OPTS=
PGM_NAME="`echo $PGM | sed -e 's/^.*\///'`"

# determine the correct options for ps

case "`uname -s`" in
   Linux|Darwin|*BSD) PS="/bin/ps auwxx" ;;
   *) PS="/bin/ps -ef" ;;
esac

# evaluate each argument

for ARG in "$@"
do
case "$ARG" in
   start)

      # check if the program is disabled

      if [ -e "/etc/.no-$PGM_NAME" ] ; then
         echo "Error: Program disabled: $PGM" 1>&2
         exit 1
      fi

      # verify that the program is executable

      if [ ! -x "$PGM" ] ; then
         echo "Error: Not Executable: $PGM" 1>&2
         exit 1
      fi

      # check if the program is running

      RUNNING=`$PS | grep "$PGM" | grep -v grep | head`
      if [ -n "$RUNNING" ] ; then
```

LISTING 22.1 Continued

```
         echo "Error: Already running: $PGM" 1>&2
         exit 1
      fi

      # start the program

      "$PGM" $PGM_OPTS
      ;;

   stop)

      # stop the program

      $PS | grep "$PGM" | grep -v grep | \
      awk '{ print $2 ; }' | xargs kill
      ;;

   enable)

      # remove the .no file to enable this program

      rm -f "/etc/.no-$PGM_NAME"
     ;;

   disable)

      # create the .no file to disable this program

      touch "/etc/.no-$PGM_NAME"
      ;;

   *) echo "$USAGE"
      exit 1
      ;;
esac
done

exit 0
```

Adapting the Script

This script is fairly adaptable and can be modified to start, stop, enable, and disable almost any program by just modifying two variables, `$PGM` and `$PGM_OPTS`. Currently these are set as follows:

```
PGM=/usr/local/bin/sshd
PGM_OPTS=
```

If you need to reuse the script for a different program, for example a Web server, you could simply make a copy of the script as follows:

```
# cd /sbin/init.d
# cp sshd httpd
```

This assumes that the script is stored in the directory `/sbin/init.d` and that the name you want to give the Web servers startup script is `httpd`. The actual location of startup scripts differs from system to system as discussed previously. Once you have a copy, you can modify just the variable definitions for `$PGM` and `$PGM_OPTS` as follows:

```
PGM=/usr/local/bin/httpd
PGM_OPTS=-DSSL
```

This assumes that the Web server named `httpd` is located in `/usr/local/bin` and that it needs to be started with the `-DSSL` option. After making this modification, you can start the Web server as follows:

```
# /sbin/init.d/httpd start
```

To stop it, you can do the following:

```
# /sbin/init.d/httpd stop
```

All that would remain is to make the start and stop links in the appropriate run-level directories. Usually the start link is in the `rc3.d` directory, whereas the stop link is in the `rc5.d` and `rc6.d` directories (except on Linux where it is only in the `rc6.d` directory). You can create these links as follows:

```
# cd /sbin/rc3.d && ln -s ../init.d/httpd S98httpd
# cd /sbin/rc5.d && ln -s ../init.d/httpd K02httpd
# cd /sbin/rc6.d && ln -s ../init.d/httpd K02httpd
```

The actual directories where the links need to be created are system-dependent as discussed previously. As an example, the commands that might be used on Solaris are

```
# cd /etc/rc3.d && ln -s ../init.d/httpd S98httpd
# cd /etc/rc5.d && ln -s ../init.d/httpd K02httpd
# cd /etc/rc6.d && ln -s ../init.d/httpd K02httpd
```

On Linux you need something like the following:

```
# cd /etc/rc.d/rc3.d && ln -s ../init.d/httpd S98httpd
# cd /etc/rc.d/rc6.d && ln -s ../init.d/httpd K02httpd
```

Maintaining an Address Book

In this section, you will look at solving a common problem for many people: tracking addresses and phone numbers. Many people, myself included, often get business cards or e-mail messages from people they need to keep in touch with. E-mail messages and business cards have a tendency to get lost, leading to problems when you need to contact someone. A nice solution to this problem is to store all the contact information on the computer so that you can access and manipulate it easily.

In this section, you will develop a set of scripts that work together to maintain a simple address book. The address book will store the following information:

- Name
- E-mail address
- Postal address
- Phone number

Each of these pieces of information can contain almost any character including spaces or other special characters such as the dash (-), period, (.), or single quote ('). Thus you need to hold the information in a format that allows for such a wide range of characters. A commonly used format is to separate each piece of information using the colon (:) character. For example, the following information:

```
Sriranga Veeraraghavan
ranga@soda.berkeley.edu
1136 Wunderlich Dr. San Jose CA 95129
408-444-4444
```

can be stored as:

```
Sriranga Veeraraghavan:ranga@soda.berkeley.edu:1136 Wunderlich Dr.
➥San Jose CA 95129:408-444-4444
```

Here any special character, except the colon, can be used. Also this format enables you to make any field optional. For example,

```
:vathsa@kanchi.bosland.us::408-444-4444
```

can indicate that only the e-mail address and phone number were known for a particular person.

To maintain your address book, you need a few scripts:

- `showperson` to show information about one or more people in the address book
- `addperson` to add a person to the address book
- `delperson` to delete a person from the address book

The following examples assume that the address book is stored in the file `$HOME/addressbook`.

Showing People

One of the main tasks any address book must perform is looking up information about a person and then displaying it. You will develop a script called `showperson` to handle this task.

To find information about a person, you can use `grep`. For example,

```
$ grep vathsa addressbook
```

lists all the lines that contain the word *`vathsa`* in the file `addressbook`. For your address book, the output might look like the following:

```
:vathsa@kanchi.bosland.us::408-444-4444
```

As you imagine, your script should format the results of the `grep` command. A nice format would be to list the name, e-mail address, postal address, and phone number on separate lines. You can do this using an `awk` command:

```
awk -F: '{ printf "Name: %s\nEmail: %s\nAddress: %s\nPhone:
➥%s\n\n",$1,$2,$3,$4 ; }'
```

By putting these commands together, you can construct the `showperson` script as given in Listing 22.2 (the line numbers are provided for your reference).

LISTING 22.2 Listing of the showperson Script

```
#!/bin/sh
# Name: showperson
# Desc: show matching records in addressbook
# Args: $1 -> string to look for in addressbook

PATH=/bin:/usr/bin

# check that a string is given

if [ $# -lt 1 ] ; then
    echo "USAGE: `basename $0` name"
    exit 1
fi

# check that the address book exists

MYADDRESSBOOK="$HOME/addressbook"
if [ ! -f "$MYADDRESSBOOK" ] ; then
    echo "ERROR: $MYADDESSBOOK does not exist, or is not a
    ➥file." >&2
    exit 1
fi

```

Listing 22.2 Continued

```
23  # get all matches and format them
24
25  grep "$1" "$MYADDRESSBOOK" |
26      awk -F: '{
27          printf "%-10s %s\n%-10s %s\n%-10s %s\n%-10s %s\n\n",\
28                  "Name:",$1,"Email:",$2,"Address:",$3,
                ➥"Phone:",$4 ;
29      }'
30
31  exit $?
```

There are three main actions in the script:

1. Verify the number of arguments.
2. Check to see whether the address book exists.
3. Find all matches and print them.

In the first part (lines 10–13), the script checks to see whether at least one argument is given. If so, the script continues; otherwise, it prints a usage message and exits. In the second part, the script checks to see whether the address book exits. If it does not, the script prints an error and then exits; otherwise, it continues. In the last part of the script, `grep` obtains a list of matches and `awk` formats this list. To ensure even spacing of the output, the `awk` command uses formatting for both the information and its description. As an example,

```
$ ./showperson ranga
```

produces output similar to the following:

```
Name:      Sriranga Veeraraghavan
Email:     ranga@soda.berkeley.edu
Address:   1136 Wunderlich Dr. San Jose CA
Phone:     408-444-4444
```

Notice how all the information in the second column is correctly aligned.

You can also use `showperson` to look for matches of a particular string. For example,

```
$ ./showperson va
```

produces two matches:

```
Name:      Sriranga Veeraraghavan
Email:     ranga@soda.berkeley.edu
Address:   1136 Wunderlich Dr. San Jose CA
Phone:     408-444-4444
```

```
Name:
Email:    vathsa@bosland.us
Address:
Phone:    408-444-4444
```

Adding a Person

One of the most important things about any address book is the capability to easily add information to it. If you need to edit the address book manually to add information, you are bound to make errors such as forgetting to add a colon to separate fields. By using a script, you can avoid such errors.

In this section you will look at the `addperson` script. It enables you to add entries into the address book by either providing information interactively or by providing information on the command line via command-line options. The script enters interactive mode when no options are given. In non-interactive mode it tries to obtain the necessary information from the command-line options.

Regardless of the mode, the script stores the user-provided information into the following variables:

- `NAME` stores the name given by the user.
- `EMAIL` stores the e-mail address given by the user.
- `ADDR` stores the postal address given by the user.
- `PHONE` stores the phone number given by the user.

In interactive mode, you prompt for the information in each record as follows:

```
printf "%-10s " "Name:"    ; read NAME
printf "%-10s " "Email:"   ; read EMAIL
printf "%-10s " "Address:" ; read ADDR
printf "%-10s " "Phone:"   ; read PHONE
```

After each prompt, you read and store the user's input, including spaces and special characters, inside the appropriate variable. In non-interactive mode, you use `getopts` to scan the options:

```
while getopts n:e:a:p: OPTION
do
        case $OPTION in
            n) NAME="$OPTARG" ;;
            e) EMAIL="$OPTARG" ;;
            a) ADDR="$OPTARG" ;;
            p) PHONE="$OPTARG" ;;
            \?) echo "USAGE: $USAGE" >&2 ; exit 1 ;;
        esac
done
```

As you can see, the options understood by the script in non-interactive mode are

- -n for the name (sets NAME)
- -e for the e-mail address (sets EMAIL)
- -a for the postal address (sets ADDR)
- -p for the phone number (sets PHONE)

After you have obtained the required information, you can update the file by appending a formatted record to the end of the addressbook file as follows:

```
echo "$NAME:$EMAIL:$ADDR:$PHONE" >> "$MYADDRESSBOOK"
```

Here you are assuming that the variable MYADDRESSBOOK contains the pathname to the address book file.

The complete addperson script is given in Listing 22.3 (the line numbers are provided for your reference).

LISTING 22.3 Complete Listing of the addperson Script

```
#!/bin/sh
# Name: addperson
# Desc: add a person addressbook
# Args: -n <name>
#       -e <email>
#       -a <postal address>
#       -p <phone number>

# initialize the variables

PATH=/bin:/usr/bin
MYADDRESSBOOK=$HOME/addressbook
NAME=""
EMAIL=""
ADDR=""
PHONE=""

# create a function to remove the : from user input

remove_colon() { echo "$@" | tr ':' ' ' ; }

if [ $# -lt 1 ] ; then

    # this is interactive mode

    # enable erasing input

    stty erase '^?'
```

LISTING 22.3 Continued

```
29
30      # prompt for the info
31
32      printf "%-10s " "Name:"    ; read NAME
33      printf "%-10s " "Email:"   ; read EMAIL
34      printf "%-10s " "Address:" ; read ADDR
35      printf "%-10s " "Phone:"   ; read PHONE
36
37  else
38
39      # this is noninteractive mode
40
41      # initialize a variable for the usage statement
42
43      USAGE="`basename $0` [-n name] [-e email] [-a address]
        ➥[-p phone]"
44
45      # scan the arguments to get the info
46
47      while getopts n:e:a:p:h OPTION
48      do
49          case $OPTION in
50              n) NAME="$OPTARG" ;;
51              e) EMAIL="$OPTARG" ;;
52              a) ADDR="$OPTARG" ;;
53              p) PHONE="$OPTARG" ;;
54              \?|h) echo "USAGE: $USAGE" >&2 ; exit 1 ;;
55          esac
56      done
57  fi
58
59  NAME="`remove_colon $NAME`"
60  EMAIL="`remove_colon $EMAIL`"
61  ADDR="`remove_colon $ADDR`"
62  PHONE="`remove_colon $PHONE`"
63
64  echo "$NAME:$EMAIL:$ADDR:$PHONE" >> "$MYADDRESSBOOK"
65
66  exit $?
```

This script first initializes its variables (lines 11–16). Then you set the internal variables that store the user information to null in order to avoid conflicts with exported variables from the user's environment.

The next step is to create the following function (line 20):

```
remove_colon() { echo "$@" | tr ':' ' ' ; }
```

You use this function to make sure that the user's input doesn't contain any colons.

Then you check to see whether any arguments are given (line 22). If no arguments are given, you enter interactive mode (lines 23–36); otherwise, you enter non-interactive mode (lines 38–56).

In interactive mode, you prompt for each piece of information and read it in. Before you produce the first prompt, you issue a `stty` command (line 28) to make sure the user can erase any mistakes made during input.

In non-interactive mode, you use `getopts` to obtain the information provided on the command line. In this section you also initialize the variable `USAGE` that contains the usage statement for this command.

After you have obtained the necessary information, you call the `remove_colon` function for each variable (lines 59–62). Because the user can potentially specify information that contains colons, skipping this step could corrupt the address book and confuse the `showperson` script. Finally you update the address book and exit.

An example of using the script in interactive mode is

```
$ ./addperson
Name:      James Kirk
Email:     jim@enterprise-a.starfleet.mil
Address:   1701 Main Street James Town Iowa UFP
Phone:
```

Here you provided only the name, e-mail address, and postal address for *Jim Kirk*. Thus when you look up *James Kirk* in the address book, you find that his phone number is empty:

```
$ ./showperson
Name:      James Kirk
Email:     jim@enterprise-a.starfleet.mil
Address:   1701 Main Street James Town Iowa UFP
Phone:
```

You can do the same operation using the non-interactive form of the command as follows:

```
$ ./addperson -n "James Kirk" -e jim@enterprise-a.starfleet.mil \
-a "1701 Main Street James Town Iowa UPF"
```

Notice that on the command line you need to quote the entries that contain spaces.

Deleting a Person

Occasionally, you will need to delete a person from the address book. In this section, you will look at a script called `delperson` that deletes people from the address book.

Deleting a person from the address book is a harder task because you have to confirm each record selected for deletion. The two main tasks you need to perform are

1. Make a list of the lines in the address book that match the specified name.
2. Based on user feedback, delete the appropriate entries from the address book.

Because the delete operation can potentially remove information from the address book, you have to be extra careful about making backups and working on a copy of the address book rather than on the original address book.

To simplify prompting and printing error messages, this script uses the shell function library `libTYSP2.sh` that was introduced in Chapter 21.

The basic flow of the script is as follows:

1. Make a copy of the address book and use the copy for all modifications.
2. Get a list of all matching lines from this copy and store them in a deletion file.
3. For each record in the deletion file, print out the record and ask the user whether that line should be deleted.
4. If the user wants the record deleted, remove that record from the copy of the address book.
5. After the deletions are complete, make a backup of the original address book.
6. Make the edited copy the address book.
7. Clean up temporary files and exit.

For each of these steps, you use a function to make sure that the operations performed succeeded.

The complete `delperson` script is given in Listing 22.4 (the line numbers are provided for your reference).

LISTING 22.4 Complete Listing of the `delperson` Script

```
#!/bin/sh
# Name: delperson
# Desc: del a person addressbook
# Args: $1 -> name of person to delete

# get the helper functions

. $HOME/lib/sh/libTYSP2.sh

PATH=/bin:/usr/bin

```

LISTING 22.4 Continued

```
# check that a name is given
if [ $# -lt 1 ] ; then
    printUSAGE "`basename $0` name"
    exit 1
fi
# check that the address book exists
MYADDRESSBOOK="$HOME/addressbook"
if [ ! -f "$MYADDRESSBOOK" ] ; then
    printERROR "$MYADDESSBOOK does not exists, or is
    ➥not a file."
    exit 1
fi
# initialize the variables holding the location of the
# temporary files
TMPF1=/tmp/apupdate.$$
TMPF2=/tmp/abdelets.$$
# function to clean up temporary files
doCleanUp() { rm "$TMPF1" "$TMPF1.new" "$TMPF2" 2>
➥/dev/null ; }
# function to exit if update failed
Failed() {
    if [ "$1" -ne 0 ] ; then
        shift
        printERROR $@
        doCleanUp
        exit 1
    fi
}
# make a copy of the address book for updating,
# proceed only if sucessful
cp "$MYADDRESSBOOK" "$TMPF1" 2> /dev/null
Failed $? "Could not make a backup of the address book."
# get a list of all matching lines from the address book copy
# continue if one or more matches were found
grep "$1" "$TMPF1" > "$TMPF2" 2> /dev/null
Failed $? "No matches found."
# prompt the user for each entry that was found
```

LISTING 22.4 Continued

```

exec 5< "$TMPF2"
while read LINE <&5
do

    # display each line formatted

    echo "$LINE" | awk -F: '{
        printf "%-10s %s\n%-10s %s\n%-10s %s\n%-10s %s\n\n",\
               "Name:",$1,"Email:",$2,"Address:",$3,
               ➥"Phone:",$4 ;
    }'

    # prompt for each line, if yes try to remove the line

    promptYESNO "Delete this entry" "n"
    if [ "$YESNO" = "y" ] ; then

        # try to remove the line, store the updated version
        # in a new file

        grep -v "$LINE" "$TMPF1" > "$TMPF1.new" 2> /dev/null
        Failed $? "Unable to update the address book"

        # replace the old version with the updated version

        mv "$TMPF1.new" "$TMPF1" 2> /dev/null
        Failed $? "Unable to update the address book"

    fi
done
exec 5<&-

# save the original version

mv "$MYADDRESSBOOK" "$MYADDRESSBOOK".bak 2> /dev/null
Failed $? "Unable to update the address book"

# replace the original with the edited version

mv "$TMPF1" "$MYADDRESSBOOK" 2> /dev/null
Failed $? "Unable to update the address book"

# clean up

doCleanUp

exit $?
```

In the first part of the script (lines 8–30), you perform some initialization steps:

1. Retrieve the helper functions from `libTYSP2.sh` (line 8).
2. Check to make sure a name to delete is given (lines 14–17).
3. Check to make sure that the address book exits (lines 21–25).
4. Initialize the variables for the temporary files (lines 29 and 30) and the `PATH` (line 10).

After initialization, you create a few additional helper functions:

- `doCleanUp` to remove the temporary files (line 34)
- `Failed` to issue an error message, remove the temporary files, and exit if a critical command fails (lines 37–44)

The first step in the script is to make a copy of the address book (line 49). If this step fails, you exit (line 50). If this step is successful, you make a list of all the lines in the address book that match the name specified by the user (line 55). If you cannot successfully make this file, you exit (line 56).

Next you enter the delete loop (lines 60–89). For each line that matches the name provided by the user, you print a formatted version of the line (lines 66–69). Notice that you are using the same `awk` statement used in the `showperson` script.

For each matching line, ask the user whether the entry should be deleted (line 73). If the user agrees (line 74), you do the following:

1. Try to delete the line from the copy of the address book. Store the modified version in a different file (line 79).
2. Replace the copy of the address book with the modified copy (line 84).

If either of these operations fails, you exit (lines 80 and 85).

After the deletions are finished, you make a backup of the original address book (line 93). Then you replace the address book with the edited version (line 98). Again you exit if either operation fails (lines 94 and 99).

Finally you clean up and exit.

Here is an example of this script in action:

```
$ ./delperson Sriranga
Name:       Sriranga Veeraraghavan
Email:      ranga@soda.berkeley.edu
Address:    1136 Wunderlich Dr. San Jose CA
Phone:      408-444-4444

Delete this entry (y/n)? [n] y
```

Here you replied *yes* to the question. You can confirm that the delete worked as follows:

```
$ ./showperson Sriranga
$
```

Because there is no output from `showperson`, you know that this entry has been deleted.

Summary

This chapter covered using shell scripts to solve two problems:

- Creating init or startup scripts
- Maintaining an address book

In the first example, you learned how the system boots and how scripts are used to streamline this process. In the second example, you developed three scripts that modify and view the contents of an address book. Some of the highlights of these scripts are

- The `showperson` script showed you how the `grep` and `awk` commands can be used to format input.
- The `addperson` script showed you how a single script can be used in both interactive and non-interactive modes.
- The `delperson` script showed you how to use the `grep` command and file descriptors to update a file accurately.

The examples in this chapter demonstrate how you can apply the tools covered in previous chapters to solve real problems. Using these scripts as examples, you can see some of the techniques used to solve everyday problems.

The next chapter explores several methods of writing scripts to ensure that they are portable between different versions of UNIX.

Questions

1. Add a check to the `sshd` init script that verifies if the user is root. (Init scripts should only be executed by root).

   HINT: Use the `id` and `sed` commands.
2. The `showperson` script lists all matching entries in the address book based on a name provided by the user. The matches produced are case sensitive. How can you change the script matches so they aren't case sensitive?

3. Both the `showperson` and `delperson` scripts reproduce the following code

```
PATH=/bin:/usr/bin

# check that a name is given

if [ $# -lt 1 ] ; then
    printUSAGE "`basename $0` name"
    exit 1
fi

# check that the address book exists

MYADDRESSBOOK="$HOME/addressbook"
if [ ! -f "$MYADDRESSBOOK" ] ; then
    printERROR "$MYADDESSBOOK does not exists, or is
    ➥not a file."
    exit 1
fi
```

   and

```
awk -F: '{
        printf "%-10s %s\n%-10s %s\n%-10s %s\n%-10s
        ➥%s\n\n",\
                "Name:",$1,"Email:",$2,"Address:",$3,
                ➥"Phone:",$4 ;
    }'
```

   How might you rewrite these scripts so that this code can be shared between the two scripts instead of being replicated in both?

4. The `delperson` script uses the `grep` command to generate a list of matching entries. This might confuse the user in the following instance:

```
$ ./delperson to
Name:       James T. Kirk
Email:      jim@enterprise.mil
Address:    1701 Main Street Anytown Iowa
Phone:      555-555-5555

Delete this entry (y/n)? [n]
```

   Here the `to` in `Anytown` was matched.

   What changes should be made to the `delperson` script so that only those entries whose names match the user-specified name are selected for deletion?

   (HINT: Use the `sed` command instead of `grep`.)

5. If `delperson` gets a signal while it is processing deletes, all the intermediate files are left behind. What can be done to prevent this?

Terms

Init Scripts Simple scripts, originally stored in `/sbin/init.d`, that are responsible for starting and stopping a program.

Run-levels Partition the system startup into seven levels (zero through six) and provide a method for enforcing startup dependencies and partitioning the startup of system services into the different levels.

HOUR 23

Scripting for Portability

Shell programming is an important part of UNIX because shell scripts are easily portable to many different versions of UNIX. In many cases, shell scripts will function correctly on multiple systems without modification.

The easiest way to ensure that a shell script is completely portable is to restrict the script to using only those commands and features that are available on all versions of UNIX. Sometimes this means that the script must implement workarounds to deal with the limitations of a particular version of UNIX.

In this chapter, we will examine the following topics that relate to shell script portability:

- Determining the version of UNIX a system is running
- Adapting shell scripts to different versions of UNIX

Determining UNIX Versions

Before you can begin adjusting shell scripts to be portable, you need to know what the different types of UNIX are and how to tell them apart. The three major types of UNIX are

- BSD (Berkeley Software Distribution)
- System V
- Linux

The locations of commands and the options supported by certain commands are different among these three types of UNIX. This chapter highlights some of the major differences pertaining to commands in particular.

BSD

UNIX was first developed in the 1970s at AT&T's Bell Labs. For many years it remained restricted to AT&T and a few universities. In the early 1980s, the University of California at Berkeley acquired the source code to UNIX from AT&T Bell Labs. Throughout the 1980s and into the early 1990s, the Berkeley Systems Research Group made significant improvements and advancements to UNIX. These improvements were periodically distributed under the name Berkeley Software Distribution or BSD.

In the early 1990s, the Berkeley team disbanded and released the source code to the public. Several groups and companies adopted the BSD source and provided their own versions of BSD. The three major groups currently developing freely available versions BSD are

- The FreeBSD Project: `http://www.freebsd.org`
- The NetBSD Foundation: `http://www.netbsd.org`
- OpenBSD: `http://www.openbsd.org`

Currently the two major companies involved in BSD development and distribution are Apple Computer and Wind River Systems. Apple's MacOS X is based on FreeBSD. Wind River's BSD/OS is also based on FreeBSD. Another commercial version of BSD is Sun Microsystems' SunOS4. Sun has not supported or developed SunOS4 since the early 1990s, but it is still quite popular at some universities.

System V

System V (sometimes abbreviated as SysV) is the latest version of UNIX released by AT&T Bell Labs. System V UNIX is the standard for most commercial versions of UNIX. Both Sun Microsystems' Solaris and Hewlett-Packard's HP-UX are based on System V UNIX.

Some of the new features added to UNIX in System V are

- A new boot system
- A networking subsystem known as STREAMS
- A process-to-process communication and memory sharing system
- Standardized system administration tools
- A prepackaged software installation and removal system

System V UNIX also changed the layout of the file system. Table 23.1 lists the BSD directories and their System V equivalents.

TABLE 23.1 System V Equivalents of BSD Directories

BSD	*System V*
`/bin`	`/usr/bin`
`/sbin`	`/usr/sbin`
`/usr/adm`	`/var/adm`
`/usr/mail`	`/var/mail` or `/var/spool/mail`
`/usr/tmp`	`/var/tmp`

The directories `/bin` and `/sbin` still exist on some System V–based UNIX versions. On Solaris, these directories are links to `/usr/bin` and `/usr/sbin`, respectively. On HP-UX, these directories still contain some commands essential at boot time. The commands stored in these directories are not the same commands as in BSD. Most vendors who have switched from BSD to System V still provide BSD versions in the directory `/usr/ucb`.

In addition to these changes, many System V–based UNIX versions have introduced the directory `/opt` in an attempt to standardize the installation locations of prepackaged software products. On older systems, many different locations, including `/usr`, `/usr/contrib`, and `/usr/local`, were used to install optional software packages.

Linux

Linux can be considered as a third version of UNIX. It was developed independent of either the BSD or the System V source code. Linux was written by Linus Torvalds at the University of Helsinki in the early 1990s. It incorporates the best features found in both System V and BSD. The commands and the networking layer in Linux are similar to BSD, whereas the standardized tools for system configuration and installation of prepackaged software are similar to System V. Some of the major vendors of Linux are Caldera, Debian, Mandrake, Red Hat, Slackware, and SuSE.

Using `uname` to Determine the UNIX Version

The first step in writing portable shell scripts is to determine which version of UNIX is executing your shell script. This can be determined this using the `uname` command:

```
uname options
```

Here, *`options`* is one or more of the options given in Table 23.2.

TABLE 23.2 Options for the `uname` Command

Option	*Description*
`-a`	Prints all information
`-m`	Prints the current hardware type
`-n`	Prints the hostname of the system
`-r`	Prints the operating system release level
`-s`	Prints the name of the operating system (default)

On SunOS, the `-a` option of `uname` displays summary information about the system. To get complete information, use the `-X` option of `uname`.

By default, the `uname` command prints the name of the operating system. The output looks like the following:

```
$ uname
Linux
```

Here, the output indicates that the operating system name of the machine is `Linux`. Usually, this is enough to determine the UNIX version, as you can see from the values listed in Table 23.3.

TABLE 23.3 Selected UNIX Version names as Displayed by `uname`

Name	*Description*
Linux	A system running Linux
HP-UX	A system running Hewlett-Packard's HP-UX
FreeBSD	A system running FreeBSD
OpenBSD	A system running OpenBSD
Darwin	A system running Apple's MacOS X
SunOS	A system running Sun Microsystem's SunOS (BSD based) or Solaris (System V based)

Dealing with SunOS

SunOS is the name of the UNIX operating system developed by Sun Microsystems. SunOS was originally based on BSD UNIX but has since changed to be based on System V UNIX. Although the marketing name has been changed to Solaris, `uname` still produces the output `SunOS`. Shell scripts that have to run on both Solaris and earlier BSD-based versions of SunOS, such as SunOS4, need to differentiate between these two versions.

To determine whether a system is running Solaris or SunOS, you can check the version of the operating system. SunOS versions 5 and higher are Solaris (System V–based); SunOS versions 4 and lower are SunOS (BSD-based).

To determine the version of the operating system, you can use the `-r` option of `uname`:

```
$ uname -r
5.5.1
```

This indicates that the version of the operating system is 5.5.1. If you want to add the operating system's name to this output, use the `-r` and the `-s` options:

```
$ uname -rs
SunOS 5.5.1
```

This indicates the machine is running Solaris. The output on a machine running BSD-based SunOS4 might be

```
SunOS 4.1.3
```

Determining the Hardware Type

Sometimes a shell script is written as a wrapper around a hardware-specific program. For example, install scripts are usually the same for different hardware platforms supported by a particular operating system. Although the install script might be the same for every hardware platform, the files that are installed are usually different.

To determine the hardware type, you can use the `-m` option:

```
$ uname -m
sun4m
```

Some common return values and their hardware types are listed in Table 23.4.

TABLE 23.4 Hardware Types Returned by the `uname` Command

Hardware	*Description*
`9000/`*`xxx`*	Hewlett-Packard 9000 series workstation. Some common values of *xxx* are 700, 712, 715, and 750.
`i386`	Intel 386-, 486-, Pentium-, or Pentium II–based workstation.

TABLE 23.4 Continued

Hardware	*Description*
`i586`	A system using an Intel Pentium II, III, or newer processor.
`sun4`*`x`*	A Sun Microsystems workstation. Some common values of *`x`* are `c` (SparcStation 1 and 2), `m` (SparcStation 5, 10, and 20), and `u` (UltraSparc).
`Power Macintosh`	An Apple Macintosh running MacOS X.

Determining the `hostname` of a System

Many shell scripts need to check the hostname of a system. The traditional method of doing this on BSD systems is to use the `hostname` command, as in the following example:

```
$ hostname
soda.CSUA.Berkeley.EDU
```

In System V and Linux, the `hostname` command is not always available. The `uname -n` command should be used instead:

```
$ uname -n
kashi
```

Because the `uname -n` command is available on both System V and BSD UNIX, it is preferred for use in portable shell scripts.

Determining the UNIX Version Using a Function

You have just looked at using the `uname` command to gather information about the version of UNIX that a particular system is running. Now you need a method for using this information in a shell script. As you saw in Chapter 21, "Problem Solving with Functions," creating a shell function to perform this task will give you the greatest flexibility:

```
getOSName() {
    case "`uname -s`" in
        *BSD)
            echo bsd ;;
        Darwin)
            echo darwin ;;
        SunOS)
            case "`uname -r`" in
                5.*) echo solaris ;;
                  *) echo sunos ;;
            esac
            ;;
        Linux)
            echo linux ;;
        HP-UX)
```

```
            echo hpux ;;
        AIX)
            echo aix ;;
        *)  echo unknown ;;
    esac
}
```

As you can see, this function is not very complicated. It checks the output of `uname -s` and looks for a match. In the case of SunOS, it also checks the output of `uname -r` to determine whether the operating system is Solaris or SunOS.

In many cases, you need to tailor the options of a command, such as `ps` or `df`, for a particular system in order to obtain the desired output from that command. In such cases, you need the capability to "ask" whether the operating system is of a certain type:

```
isOS() {
    if [ $# -lt 1 ] ; then
        echo "ERROR: Insufficient Aruments." >&2
        return 1
    fi

    REQ=`echo $1 | tr '[A-Z]' '[a-z]'`
    if [ "$REQ" = "`getOSName`" ] ; then return 0 ; fi
    return 1
}
```

This function compares its first argument to the output of the function `getOSName` and returns `0` (true) if they are the same; otherwise, it returns `1` (false).

Using this function, it is possible to write `if` statements similar to the following:

```
if isOS hpux ; then
    : # HP-UX specific commands here
elif isOS solaris ; then
    : # Solaris specific comands here
else
    : # generic unix commands here
fi
```

The reason that the `isOS` function does not directly check the value of `$1`, but uses the variable `REQ` instead, is to allow for greater flexibility on the part of the function's user. For example, this implementation allows any of the following to be used to check whether a system is running Linux:

```
isOS LINUX
isOS Linux
isOS linux
```

Techniques for Increasing Portability

There are two common techniques to increase the portability of a shell script between different versions of UNIX:

- Conditional execution
- Abstraction

Conditional execution alters the execution of a script based on the system type, whereas *abstraction* retains the same basic flow of the script by placing the conditional statements within functions.

Conditional Execution

A script that uses conditional execution for portability contains an `if` statement at the beginning that sets several variables indicating the set of commands to use on a particular platform. This section looks at two common cases in which conditional execution is used:

- Determining the remote shell command
- Determining the proper method of using the `echo` command in prompts

The first case illustrates setting a variable based on the operating system type. The second case illustrates setting variables based on the behavior of a command (`echo`) on a particular system.

Executing Remote Commands

A common use of conditional execution is found in scripts that need to execute commands on remote systems. On most versions of UNIX, you can use the `rsh` (remote shell) command to execute commands on a remote system. Unfortunately, this command is not available on all versions of UNIX. On HP-UX, for example, `rsh` is available but it is not the remote shell program—it is the restricted shell program. On HP-UX, you need to use the command `remsh` to execute commands on a remote system.

A script that needs to execute commands on a remote system might have an `if` statement of the following form at its beginning:

```
if SystemIS HPUX ; then
    RCMD=remsh
else
    RCMD=rsh
fi
```

After the variable `$RCMD` is set, remote commands can execute as follows:

```
"$RCMD" host command
```

Here, *`host`* is the hostname of the remote system, and *`command`* is the command to execute.

Problems with the `echo` Command in Prompts

Most programs that need to prompt the users need to be able to print a prompt that is not terminated by a newline. In Chapter 5, "Input and Output," there were several problems with using the `\c` escape sequence of the `echo` command to do this. The workaround was to use the `/bin/echo` command.

Although this works for UNIX versions based on System V, on some BSD-based systems this does not work. You need to specify the `-n` option to `echo` instead. By using the following shell script, you can create a shell function, `echo_prompt`, to display a prompt reliably across all versions of `echo`:

```
_ECHO=/bin/echo
_N=
_C="\c"
ECHOOUT=`$_ECHO "hello $_C"`
if [ "$ECHOOUT" = "hello \c" ] ; then
    _N="-n"
    _C=
fi
export _ECHO _N _C

echo_prompt() {  $_ECHO $_N $@ $_C ; }
```

This script fragment uses the `/bin/echo` workaround as the base from which to construct the correct `echo` command. It checks the output of an `echo` command to determine whether the `\c` sequence is handled correctly. If it is not, the `-n` option is enabled.

After the appropriate values have been determined, the function echo_prompt is created using these values. This function enables you to reliably output prompts on every system.

Abstraction

Abstraction is a technique used to hide the differences between the versions of UNIX inside shell functions. By doing this, the overall flow of a shell script is not affected. When a function is called, it makes a decision as to what commands to execute.

You will learn about two different examples of abstraction:

- Adapting the `getSpaceFree` function to run on HP-UX
- Adapting the `getPID` function to run on both BSD and System V

This section uses the functions `getOSName` and `isOS`, given earlier in this chapter.

Adapting `getSpaceFree` for HP-UX

Recall the `getSpaceFree` function introduced in Chapter 21:

```
getSpaceFree() {
    if [ $# -lt 1 ] ; then
```

```
        echo "ERROR: Insufficient Arguments." >&2
        return 1
    fi

    DIR="$1"
    if [ ! -d "$DIR" ] ; then
        DIR=`/usr/bin/dirname $DIR`
    fi

    df -k "$DIR" | awk 'NR != 1 { print $4 ; }'
}
```

This function prints the amount of free space in a directory in kilobytes. Its output is used in the `isSpaceAvailable` function to determine whether there is enough space in a particular directory. Although this works for most systems (Solaris, Linux, BSD), it does not work on HP-UX systems because the output of `df -k` on HP-UX systems is quite different from other versions of UNIX:

```
$ df -k /usr/sbin
/usr            (/dev/vg00/lvol8       ) :   737344 total allocated Kb
                                             368296 free allocated Kb
                                             369048 used allocated Kb
                                                 50 % allocation used
```

To get the output in a format that is easier to parse, you need to use the command `df -b` instead:

```
$ df -b /usr/sbin
/usr                    (/dev/vg00/lvol8       ) :   392808 Kbytes free
```

In order to use `isSpaceAvailable` on all systems, including HP-UX, you need to change the function `getSpaceFree` to take this into account. The modified version looks like the following:

```
getSpaceFree() {
    if [ $# -lt 1 ] ; then
        echo "ERROR: Insufficient Arguments." >&2
        return 1
    fi

    DIR="$1"
    if [ ! -d "$DIR" ] ; then
        DIR=`/usr/bin/dirname $DIR`
    fi

    if isOS HPUX ; then
        df -b "$DIR" | awk '{ print $5 ; }'
    else
        df -k "$DIR" | awk 'NR != 1 { print $4 ; }'
    fi
}
```

Here, the `isOS` function is called in order to determine the command to execute.

Adapting getPID for BSD

Recall the getPID function introduced in Chapter 21:

```
getPID() {

    if [ $# -lt 1 ] ; then
        echo "ERROR: Insufficient Arguments." >&2
        return 1
    fi

    PSOPTS="-ef"

    /bin/ps $PSOPTS | grep "$1" | awk '/grep/ { next; } { print $2; }'
}
```

This function works correctly only on systems where the ps -ef command produces a listing of all running processes. On BSD systems and older Linux systems, you need to use the command

```
ps -auwx
```

to get the correct output. This command works correctly on BSD system but older Linux systems produce the following warning message:

```
warning: '-' deprecated; use 'ps auwx', not 'ps -auwx'
```

By using the getOSName function given earlier in this chapter, you can adapt the getPID function to work with the BSD, Linux, and System V versions of ps. The modified version of getPID is as follows:

```
getPID() {

    if [ $# -lt 1 ] ; then
        echo "ERROR: Insufficient Arguments." >&2
        return 1
    fi

    case `getOSName` in
        bsd|sunos|linux|darwin)
            PSOPTS="-auwx" ;;
        *)
            PSOPTS="-ef" ;;
    esac

    /bin/ps $PSOPTS 2>/dev/null | grep "$1" | \
    awk '/grep/ { next; } { print $2; }'
}
```

The two main changes to the function are

- A `case` statement sets the variable `PSOPTS` based on the operating system name.
- The STDERR of `ps` is redirected to `/dev/null` in order to discard the warning message generated on older versions of Linux.

Linux ps

In Linux the `ps` command varies between different versions. In older versions of Linux (2.0), the hyphen in the `-auwx` command is not properly supported, whereas in current versions the hyphen is supported, as are the System V style `-ef` options. Taking this into account, you could modify the `getPID()` functions as follows:

```
getPID() {

    if [ $# -lt 1 ] ; then
        echo "ERROR: Insufficient Arguments." >&2
        return 1
    fi

    PSOPTSPTS="-ef"
    case `getOSName` in
        bsd|sunos|darwin)
            PSOPTSPTS="-auwx" ;;
        linux)
            case `uname -r` in
               [01].*) PSOPTS="-auwx" ;;
               2.0*) PSOPTS="auwx" ;;
            esac
            ;;
    esac

    /bin/ps $PSOPTS | grep "$1" | \
    awk '/grep/ { next; } { print $2; }'
}
```

This version avoids having to redirect STDERR to `/dev/null` and allows you to detect any problems that might be reported by the `ps` command.

Summary

In this chapter, you learned how to determine which version of UNIX is running using `uname`. In addition, you developed the `getOSName` and `isOS` functions to help adapt shell scripts to multiple versions of UNIX. You also looked at the following techniques for improving the portability of shell scripts:

- Conditional execution
- Abstraction

In conditional execution, the flow of a script was modified depending on the version of UNIX being used. In abstraction, function implementations were altered to account for the differences between versions of UNIX; the overall flow of the script remained the same.

Using the techniques and tips in this chapter, you can port shell scripts across different versions of UNIX.

Question

1. Write a function called `getCharCount` that prints the number of characters in a file. Use `wc` to obtain the character count.

   Linux, FreeBSD, and SunOS (not Solaris), use the `-c` option for `wc`, whereas other versions of UNIX use the `-m` option. Feel free to use the function `getOSName`.

Terms

Abstraction Scripts that use abstraction retain the same basic flow by placing the conditional execution statements within functions. When a function is called, it decides which commands to execute on a given platform.

Conditional Execution Alters the execution of a script based on the system type. A script that uses conditional execution usually contains an `if` statement at the beginning of the script that sets variables to indicate the commands to use on a particular platform.

HOUR 24

Shell Programming FAQs

Each of the previous chapters has focused on an individual topic in shell programming, such as variables, loops, or debugging. As you progressed through the book, you worked on problems that required knowledge from previous chapters. This chapter takes a slightly different approach by trying to answer some frequently asked shell programming questions. Specifically, this chapter covers questions from three main areas of shell programming:

- The shell and commands
- Variables and arguments
- Files and directories

Each section includes several common shell programming questions (and answers!). These questions are designed to help you solve or avoid common problems. Some of the questions provide deeper background information about UNIX, whereas others illustrate concepts covered in previous chapters.

Shell and Command Questions

This section covers some of the common questions about the shell itself and how the shell executes commands.

Why does `#!/bin/sh` have to be the first line of my scripts?

Chapter 2, "Script Basics," stated that `#!/bin/sh` must be the first line in your script to ensure that the correct shell is used to execute your script. This line must be the first line in your shell script because of the underlying mechanism used by a shell to execute commands.

When you ask a shell to execute a command as follows

```
$ date
```

The shell uses the `exec` *system call* to ask the UNIX kernel to execute the command you requested. System calls are C language functions built in to the UNIX kernel that enable you to access features of the kernel. The shell passes the name of the command that should be executed to the `exec` system call. This system call reads the first two characters in a file to determine how to execute the command. In the case of shell scripts, the first two characters are `#!`, indicating that the script needs to be interpreted by another program instead of executed directly. The rest of the line is treated as the name of the interpreter to use.

Usually the interpreter is `/bin/sh`, but you can also specify options to the shell on this line. Sometimes options such as `-x` or `-nv` are specified to enable debugging. This also enables you to write scripts tuned for a particular shell such as `ksh`, `bash`, or `zsh` by using `/bin/ksh`, `/bin/bash`, or `/bin/zsh` instead of `/bin/sh`. (The exact path to the shell may vary from system to system.)

How can I access the name of the current shell in my initialization scripts?

In your shell initialization scripts, the name of the current shell is stored in the variable `$0`.

Users who have a single `.profile` that is shared by `sh`, `ksh`, and `bash` use this variable in conjunction with a `case` statement near the end of this file to execute additional shell–specific startups. For example, you can use the following `case` statement in your `.profile` to set up the prompt, `PS1`, differently depending on the shell:

```
case "$0" in
    *bash) PS1="\t \h \#$ " ;;
    *ksh) PS1="`uname -n` !$ " ;;
    *sh) PS1="`uname -n`$ " ;;
esac
export PS1
```

Here, you have specified the shells as `*bash`, `*ksh`, and `*sh`, because some versions of UNIX place the `-` character in front of login shells, but not in front of other shells.

How do I tell whether the current shell is interactive or non-interactive?

Some scripts need the capability to determine whether they are running in an interactive shell or a non-interactive shell. Usually this is restricted to your shell initialization scripts because you don't want to perform a full-blown initialization every time these scripts execute. Some other examples include scripts that can run from the `at` or `cron` commands.

You can tell whether a shell is interactive by checking the value of the variable `$-`. If the value contains the letter *i*, the shell is interactive. Otherwise, it is non-interactive. The following `case` statement illustrates one method for checking the value of `$-`:


```
case $- in
   *i*) : # interactive
          # commands for interactive shells go here
        ;;
   *)   : # non interactive
          # commands for non-interactive shells go here
        ;;
esac
```

The following example illustrates the use of this `case` statement:

```
isInteractive () {
  case $- in
     *i* ) echo Interactive ; ec=0 ;;
     *) echo Non-Interactive ; ec=1 ;;
  esac
  return $ec
}
```

This function can be used to determine whether the current shell is interactive.

How do I discard the output of a command?

Sometimes you will need to execute a command, but you don't want the output displayed to the screen. In these cases you can discard the output by redirecting it to the file `/dev/null`:

```
cmd > /dev/null
```

Here *`cmd`* is the name of the command you want to execute. The file is a special file (called the *bit bucket*) that automatically discards all its input. For example, the following command discards the output of the `grep` command:

```
if grep soda /etc/hosts > /dev/null ; then
   echo 'Soda found!'
fi
```

Because commands also output error messages, you will often have to redirect STDERR to `/dev/null`. If you do not redirect STDERR, when a command fails your script will display that error message, which can be confusing to a user. To discard both output of a command and its error output, you can redirect STDERR (file descriptor 2) to STDOUT (file descriptor 1) and redirect STDOUT to `/dev/null` as follows:

```
cmd > /dev/null 2>&1
```

The following example illustrates redirecting both STDERR and STDOUT to `/dev/null`:

```
if grep soda /etc/hosts > /dev/null 2>&1 ; then
   echo 'Soda found!'
fi
```

How can I display messages on STDERR?

You can display a message on to STDERR by redirecting STDIN into STDERR as follows:

```
echo msg 1>&2
```

Here *msg* is the message you want to display. For example, the output of the following command is displayed on STDERR instead of STDOUT:

```
$ echo 'This is an error message' 1>&2
```

If you are interested in shell functions that perform additional formatting, please consult Chapter 21, "Problem Solving with Functions," which covers several shell functions that display messages on to STDERR.

How can I determine whether a command executed successfully?

You can determine whether a command executed successful by checking the command's exit code, which the shell stores in the variable `$?`. By convention, the exit code of a successful command is `0`. A nonzero exit code indicates a failure.

An `if` statement of the following form is often used to check whether a command executed successfully:

```
cmd
if [ $? -eq 0 ] ; then
   : # cmd successful
else
   : # cmd failed
fi
```

Here *cmd* is a command whose exit status needs to be checked. The following example illustrates this:

```
grep soda /etc/hosts > /dev/null 2>&1
if [ $? -ne 0 ] ; then
   echo "Soda Found!"
else
   echo "No entry in /etc/hosts for soda."
fi
```

Here you execute a `grep` command and then check the exit status of that command using the value stored in `$?`.

How do I determine whether the shell can find a particular command?

You can check to make sure that the shell can find a command or shell function by using the `type` command covered in Chapter 18, "Other Tools":

```
type cmd > /dev/null 2>&1
if [ $? -eq 0 ] ; then
   : # we have cmd, execute commands that require cmd
else
   : # we don't have cmd, execute alternate commands (if any)
fi
```

Here *cmd* is the name of the command you want check for. The `type` command is a built-in in `sh`, `bash`, and `zsh`. In `ksh`, `type` is usually an alias, `whence -v`.

An alternate form omits the explicit checking of the exit status stored in `$?`:

```
if type cmd > /dev/null 2>&1 ; then
   : # we have cmd, execute commands that require cmd
else
   : # we don't have cmd, execute alternate commands (if any)
fi
```

This form relies on the fact that `if` interprets an exit code of 0 as true.

The following example illustrate a possible use of the `type` command:

```
if type basename > /dev/null 2>&1 ; then
   : # we have basename, nothing to do
else
   # we don't have basename, define a function that
   # implements the same functionality
   basename () {
      if [ -n "$1" ] ; then
         echo "$1" | sed -e 's/^.*\///'
      else
         echo "Usage: basename [file]" 1>&2
         return 1
```

```
        fi
        return 0
    }
fi
```

This `if` statement checks to see if `basename` exists; if it does not, a function implementation is defined.

Can I use the `&&` and `||` operators to conditionally execute commands?

The && and `||` operators are often used to conditionally execute commands. The basic syntax for using these operators is

```
cmd1 op cmd2
```

Here *`cmd1`* and *`cmd2`* are two commands and *`op`* is the `&&` or `||` operator. If *`op`* is `&&` then *`cmd2`* is executed only when *`cmd1`* is successful. If *`op`* is `||` then *`cmd2`* is executed only when *`cmd1`* fails.

The following example illustrates the use of `&&`:

```
type bash > /dev/null 2>&1 &&
{ HAVE_BASH=1 ; echo "bash found" ; }
```

This command is equivalent to the following `if` statement:

```
type bash > /dev/null 2>&1
if [ $? -eq 0 ] ; then
   HAVE_BASH=1
   echo "bash found"
fi
```

The following example illustrates the use of `||`:

```
grep soda /etc/hosts > /dev/null 2>&1 || echo 'Soda not found!'
```

This command is equivalent to the following `if` statement:

```
grep soda /etc/hosts > /dev/null 2>&1
if [ $? -ne 0 ] ; then
   echo 'Soda not found!'
fi
```

How do I execute some commands in a separate shell?

The easiest way to execute a set of commands in a separate shell is to use the parentheses, `()`, as follows:

```
( list ; )
```

Here *list* is executed in a separate shell (called a sub-shell) and any changes the commands in *list* make to the working directory (via calls to `cd`) or environment variables will not affect the values in the script that invoked *list*.

As an example, the following function allows you to determine the absolute pathname of a directory without altering your current working directory:

```
abspath () { ( cd "$1" && pwd ; ) ; }
```

Variable and Argument Questions

This section examines some questions that relate to variables and their use in shell scripts. It also covers questions related to command-line arguments.

How can I include functions and variable definitions located in one script in to another script?

To include functions and variable definitions defined in one script in to another script, you need to use the `.` command as follows:

```
. file
```

Here *file* is the pathname of the script you want to include. This topic is covered in detail in Chapter 21, "Problem Solving with Functions."

When you include a file using the `.` command, make sure that the file does not contain the `exit` command as this will cause the current instance of the shell to exit.

If you are using the `.` command to include a file in your login session, your session will be terminated and you will have to log in again.

Is it possible to consider each argument to a shell script one at a time?

This can be accomplished using a `for` loop of the following form:

```
for arg in "$@"
do
    list
done
```

Here the variable arg will be set to each argument in turn. The specified list of commands, *list*, will be executed for each argument. The following function illustrates the use of this for loop:

```
echoargs () {
   for arg in "$@"
   do
      echo $arg
   done
   return 0
}
```

How can I forward all the arguments given to my script to another command?

A common task of shell programmers is writing a wrapper script for a command. A wrapper script might need to define a set of variables or change the environment in some way before a particular command starts executing.

When writing wrapper scripts, you need to forward all the arguments given to your script to a command. Usually the following is sufficient:

```
cmd "$@"
```

Here *cmd* is the name of the command you want to execute.

The one problem with this is that if no arguments were specified to your script, some versions of the shell will expand "$@" to "". If no arguments were specified, you want to execute *cmd*, not *cmd* "". To avoid this problem, you can use the following:

```
command ${@:+"$@"}
```

Here you are using one of the forms of variable substitution discussed in Chapter 9, "Substitution." In this case you check to see whether the variable $@ has a value. If it does, you substitute the value "$@" for it. If your script was not given any command-line arguments, $@ will be null; thus no value will be substituted.

How do I use the value of a shell variable in a sed command?

The simplest method to use variables in a sed command is to enclose your sed command in double quotes (") instead of single quotes ('). Because the shell performs variable substitution on double-quoted strings, the shell will substitute the value of any variables you specify before sed executes.

For example, the command

```
sed "/$DEL/d" file1 > file2
```

deletes all the lines in *file1* that contain the value stored in the variable $DEL.

How can I store the output of a command in a variable?

You can store the output of a command in a variable by combining the assignment operator, =, and the backquotes, ' ':

```
var=`cmd`
```

Here *var* is the name of a variable and *cmd* is the command whose output you want to store. For example, the following command stores the current date in the variable THEDATE:

```
THEDATE=`date`
```

How do I check to see whether a variable has a value?

There are several methods for determining this. The simplest is the `if` statement:

```
if [ -z "$VAR" ] ; then
   list ;
fi
```

Here *VAR* is the name of the variable, and *list* is the list of commands to execute if *VAR* does not have a value. Usually *list* initializes *VAR* to some default value. For example, the following command initializes the variable THDATE if it does not have a value:

```
if [ -z "$THEDATE" ] ; then
   THEDATE=`date`
fi
```

If you are just interested in variable initialization, this can be accomplished in a much more succinct fashion using variable substitution. For example, the previous `if` statement can be written as

```
: ${VAR:=default}
```

Here *default* is the default that should be assigned to *VAR*, if *VAR* does not have a value. If you need to execute a set of commands to obtain a default value, the backquotes (``) can be used to obtain the value to be substituted:

```
: ${VAR:=`default`}
```

Here *default* is a list of commands to execute. If *VAR* does not have a value, the output of these commands will be assigned to it. The following command also initializes the variable THEDATE:

```
: ${THEDATE:=`date`}
```

File and Directory Questions

This section looks at some questions about files and directories. These questions include issues with specific commands and examples that illustrate the use of commands to solve particular problems.

How do I determine the absolute pathname of a directory?

Shell scripts that work with directories often need to determine the absolute pathname of a directory to perform the correct operations on these directories.

You can determine the absolute pathname of a directory by using the `cd` and `pwd` commands as follows:

```
ABSPATH=`(cd dir 2> /dev/null && pwd ;)`
```

Here *`dir`* is the name of a directory. This command changes directories to the specified directory, *`dir`*, and then displays the full pathname of the directory using the `pwd` command. Then you assign the output of `pwd`, which is the full path to *`dir`*, to the variable `ABSPATH`. Because the `cd` command changes the working directory of the current shell, you execute it in a sub-shell. Thus the working directory of the shell script is unchanged.

The following function also provides this functionality:

```
abspath () { [ -n "$1" ] && ( cd "$1" 2> /dev/null && pwd ; ) }
```

Here, you determine whether the first argument is given and if it is, you `cd` to that directory and print its absolute path.

How do I determine the absolute pathname of a file?

Determining the absolute pathname of a file is slightly harder than determining the absolute pathname of a directory. You need to use the `dirname` and `basename` commands in conjunction with the `cd` and `pwd` commands to determine the absolute pathname of a file:

```
CURDIR=`pwd`
cd `dirname file`
ABSPATH="`pwd`/`basename file`"
cd $CURDIR
```

Here *`file`* is the name of a file whose absolute pathname you want to determine. First you save the current path of the current directory in the variable `CURDIR`. Next you move to the directory containing the specified file, *`file`*.

Then you join the output of the `pwd` command and the name of the *`file`* determined using the `basename` command to get the absolute pathname. At this point the absolute pathname of the file is stored in the variable `ABSPATH`. Finally you change back to the original directory.

As an example, the following function implements this functionality:

```
absfpath () {
   if [ -z "$1" ] ; then
      return 1
   fi
   CURDIR="`pwd`"
   cd "`dirname $1`"
   ABSPATH="`pwd`/`basename $1`"
   cd "$CURDIR"
}
```

How can I locate a particular file?

The structure of the UNIX directory tree sometimes makes locating files and commands difficult. To locate a file, often you need to search through a directory and all its subdirectories. The easiest way to do this is with the `find` command:

```
find dir -name file -print
```

Here *`dir`* is the name of a directory where `find` should start its search, and *`file`* is the name of the file it should look for.

The `name` option of the `find` command also works with the standard filename substitution operators covered in Chapter 9. For example, the command

```
find /home/ranga -name "*.txt" -print
```

displays a list of all the files in the directory `/home/ranga` and all its subdirectories that end with the string `.txt`.

How can I `grep` for a string in every file in a directory?

When you work on a large project involving many files, remembering the contents of the individual files becomes difficult. It is much easier to look through all the files for a particular piece of information.

You can use the `find` command in conjunction with the `xargs` command to look for a particular string in every file contained within a directory and all its subdirectories:

```
find dir -type f -print | xargs grep "string"
```

Here *`dir`* is the name of a directory in which to start searching, and *`string`* is the string to look for. Here you specify the `-type` option to the `find` command so that only regular files are searched for the *`string`*. As an example, the following command searches all of the C language include files in `/usr/include` for the string `pid_t`:

```
$ find /usr/include -type f -print | xargs grep pid_t
```

24

How do I remove all the files in a directory matching a particular name?

Some editors and programs create large numbers of temporary files. Often you need to clean up after these programs, to prevent your hard drive from filling up. The simplest method to remove a set of files that matches a particular name is to use the `find` and `xargs` commands as follows:

```
find dir -type f -name "name" -print | xargs rm
```

Here *`dir`* is the pathname of a directory and *`name`* is the filename that you want to remove. For example, the following command removes all of the files that end with ~ from the directory `/home/cvs`:

```
find /home/cvs -type f -name "*~" -print | xargs rm
```

The only limitation in using `find` and `xargs` is that `xargs` cannot properly deal with pathnames that contain spaces. If you need to delete files whose pathnames contain spaces you will need to use the `-exec` option of `find` rather than `xargs`:

```
find dir -type f -name "name" -exec rm '{}' \; -print
```

What command can I use to rename all the `*.aaa` files to `*.bbb` files?

In DOS and Windows, you can rename all the `*.aaa` files in a directory to `*.bbb` by using the `rename` command as follows:

```
rename *.aaa *.bbb
```

In UNIX you can use the `mv` command to rename files, but you cannot use it to rename more than one file at the same time. To do this, you need to use a `for` loop:

```
OLDSUFFIX=aaa
NEWSUFFIX=bbb
for FILE in *."$OLDSUFFIX"
do
    NEWNAME=`echo "$FILE" | sed -e "s/${OLDSUFFIX}\$/$NEWSUFFIX/"`
    mv "$FILE" "$NEWNAME"
done
```

Here you generate a list of all the files in the current directory that end with the value of the variable `OLDSUFFIX`. Then you use `sed` to modify the name of each file by removing the value of `OLDSUFFIX` from the filename and replacing it with the value of `NEWSUFFIX`. You use the `$` character in our `sed` expression to anchor the suffix in `OLDSUFFIX` to the end of the line; this ensures that the pattern is really a filename suffix. After you have the new name, you rename the file from its original name, stored in `FILE`, to the new name stored in `NEWNAME`.

To prevent a potential loss of data, you might consider modifying this loop to specify the -i option to the mv command. For example, if the files 1.aaa and 1.bbb exist prior to executing this loop, after the loops exits, the original version of 1.aaa will be overwritten when 1.bbb is renamed as 1.aaa. If mv -i is used, you will be prompted before 1.bbb is renamed:

```
mv: overwrite 1.aaa (yes/no)?
```

You can answer no to avoid losing the information in this file. The actual prompt produced by mv might be different on your system.

What command can I use to rename all the aaa* files to bbb* files?

The technique used in the last question can be used to solve this problem as well. In this case, you can use the variables OLDPREFIX to hold the prefix a file currently has and NEWPREFIX to hold the prefix you want the file to have. As an example, you can use the following for loop to rename all files that start with aaa to start with bbb instead:

```
OLDPREFIX=aaa
NEWPREFIX=bbb
for FILE in "$OLDPREFIX"*
do
    NEWNAME=`echo "$FILE" | sed -e "s/^${OLDPREFIX}/$NEWPREFIX/"`
    mv "$FILE" "$NEWNAME"
done
```


How can I set my filenames to lowercase?

When you transfer a file from a Windows or DOS system to a UNIX system, the filename can end up in all capital letters. You can rename these files to lowercase using the following command:

```
for FILE in *
do
    mv -i "$FILE" `echo "$FILE" | tr '[A-Z]' '[a-z]'` 2> /dev/null
done
```

Here, you are using the mv -i command in order to avoid overwriting files. For example, if the files APPLE and apple both exist in a directory, you might not want to rename the file APPLE.

How do I eliminate carriage returns (^M) in my files?

If you transfer text files from a DOS machine to a UNIX machine, you might see a ^M (Ctrl-M) before the end of each line. This character corresponds to a carriage return. In DOS, a newline is represented by the character sequence \r\n, where \r is the carriage return and \n is newline. In UNIX a newline is represented by just \n. When text files created on a DOS system are viewed in UNIX, the `\r` is displayed as `^M`. The `^M` can be removed from a file by using the `tr` command as follows:

```
tr -d '\015' < file > newfile
```

Here *`file`* is the name of the file that contains the carriage returns, and *`newfile`* is the name you want to give the file after the carriage returns have been deleted. You are using the octal representation `\015` for carriage return, because the escape sequence `\r` is not correctly interpreted by some versions of `tr`.

Summary

This chapter has looked at some common questions encountered in shell programming. These questions and their answers will help you write bigger and better scripts.

Now that you have finished all 24 chapters, you have learned about using both the basics of the shell and its advanced features. As you continue to program, use this book as a reference to help you remember the intricacies of shell programming.

I hope that you learned not only to program efficiently using the shell but also to enjoy shell programming. Thanks for reading!

Part IV
Appendixes

APPENDIX A

Command Quick Reference

This appendix summarizes and reviews the following script elements:

- Reserved words and built-in shell commands
- Conditional expressions
- Arithmetic expressions (`ksh`, `bash`, and `zsh` only)
- Parameters and variables
- Parameter substitution
- Pattern matching
- I/O
- Miscellaneous command summaries
- Regular expression wildcards

Reserved Words and Built-in Shell Commands

Most of the following commands are built-in commands; they are present within the shell and are not external programs. Some of the shells discussed in this book do not contain all of these commands, so those commands that are restricted to a particular shell or shells are noted as so in the description of that command.

Although most of these commands functions the same under the shells covered in this book, some do not. This appendix describes the commands in general, for the specific information for your system you should consult the man page for the command of interest using the `man` command.

`. (period)` executes a script in the current shell rather than as a child process.

`: (colon)` no-op command. It does nothing, but the shell still processes the arguments of this command for variable and command substitution.

`alias` (`ksh`, `bash` and `zsh` only) creates a short name for the command.

`bg` (Korn/Bash) starts a suspended job running in background.

`break` exits from the current `for`, `while`, or `until` loop.

`case` executes the commands corresponding to the pattern that matches *`expr`*. Patterns can contain filename expansion wildcards.

```
case expr in
   pattern1) list1 ;;
   ...
   patternN) listN ;;
esac
```

`cd` changes the directory. If an argument is specified, `cd` changes the current directory to that directory (if possible). Otherwise `cd` changes the directory to the user's home directory.

`continue` skips the rest of the commands in a loop and starts the next iteration of a loop.

`do` indicates the start of the body of a loop.

`done` indicates the end of the body of a loop.

`echo` displays its arguments to standard output. In `ksh`, `bash`, and `zsh` `echo` is a built-in command. In the Bourne shell it is an external command located in `/bin/echo`.

`esac` denotes the end of a `case` statement.

`eval` causes the shell to reinterpret the command that follows.

exec executes the following command, which replaces the current process instead of running it as a child process.

exit *n* ends the shell script with status code *n*.

export marks variables as environment variables, allowing them to be passed to any child processes and called programs.

false (ksh, bash, and zsh only) always returns an unsuccessful or logical false result.

fg (Korn/Bash) brings a background or suspended job to the foreground.

fi denotes the end of an `if` statement.

for executes a block of code multiple times.

```
for var in list1
do
     list2
done
```

function (Korn/Bash) keyword to define a function.

getopts a function called repeatedly in a loop to process the command-line arguments.

if allows conditional execution.

```
if list1 ; then
   list2 ;
elif list3 ; then
   list4 ;
...
else
   listN ;
fi
```

integer (ksh, bash and zsh only) specifies an integer variable.

jobs (ksh, bash, and zsh only) list the background and suspended jobs.

kill sends a signal to a process; often used to terminate a process or to reinitialize a daemon background process.

let (ksh, bash, and zsh only) performs integer arithmetic.

pwd prints the present working or current directory.

read waits for one line of standard input and saves each word in the variables specified to it as arguments. If there are more words than variables, it saves the remaining words in the last variable.

A

readonly marks variables as read-only, so that their values cannot be changed.

return *n* returns from a function with the return code *n*.

select (`ksh`, `bash`, and `zsh` only) presents a menu and enables user selection.

set displays or changes shell options.

shift discards `$1` and shifts all the positional parameters up one to take its place.

test provides many options to check files, strings, and numeric values. Often denoted by `[` (left bracket). This command is a built-in command in `ksh`, `bash`, and `zsh`. Bourne Shell uses the external version located at `/bin/test`.

trap designates code to execute if a specific signal is received.

type displays the pathname of the following command or indicates whether it is built-in or an alias.

typeset (`ksh`, `bash`, and `zsh` only) sets the type of variable and optionally its initial value.

ulimit displays or sets the largest file or resource limit.

umask displays or sets a mask to affect permissions of any new file or directory you create.

unalias (`ksh`, `bash`, and `zsh` only) removes an alias.

unset undefines the variables that follow.

until (`ksh`, `bash`, and `zsh` only) loops until the test command is true (successful).

```
until test
do
    list
done
```

wait pauses until all background jobs are complete.

whence (`ksh` and `zsh` only) similar to the `type` command.

while loops while a test command is true (successful).

```
while list1
do
    list2
done
```

Conditional Expressions

This section summarizes conditional expressions or tests. Conditional expressions are mainly used with the `test` command in conjunction with `if` statements and `while` and `until` loops.

File Tests

The following conditional expressions are used to perform file and directory related tests.

`-a` ***`file`***	true if *file* exists (`ksh`, `bash`, and `zsh` only)
`-b` ***`file`***	true if *file* is a block special device
`-c` ***`file`***	true if *file* is a character special device
`-d` ***`dir`***	true if *dir* is a directory
`-e` ***`file`***	true if *file* exists
`-f` ***`file`***	true if *file* is a regular file
`-g` ***`file`***	true if *file* has the SGID permission bit set
`-G` ***`path`***	true if *`path`* exists and its group matches the user's current group ID (Linux and BSD systems only)
`-h` ***`file`***	true if *file* is a symbolic link
`-k` ***`path`***	true if *path* has the sticky bit set
`-L` ***`file`***	true if *file* is a symbolic link (`ksh`, `bash`, and `zsh` only)
`-O` ***`file`***	true if the user running this command owns *file* (`ksh`, `bash`, and `zsh` only)
`-p` ***`file`***	true if *file* is a named pipe or fifo
`-r` ***`path`***	true if *path* is readable
`-s` ***`file`***	true if *file* has a size greater than zero
`-S` ***`file`***	true if *file* is a socket
`-t` ***`des`***	true if *des* is a file descriptor associated with a terminal device
`-u` ***`file`***	true if *file* has its SUID permission bit set
`-w` ***`path`***	true if *path* is writable
`-x` ***`path`***	true if *path* is executable

String Tests

The following conditional expressions are used to evaluate strings and their contents.

`-z string`	true if *string* is empty
`-n string`	true if *string* has nonzero size
`string`	true if *string* is not null ("")
`s1 = s2`	true if string s1 equals s2
`s1 != s2`	true if the strings are not equal

Integer Comparisons

The following conditional expressions are used to evaluate integers. Comparisons stop on first non-digit.

`n1 -eq n2`	true if *n1* is equal in value to *n2*.
`n1 -ne n2`	true if *n1* is not equal to *n2*
`n1 -gt n2`	true if *n1* is greater than *n2*
`n1 -ge n2`	true if *n1* is greater than or equal to *n2*
`n1 -lt n2`	true if *n1* is less than *n2*
`n1 -le n2`	true if *n1* is less than or equal to *n2*

Compound Expressions

The following conditional operators are used to construct compound conditional expressions.

`[ ! expr ]`	true if *expr* is false (logical NOT)
`[ expr1 -a expr2 ]`	true if *expr1* and *expr2* are true (logical AND)
`[ expr1 ] && [ expr2 ]`	true if *expr1* and *expr2* are true (logical AND)
`[ expr1 -o expr2 ]`	true if either *expr1* or *expr2* is true (logical OR)
`[ expr1 ] || [ expr2 ]`	true if either *expr1* or *expr2* is true (logical OR)

Arithmetic Expressions (ksh, bash, and zsh Only)

The general format for integer variable assignment is as follows:

```
let "VARIABLE=integer_expresson"
```

To embed integer calculations within a command, you can use the following syntax:

```
$((integer_expression))
```

Integer Expression Operators

The integer operators are used to perform simple arithmetic operations on integer values. The following list (order from highest to lowest operator precedence) describes the integer operators supported in `ksh`, `bash` and `zsh`. The logical operators described in this list return 1 for true and 0 for false.

`-` unary minus (negates the following value)

`! ~` logical NOT, binary one's complement

`* / %` multiply, divide, modulus (remainder operation)

`+ -` add, subtract

`>> <<` right, left shift, for example: `$((32 >> 2))` gives 8 (right shift 32 by 2 bits is the same as division by 4)

`<= >=` less than or equal to, greater than or equal to

`> <` greater than, less than

`== !=` equal to, not equal to

`&` bitwise AND operation, for example: `$((5 & 3))` converts 5 to binary 101 and 3 to binary 011 and ANDs the bits to give 1 as the result

`^` bitwise exclusive OR operation

`|` bitwise regular OR operation

`&&` logical AND

`||` logical OR

`*= /= %=` C programming type assignment, for example, `$((A *= 2))` means multiply variable `A` by `2`, save result in `A`, and substitute result

`= += -=` more C programming type assignments

`>>= <<=` more C programming type assignments using shift right, shift left

`&= ^= |=` more C programming type assignments using AND, exclusive OR, and regular OR

Parameters and Variables

This section describes parameters and variables.

User-Defined Variables

Any variable defined by a programmer is a user defined variable. User-defined variable names

- Must start with letters
- Can contain only letters or digits
- Are often in capital letters to differentiate them from UNIX commands

Variables are assigned values using the assignment operator, =, as follows:

```
VAR=value
```

Here, *VAR* is the name of the variable and *value* is the value you want to assign to it.

Variables are unset using the `unset` command as follows:

```
unset var1 … varN
```

Here *var1* … *varN* are the names of the variables to unset.

Variable Substitution

The value stored in a variable can be accessed using the $ operator as follows:

```
$VAR
```

Here *VAR* is the name of the variable whose value you want to access. Other forms of variable substitution include the following:

`${var}` substitutes the contents of *var*, which can be a variable name or digit indicating a positional parameter

`${var:-word}` substitutes the contents of *var* but if it is empty or undefined, it substitutes *word*, which might contain unquoted spaces

`${var:=word}` substitutes the contents of *var* but if it is empty or undefined, it sets *var* equal to *word* and substitutes *word*

`${var:?var}` substitutes the contents of *var*, but if it is empty or undefined, aborts the script and gives the *message* as a final error. Message might contain unquoted spaces.

`${var:+word}` if *var* is not empty, it substitutes *word*; otherwise it substitutes nothing

Array Variables (ksh, bash, and zsh Only)

Arrays provide a method for grouping variables using a single variable name coupled with an index. The index must always be a positive integer. In ksh the maximum value for index is 1024. No such limit exists in bash or zsh.

In ksh and zsh array variables are initialized using the set command as follows:

```
set -A ARRAY val1 … valN
```

In bash, array variables are initialized as follows:

```
ARRAY=(val1 … valN)
```

In either case *ARRAY* is the name of the array and *val1 … valN* are the values for the first *N* elements in the array.

Arrays are not available in the Bourne shell and 1.x and earlier versions of bash.

ARRAY[index]=value	sets the value of the element denoted by *index* in *ARRAY* to *value*
${ARRAY[index]}	substitutes the value of the element *index* in *ARRAY*.
${ARRAY[*]}	substitutes all elements in *ARRAY*
${ARRAY[@]}	substitutes all array elements in *ARRAY* and treats each element as if individually double-quoted

Special Variables

The following are special variables that are created and modified by the shell itself. These variables cannot be changed by scripts.

$0	name of the command or script being executed
$n	positional parameters—that is, arguments given on the command line numbered 1 through 9
$#	number of positional parameters given on command line
$*	a list of all the command-line arguments
$@	a list of all command-line arguments individually double-quoted
$?	The numeric exit status (that is, return code) of last command executed
$$	PID (process ID) number of current shell
$!	PID (process ID) number of last background command

Shell Variables

The following variables are used by the shell, but can be modified by scripts.

CDPATH contains a colon-separated list of directories to facilitate the `cd` command.

HOME is your home directory.

IFS contains internal field separator characters.

OPTARG is the last `cmd` line `arg` processed by `getopts` (Korn/Bash).

OPTIND is the index of the last `cmd` line `arg` processed by `getopts` (Korn/Bash).

PATH contains a colon-separated list of directories to search for commands that are given without any slash.

PS1 is the primary shell prompt string.

PS2 is the secondary shell prompt string for continuation lines.

PWD returns the current directory.

RANDOM returns a different random number (from 0 to 32,767) each time it is invoked (`ksh`, `bash`, and `zsh` only).

REPLY is the last input line from read via the select command (`ksh`, `bash`, and `zsh` only).

SECONDS returns the numbers of seconds since shell invocation (`ksh`, `bash`, and `zsh` only).

SHLVL returns the number of shells currently nested.

UID is the numeric user ID number.

Input/Output

This section discusses I/O. Table A.1 describes the standard UNIX file descriptors, whereas other sections describe input and output redirections and "here" documents.

TABLE A.1 Summary of Standard UNIX I/O

Abbreviation	*I/O description*	*File Descriptor*
STDIN	Standard input	0
STDOUT	Standard output	1
STDERR	Standard error	2

Input and Output Redirection

Input and output redirection can be performed as follows:

`cmd > file`	save STDOUT from UNIX command in `file`
`cmd 1> file`	same as above
`cmd >> file`	append STDOUT from UNIX command to `file`
`cmd 1>> file`	same as above
`cmd 2> file`	save STDERR from UNIX command in `file`
`cmd 2>> file`	append STDERR from UNIX command in `file`**`cmd < file`** provide STDIN to UNIX command from `file` instead of keyboard
`cmd 0< file`	same as above
`cmd1 | cmd2`	pipe STDOUT of *`cmd1`* as STDIN to *`cmd2`*
`cmd | tee file`	save STDOUT of UNIX command in `file` but also pass same text as STDOUT
`exec n> file`	redirect output of file descriptor *n* to (overwrite) file. This applies to subsequent UNIX commands.
`exec n>> file`	same as above but append to `file` instead of overwriting
`cmd 2>&1`	redirect STDERR from UNIX command to wherever STDOUT is currently going
`cmd 1>&2`	
`cmd >&2`	redirect STDOUT as STDERR. This should be done when `echo` displays an error message.
`cmd n>&m`	redirect file descriptor *n* to wherever file descriptor *m* is currently going. This is a generalization of the previous examples.
`exec n>&-`	close file descriptor *n*

Here Document

Here documents provide STDIN to UNIX commands from lines that follow until `delimiter` is found at the start of line:

```
cmd << delimiter
line1
...
lineN
delimiter
```

Pattern Matching and Regular Expressions

This section describes the meta-characters and rules for filename expansion, pattern matching for the `case` statement, and regular expressions.

Filename Expansion and Pattern Matching

The rules for filename expansion are as follows:

- Any word on the command line that contains a meta-character is expanded to a list of files that match the pattern word.
- If no filename matches are found, the pattern word is not substituted.
- Meta-characters cannot match a leading period or a slash.

The filename expansion meta-characters are

`*`	matches 0 or more of any character
`?`	matches exactly 1 of any character
`[list]`	matches exactly 1 of any character in *list*
`[!list]`	matches exactly 1 of any character not in *list*

Limited Regular Expression Wildcards

All regular expression patterns can include these wildcards:

`^pattern`	only matches if *pattern* is at the start of a line
`pattern$`	only matches if *pattern* is at the end of a line
`.`	matches exactly 1 of any character
`[list]`	matches exactly 1 of any character in *list*
`[^list]`	matches exactly 1 of any character not in *list*
`*`	matches 0 or more repetitions of the previous element (char or expression)
`.*`	matches 0 or more of any characters

Extended Regular Expression Wildcards

These are additional regular expression wildcards that are only supported in some commands:

`\{n\}`	matches *n* repetitions of the previous element
`\{n,\}`	matches *n* or more repetitions of the previous element

`\{n,m\}`	matches at least *n* but not more than *m* reps of the previous element
`?`	matches 0 or 1 occurrences of the previous element
`+`	matches 1 or more occurrences of the previous element

APPENDIX B

Glossary

Absolute Pathname Represents the location of a file or directory starting from / and listing all the directories between / and the file or directory of interest. The pathname `/etc/hosts` is an absolute pathname.

Abstraction Scripts that use abstraction retain the same basic flow by placing the conditional execution statements within functions. When a function is called, it makes a decision as to which commands execute on a given platform.

Alias An abbreviation or an alternative name, usually mnemonic, for a command.

Anchoring Anchoring a regular expression limits matches to lines that begin or end with the expression.

Arguments Command modifiers that change the behavior of a command.

Array Variable A variable that groups multiple scalar variables together using a single name. Each of the individual scalar variables is accessed through an index.

Background Describes processes usually running at a lower priority and with their input disconnected from the interactive session. Input and output are usually directed to a file or other process.

Background Processes Autonomous processes that run under UNIX without requiring user interaction.

Bash See *Bourne-Again Shell.*

Block Special Files Provide a mechanism for communicating devices by transferring large blocks of data.

Body The set of commands executed by a loop.

Bourne Shell The original UNIX shell was written at AT&T Bell Labs in New Jersey during the mid-1970s by Steve Bourne. Because the Bourne shell was the first to appear on UNIX systems, it is often referred to as "the shell."

Bourne-Again Shell A shell written by Brian Fox of the Free Software Foundation as a replacement for the Bourne shell. At present `bash` is maintained by Chet Ramey. It incorporates most of the features of `csh`, `tcsh`, and `ksh` while retaining compatibility with the original Bourne shell and compliance with the POSIX standard.

Character Range A method for specifying a set of characters by just giving the first and last character in the set.

Character Special Files Provide a mechanism for communicating with a device one character at a time.

Child Processes See *Subprocesses.*

Child Shells See *Subshells.*

Command Separators Indicate where one command ends and another begins. The most common command separator is the semicolon character (`;`).

Command Comprised of the name of a program along with zero or more arguments. You might see the term *command* used instead of the term utility for simple commands, when only the program name is given.

Comment A statement that is embedded in a shell script but is not executed by the shell. Comments are intended to be internal human-readable documentation that cover the inner workings of the script.

Complex Command A command that consists of a command name and a list of arguments.

Compound Command A command that consists of a list of simple and complex commands separated by the semicolon character (`;`).

Conditional Execution Alters the execution of a script based on the system type. A script that uses conditional execution usually contains an `if` statement at the beginning of the script that sets variables to indicate the commands to use on a particular platform.

Conditional Flow Control Commands Commands that allow the flow of a script to be conditionally changed; also called flow control commands.

`csh` See *C-Shell.*

C-Shell A shell written at the University of California at Berkeley in the early 1980s by Bill Joy. C-Shell was designed to make the shell easier to use interactively. It first appeared in BSD UNIX and was later incorporated into AT&T's version of UNIX. C shell is usually installed as `/bin/csh`.

Default Action The action that the system takes on behalf of the program in the absence of a signal handler.

Default Behavior The default behavior of a command is the output generated by a command when it is run as a simple command.

Directories Used to hold ordinary and special files. Directories are similar to folders in MacOS or Windows.

Directory Tree The hierarchical structure used in UNIX for organizing files and directories.

Environment A set of variables that the shell passes to every program it starts. The environment provides useful information to commands about the current user and the system. The command search path, the online help search path, the time zone and the local language settings are examples of the type of information typically stored in the environment.

Environment Variable A variable that is a member of the environment.

Escape Sequence A special sequence of characters that represents another character.

Escaping Placing a backslash (\) just before a character. Escaping can either remove the special meaning of a character in a shell command, or it can add special meaning as with `\n` in the `echo` command. The character following the backslash is called an escaped character.

Executable Code All the commands in a script outside of the function definitions.

Exporting The process of placing a variable in the environment.

Field A set of characters that are separated by one or more field separator characters. The default field separator characters are tab and space.

Field Separator Controls the manner in which an input line is broken into fields. In the shell, the field separator is stored in the variable `IFS`. In `awk`, the field separator is stored in the `awk` variable `FS`. Both the shell and `awk` use the default value of space and tab for the field separator.

File Descriptor An integer that is associated with a file. Enables you to read and write from a file using the integer instead of the file's name.

Filename The name of a file. The name of the file `/etc/hosts` is `hosts`.

Function chaining The process of calling a function from another function.

Functions Provide a way of mapping a name to a list of commands. Functions are similar to subroutines and procedures in other programming languages.

Global Scope If a variable has global scope, its value can be accessed from anywhere within a script.

Global Variables Variables with global scope.

Globbing The process used by the shell to produce a list of files that match a particular expression. Globbing is also known as filename substitution.

Hard Link A special directory entry that points to another file. A hard link cannot point to a directory; it can only point to a file. A hard link is also indistinguishable from the file that it points to; there is no way to tell whether a particular file is a hard link or the original file.

Home Directory The directory where you start after logging in.

Infinite Loops Loops that execute forever without terminating.

Input Redirection In UNIX, the process of sending input to a command from a file.

Interactive Mode A mode in which the shell reads input from the user and executes the specified commands. This mode is called interactive because the shell is interacting with a user.

Invisible Files Files whose first characters are dots or periods (`.`). Many programs (including the shell) use such files to store configuration information. Invisible files are also referred to as hidden files.

Iteration A single execution of the body of a loop.

Kernel The heart of the UNIX system. It provides utilities with a means of accessing a machine's hardware. It also handles scheduling and executing commands.

Korn Shell David Korn of AT&T Bell Labs wrote the Korn shell, `ksh`. It incorporates all the C shell's interactive features while preserving the Bourne shell's ALGOL-like syntax. The Korn shell is usually installed as `/bin/ksh` or `/usr/bin/ksh`.

`ksh` See *Korn Shell*.

Library A repository of functions that can be accessed by your shell scripts.

Link A file that points to another file on the system.

Literal Characters These characters have no special meaning and cause no extra action to be taken. Quoting causes the shell to treat a wildcard as a literal character.

Local Scope If a variable has local scope, its value can only be accessed within the function where it is declared.

Local Variable A variable that is present within the current instance of the shell. It is not available to programs that are started by the shell. Local variables are also variables that have local scope.

Loops Enable you to execute a series of commands multiple times. Two main types of loops are the `while` and `for` loops.

Man Pages Every version of UNIX comes with an extensive collection of online help pages called man pages (short for manual pages). The man pages are the authoritative source about your UNIX system. They contain complete information about both the kernel and most of the utilities.

Meta-characters Characters that have a special meaning in the shell.

Newline This is literally the linefeed character whose ASCII value is 10. In general, the newline character is a special shell character that indicates a complete command line has been entered and can now be executed.

Nested Loops When a loop is located inside the body of another loop it is said to be nested within another loop.

Non-interactive Mode A mode in which the shell does not interact with the user; instead it reads commands stored in a file and executes them. When the shell reaches the end of the file, it exits.

Option An argument that starts with the hyphen or dash character, `-`.

Ordinary File A file that contains data, text, or program instructions. Almost all the files on a UNIX system are ordinary files.

Output Redirection In UNIX, the process of capturing the output of a command and storing it in a file is called *output redirection* because it redirects the output of a command into a file instead of the screen.

Parent Directory The directory that contains a given directory. If directory `B` is contained within directory `A`, directory `A` is considered the parent directory of `B`.

Parent Process Identifier Shown in the heading of the `ps` command as `PPID`. This is the process identifier of the parent process. See also *Parent Processes*.

Parent Processes These processes control other processes that are often referred to as child processes or subprocesses. See *Processes*.

Parent Shell This shell controls other shells, which are often referred to as child shells or subshells. The login shell is typically the parent shell. See *Shell*.

Pathname The filename of a file combined with the filenames of its parent directories. The pathname of the file `hosts` located in the directory `/etc` is `/etc/hosts`.

Pipe Used to connect the standard output of a command to the standard input another command.

Process Identifier (PID) Shown in the heading of the `ps` command as PID. It is the unique number assigned to every process running in the system.

Processes Discrete, running programs under UNIX. The user's interactive session is a process. A process can invoke (run) and control another program that is then referred to as a subprocess. Ultimately, everything a user does is a subprocess of the operating system.

Prompt Displayed by the shell. When the prompt is present, the shell can be given a command to execute. In this book, the `$` character is used to indicate the prompt.

Quoting The process that literally encloses selected text within some type of quotation marks. When applied to shell commands, quoting disables shell interpretation of special characters by enclosing the characters within single or double quotes or by escaping the characters.

Read-only Variable A variable whose value cannot be changed.

Recursion A special instance of function chaining in which a function calls itself.

Regular files The most common type of files on UNIX systems and can be used to store any kind of data, including binary data that the system can execute.

Relative Pathname Represents the location of a file or directory relative to the current directory. The pathname `../etc/hosts` is a relative pathname.

Return code The exit status from a function. The convention for return codes is the same as for exit codes; 0 equals success and nonzero equals failure.

Root Directory The topmost directory in the UNIX directory tree, `/`, is called the root directory.

Scalar Variable A variable that can hold only one value at a time.

Scope Refers to the region within a program where a variable's value can be accessed.

Shell An interface to the UNIX system. It reads input and executes programs based on that input. When a program has finished executing, it displays that program's output. The shell is sometimes called a command interpreter.

Shell Initialization After a shell is started, it undergoes a phase called initialization in which important parameters are set up.

Shell Script A list of commands stored in a file.

Shell Variable A variable that is set by the shell and is required by the shell in order to function correctly.

Signal A software interrupt sent to a program to indicate that an important event has occurred.

Signal Handler A function provided by a program that defines the actions to take when a signal is received.

Simple Command A command that can be executed by giving just its name at the prompt.

Special Files Files mainly used to provide access to hardware such as hard drives, CD-ROM drives, modems, and Ethernet adapters. Some special files are similar to aliases or shortcuts and enable you to access a single file using different names.

STDERR Standard Error. A special type of output used for error messages. The file descriptor for STDERR is 2.

STDIN Standard Input. User input is read from STDIN. The file descriptor for STDIN is 0.

STDOUT Standard Output. The output of commands and scripts is normally written to STDOUT, which is connected to the terminal. The file descriptor for STDOUT is 1.

Subdirectory A directory that is contained within another directory. If directory `A` contains directory `B`, directory `B` is considered a subdirectory of `A`.

Subprocesses Run under the control of other processes, which are often referred to as parent processes. See *Processes*.

Subshells Run under the control of another shell, which is often referred to as the parent shell. Typically, the login shell is the parent shell. See *Shells*.

Symbolic Link A special file that stores a pathname to another file. A symbolic link is often referred to as a symlink.

Uninitialized Shell A shell that has not yet read its init files in order to set up the parameters required for its proper operation.

Unsetting Removing a variable from the list of variables tracked by the shell.

Usage Statement A short message that a script outputs in order to inform a user of the proper invocation syntax for the script.

Utilities Programs, such as `who` and `date`, that can be executed.

Variable A word that holds a value. The value can be any text string.

Variable Substitution The process by which the shell replaces the name of a variable with its value.

Wildcards Meta-characters used in globbing. The two main wildcards are `*` and `?`.

Words Sets of characters separated by spaces and tabs.

zsh See *Z-Shell*.

Z-Shell A shell written by Paul Falstad while he was a student at Princeton University. It is extremely customizable and is mostly compatible with `ksh`.

APPENDIX C

Answers to Questions

This appendix presents the answers to the questions at the end of each hour.

Hour 1

1. The first is a simple command. The second is a compound command constructed from two simple commands. The last two are complex commands.
2. There is no effect. The output will be the same for both commands.
3. The two types are Bourne (includes `ksh`, `bash`, and `zsh`) and C (`csh` or `tcsh`).

Hour 2

1. The files are `/etc/profile` and `.profile`.
2. If `PATH` is not set, the shell cannot find the commands you want to execute. If `MANPATH` is not set, the shell cannot locate the online help.
3. It specifies that the shell `/bin/sh` should be used to execute the script.
4. The `man` command.

Hour 3

1. Invisible files are files with names that start with the `.` character. You can list them by specifying the `-a` option to `ls`.
2. No. Each of these commands will produce the same results.
3. On Solaris, HPUX and BSD (including MacOS X), use the command

   ```
   $ wc -lm
   ```

   On Linux use the command

   ```
   $ wc -lc
   ```
4. (b) and (c) will generate error messages indicating that `homework` is a directory.

Hour 4

1. (a) and (d) are absolute pathnames. (b) and (c) are relative pathnames.
2. The `pwd` command will output the full path to your home directory.
3. The following command will work:

   ```
   cp -r /usr/local /opt/pgms
   ```
4. The following commands will work:

   ```
   cp -r /usr/local /opt/pgms ; rm -r /usr/local
   ```
5. No, you cannot use the `rmdir` command, because the directory is not empty. You can use the following command:

   ```
   $ rm -r backup
   ```

Hour 5

1. The file descriptors associated with STDOUT, STDERR, and STDIN are 0, 2, and 1 respectively.
2. You can use the following `printf` statements:

   ```
   printf "0%o 0%o 0%o \n" 16 255 65535
   printf "0x%x 0x%x 0x%x\n" 16 255 65535
   ```
3. The output ends up in the file `out.txt`.

Hour 6

1. The file types of these files are

/dev/rdsk/c0t1d0	character special file
/etc/passwd	regular file

/usr/local	directory
/usr/sbin/ping	regular file

2. The owner and groups of these files are

/dev/rdsk/c0t1d0	owner bin	group sys
/etc/passwd	owner root	group sys
/usr/local	owner bin	group bin
/usr/sbin/ping	owner root	group bin

3. The permissions of these files are

`/dev/rdsk/c0t1d0`	owner `read` and `write`
	group `read`
	other `none`
`/etc/passwd`	owner `read`
	group `read`
	other `read`
`/usr/local`	owner `read`, `write`, and `execute`
	group `read`, `write`, and `execute`
	other `read`, `write`, and `execute`
`/usr/sbin/ping`	owner `read` and SUID `execute`
	group `read` and `execute`
	other `read` and `execute`

Hour 7

1. By putting an ampersand (`&`) at the end of the command line.
2. With the `ps` command.
3. Use the suspend key (usually Ctrl+Z) to stop the foreground process, and then use the `bg` command to resume it in the background.

C

Hour 8

1. (a) and (d) are valid variable names. (b) starts with a number thus it is invalid. (c) contains the `&` character, which is not a valid character for variable names.
2. These assignments are valid in `ksh`, `bash`, and `zsh`, but not in Bourne shell. Bourne shell only supports scalar variables.

3. To access the array item at index 5 use the following:

   ```
   ${adams[5]}
   ```

   To access every item in the array use the following:

   ```
   ${adams[@]}
   ```

4. An environment variable is one whose value can be accessed by child processes of the shell. A local variable is restricted to a particular shell; its value cannot be accessed by child processes.

Hour 9

1. The following command will accomplish this task:

   ```
   $ ls *hw[0-9][0-9][2-6].???
   ```

2. If `MYPATH` is unset, it is set to the given value, which is then substituted.
3. If `MYPATH` is unset, the given value is substituted for it. `MYPATH` remains unset.
4. 10.

Hour 10

1. You can use double quotes as follows:

   ```
   $ echo "It's <party> time!"
   ```

2. The following command will accomplish this task:

   ```
   $ echo "$USER owes       \$$DEBT"
   ```

Hour 11

1. The difference is that the first command will try to run the command without checking if it is executable. Thus if the file exists but is not executable, the command will fail. The second command takes this into account and attempts to run the command only if it is executable.
2. The output is

   ```
   Your binaries are stored in your home directory.
   ```

3. Any of the following commands are valid:

   ```
   $ test -d /usr/bin || test -h /usr/bin
   $ [ -d /usr/bin ] || [ -h /usr/bin ]
   $ test -d /usr/bin -o -h /usr/bin
   $ [ -d /usr/bin  -o -h /usr/bin ]
   ```

4. The following case statement covers the given combinations and several more:

```
case "$ANS" in
    [Yy]|[Yy][Ee][Ss]) ANS="y" ;;
    *) ANS="n" ;;
esac
```

Hour 12

1. Here is one possible implementation:

```
x=0
while [ $x -lt 10 ]
do
    x=$(($x+1))
    y=0
    while [ $y -lt $x ] ; do
 echo "$y \c"
        y=$(($y+1))
    done
    echo
done
```

2. Here is one possible implementation:

```
#!/bin/bash

select FILE in * "Exit Program"
do

    if [ -z "$FILE" ] ; then continue ; fi

    if [ "$FILE" = "Exit Program" ] ; then break ; fi

    if [ ! -f "$FILE" ] ; then
        echo "$FILE is not a regular file."
        continue
    fi

    echo $FILE
    cat $FILE
done
```

Hour 13

1. One correct implementation is as follows:

```
#!/bin/sh

USAGE="Usage: `basename $0` [-c|-t] [files|directories]"
```

```
if [ $# -lt 2 ] ; then
    echo "$USAGE" ;
    exit 1 ;
fi

case "$1" in
    -t|-x) TARGS=${1}vf ; shift
        for i in "$@" ; do
            if [ -f "$i" ] ; then
                FILES=`tar $TARGS "$i" 2>/dev/null`
                if [ $? -eq 0 ] ; then
                    echo ; echo "$i" ; echo "$FILES"
                else
                    echo "ERROR: $i not a tar file."
                fi
            else
                echo "ERROR: $i not a file."
            fi
        done
        ;;
    -c) shift ; TARGS="-cvf" ;
        tar $TARGS archive.tar "$@"
        ;;
     *) echo "$USAGE"
        exit 0
        ;;
esac
exit $?
```

2. One possible implementation is as follows:

```
#!/bin/sh

USAGE="Usage: `basename $0` [-v] [-x] [-f] [filename] [-o] [filename]";

VERBOSE=false
EXTRACT=false

while getopts f:o:x:v OPTION ; do
    case "$OPTION" in
        f) INFILE="$OPTARG" ;;
        o) OUTFILE="$OPTARG" ;;
        v) VERBOSE=true ;;
        x) EXTRACT=true ;;
       \?) echo "$USAGE" ;
           exit 1
           ;;
    esac
done

shift `echo "$OPTIND - 1" | bc`
```

```
if [ -z "$1" -a -z "$INFILE" ] ; then
    echo "ERROR: Input file was not specified."
    exit 1
fi
if [ -z "$INFILE" ] ; then INFILE="$1" ; fi

: ${OUTFILE:=${INFILE}.uu}

if [ -f "$INFILE" ] ; then
    if [ "$EXTRACT" = "true" ] ; then
        if [ "$VERBOSE" = "true" ] ; then
            echo "uudecoding $INFILE... \c"
        fi
        uudecode "$INFILE" ; RET=$?
    else
        if [ "$VERBOSE" = "true" ] ; then
            echo "uuencoding $INFILE to $OUTFILE... \c"
        fi
        uuencode "$INFILE" "$INFILE" > "$OUTFILE" ; RET=$?
    fi

    if [ "$VERBOSE" = "true" ] ; then
        MSG="Failed" ; if [ $RET -eq 0 ] ; then MSG="Done." ; fi
        echo $MSG
    fi
else
    echo "ERROR: $INFILE is not a file."
fi
exit $RET
```

Hour 14

1. A possible implementation is

```
inPath () {
   OLDIFS="$IFS"
   IFS=:
   RC=1
   for i in $PATH
   do
      if [ -x "$i/$1" ] ; then
         echo "$i/$1"
         RC=0
         break
      fi
   done
   IFS="$OLDIFS"
   return $RC
}
```

2. A possible implementation is

```
mymkdir() {

    if [ $# -lt 1 ] ; then
        echo "ERROR: Insufficient arguments." >&2
        return 1
    fi

    mkdir -p "$1" > /dev/null 2>&1
    if [ $? -eq 0 ] ; then
        cd "$1" > /dev/null 2>&1
        if [ $? -eq 0 ] ; then
            pwd ;
        else
            echo "ERROR: Could not cd to $1." >&2
        fi
    else
        echo "ERROR: Could not mkdir $1." >&2
    fi
}
```

3. You can replace `mkdir -p` in Question 2 with a call to the following function:

```
mkdirp () {
   OLDIFS="$IFS"
   IFS=/
   for i in $@
   do
      if [ -z "$i" ] ; then i="/" ; fi

      if [ -z "$parent" ] ; then
         parent="$i"
      elif [ "$parent" = "/" ] ; then
         parent="$parent$i"
      else
         parent="$parent/$i"
      fi

      if [ ! -d "$parent" ] ; then

         if [ ! -e "$parent" ] ; then
            mkdir "$parent"
            if [ $? -ne 0 ] ; then
               echo "mkdir $parent failed."
               IFS="$OLDIFS"
               return 1
            fi
         else
            echo "$parent exists, but is not a dir."
            IFS="$OLDIFS"
            return 1
         fi
```

```
        fi

    done
    IFS="$OLDIFS"
    return 0
}
```

4. A possible solution is

```
readPass () {
    stty -echo
    while : ;
    do
        PASS1=""
        PASS2=""
        echo -n "Enter Password: "
        read PASS1
        if [ -z "$PASS1" ] ; then
            echo
            echo "Error: Password must not be blank. Try again." 1>&2
            continue
        fi
        echo
        echo -n "Enter Password (confirm): "
        read PASS2
        if [ "$PASS1" != "$PASS2" ] ; then
            echo
            echo "Error: Passwords do not match. Try again." 1>&2
            continue;
        fi
        PASS="$PASS1"
        break;
    done
    stty echo
    echo
}
```

5. A possible implementation is

```
Prompt_RESPONSE() {

    if [ $# -lt 1 ] ; then
        echo "ERROR: Insufficient arguments." >&2
        return 1
    fi

    RESPONSE=
    while [ -z "$RESPONSE" ]
    do
        echo "$1 \c "
        read RESPONSE
    done

    export RESPONSE
}
```

Hour 15

1. A sample implementation is

   ```
   lspids() {

       USAGE="Usage: lspids [-h] process"
       HEADER=false
       PSCMD="/bin/ps -ef"

       case "$1" in
           -h) HEADER=true ; shift ;;
       esac

       if [ -z "$1" ] ; then
           echo $USAGE ;
           return 1 ;
       fi


       if [ "$HEADER" = "true" ] ; then
           $PSCMD 2> /dev/null | head -n 1 ;
       fi

       $PSCMD 2> /dev/null | grep "$1"| grep -v grep
   }
   ```

   For Linux or FreeBSD, change the variable `PSCMD` from

   ```
   PSCMD="/bin/ps -ef"
   ```

   to

   ```
   PSCMD="/bin/ps -auwx"
   ```

2. The following is one possible implementation:

   ```
   lspids ()
   {
       USAGE="Usage: lspids [-h|-s] process";
       HEADER=false;
       SORT=false;
       PSCMD="/bin/ps -ef";
       SORTCMD="sort -rn -k 2,2";
       for OPT in $@;
       do
           case "$OPT" in
               -h)
                   HEADER=true;
                   shift
               ;;
               -s)
                   SORT=true;
                   shift
               ;;
   ```

```
            -*)
                echo $USAGE;
                return 1
            ;;
        esac;
    done;
    if [ -z "$1" ]; then
        echo $USAGE;
        return 1;
    fi;
    if [ "$HEADER" = "true" ]; then
        $PSCMD | head -1;
    fi;
    if [ "$SORT" = "true" ]; then
        $PSCMD 2> /dev/null | grep "$1" | grep -v grep | $SORTCMD;
    else
        $PSCMD 2> /dev/null | grep "$1" | grep -v grep;
    fi
}
```

For Linux and FreeBSD, change the variable `SORTCMD` to

```
SORTCMD="sort -rn"
```

instead of

```
SORTCMD="sort -rn -k 2,2"
```

You will also need to change the variable `PSCMD` from

```
PSCMD="/bin/ps -ef"
```

to

```
PSCMD="/bin/ps -auwx"
```

Hour 16

1. One possible implementation is

```
sgrep() {
    if [ $# -lt 2 ] ; then
        echo "USAGE: sgrep pattern files" >&2
        exit 1
    fi

    PAT="$1" ; shift ;

    for i in $@ ;
    do
        if [ -f "$i" ] ; then
            sed -n "/$PAT/p" $i
        else
            echo "ERROR: $i not a file." >&2
```

C

```
        fi
    done

    return 0
}
```

2. The following command does the job:

```
$ uptime | sed 's/.* load/load/'
```

3. There are two possible solutions:

```
$ df -k | sed -n '/^\//p'
$ df -k | sed '/^[^\/]/d'
```

4. The following command will solve this problem:

```
/bin/ls -al | sed -e '/^[^\-]/d' -e 's/ *[0-9].* / /'
```

Hour 17

1. A possible implementation is as follows:

```
#!/bin/sh

if [ $# -lt 1 ] ; then
    echo "USAGE: `basename $0` files"
    exit 1
fi

awk '{
    for (i=NF;i>=1;i--) {
        printf("%s ",$i) ;
    }
    printf("\n") ;
}' $@
```

2. A possible solution is

```
#!/bin/sh
awk 'BEGIN { FS=":" ; }
    $1 == "B" {
        BAL=$NF ; next ;
    }
    $1 == "D" {
        BAL += $NF ;
    }
    ($1 == "C") || ($1 == "W") {
        BAL-=$NF ;
    }
    ($1 == "C") || ($1 == "W") || ($1 == "D") {
        printf "%10-s %8.2f\n",$2,BAL ;
    }
' account.txt ;
```

Alternatively, you can use the `-F` option:

```
#!/bin/sh
awk -F: '
    $1 == "B" {
        BAL=$NF ; next ;
    }
    $1 == "D" {
        BAL += $NF ;
    }
    ($1 == "C") || ($1 == "W") {
        BAL-=$NF ;
    }
    ($1 == "C") || ($1 == "W") || ($1 == "D") {
        printf "%10-s %8.2f\n",$2,BAL ;
    }
' account.txt ;
```

3. The following is a possible implementation:

```
#!/bin/sh
awk -F: '
    $1 == "B" {
        BAL=$NF ;
        next ;
    }
    $1 == "D" {
        BAL += $NF ;
    }
    ($1 == "C") || ($1 == "W") {
        BAL-=$NF ;
    }
    ($1 == "C") || ($1 == "W") || ($1 == "D") {
        printf "%10-s %8.2f\n",$2,BAL ;
    }
    END {
        printf "-\n%10-s %8.2f\n","Total",BAL ;
    }
' account.txt ;
```

4. A possible implementation is

```
#!/bin/sh
awk -F: '
    $1 == "B" {
        BAL=$NF ;
        next ;
    }
    $1 == "M" {
        MIN=$NF ;
        next ;
    }
    $1 == "D" {
        BAL += $NF ;
```

C

```
    }
    ($1 == "C") || ($1 == "W") {
        BAL-=$NF ;
    }
    ($1 == "C") || ($1 == "W") || ($1 == "D") {
        printf "%10-s %8.2f",$2,BAL ;
        if ( BAL < MIN ) { printf " * Below Min. Balance" }
        printf "\n" ;
    }
    END {
        printf "-\n%10-s %8.2f\n","Total",BAL ;
    }
' account.txt ;
```

Hour 18

1. The following command will accomplish this task:

   ```
   $ type process2
   ```

2. The following command will accomplish this task:

   ```
   $ find /data -name '*process2*' -print
   ```

3. The following command will accomplish this task:

   ```
   PRICE=`echo "scale=2; 3.5 \* $PRICE" | bc`
   ```

Hour 19

1. Here is a possible implementation:

   ```
   trap CleanUp 2 15
   trap Init 1
   trap "quit=true" 3
   PROG="$1"
   Init

   while : ;
   do
       wait $!
       if [ "$quit" = true ] ; then exit 0 ; fi
       $PROG &
   done
   ```

2. Here is a possible implementation:

   ```
   #! /bin/sh

   AlarmHandler() {
       echo "Got SIGALARM, cmd took too long."
       KillSubProcs
       exit 14
   ```

```
}

IntHandler() {
    echo "Got SIGINT, user interrupt."
    KillSubProcs
    exit 2
}

KillSubProcs() {
    kill ${CHPROCIDS:-$!}
    if [ $? -eq 0 ] ; then echo "Sub-processes killed." ; fi
}

SetTimer() {
    DEF_TOUT=${1:-10};
    if [ $DEF_TOUT -ne 0 ] ; then
        sleep $DEF_TOUT && kill -s 14 $$ &
        CHPROCIDS="$CHPROCIDS $!"
        TIMERPROC=$!
    fi
}

UnsetTimer() {
    kill $TIMERPROC
}

# main()

trap AlarmHandler 14
trap IntHandler 2

SetTimer 15
$PROG &
CHPROCIDS="$CHPROCIDS $!"
wait $!
UnsetTimer
echo "All Done."
exit 0
```

C

Hour 20

1. The three main methods are
    - Issue the script in the following fashion:

      `$ /bin/sh option script arg1 arg2 arg3`
    - Change the first line of the script to

      `#!/bin/sh option`
    - Use the `set` command as follows:

      `set option`

Here *option* is the debugging option you want to enable.

2. Here is one possible implementation:

```
Debug() {
    if [ "$DEBUG" = "true" ] ; then
        if [ "$1" = "on"  -o "$1" = "ON" ] ; then
            set -x
        else
            set +x
            echo " >Press Enter To Continue< \c"
            read press_enter_to_continue
        fi
    fi
}
```

Hour 21

1. One possible implementation is

```
################################################
# Name: toLower
# Desc: changes an input string to lower case
# Args: $@ -> string to change
################################################

toLower() {
    echo $@ | tr '[A-Z]' '[a-z]' ;
}
```

2. One possible implementation is

```
################################################
# Name: toUpper
# Desc: changes an input string to upper case
# Args: $@ -> string to change
################################################

toUpper() {
    echo $@ | tr '[a-z]' '[A-Z]'
}
```

3. One possible solution is

```
################################################
# Name: isSpaceAvailable
# Desc: returns true (0) if space available
# Args: $1 -> The directory to check
#       $2 -> The amount of space to check for
################################################

isSpaceAvailable() {
```

```
    if [ $# -lt 2 ] ; then
        printERROR "Insufficient Arguments."
        return 1
    fi

    if [ ! -d "$1" ] ; then
        printERROR "$1 is not a directory."
        return 1
    fi

    if [ `getSpaceFree "$1"` -gt "$2" ] ; then
        return 0
    fi

    return 1
}
```

4. One possible solution is

```
################################################
# Name: isSpaceAvailable
# Desc: returns true (0) if space available
# Args: $1 -> The directory to check
#       $2 -> The amount of space to check for
#       $3 -> The units for $2 (optional)
#                 k for kilobytes
#                 m for megabytes
#                 g for gigabytes
################################################

isSpaceAvailable() {

    if [ $# -lt 2 ] ; then
        printERROR "Insufficient Arguments."
        return 1
    fi

    if [ ! -d "$1" ] ; then
        printERROR "$1 is not a directory."
        return 1
    fi

    SPACE_MIN="$2"

    case "$3" in
        [mM]|[mM][bB])
            SPACE_MIN=`echo "$SPACE_MIN * 1024" | bc` ;;
        [gG]|[gG][bB])
            SPACE_MIN=`echo "$SPACE_MIN * 1024 * 1024" | bc` ;;
    esac
```

```
    if [ `getSpaceFree "$1"` -gt "$SPACE_MIN" ] ; then
        return 0
    fi

    return 1
}
```

5. One possible solution is

```
################################################
# Name: isUserRoot
# Desc: returns true (0) if the users UID=0
# Args: $1 -> a user name (optional)
################################################

isUserRoot() {
    if [ "`getUID $1`" -eq 0 ] ; then
        return 0
    fi
    return 1
}
```

Hour 22

1. You can add a check similar to the following to the beginning of the init script:

```
CURUID="`id | sed -e 's/(.*$//' -e 's/^.*\=//'`"
if [ "$CURUID" -ne 0 ] ; then
    echo "Error: Only root (uid=0) can run this script." 1>&2
    exit 1
fi
unset CURUID
```

2. Use `grep -i` instead of `grep`.
3. They can be rewritten as functions and stored in a shell library that both scripts can access.
4. You can change the lines

```
55  grep "$1" "$TMPF1" > "$TMPF2" 2> /dev/null
56  Failed $? "No matches found."
```

to

```
55  sed -n "/^$1[^:]*:/p" "$TMPF1" > "$TMPF2" 2> /dev/null
56  test -s "$TMPF2" > /dev/null
57  Failed $? "No matches found."
```

You can also change the line

```
79          grep -v "$LINE" "$TMPF1" > "$TMPF1.new" 2> /dev/null
```

to

```
sed -e "s/^$LINE$//" "$TMPF1" > "$TMPF1.new" 2> /dev/null
```

5. Add a signal handler. A simple one might be

```
trap 'echo "Cleaning Up." ; doCleanUp ; exit 2; ' 2 3 15
```

You should add this to the script before the line:

```
cp "$MYADDRESSBOOK" "$TMPF1" 2> /dev/null
```

Hour 23

1. A possible implementation is

```
getCharCount() {
    case `getOSName` in
        bsd|sunos|linux)
            WCOPT="-c" ;;
        *)
            WCOPT="-m" ;;
    esac

    wc $WCOPT $@
}
```

APPENDIX D

Shell Function Library

This appendix contains the complete shell function library from Chapter 21, "Problem Solving with Functions." The library can be downloaded using the following URL:

http://www.csua.berkeley.edu/~ranga/downloads/tysp2/libtysp2.sh

LISTING D.1 Listing of the Library `libTYSP2.sh`

```
# Name: printError
# Desc: prints an message to STDERR
# Args: $@ -> message to print

printError () {
    echo "ERROR:   $@" 1>&2
}

# Name: printWarning
# Desc: prints an message to STDERR
# Args: $@ -> message to print

printWarning () {
    echo "WARNING: $@" 1>&2
}
```

LISTING D.1 Continued

```
# Name:    promptYESNO
# Desc:    Asks a yes/no question
# Args:    $1 -> The prompt
#          $2 -> The default answer (optional)
# Globals: YESNO -> set to the users response y for yes, n for no

promptYESNO () {

   YESNO=""

   if [ $# -lt 1 ] ; then
      return 1
   fi

   _YNPROMPT="$1 (y/n)? "
   _YNDEFANS=""

   case "$2" in
      [yY]|[yY][eE][sS]) _YNDEFANS="y" ;;
      [nN]|[nN][oO])     _YNDEFANS="n" ;;
   esac

   _YNPROMPT="$_YNPROMPT${_YNDEFANS:+[$_YNDEFANS] }"

   while :
   do
      printf "$_YNPROMPT"
      read YESNO
      case "${YESNO:-$_YNDEFANS}" in
         [yY]|[yY][eE][sS])
             YESNO="y"
             break
             ;;
         [nN]|[nN][oO])
             YESNO="n"
             break
             ;;
         *) YESNO="" ;;
      esac
   done

   unset _YNPROMPT _YNDEFANS
   export YESNO
   return 0
}

# Name:    promptRESPONSE
# Desc:    Asks a question
# Args:    $1 -> The prompt
```

Listing D.1 Continued

```
#         $2 -> The default answer (optional)
# Globals: RESPONSE -> set to the users response

promptRESPONSE () {

   RESPONSE=""

   if [ $# -lt 1 ] ; then
      return 1
   fi

   _RDEFANS="${2:+$2}"
   _RPROMPT="$1? ${_RDEFANS:+[$_RDEFANS] }"

   while :
   do
      printf "$_RPROMPT"
      read RESPONSE
      RESPONSE="${RESPONSE:-$_RDEFANS}"
      if [ -n "$RESPONSE" ] ; then
         break
      fi
      RESPONSE=""
   done

   unset _RDEFANS _RPROMPT
   export RESPONSE
   return 0
}

# Name: getSpaceFree
# Desc: Outputs the space avail for a directory
# Args: $1 -> The directory to check

getSpaceFree () {
   if [ $# -ge 1 ] ; then
      df -k "$1" 2> /dev/null | awk 'NR != 1 { print $4; }'
      return $?
   fi
   return 1
}

# Name: getSpaceUsed
# Desc: output the space used for a directory
# Args: $1 -> The directory to check

getSpaceUsed () {
   if [ -d "$1" ] ; then
      du -sk "$1" | awk '{ print $1; }'
```

LISTING D.1 Continued

```
        return $?
    fi
    return 1
}

# Name: getPID
# Desc: Outputs a list of process id matching $1
# Args: $1 -> the command name to look for

getPID() {

    if [ $# -lt 1 ] ; then
        return 1
    fi

    PSOPTS="-ef"

    /bin/ps $PSOPTS | grep "$1" | grep -v grep | awk '{ print $2; }'
}

# Name: getUID
# Desc: outputs a numeric user id
# Args: $1 -> a user name (optional)

getUID() {
    id $1 | sed -e 's/(.*$//' -e 's/^uid=//'
}

# Name: toLower
# Desc: changes an input string to lower case
# Args: $@ -> string to change

toLower() {
    echo $@ | tr '[A-Z]' '[a-z]' ;
}

# Name: toUpper
# Desc: changes an input string to upper case
# Args: $@ -> string to change

toUpper() {
    echo $@ | tr '[a-z]' '[A-Z]'
}
```

INDEX

Symbols

A

D

E

F

G

T

U

Z